RENEWALS 458-4574
DATE DUE

**WITHDRAWN
UTSA Libraries**

The Meaning of Work in the New Economy

The Future of Work Series

Series Editor: **Peter Nolan**, Director of ESRC Future of Work Programme and the Montague Burton Professor of Industrial Relations at Leeds University Business School in the UK.

Few subjects could be judged more vital to current policy and academic debates than the prospects for work and employment. *The Future of Work* Series provides much needed evidence and theoretical advances to enhance our understanding of the critical developments most likely impact on people's working lives.

Titles include:

Chris Baldry, Peter Bain, Phil Taylor, Jeff Hyman, Dora Scholarios, Abigail Marks, Aileen Watson, Kay Gilbert, Gregor Gall and Dirk Bunzel
THE MEANING OF WORK IN THE NEW ECONOMY

Julia Brannen, Peter Moss and Ann Mooney
WORKING AND CARING OVER THE TWENTIETH CENTURY
Change and Continuity in Four-Generation Families

Michael White, Stephen Hill, Colin Mills and Deborah Smeaton
MANAGING TO CHANGE?
British Workplaces and the Future of Work

Andy Danford, Michael Richardson, Paul Stewart, Stephanie Tailby and Martin Upchurch
PARTNERSHIP AND THE HIGH PERFORMANCE WORKPLACE
Work and Employment Relations in the Aerospace Industry

Geraldine Healy, Edmund Heery, Philip Taylor, William Brown (*editors*)
FUTURE OF WORKER REPRESENTATION

Diane Houston (*editor*)
WORK-LIFE BALANCE IN THE 21ST CENTURY

Theo Nichols and Surhan Cam
TFW; LABOUR IN A GLOBAL WORLD

Paul Stewart (*editor*)
EMPLOYMENT, TRADE UNION RENEWAL AND THE FUTURE OF WORK

Clare Ungerson, Susan Yeandle (*editors*)
CASH FOR CARE SYSTEMS IN THE DEVELOPED WELFARE STATES

The Future of Work Series
Series Standing Order ISBN 1–4039–1477–X

You can receive future titles in this series as they are published by placing a standing order. Please contact your bookseller or, in case of difficulty, write to us at the address below with your name and address, the title of the series and one of the ISBNs quoted above.

Customer Services Department, Macmillan Distribution Ltd, Houndmills, Basingstoke, Hampshire RG21 6XS, England

The Meaning of Work in the New Economy

Chris Baldry, Peter Bain, Phil Taylor, Jeff Hyman, Dora Scholarios, Abigail Marks, Aileen Watson, Kay Gilbert, Gregor Gall and Dirk Bunzel

The Future of Work Series
Edited by Peter Nolan

© Chris Baldry, Jeff Hyman, Phil Taylor, Peter Bain, Dora Scholarios, Abigail Marks, Aileen Watson, Kay Gilbert, Gregor Gall and Dirk Bunzel 2007
Foreword © Peter Nolan 2007

All rights reserved. No reproduction, copy or transmission of this publication may be made without written permission.

No paragraph of this publication may be reproduced, copied or transmitted save with written permission or in accordance with the provisions of the Copyright, Designs and Patents Act 1988, or under the terms of any licence permitting limited copying issued by the Copyright Licensing Agency, 90 Tottenham Court Road, London W1T 4LP.

Any person who does any unauthorized act in relation to this publication may be liable to criminal prosecution and civil claims for damages.

The authors have asserted their rights to be identified as the authors of this work in accordance with the Copyright, Designs and Patents Act 1988.

First published 2007 by
PALGRAVE MACMILLAN
Houndmills, Basingstoke, Hampshire RG21 6XS and
175 Fifth Avenue, New York, N.Y. 10010
Companies and representatives throughout the world

PALGRAVE MACMILLAN is the global academic imprint of the Palgrave Macmillan division of St. Martin's Press, LLC and of Palgrave Macmillan Ltd. Macmillan® is a registered trademark in the United States, United Kingdom and other countries. Palgrave is a registered trademark in the European Union and other countries.

ISBN 13: 978–1–4039–3407–9   hardback
ISBN 10: 1–4039–3407–X   hardback

This book is printed on paper suitable for recycling and made from fully managed and sustained forest sources. Logging, pulping and manufacturing processes are expected to conform to the environmental regulations of the country of origin.

A catalogue record for this book is available from the British Library.

Library of Congress Cataloging-in-Publication Data

The meaning of work in the new economy / Chris Baldry ... [et al.].
   p. cm. – (The future of work)
   Includes bibliographical references and index.
   Contents: Work attachment, work centrality and the meaning of work in life – Into the new century: the changing terrain for work and employment – Organizational life: the nature of work – Organizational life: the management of commitment – Occupational life – Household and community life – Women and men – Class and status – Back to the future? change and continuity at work.
      ISBN-13: 978–1–4039–3407–9 (cloth)
      ISBN-10: 1–4039–3407–X (cloth)
   1. Quality of work life. 2. Work–Social aspects. 3. Organizational change–Social aspects. I. Baldry, Christopher.

HD6955.M43 2007
306.3'6—dc22   2006048788

10   9   8   7   6   5   4   3   2   1
16   15   14   13   12   11   10   09   08   07

Printed and bound in Great Britain by
Antony Rowe Ltd, Chippenham and Eastbourne

For Harvie
Who argued with us, inspired us, drove us crazy, and made us laugh. Who was our great friend.

Contents

List of Tables and Figure viii
Foreword by Peter Nolan ix
Acknowledgments xi

1 Work Attachment, Work Centrality and the Meaning of Work in Life 1
2 Into the New Century: The Changing Terrain for Work and Employment 27
3 Organizational Life: The Nature of Work 50
4 Organizational Life: The Management of Commitment 85
5 Occupational Life 109
6 Household and Community Life 134
7 Women and Men 165
8 Class and Status 196
9 Back to the Future? Change and Continuity at Work 223
Appendix A Research methods and data collection 237
Appendix B Survey respondent characteristics 239
Bibliography 241
Index 260

List of Tables and Figure

Tables

1.1	Profile of call centre case studies	21
1.2	Profile of software case studies	24
2.1	Scottish employment by sector, 2000	44
3.1	Most important reasons for working paid or unpaid overtime	62
3.2	Call centre operating hours and extent of 'atypical' working	64
3.3	Perceptions of degree of control	76
4.1	Measures of commitment among call centre employees	101
4.2	Measures of commitment among software employees	102
4.3	Satisfaction ratings for different job facets: call centres	106
4.4	Satisfaction ratings for different job facets: software	107
5.1	Perceptions of current job as career	121
5.2	Career patterns and attitudes	122
5.3	Prediction of career attitudes	124
6.1	Household life: sample characteristics for men and women	140
6.2	Work-life interface	143
6.3	Family-friendly culture	151
6.4	Work values	154
7.1	Sample characteristics for men and women (survey respondents)	167
7.2	Contribution to household income	169
7.3	Attitudes to equality and women's roles for men and women	171
7.4	Importance of work, leisure and family for men and women	177
7.5	Reasons for current job choice	180
7.6	Importance of company career for men and women, with and without children	181
7.7	Family friendly cultures	187
7.8	Managers and non-managers in call centres, by gender	191
7.9	Perception of job characteristics in software, by gender	194
8.1	Positive self-location of class identity for software workers	208
8.2	Attitudes to management in respondents' own workplace	210
8.3	Attitudes to management in Britain generally	210
A.1	Description of data and research methods	237
A.2	Survey response rates and sample	238
A.3	Interviewee profile	238
B.1	Call centre and software employee characteristics	239

Figure

3.1	Spectrum of control	81

Foreword

The 'new' economy has featured prominently in recent policy analysis and debate. Although the concept remains ill-defined, the new economy has served as a touchstone for the present UK government's strategic approach to work and employment issues. There is a working assumption that the character, rhythms and places of work are changing and that transactions between workers and entrepreneurs in the 'dematerialised' world of the twenty-first century will be very different from the past.

Treated theoretically as a break from the 'old' economy that supposedly dominated work in the twentieth century, the new economy has been presented by many writers as a brave new world encompassing innovative forms of business organisation, employment patterns and work spaces. Why work for a firm, office, or bank when you can work for yourself from home with a laptop? According to some commentators the advancing army of e-lancers is challenging, root and branch, established business structures, social relations and individual ways of working.

Poor theory thrives on sensational vignettes and limited data. The difficulties are nowhere more acute than in the world of work where even marginal shifts in behaviour and conduct raise the spectre in the minds of many observers of paradigm shifts in employment and labour markets. Yet cutting across the new economy concept is the unimpeachable evidence of the enduring presence of traditional occupations and the stressful conditions, long working hours, and fitful careers of many new economy workers.

The *Future of Work* Programme was established to investigate contemporary developments in the changing world of work. It set out to generate new data, refine established concepts, and develop rigorous theories that better explained the complex changes taking place in different sectors of the economy. It aimed to illuminate the changing boundaries between paid and unpaid work, the interplay of employment and family life, and the shifting attitudes to work of both workers and their bosses.

This rigorous and searching new study by Professor Chris Baldry and his colleagues, focusing on the nature of work in two sectors commonly connected to the new economy, could not be more timely. Focusing on call and contract centres and software engineering in Scotland, the study asks what it is like to be a new economy worker. Do such workers have more or less autonomy in their jobs, more or less job satisfaction, superior or inferior material terms and conditions than workers in the so-called old economy? Is the new economy providing jobs that represent a break from the past or are there lines of continuity that render the distinction between new and old meaningless? What are the changing boundaries between paid and unpaid work, and how does the work in these important sectors in Scotland impact on gender divisions, home and work-life, and the meaning of work in people's lives.

These crucial questions are addressed with a battery of advanced research techniques – both quantitative and qualitative – that highlight the benefits of interdisciplinary research teams. The results reported in this study will attract widespread attention and will serve as a starting point for subsequent studies of the changing world of work in the twenty-first century.

Acknowledgments

The work for this project was financed by the ESRC under the national *Future of Work* Programme [Award no: L212252006]. In addition to the current authors the research team at different times included, Gareth Mulvey, Cliff Lockyer, Ann Witz and Nick Bozionelos and the late Harvie Ramsay. Valuable encouragement at the start of the project was given by both Richard Brown and Peter Nolan and we thank them for their ideas and suggestions. Thanks are due to Linda Brisbane for invaluable secretarial support during the life of the project and to Karen Hill and Andrew Watson for their coding work. Above all we thank all the software and call centre organizations who cooperated so fully with the research.

1
Work Attachment, Work Centrality and the Meaning of Work in Life

Introduction: aims of the book

In recent times, a new orthodoxy has become established, claiming simultaneously to describe, explain and indeed shape contemporary economy and society. Concepts associated with the knowledge economy now permeate academic, populist, policy maker and practitioner thinking, to such an extent that they have become axiomatic nostrums informing government agendas (e.g. DTI, 1998; 2004a, b). Accordingly, it is widely accepted that we are living through a new and distinctive epoch, in which the dominant principles organizing human society have changed fundamentally and dramatically. Yet, the 'big picture franchise' (Thompson, 2003) of the knowledge economy is but the latest in a succession of paradigm break theories proclaiming the end of industrialism and Fordism, meta-characterizations themselves fraught with definitional and conceptual difficulties (Williams et al., 1987). Since the 1980s, post-Fordism, post-modernism and the surveillance society have been advanced as models, each successively claiming to provide *the* indispensable framework for understanding socio-economic phenomena of all kinds.

Although incorporating core assumptions derived from these earlier models, the contemporary knowledge economy variant can claim key distinguishing features which demarcate it from its immediate predecessors, whilst drawing upon longer-established antecedents. Various social theorists in the post-war period asserted the increased importance of knowledge in contemporary society. Aaron, Dahrendorf, Kerr, Bell and Giddens all emphasized the increasing relevance of codified and theoretical knowledge to social development and work organizations (Ackroyd et al., 2000). However, the continued influence of such ideas also owes much to the work of Drucker (1968) who, as early as the mid-1960s, was suggesting the importance of the 'knowledge industries' to the 'knowledge economy'. Notwithstanding continuity with earlier theories of information society, the novelty of the pre-millennial versions of the knowledge economy, or 'informationalism' as propounded by Castells (1996), lies in the claimed emergence of the network society, where the widespread dissemination of information technologies is facilitated by, and contributes to, economic and cultural globalization. This claimed shift to an information-based society brings into sharp focus the actual nature of work undertaken in contemporary society, with expected decline in the demands for 'old economy' physical and unskilled labour and the growth of knowledge-intensive work within an information based and networked economy. In turn, these networked processes are forecast to dominate the execution, direction and experience of work for the foreseeable future.

In this book, we look at two contemporary sectors, call centres and software development, where information and communications technologies (ICT) are a dominant feature of the labour process. With ICT at the productive core, the main aim of this book is to provide a comprehensive account of a major Economic and Social Research Council-funded research study designed to explore connections between changing forms and conditions of employment and the meaning of work at the beginning of the twenty-first century. A central premise of the project was that examination of work should focus not only on the workplace but also on the significance of work in people's wider lives (and *vice versa*).

A glance at the burgeoning future of work literature confirms that there is no shortage of predictions of end-of career, portfolio working and even doomsday, end-of-work scenarios (see for example, Aronowitz and Fazie, 1995), but few of these proclamations have been located in empirically-grounded research (and even fewer have yet to be realized). By contrast, the prime aim of this book is to present an in-depth investigation of the actual experience and meanings of work to participants engaged in two different growth sectors in the so-called new or knowledge economy, in order to provide an analytically constructed and theoretically informed basis for examining the nature of work in the early twenty-first century. Our choice of two contrasting but information-based sectors, call centres and software, allows us to examine continuities and disjunctures from earlier analyses of the significance and experience of work. In particular, a significant intention is to return to earlier sociological examinations of work meanings within broader contexts of family and community attachments.

Debates about the nature of work have always been central to and suggestive of debates about the nature of society and, by a sort of converse logic, it has been periodically claimed that perceived changes in the nature of society and economy will or must have consequences for how work is organized and experienced. The starting point is to ground our enquiry in the intellectual traditions and legacies that have informed studies of work and its meanings, and then to reunite these with present concerns.

The classical legacy

A contemporary philosopher has observed that work 'is not only a kind of activity but a set of ideas and values related to that activity' (Ciulla, 2000: 25). Whilst the underlying values and meanings of physical, spiritual and mental work have always attracted debate (Donkin, 2001), it was the rise of industrial society with its routinized and disciplined production schedules which elevated the institution of paid work to one of the fundamental foci of social analysis. Clearly any book which lays claim to examine the meaning or meanings of work needs first to confront the contemporary relevance of ideas of personal deprivation which the classical social theorists associated with paid work more than one hundred years ago.

One of the longest running themes in social science has been the dialogue between the observation that work can be a dehumanizing or alienating experience and the assertion that this need not be the case. As early industrialism began to reveal its true characteristics, observers such as Adam Smith and Adam Ferguson through to Marx came to the conclusion that employed work in capitalist industrial society seems to divorce us from our true selves as human beings. For the first time, work became abstract and separate from intrinsic human nature, a factor of production that could be measured and combined with technology, land and money to create products with market value. And here was the paradox for, in Kumar's words:

> With industrialism, work is placed at the centre, not just of man but of history. Work is the means by which man makes himself... The question 'who am I?', which would formerly have been answered almost everywhere in terms of religion, family or place of origin, could now really be answered only in terms of the occupation a man worked in (Kumar, 1984: 8–9).

Essentially, it was held that the nature of capitalist employment, centred on the cash nexus, denied the worker control over and access to his or her own creativity as a human being, the common factor which linked the critiques of the classical social theorists. The starting point for our exploration, therefore, commences with the works of Marx, Weber and Durkheim, who each arrived at different pathologies in their analysis of work and its meanings under capitalist forms of organization and production.

Marx essentially believed in the redemptionist value of meaningful work performed under worker control. In contrast, capitalism alienated workers both from the end products of their labour and from the labour process itself. Labour power is sought at minimum cost by owners of capital, whose sources of profit rest in cost-minimization through worker exploitation, division and domination, work intensification and ever-increasing control over production. Under these conditions, work has little meaning other than of oppression:

> [The worker] does not fulfill himself in his work but denies himself, has a feeling of misery rather than well-being, does not develop freely his mental and physical energies but is physically exhausted and mentally debased (Marx, 1982: 15).

Under capitalism, Marx argued, work becomes an instrumental means for employed workers to acquire money but has little intrinsic value or meaning for them. Neither is the system *expected* to offer meaning or satisfaction and consequently workers' motivations are based on limiting the level of exploitation through reduced effort, by collective action and seeking higher pay, all vigorously contested by their masters. Concepts of alienation, consciousness and class relations between owners of capital and propertyless workers have provided a central theme of subsequent Marxist analysis and the impetus for continuing analysis of the meaning of work under different technological and productive conditions (see, for example, Gorz, 1967; Mallet, 1975; Poulantzas, 1975).

Whilst Marx contended that the system of exploitation could only be overturned through revolutionary means, Durkheim, writing at the end of the nineteenth century and also preoccupied by societal instability provoked by tensions between privileged (owners) and exploited (workers) groups (Salaman, 1981: 42), believed that capitalist oppression could be overcome through reform rather than revolution. He argued that growing economic and social disparities between owners and workers resulted in a state of *anomie* or normlessness, which could be resolved through establishing a new, and shared, moral order based on organic solidarity (Durkheim, 1984). This order would promote societal stability through uniting the different interests reflected in the increasing division of labour found in capitalist societies. Organic solidarity between different interest groups would be sustained through establishing voluntary collective occupational associations which by binding and uniting group interests through shared norms would 'give direction and meaning to work and ... provide safeguards against abuse, exploitation, and overwork' (Hodson, 2001: 27).

Max Weber's ideas developed from his analysis of large organizations, which he saw as operating as rational hierarchies or bureaucracies, bound together by shared beliefs in the legitimacy of the control system which both ensured efficient operation and shared rewards. These bureaucratic organizations also operated according to the rationality of increasing specialization at work and the use of profit and loss accounting procedures leading to 'more systematic, rational and intensive use of labour' (Salaman, 1981: 49) in which 'all the workers become "hands"' (Weber, 1964: 259). According to Hodson, in his development of a theory of dignity at work, it is this 'formal economic rationality that displaces shared values and sentiments and that undermines meaning and dignity at work' (2001: 27). Consent is given to subordination and domination through the legitimacy proffered to the formal rules associated with each level of the bureaucratic hierarchy, and the allocation of legitimate rewards which derive from the office. The technological accomplishments of the 'iron cage' of bureaucracy carry a cost, however: 'already now ... in all economic enterprises run on modern lines, rational calculation is manifest at every stage. By it, the performance of each individual worker is mathematically measured, each man becomes a little cog in the machine' (Weber, quoted in Hodson, 2001: 28).

The meaning of work in the workplace

From these classical accounts, two factors emerge which are highly relevant for the present enquiry. Firstly, in the early years of industrialization, owners and their managers ruled by imposed control and rarely by consent. Secondly, it was believed that work had little intrinsic meaning for workers other than to satisfy economic needs in this world or to serve as a possible means of salvation in the next. To these we could add a third element that needs to be considered when addressing the issue of work centrality, namely that of context: in other words, meanings of work can be mediated according to different micro (for example organizational) or macro (for example societal) influences. An important and underlying theme of this book, therefore, is the extent to which these twin aspects, control and consent, have been continuously re-enacted and applied through succeeding decades and in different socio-economic contexts.

Early management approaches to work organization took the idea of alienated labour and turned it on its head. At the turn of the nineteenth century, F.W. Taylor's prescriptions were based on the doctrine of the 'rational economic man', in which workers are represented as isolated individuals seeking income maximization. Taylorism was not just an assault on craft control (Braverman, 1974) but also on the craft workers' values of pride in the job. Taylor argued that if workers only want money from work then jobs should be so designed as to eliminate any other bond and to offer the promise of monetary gain in return for enhanced performance.

In return, through the process of scientific management, all discretion and autonomy were to be stripped from work tasks and located in the management function which alone was to determine the ways in which work could be rationalized and conducted to provide the 'one best way' of performing tasks (Rose, 1988; Ritzer, 1996: 24). Arguably, scientific management and its assembly line derivatives are still reflected in wide areas of work organization today. Recent studies suggest that fast-food restaurants demonstrate both elements of Taylorist rationality and of assembly-line technique (Ritzer, 1996: 26). Work in call centres, one of the prime subjects of our enquiry, has been portrayed metaphorically as 'an assembly line in the head' (Taylor and Bain, 1999).

Drawing upon the Workplace Employee Relations Survey (WERS) 1998 findings and demonstrating continuity with the labour process of an earlier industrialized era (see Baldamus, 1961), Cully *et al.* (1999: 106) also pointed to the presence of another stark and enduring feature of the nature of latter-day capitalism: 'at its heart, the employment relationship is an exchange of effort for earnings'.

From these perspectives, it would appear that work is unlikely to possess intrinsic meaning for those who undertake it. Nevertheless, these consistent but pessimistic conclusions have provoked equally regular responses offering the possibility of replacing such alienating labour with work which is creative, psychologically rewarding and self-fulfilling. These responses have either been pitched at the level of societal change or at the level of organizational reform. For all the historic impact of Marx's revolutionary response, requiring the overthrow of capitalism and its replacement with a more humanistic system, far more numerous have been the evolutionary hopes for a better future. As we shall see in the next chapter, these are usually based on detecting in current socio-economic changes the signs of a new societal epoch, such as post-capitalism (Dahrendorf, 1959), post-industrialism (Bell, 1974), the Information Society (Stonier, 1983; Bell, 1976) and latterly, the knowledge economy (Reich, 1993) and network society (Castells, 1996), under which new socio-economic regimes work would be intrinsically more creative and rewarding.

At the sub-societal level there has been a reiterated theme that capitalist work itself is not intrinsically bad but that it has been, in the past, badly designed and organized. Although, as we have seen above, such a perspective can be traced to Durkheim, it is the human relations school developed by Elton Mayo and his successors that has consistently advocated the redesigning of work in order to enhance its intrinsic satisfactions. Whilst the human relations movement arose to serve managerial interests in response to the perceived failings of Taylorist prescriptions, it did so on an understanding that workers can derive substantive meaning and satisfaction from social relationships and from the intrinsic value of work tasks, expressed in autonomy, praise and fulfillment. The idea that appropriate management strategies can provide satisfying conditions of work was taken up by the neo-human relations theorists such as Maslow (Rose, 1988), in the ubiquitous depiction of whose hierarchy of needs model we find words like vocation, calling, mission, duty, beloved job, even oblation, to describe the sense of dedication and devotion to their work experienced by self-actualizing people. In response came Braverman's (1974) seminal reminder that jobs can be, and frequently have been, deliberately designed to offer *little* intrinsic or extrinsic task satisfaction and that this was not a regrettable by-product of any given phase of technological development but a conscious organizational strategy to maximize surplus value.

Job re-redesign, when it has occurred, has always been within the limits of managerial rationality, that is to say the goal has been to increase efficiency rather than create optimally satisfying jobs. There is, nevertheless, in the human relations approach the recognition that there *can* be intrinsic rewards from the performance of work tasks, the closer these get to non-alienative labour; for example, in the greater control the worker has over the whole job. Also, many of the meanings attached to work are not necessarily a direct reflection of either an individual psychological state or the quality of the jobs that people do, but arise from the context in which the work is performed. In this sense, it could be argued that there has been a shift in context over recent years, as increasing numbers of so-called knowledge jobs (it is claimed) depend upon marshalling employees' non-physical cognitive, attitudinal and emotional attributes to contribute to organizational success. In response to perceived cumulative failings in the post-war industrial relations settlement (MacInnes, 1987) and a putative shift at company level towards quality-based competition, there has been a neo-neo human relations reaction proposing a shift from a managerial strategy based on control to one aimed at gaining commitment, in which operational controls over employees are exerted in less direct and visible ways through value-based normative means.

Furthermore, the pre-eminence of Japanese companies in the 1980s generated not only the 'excellence' literature typified by Peters and Waterman (1982), but also led to efforts by many Western companies to emulate the customer-orientated employment practices perceived to have contributed significantly to Japanese economic success (Oliver and Wilkinson, 1992). As the cult of the customer has deepened (du Gay and Salaman, 1992; du Gay, 1996) so management have increasingly publicized their ambitions to seek to win workers' hearts and minds as a critical element in their proclaimed mission to provide high levels of service, quality and efficiency – all at low cost. These ideas were incorporated into the agenda of the new philosophy of human resource management (HRM), which aims to promote direct links between employee feelings of well-being and productivity. Thus, central to every model of HRM is the concept of employee commitment to the organization, with the underlying 'assumption that committed employees will be more satisfied, more productive and more adaptable' (Guest, 1987: 513).

The 1998 Workplace Employee Relations Survey found that differences in employee commitment were 'most closely related to job influence' a factor which 'more than any other indicator ... appears to have captured the essence of the implicit aspects of the employment contract' (Cully *et al.*, 1999: 191). In other words, management have the option to exercise the potential 'to expand the realm of worker power and autonomy' (Hodson,

2001: 198), at least over individual tasks and jobs, and in so doing, contribute positively to workers' orientations toward their employer and to their work. Similar benefits are also anticipated by Heller *et al.* (1998: 190) who point out that participation by employees in organizational decision-making 'works', at least, in the authors' words, 'if conditions are appropriate'. Gaining this commitment, therefore, can be seen as the key to, if not guarantor of, organizational success and has been favourably contrasted with the 'resigned behavioural compliance' exhibited by employees in other (or Taylorist) work regimes. According to Walton (1985), adoption of a strategy of employer-employee 'mutuality' necessitated a radical break with traditional control-orientated approaches to managing the workforce. Instead, managerial style had to move decisively and visibly from a philosophy of seeking to exert control over the workforce to one of developing positive feelings of commitment to the organization by employees.

In his influential article, Walton summarized the essential features of such a 'high commitment work practices' (HCWP) strategy:

> Jobs are designed to be broader than before, to combine planning and implementation, and to include efforts to upgrade operations, not just to maintain them. Individual responsibilities are expected to change as conditions change, and teams, not individuals, often are the organization units accountable for performance. With management hierarchies relatively flat and differences in status minimized, control and lateral coordination depend on shared goals. And expertise rather than formal position determines influence. (Walton, 1985: 80)

From this HCWP perspective, work itself is (re)defined and viewed exclusively in relation to the objectives of the organization and to its perceived measures and criteria of success. While the worker is seen as making an important or crucial contribution to these outcomes, and may gain skills and rewards in the process, these potential developments are predicated upon his/her identification with the need for the organization itself to be successful (however this may be measured). Thus, workers' previous formal compliance with work regimes is to be replaced by positive attitudinal and behavioural commitment to the employing organization (Guest, 1987). This expression of worker commitment is reciprocated by management's abandonment of low trust control strategies as they, in turn, exhibit an approach towards the workforce 'expressive of an individualistic "high trust" organisational culture' (Legge, 1995: 175). Nevertheless, contradictions (and continuities) remain: the perennial question of how to materially reward worker commitment has been widely perceived to lie in some form of individualized performance related pay scheme, but:

> ...with the rise of other ideas, it [incentive pay] became for a time regarded as old-fashioned. Now the pendulum has swung back and

incentive pay is widely seen by management theorists as an essential part of high performance work systems (White *et al.*, 2004: 49)

Whatever the incentive link, it can be seen that the concept and operational framework of mutual commitment is unitarist in character, aimed at not only fusing together the previously discreet interests of employees and employer in 'win-win' work and employment practices and policies but, in the process, banishing conflict from the workplace as well. Images abound of the workforce and management as a team, ship crew or even as a family, with 'senior management as parents and employees as children – at worst rebellious adolescents' (Legge, 1995: 205). For employees, the meaning of work is expressed exclusively in terms of commitment to the organization, which was privileged over any other rival affective source, whether it be trade union, family, craft or profession (Legge, 1995). Organizationally and ideologically, under such a regime, the workplace is transformed into a community in which all have the same interests. The organizational embrace of the 'complete person', in Flecker and Hofbauer's (1998) words, anticipates beyond-contract commitment complemented with deep emotional inputs (Hochschild, 1983). The effects of these can penetrate into all aspects of living, ascribing a dedicated meaning to work which is all-consuming, and epitomized by the 'organization man' first propounded by William H. Whyte Jr. (1956) fifty years ago.

A radically different re-definition of the meaning of work has been proposed by Cappelli (1999), against the background of sustained economic boom and growing labour market supply problems in the USA in the late 1990s. This perspective bears certain similarities to earlier notions that work was being increasingly characterized by those pursuing 'portfolio careers' (Handy, 1994), and that few people would be in long-term salaried employment (Reich, 1993). Cappelli argued that the traditional (and 'psychological') employment contract between employer and employee had been torn asunder by the pull of market forces, and the rise of the labour market had been 'perhaps the most important development in the world in the past generation' (Cappelli, 1999: viii). While the traditional career-based employment relationship was like a marriage, the new one 'is like a lifetime of divorces and remarriages' (Cappelli, 1999: 2). Accordingly, long-term commitment by either employer or employee should be accepted as a thing of the past: 'the old goal of HR management – to minimize overall employee turnover – needs to be replaced by a new goal: to influence who leaves and when'. (Cappelli, 1999: 9) Nevertheless, some form of employee commitment was clearly still necessary, and this was to be achieved through careful selection of new employees, and by encouraging 'ownership' of the project and identification with team rather than with the organization (Cappelli, 1999: 11).

The optimistic view of free worker choice predicated on strong and secure labour markets may then be contrasted with an alternative perspective in which labour market fragmentation is actively promoted and pursued by employers unwilling or unable to offer employee security in a competitive economic environment. For peripheral employees and marginal groups, employment stability and progression can be jettisoned as employers turn to labour market flexibility, whilst contemporaneously and one-sidedly seeking loyalty and commitment from their workers. Here, the meaning of work becomes infused with potential ambiguity, as workers attempt to come to terms both ideologically and practically with their apparent disposability and short-term value whilst confronted with senior executive rhetoric about their worth as their company's valued assets.

Arguably, it is in those areas where employees possess sought-after skills and qualities that commitment approaches may be most eagerly applied by employers. One might also anticipate that knowledge workers would be recipients (and promoters) of such high trust initiatives. Emerging from this analysis, the central linked questions which this book raises concern both the extent and depth of application of these commitment initiatives. We also ask whether under contemporary managerial commitment-seeking regimes operating in changing socio-economic conditions, employees do find greater meaning to their work than in earlier epochs, or simply respond to management initiatives on pragmatic and defensive grounds. Certainly, the omens to date have not been too encouraging. The response of the 'human resources' themselves to the plethora of high commitment techniques, not to mention the ascendancy of HRM practice in management circles generally, has been, in the main, to exhibit few of the characteristics associated with greater commitment to work (however this was defined or measured). Contrary to what might have been expected after almost twenty years of HRM and latterly the application of bundles of high commitment practices, 'workers reveal no widespread belief in any sense of obligation to the firms who employ them' (Taylor, 2002a: 11). People may be working harder (Green, 2001), but the reasons for this may not necessarily derive from greater employee attachment to their work (see for example, Ramsay *et al.*, 2000: 521). Our analysis in later chapters takes us further, however, as the very concept of organizational commitment, a prime objective of modern management and their advisors, begins to dissolve when placed under analytical scrutiny.

Hence, a related area of our enquiry centres around organizational contexts – the work group, the craft or profession, the employing organization – all of which offer sources of meaning and identity which are not necessarily intrinsic to the work tasks themselves. In addition to its economic reward, work has always been looked to for opportunities for social interaction and a source of personal identity (du Gay, 1996: 10). Hodson (2001: 203) identifies four principal ways in which co-workers can offer significant layers of meaning to work: socialization to occupational norms; solidarity and mutual defense; resistance to authority and role distancing; and affirmation of occupational, class and gender identities. Occupational norms are sustained through a combination of interaction with group members, self-regulation and internalization of informal rules which, by competing with managerial (or indeed other work group) definitions of occupational boundaries and limits of control, serve to provide distinctive meanings to work. These meanings can also be deepened through association with specific occupational qualities such as exposure to danger, traditions of loyalty to co-workers and expectations of fairness of treatment.

Hodson points out that group identity, solidarity and mutual defense can arise from potential challenges from managers or other workers and is based on Goffee's (1981) formulation of 'the sense of involvement and attachment' which arises from 'shared experiences of work' (Hodson, 2001: 204). Working groups can create the potential to resist management through the social sabotage of undermining authority (see Ackroyd and Thompson, 1999) and at the same time create personal bonds which can serve to add meaning to otherwise meaningless labour. This latter point is ably demonstrated by early ethnographic work accounts such as those by Terkel (1974) and more recently in a participant study by Cavendish. When asked why she stuck with dirty work conducted in highly uncongenial assembly line conditions, one of Cavendish's female colleagues replied simply: 'because they are such a wonderful crowd in here'. Cavendish (1982: 147) reported that 'everyone pulled together, and looked after each other – otherwise she [her colleague] would have left long ago. She hadn't a bad word to say against any of them, and she thought that was the reason they all stayed'. Similar sentiments can be found in Ehrenreich's (2001) contemporary account of low-wage labour in the US. These comments link in directly with Hodson's (2001: 205) fourth point, that co-workers 'provide a forum for affirming group identities, including class and gender identities'. The case study conducted by Cavendish examined women working on an assembly line. Other studies have demonstrated that gendered workplace norms can be mobilized to emphasize masculine qualities embedded in and protective of prestigious occupations and tasks (Ledwith and Colgan, 1996). As is examined in later chapters, gendered work can therefore add a substantial layer of subjective meaning to work.

These contextual perspectives, where social and group identity can offer meanings to work which prevail over mundane or even oppressive work conditions, possibly help to explain the reasons why nearly fifty years of asking variants of the Morse and Weiss (1955) 'lottery' question have provided repeated demonstrations that a majority of employees would wish to continue working even if they had the financial means to exist without it.

The meaning of work in social life

In examining the meaning of work in the contemporary economy, the contextual interface between work and domestic life is also a vital factor. As we saw above, the Marxian concept of alienation is key to any attempt to answer questions concerning the role that work plays in the worker's life. For Marx (1982: 15) 'the worker therefore feels himself at home only during his leisure time, whereas at work he feels homeless'. It is significant that Marx, in demonstrating alienation within capitalist employment, was also demonstrating the sharp distinction that had arisen between work and non-work life. The industrial era consolidated a social and geographical separation of work from all other areas of social life and from the sets of social relationships which characterized family, household, community, leisure, politics and religion.

Yet, although work under capitalism is not imbued with the intricacies of meaning it may possess in societies where these areas of social action are less functionally specialized, work and non-work do impinge on each other in ways that, because they are seen as nominally separate, can be problematic. For Marx, for example, the worker is also physically exhausted and mentally debased by wage-labour. For workers under early industrialism, work was undoubtedly a central issue in their lives not least because it occupied such a large amount of their waking time. It is important though to distinguish between such quantitative work centrality and situations of qualitative centrality where people may find the endeavour of work to be intrinsically important and meaningful. The 'meaning of work' for the individual, as a combination of both of these dimensions, is the part that work plays in the totality of his/her life. Thus, the non-work part of our lives, including family, class, educational background, position in the life-cycle, local community structures and values, is another mediating and meaning-creating context for attaching meaning to our work. These issues are addressed in the central empirical chapters of this book.

One of the major contributions of British post-war sociology of work was to move away from a narrow concern with job satisfaction and explore the meaning which work held for employees within this wider social setting. This was pursued through a series of classic occupational studies of miners, steelworkers, shipbuilders, dockworkers, farmworkers and fishermen (see for example, Brown *et al.*, 1972; Dennis *et al.*, 1956; Newby, 1972; Bulmer, 1975). The early single-industry community studies seem to demonstrate, in retrospect, that the cash nexus basis of the employment relationship could, under specific historical circumstances, be overlain with orientations of collectivism and occupational identity which permeated not just work, but community and social life, to the extent that work could become a central life interest (Dubin, 1956) even though that work might be hazardous and performed under unpleasant conditions. Focusing on the interactions between work and wider social life inevitably involved engaging not just with contemporary forms of work organization but with the more elusive concepts of community and class, whose traditional patterns appeared to be challenged at the time by the growth of newer industries and related emergence and expansion of technical, white-collar and professional workers (Armstrong et al., 1986; Smith, 1987).

This concern with the role of work in social life reached its culmination with the *Affluent Worker* studies of workers' orientations to work and life in the 1960s (Goldthorpe et al., 1968). Goldthorpe, Lockwood and their colleagues found that, for the car workers, engineers and chemical workers of Luton, the traditional attitudes of 'solidaristic collectivism' had been replaced, not by middle-class identification as was widely claimed at the time, but by a working-class privatized orientation in which employees related to work instrumentally in order to support household based social and economic activities. As had been concluded earlier by Dubin (1956), most industrial workers, outside a few atypical occupational communities, did not see work as a 'central life interest'. Instead, work seems to provide the basis for social and domestic consumption but workers' prime focus of loyalty now lay with home and family. Family structures were nuclear rather than extended and there was little coincidence between patterns of socializing and workplace relationships.

These classic studies of the interaction between workplace and household were carried out in an era of Fordist industrialism, characterized by big workplaces, with predominantly male manual employees, high levels of trade union membership, extensive collective bargaining coverage and full and secure employment. Ironically, however, the publication of the *Affluent Worker* studies coincided with the beginning of the twilight of the post-war consensus; the next few years would see the end of more than twenty years of full employment, and the abandoning of a shared belief in Keynesian demand management allied to a redistributive welfare system. At the same time, the profile of the labour market would shift away from manufacturing towards services (the Vauxhall plant at Luton finally ceased car production during this research project). Observers of the remaining decades of the century again claimed to see a time of structural and attitudinal change.

When examining the meaning of work in the lives of employed people in the early twenty-first century, it is useful to compare the characteristics of mid-century industrialism, above, with the currently widely disseminated models of the 'information society' or 'knowledge economy', where 'economic value is found more in the intangibles, such as new ideas, software, services and relationships, and less in tangibles, like physical products, tons of steel or acres of land' (Newell et al., 2002). Economic activity is held to be characterized by different organizational forms and trends towards geographically dispersed smaller scale workplaces, a more feminized workforce, a far wider range of contractual employment arrangements, flexibility of work organization resulting in significant variability in such fundamental conditions of employment as patterns of working time, and the almost universal use of information and communication technologies. This is also, as we have seen above, the context for propagation of the HRM agenda, stressing employee commitment to the organization.

Nevertheless, the extent to which this all-pervasive model is found in organizational settings may be diminished by the uncertain and pressurized reality of people's working and domestic lives which, in turn, points to more instrumental and contingent meanings extended to work. On one hand, employees may recognize more readily their insecure and commodity status under tight and dynamic economic conditions, under which employers are unable to extend to employees the institutional and behavioural commitment (in terms of security, career, development, progression etc) which can provide the reciprocal context for employee attachment to their work (Thompson, 2003). It has been persuasively argued that recognition of one's career vulnerability in the contemporary organization may be accompanied by profound and disturbing effects: disillusionment and fragmentation of occupational *and* personal identities leading, in Sennett's (1998) words, to an inevitable 'corrosion of character'. At the same time, the meaning of work to employees is likely to be affected by complex interactions between work and non-work influences, such as child-rearing and domestic responsibilities. Labels such as 'working Mum' and 'part-time Father' testify to the potential identity tensions lurking in the contemporary economy, tensions which may be exacerbated by Hochschild's (1997) claimed contrast between the relative order and continuity associated with paid labour and the disorder, frustration and lack of control experienced in coping with domestic life, such that 'work becomes home and home becomes work'.

An invisible, and more subtle, mediating and legitimizing context which contributes to the meanings we attach to work and employment is provided by the wider society and its hegemonic or 'taken for granted' values, more usually referred to as the 'work ethic'. The changes in the societal work ethic which accompanies the industrial separation of work from life have been the subject of historical analysis by Weber (1992), Tawney (1926), Bendix (1967) and Anthony (1977). The Protestant Work Ethic, as interpreted by nineteenth-century employers, legislators and educationalists, emphasized the moral significance and value of effort, obedience and duty, and paid work became both symbolic of this ethic and a universal moral obligation for everyone (Anthony, 1977). Similar manifestations of a culturally-shrouded duty-based work ethic abound across other countries, including those where its assimilation has been stimulated through trade, commerce, conquest and more recently, through globalization (Castells, 2000: 132). For example, in a popular text, Donkin (2001:

212–13) argues that: 'the background to the Japanese work ethic is not so very different to that of the West. There are strong parallels between the rise of the work ethic in western Nonconformism and the way that different social classes under the Tokugawa Shogunate drew on elements of Confucianism and Buddhism to deal with a strictly imposed social order'.

Whilst a work ethic may be embedded in the cultures of industrialized and post industrialized countries, its existence can also be promoted to serve the practical and political purposes of ensuring that sufficient labour is available to meet the needs of the economy. Hence in a recent report, it was pointed out that 'the [UK] Department of Trade and Industry emphasized the need to encourage more women to participate in the labour market in order to help improve the country's competitive performance' (Taylor, 2002b). One consequence of this has been, through a combination of incentives and sanctions, to attempt to inculcate labour market awareness and heightened sense of social responsibility into single non-employed mothers and other disadvantaged groups:

> The paid work ethic lies at the core of the Government's social and economic policies. Employment opportunities for all has become one of its favourite mantras... It is widely argued that it is only through active and paid participation in formalized labour markets that men and women as worker citizens can achieve both increased prosperity and personal salvation... Integration into active participation in paid work has become a crucial test for the Government of what it constitutes as social citizenship. (Taylor, 2002b: 7–8)

Notwithstanding any tendencies toward universal conformity, there can still remain significant national cultural differences in the values attached to work (Hofstede, 1991). This was shown by the international *Meaning of Work* survey in which work centrality was defined as 'the degree of general importance that work has in the life of an individual at any given time,' (MOW, 1987: 81). Although the study did not find work as *the* most important activity in respondents' lives, it did find that work came second only to family (40 per cent placed family as most important as opposed to 27 per cent who placed work as being most important). In this early cross-national study, British workers were apparently found to be less work focused than other countries, particularly Japan. Nevertheless, more recent studies paint a different picture, suggesting that British employees work longer hours than most (Green, 2001), although they may express rising levels of dissatisfaction at doing so. Their application and commitment to work are demonstrated in the ways in which work impacts upon the daily lives of workers and managers in both qualitative and quantitative ways (Hyman *et al.*, 2003).

It is not external contextual factors alone that shape meanings attributed to paid work. The international *Meaning of Work* survey (MOW, 1987) found that age, nationality and gender had an impact on work centrality. Work centrality appears to increase with age, which may provide one explanation as to why older people believe that their work ethic is greater than the next generation. Work centrality also appears to be affected by gender, with men attaching greater importance to work than women (Harpaz and Snir, 2003; Hakim, 1996). Clearly this may reflect divisions of domestic labour in society and the higher representation of women within the part time labour force. One of the factors that the MOW survey did not examine was the impact of 'newer' societal structures on work centrality. A recent US study indicated that between 1970 and 1997, a major shift took place from male-breadwinner to dual-earner couples. During the same period, total working hours for men and women increased, and in a growing number of cases substantially, raising concerns both about the 'over-worked American' and the consequent capacities of these employees to undertake domestic responsibilities (Schor, 1991). High growth in working hours was further concentrated in higher-educated workers, a demographic trend also found in the UK (Jacobs and Gerson, 2001; Dex, 1999; Wolf, 2002).

These factors may also mediate between feelings about work. As we saw above, high proportions of respondents to the *Meaning of Work* survey placed family as their most important activity. If work is hardening both in its intensity and number of hours worked whilst demands are made upon employees from domestic commitments, it is clear that heightened tensions between the two domains may emerge. This may be especially relevant for women, who are participating more in the paid labour market, whilst still continuing as the major contributor to domestic labour in the 'second shift' (Newell, 1993).

Structure of the book

It is clear from the above, necessarily concentrated, overview that, when an employee talks about 'the meaning' of his or her work, they can be referring to a complex amalgam of values derived from a number of different levels of experience. There can be an element in paid employment which is something to be sought after for ethical as well as for economic cash nexus reasons. Additional meanings may be derived from the role which the work plays in wider family or community life, and the degree to which the particular job is part of an identity-sustaining professional or occupational community. How work is actually experienced will be influenced by the managerial style of the organization, the intrinsic and extrinsic reward systems in place, the structure of work organization (such as team work or assembly line) and the content and design of the actual job, tempered by prior dispositions of the employees themselves.

These different perspectives form the basis of our research objectives which are addressed in subsequent chapters. Following our opening exploration in this chapter of the contexts and meanings of work identified in earlier and more recent theoretical and empirical accounts, Chapter 2 follows thematically and analyzes in more detail the changing terrain for work and employment, focusing on the key conceptual and empirical contexts that frame and influence our study. In Chapters 3 to 8 we develop our empirical analysis to present different manifestations of working in our chosen sectors of call (or contact) centres and software development. Chapter 3 looks at the organization of work and nature of working in these two sectors. Chapter 4 focuses on a key ascribed management ambition related to working in the new economy, that of capturing and utilizing the commitment of workers, and the role of human resource management in these dynamic sectors of the economy. Chapter 5 portrays the occupational infrastructure of the two sectors by analyzing and contrasting differences in skills profiles, qualifications and career ambitions and trajectories. Chapter 6 widens the focus from the workplace to the household and community, contrasting the experiences of both sets of workers and their families in attempting to establish a measure of control and meaning to their lives. Chapter 7 builds upon this theme by analyzing the working lives and experiences of women and men in the different sectors and considers the prospects for gender equality. The final substantive chapter, Chapter 8, examines the evidence for class differentiation, based on background, experience and attitudes, in posing the question of whether class is still an issue and framework for self-location and identity in contemporary Britain. The concluding chapter draws on our empirical evidence to indicate the extent to which the experience and meaning of work in the new economy represents a departure or continuation from previous interpretations of orientations to work.

Research setting: Scottish call centre work and software development

The study is based in Scotland, which provides an excellent opportunity to explore connections between changing forms and conditions of employment and the meaning of work at the beginning of the twenty-first century. Its transformation from a base of traditional manufacturing and heavy industry provides a suitable prism for the broader study of work and change in the contemporary economy and society. Not only has Scotland been a major location for new employment sectors, but the relative compactness and self-contained nature of its labour market make a focused analysis of employment trends more feasible than in more diffuse economies. The resonance of Scotland's industrial heritage during this transition to new employment settings therefore provides an appropriate backdrop for the examination of changes in the meaning of work. Thirty years ago, Scottish society and economy was still dominated by the presence of coal, steel, shipbuilding and heavy engineering. As these large-scale industrialized workplaces declined, they were replaced by jobs in new manufacturing areas such as microelectronics and in new areas of service-sector employment. These were often held to be characterized by geographically dispersed smaller workplaces, a more feminized workforce, a diversity of employment contracts, work organization and working time flexibility and widespread use of flexible information technologies.

On the basis of ICT-based research undertaken prior to the commencement of the reported project (Taylor and Bain, 1997; Beirne et al., 1998), two sectors of the Scottish economy which we would expect to epitomize the characteristics of new work are call centres and software development. Previous studies indicate that call centres display important features of the archetypal contemporary organization: for example, the workforce is composed of a majority of women, often young and who work on a variety of temporally flexible work arrangements (Taylor and Bain, 1999). Although organization of work is arguably based on Taylorist principles, it also reflects a contemporary emphasis on flat management structures, teamworking and management attention to gaining employee commitment. Moreover, both numbers of call centres and aggregate employment have expanded spectacularly, extending to virtually every economic sector and rooted in their key role in the cost-effective transformation of the processes and loci of interactive customer servicing. In Scotland, the sector grew from 16,000 employees in 1997 to 46,000 by 2000 and continued less dramatically thereafter to 56,000 by 2003 (Taylor and Bain, 2003b: 1). Financial services, media/telecommunications, travel, information technology and utilities employed the largest numbers, and outsourcing accounted for 1-in-5 call centre jobs.

Software, at the time of the study, was the largest global knowledge-based industry. In 2000, the European market was growing at 10 per cent per annum, and even faster in Scotland (15 per cent) (Ramsay, 1999). The UK market was estimated to be worth some £32 billion (ONS, 2000a) with a further £632 million for computer services activities by other firms. The Scottish software supply industry typifies the diversity of organizations employing IT developers. These include independent houses, often owner-managed, providing customized packages for other organizations. Large concentrations of software engineers are also found in organizational subsections of finance, public service, telecommunications and other sectors. The Labour Force Survey 2000 estimated some 9,000 computer systems managers, 14,600 software engineers and 19,000 computer analysts employed in Scotland, with software divisions of large organizations representing 45 per cent, and individual contractors and sole traders accounting for 17 per cent of the workforce (ONS, 2000b).

Software supply was seen as representing the archetypal knowledge work, seeking employees with good academic qualifications and technical proficiency within a context of rapidly changing skills demands, and providing working environments with responsible autonomy and flexible employment conditions, including sub-contracting and project work (see Beirne et al., 1998). Nevertheless, little was known about the management and control of these workers or their attachment to work and organization.

Methodology

Four call centre and four software operations were originally selected as case studies for this project. The study commenced in December 1998, with fieldwork conducted between September 1999 and February 2002. During this period, there were considerable changes in the external market, and to the nature and volume of the product/service in both sectors. Actual and planned changes in ownership, through mergers and takeovers, as well as significant and continuous management reorganization and turnover, were characteristic of the extremely volatile situation in the case study organizations. This wider context, as well as a detailed description of each case study organization, is described below.

There were three principal design phases to the project. The first phase involved producing descriptive background profiles of both sector and community. Together with product and labour market statistics, this background information allowed us to identify an appropriate sampling strategy. The sampling strategy was to represent, as far as was feasible, the overall profile of the two sectors, distinguishing between city and non-city locations, establishment size and type of product or service. Owing to the diversity and large population of small software houses, the number of software case studies was expanded from four to six.[1]

Teams of four or five researchers were designated to each of the companies, with each member of the full project team participating in at least three case studies, providing researchers with exposure to both software and call centre settings. Each team was responsible for gathering key company information from documents, statistics and records, attendance at meetings, observation of work and training sessions and through guided conservations with key groups of informants. This process yielded substantial data on company history, structure, environment, key developments, employment policies, work organization, arrangements for employee voice and key themes emerging from managers' and employees' experiences of their workplaces.

---

1 The sixth company, Kappa, ceased trading during the period of the fieldwork and for this reason is not included in the subsequent analysis.

Toward the end of this data-gathering process, which typically required three or four months in each organization, a detailed written questionnaire was distributed to structured samples of respondents in call centres and whole populations in the software houses. This process was usually extended over some weeks to account for different shifts, holidays and absence. The questionnaire was designed to capture perceptions and attitudes toward the job, the company, representation, work-life linkages and biographical details. Structured information on working hours, shifts and career history was also gathered. Sections were standardized to allow cross-company comparability and questions were constructed from established scales (for example job control, satisfaction indices) or designed specifically for the project (for example on social and family networks). In total, 1,183 questionnaires were returned with a high overall response rate of 62 per cent. Further details of the survey can be found in Appendix A and B.

Employees' and managers' work experiences were investigated further through semi-structured interviews, drawing on issues that emerged from the earlier phase. Representative groups of employees were each interviewed at their workplaces, with recorded interviews lasting about 90 minutes. These interviews probed work and educational histories and their relationship to the present job; experiences of working in the company; work-life linkages and future plans; and perceptions of society, class and status. Between 17 and 26 of these interviews were conducted in each company, except for the small software start-up (Lambda) where three were undertaken. Details of these interviews can be found in Appendix A, Table A.3. To obtain further information on software workers, where the dynamics of the labour process are less accessible than in call centres, small cohorts of software workers were also asked to complete work and home diaries for one week.

The final phase of the study comprised off-site interviews conducted with a sample of respondents selected from the company interview phase. Four companies were chosen, split equally on the basis of city and non-city location. The subject-matter of these interviews shifted beyond the workplace to provide short biographies and to engage with issues of work-life boundaries, domestic and community life and non-work identity. In all, 26 of these in-depth recorded interviews were conducted.

Case study organizations

The call centre companies

The four call centre organizations, operating in financial services, travel, telecommunications/entertainment, and outsourcing, were selected to be representative of the sectoral locus of call centre work in Scotland, although the choice of industries was representative of the wider UK call centre market. The companies were also differentiated by their city and small town locations. Table 1.1 summarizes these features of each call centre case study. In addition to product diversity, the case studies exhibited other features – differing managerial emphases on quality and quantity, inbound and outbound call handling, a variety of shift arrangements – which underlined the fact that, despite common defining characteristics, call centres and their workflows are not uniform. For example, at one end are centres/workflows where simple, straightforward servicing and selling transactions predominate ('volume' operations are the most common) while, at the other, customer interaction is more complex ('value' operations).

Notably all four case studies commenced operations between 1995 and 1998, during the period of the UK call centre sector's swiftest expansion. Call centres promised significant cost savings and enhanced revenue generation as a result of the centralization of hitherto geographically dispersed front office servicing or sales operations, or through the creation of entirely new operations. In the UK the potential for economies of scale, overheads reduction and new selling opportunities was first exploited in the finance sector through the successes of branchless banking (First Direct) and insurance (Direct Line) (Bain and Taylor, 2002a; Taylor and Bain, 1999), which then acted as a catalyst for the diffusion of the call centre model through diverse economic sectors. Wherever customer servicing could be conducted remotely the call centre emerged as the dominant model.

Centralization of function and process lies at the very heart of the call centre. Thus, activities at our case studies were concentrated on single sites and conducted by sizeable workforces, from 170 to 530 employees. It should be noted, additionally, that the mean size of a call centre in Scotland was 235 during our period of study (Bain and Taylor, 2002b) and almost three-quarters of the sectoral workforce were employed in establishments of 250

Table 1.1 Profile of call centre case studies

Pseudonym	Location	Sector	Services provided	Year opened	Workforce size
Entcomm	Non-city	Telecomms/ entertainment	Customer service, sales, transfers	1998	530
Holstravel	Non-city	Holidays/ travel	Sales, enquiries, some customer service	1997	340
Moneyflow	City	Financial services	Sales, customer service	1995	170
Thejobshop	City	Various/ outsourcer	Customer service, sales, IT/technical support, telemarketing	1998	320–400

or more staff. The majority of call centres, therefore, our case studies included, are very much gathered organizations (Handy, 1985).

The financial services company Moneyflow, which specializes in mortgages, insurance and unsecured loans, employed 170 at its Glasgow call centre at the time of our research. Two discreet types of work, or workflow,[2] could be distinguished, and these reflect distinct telephonic services providing non-secured and secured loans respectively, which corresponded to the 'unregulated' and 'regulated' sides of the business.

Thejobshop is an outsourced call centre located in Glasgow whose on-site employment levels fluctuated between 320 and 400, as operations conducted on behalf of clients expanded and contracted. The core, preferred clients provided the greatest revenue and promoted Thejobshop's quality reputation, while smaller business clients took advantage of low start-up costs realized through the utilization of spare capacity, and the exploitation of a flexible internal labour market. Contractual agreements between Thejobshop and clients, closely allied to the type of service or product offered, influenced the nature of work organization. Contracts included Service Level Agreements (SLAs), a universal feature of the call centre sector, which stipulate the volume and percentage of calls to be answered within set time limits, plus variable combinations of performance criteria.

Entcomm, a large US multinational employing 530 people located in a small ex-industrial town near Glasgow, provided its UK customers with a range of services related to its cable-delivered telecommunications and entertainment products, including inquiries, billing, payments, booking or changing packages, repairs and maintenance. Holstravel is a large, long-established travel and holiday organization. At its call centre in a former industrial area in Central Scotland, 340 were employed, of whom 86 per cent were call handling staff, known as Travel Consultants.

The software companies

The five software case studies were selected to be representative of the diversity of the software supply sector. Two of the four Scottish-based firms studied were small (Pi and Lambda); one was medium (Gamma); and one medium-large (Omega). Our final case study was represented by a large division of a UK-wide organization (Beta). Four offered systems integration options to clients and all offered a combination of software maintenance and custom applications, and with on site support. Three

---

2 The use of the term 'workflow' follows that of Frenkel *et al.* (1999: 36) where it is defined 'as a structured set of tasks (work) leading to a specified output (defined to include services) oriented toward a particular market', acknowledging that workplaces often embrace multiple forms of work organization.

(Pi, Gamma and Lambda) were essentially single product companies offering a full package from installation, integration and support; Omega and Beta offered a range of custom applications, although Omega tended to use established software platforms whilst Beta was involved in more cutting edge and long-term developments within the telecommunications sector. Both Omega and Beta were multi-location organizations with a combination of company-located and virtual teams, although the latter were more evident in Beta. These features of the five case study organizations are summarized in Table 1.2.

Although at the time of the research, Scotland had a growing software industry, there were still few large indigenous firms. This has a significant impact on Scotland's ability to participate in an international market, and to attract and retain skills. Approximately 38 per cent of all software employees in Scotland were employed in indigenous software firms (the largest of which, Omega, employed about 200 people). The remaining workers were employed within autonomous software divisions of large organizations (45 per cent), sole traders (2 per cent), and individual contractors (15 per cent) (ONS, 2000b).

The software houses were selected to represent a range of employment contexts in the sector. Beta was the software arm of a former publicly owned utility and provided mainly internal support to the large established telecommunications company of which it is a part. Following some restructuring and substantial job losses in the late 1990s, the software centre had moved to a new high-tech office building in 1999. A significant proportion of the 275 employees were based at the main office in Glasgow with the remainder in a satellite office in Edinburgh.

Omega was a fast-growing software house, established in the 1980s to become one of the largest independent Scottish software houses and was still directed by one of its founders. It operated from its main office in Edinburgh and another site in southern England with 137 permanent employees and 111 contractors (not all of whom were working at any one time) based in Scotland. There were 50 employees at the southern site, mainly working on AS400 technology and combination of new build and maintenance work generally for commercial sector clients. The Edinburgh office generated much of its work on the basis of long-term links with government, the health service and some financial sector organizations. A significant proportion of Omega's work was undertaken on client sites. At the time of the study the satellite office in England had just undergone restructuring and a number of employees had been made redundant. This was the only experience of redundancies within the history of the organization.

One medium-sized and two smaller independent firms (Gamma, Pi and Lambda) employed 150, 50 and 20 employees respectively. Pi was founded in 1977 as a one person business in Aberdeen, establishing the current head

Table 1.2 Profile of software case studies

Pseudonym	Location	Primary market	Product/Services provided	Year opened	Workforce size
Beta	City	Telecommunications; internal clients	Bespoke telephone operations; robotic tools; database integration; financial systems	Former public sector utility; restructured software centre 1999	275
Gamma	Non-city	Major database users, initially manufacturing, but in recent years financial and business services	Systems integration of front/end operations; open systems development; bespoke CRM systems; subcontractor linking major platforms for clients	1986	150
Lambda	Non-city	Insurance; IT multinationals	Health and safety recording software	1996	20
Omega	City	Public sector, health services, financial services	Applications development, resourcing, testing, client support; AS400 technology	1985	248
Pi	City	Law firms	Legal and business software development, testing, support, training & maintenance.	1977/1999	50

office in Edinburgh in 1999. Pi had around 50 employees at the time of the study, with intentions to expand. The business was divided evenly between England and Scotland with additional clients in Wales, Eire and Nairobi. The nature of the work for the organization had changed considerably with the introduction of the personal computer and recently there had been much more investment into the software side of the organization. The organization also had a large development department to make sure that the software was kept up to date.

Gamma was located across five sites in the UK and with outposts in Sydney and Jakarta. The Head Office (and focus for the fieldwork) was located on the outskirts of Glasgow. The company had grown quickly in recent years, developing and providing software for front-end business solutions, principally for call centres and small and medium-sized clients. Consequently, over half of the work was outplaced to client sites, both in the UK and overseas. The owner and chief executive had designed a flat organizational structure, where staff would not be confined by formal job descriptions, job titles or reward structure. About 150 staff were employed in commercial, development and deployment teams.

Lambda was established in 1996 as a four-person management buy-out of a local engineering company's health and safety recording system, which they had developed. The software produced by Lambda filled a perceived gap in the market, and was essentially a management tool for reviewing and prompting risk assessments and recording and analyzing accidents, which could also be bolted on to personnel and training files. The company initially experienced rapid growth and, by 2001, employed twenty staff in their Scottish office. Lambda also part-owned an Australian software firm, and had also opened an office in Hong Kong. The managing director claimed that Lambda had not been making big profits, but had re-invested heavily in order to grow the company. While health and safety expertise had been their focus, the company emphasized that their skills were in software generally. As with other smaller software case studies, the organizational structure was flat, with few specialisms, and largely project-driven.

All five surviving software organizations were located in Scotland's central belt, almost equally distributed between the greater Glasgow and greater Edinburgh areas. With the exception of Beta, all were Scottish owned start-ups, still run by the founder or founders. Their demographic characteristics generally matched the profile of the software sector in the UK and Europe – a young professional workforce with over two-thirds aged between 21 and 40. The general dominance of men in software work was reflected particularly in Beta (where four-fifths of survey respondents were male) but less so in Omega (two-thirds male) where the founder was a woman.

Summary

Having outlined the historical and theoretical background to our exploration of meanings of work in the contemporary knowledge economy and provided a framework for the context and descriptions of the case study companies operating in this economy, the next chapter looks in closer conceptual, empirical and critical detail at the changing socio-economic contexts in which employment relationships are located. This leads to an examination of the impact of key distinguishing features of the knowledge economy, in terms of heightened competition, globalization and information and communication technology on work organization and working patterns.

2
Into the New Century: The Changing Terrain for Work and Employment

Discussions, assertions and policy statements concerning the nature of work at the end of the twentieth century can only be fully understood if we review them against wider socio-economic contexts. These comprise both substantive and observable trends in employment and society in the UK and, given the location of this study, in Scotland, and also of a conceptual element: the prevailing theories, models and predictions about what such trends *mean*. This latter, conceptual context – broadly that a paradigm shift has taken place in society, economy and the world of work – is associated with the knowledge economy model. This may be seen to constitute a key element of an interpretative hegemony that so pervades policy statements and popular discourse as to have become received common sense.

This chapter starts with an exposition of the knowledge economy discourse and is followed by central elements in the critique of this new orthodoxy. These serve as a point of departure, as we expand on the principal themes and conceptual underpinnings of each of the book's empirical chapters (3 to 8). Moving from this largely conceptual realm to the domain of the empirical, we begin with a consideration of some fundamental characteristics of globalization and the new political economy, and then outline the changing regulatory and legal framework that contextualises the contemporary employment relationship. Finally, summary profiles of the Scottish economy and labour market preface some of the notable dynamics of the two emerging sectors which form the specific focus of the study.

The knowledge economy

It is taken for granted by proponents that knowledge has now become the only source of value and dynamism (cf. Huws, 1999), or as Castells puts it, 'what is specific to the informational mode of development is the action of knowledge upon knowledge itself as the main source of productivity' (Castells, 1996: 17). For Drucker (1993), knowledge has rapidly become the principal economic resource, replacing capital, natural resources and labour. Consequently, there exists a weightless, or dematerialized, economy, in which intangible services are increasingly replacing physical goods as the driving force (Quah, 1997; Despres and Hiltrop, 1995) and in which invisible goods, simultaneously infinitely expandable, indivisible and inappropriable, defy the traditional laws of economics. The manipulation of symbols (Reich, 1993) demarcates the new from the old economy of mass production and consumption, Taylorism and standardization. According to an influential popularist paraphrase of more academic accounts of this ostensibly post-capitalist knowledge economy, 'We're all in the thin air business these days...the real assets of the modern economy come out of our heads not out of the ground: ideas knowledge, skills, talent and creativity' (Leadbeater, 1999: 18).

The concept of the knowledge economy is inexplicable without reference to the information technology revolution of the last twenty years which Castells, among others, holds to be 'at least as major a historical event as was the eighteenth-century industrial revolution' (Castells, 1996: 29). In this account, the transformative power of information processing and communication technologies, and their pervasive application, has created a sharp discontinuity in the material basis of economy, society, and culture. This has produced the growth of what Thurow (1996) calls 'brainpower industries', such as computers and telecommunications, and has changed the nature of the increasingly dominant service sector.

It is argued that firms are thus no longer, nor can be, large bureaucratic and vertical organizations, for their rigidities would render them unsuitable for the flexible, creative, knowledge-based capabilities indispensable for success in the new epoch (Castells, 2001: 1). Instead, as the title of the first volume of Castells' *magnum opus* indicates, the informational society generates networks which become the fundamental components of the new organizations (1996: 180). An elusive metaphor, the network essentially implies the horizontal dispersal of power among autonomous centres, each entwined in webs of mutual dependence. Thus, networks, not firms, have become 'the actual operating unit', as the boundary-less network enterprise has emerged as the characteristic form of the informational economy. So influential have been these assertions deriving from informationalism and the network society, that they have even informed texts profoundly critical of the contemporary, capitalist world order (Hardt and Negri, 2000).

Some reservations and challenges

The knowledge economy model has not been without its critics. The concept of knowledge work itself, as either a valid descriptive or analytical category, has been critiqued as being riddled with confusion (Collins, 1998), as has its claims to liberate individuals in work organizations. For example, we should make the necessary distinction between knowledge work and working knowledge, for workers have always had knowledge *of* their work, but this is not at all what is meant by knowledge work. Furthermore, it is all too easy to conflate knowledge work with the processing of information, or at a lower rung on the knowledge ladder, simple data inputting and/or data manipulation (Thompson *et al.*, 2001).

Structuralist, relatively static concepts of knowledge as expertise residing in individuals or organizations which can be manipulated and managed (for example Nonaka and Takeuchi, 1995), can be distinguished from more dynamic concepts of knowing deriving from process perspectives (Newell *et al.*, 2002). The latter criticize attempts to objectify knowledge and emphasize its socially constructed nature, deviating from any notion of knowledge as something which is possessed. Blackler (1995) acknowledges the limitations of his own structuralist categories of embrained, embodied and embedded knowledge as possessed by organizations, suggesting the increasing importance of encultured knowledge, or socially constructed ways of achieving shared understandings. Thus, he summarizes, 'knowledge is multi-faceted and complex, being both situated and abstract, implicit and explicit, distributed and individual, physical and mental, developing and static, verbal and encoded' (1995: 1032–3).

As indicated, the most influential account of the knowledge economy has been provided by Castells, although 'informationalism' is his chosen descriptor for this new mode of development. The widespread acclaim his trilogy received from both academia and the political establishment has tended to diminish the impact of the trenchant criticisms that have been made of its core concepts (see Jessop, 2000). Most significantly, Castells mistakenly ascribes to knowledge the ability to drive society, divorcing it from the fundamental processes of capital accumulation, competition and the full circuit of capital. Indeed the movement to 'higher levels of complexity in information processing' is not the result of the action of knowledge upon knowledge. As Callinicos has observed, the ceaseless pressure to upgrade computing systems is driven not by 'any autonomous technological imperative, but by the interest in profit-maximisation shared by Microsoft, Intel and the PC manufacturers' (2001: 34–5). In the final analysis, despite both his protestations to the contrary, and the apparent sophistication of his analysis, Castells falls into the very familiar trap of technological determinism. In this sense, despite his residual attachment to Marxist terminology, Castells' (1996: 25) self-confessed admiration for post-industrialists such as Bell (1973) and Touraine (1971), leads him to embrace their conviction that advanced societies have transcended the antagonisms of capitalist society.

The notion of the 'weightless' economy has been unpacked by Huws (1999, 2003) revealing the materiality of the labour processes which lie beneath the apparently intangible provision of services. Others have critiqued the exaggerated historical significance of the ICT revolution, pointing to scientific breakthroughs such as the telegraph, television or jet propulsion as equally transformative (Lyon, 1988).

While widely recognized that considerable change has taken place in the organizational structure of firms, and that traditional bureaucracies, in one sense, have been broken up with the creation of smaller units, profit centres and internal markets, it is still necessary to distinguish between the delegation of operational autonomy, and strengthened financial and other controls by the central structures. Far from power being dispersed through the nodes of the network, Thompson and McHugh (2002: 172) point out that analysis of new corporate structures demonstrates that decentralization of the form is accompanied by *centralization* of the substance of power. Furthermore, contrary to the new economy's celebration of the small-is-beautiful, e-commerce enterprise, powerful tendencies to oligopoly, merger and acquisition remain throughout the economy, even in its emergent knowledge sectors.

It is debatable whether workforce expansion has occurred mainly in occupations which can be identified as knowledge work. For example, the new economy workforce has been variously defined as those working in the most productive sectors of the economy, such as software and financial services (Henwood, 2003), those in creative occupations (Reich, 2001), or those in the fastest growing ones (Newmark and Reed, 2000). While there is evidence showing recent and future expansion in some high skill occupations, for example, in the ICT sector (European Information Technology Observatory, 2002; OECD, 2000, 2002), equally, there has been substantial growth in low-level, routinized information-handling or interactive service work (Fleming *et al.*, 2003; Henwood, 2003; Thompson *et al.*, 2001).

It is difficult to equate these lower level jobs with the ideal-typical knowledge worker, and rosy views of the diversity of jobs found in the service sector, for example, have been dismissed as exaggerated (Kumar, 1981). Thompson *et al.* (2001) argue, moreover, that far from liberating workers' creativity, new forms of work embody the same codification of workers' knowledge and inherent opportunity for exploitation typified in the scientific rationality of 'old' low-skilled jobs. Both these lines of criticism are summed up by Collins (1998) who states that 'the focus on knowledge work is a distraction, which decontextualizes the experience of work and removes questions of control from the analysis'.

Key themes and issues in working life

Organizational life and the nature of work

The implications of the knowledge economy model for assumptions about the significance of work in the lives of the twenty-first century's citizens are far-reaching. With information technologies so extensively and profoundly embedded within these networks, the old command and control bureaucratic relationships are seen as anachronistic, replaced by horizontal interaction between committed and self-motivated knowledge workers who co-operate across flattened structures. Long-established technical, financial and bureaucratic controls are claimed to have withered as patterns of 'cultural co-ordination, internalized commitment and self-discipline' (Thompson, 2003) emerge among employees. The pervasive utilization of IT is said not only to foster collaboration among colleagues, but to be a key enabler of new forms of work organization (Nohria and Berkeley, 1994).

One of the key tenets of the new orthodoxy is, therefore, that the content of work has become more skilful, challenging and creative, precisely because it is now *knowledgeable*. It is proposed, moreover, that all work can now be defined as occupying this elevated state (Cortada, 1998), and not only the work carried out by the skilled professionals or managers who were Drucker's (1993) original knowledge workers. Increasingly, flexible organizational structures designed for rapid responses to changing market conditions have led to a transformation of what once were relatively stable bundles of prescribed tasks into dynamic sets of interdependent employee roles. Some even claim that the concept of a job (meaning stable job description) is dead (Bridges, 1995). More circumspect analysis still maintains that jobs should be defined not only as task-based, but also in terms of an expanded model of desirable work performance which goes beyond narrow definitions of task performance to include contextual performance (Borman and Motowildo, 1993; Campbell *et al.*, 1993). This acknowledges a new complexity in the cognitive, social and emotional demands being placed on employees. Employees are expected to assume greater responsibility, to perform a variety of roles, to integrate regularly new knowledge and technology into existing processes, to monitor and control information produced by new technology, and to interact with a changing collection of team members representing various roles and relationships.

One example of this changing environment is provided by front-line work, where knowledge and services are seen as being inextricably connected (Frenkel *et al.*, 1999). Here, analytical skills are facilitated by new technology, and customer requirements demand customized responses, such that the creation and processing of knowledge has become a central activity. In their influential study of interactive service work, Frenkel *et al.* conclude that standardization and direct control are no longer prevalent, and even call centre work (i.e. 'service work' in their typology) as 'not as routine and uncreative as sometimes depicted' (1999: 71). The relational dimension to these new forms of work also means that supervisors will adopt facilitative, rather than directive, styles, and ascribe relatively little significance to operational data and measurement of performance (1999: 141).

In other types of knowledge work the committed, empowered employee can be more readily identifiable. Software developers, for example, have been identified as new professionals who illustrate well the prestigious status of 'gold-collar workers' (Kelley, 1985). Software work, it is said, is usually conducted in non-bureaucratic working environments with loose forms of management (Alvesson, 1995; Kunda, 1992). Software workers are more likely to be motivated by opportunities for development, autonomy and status (Cappelli, 2000; Kunda, 1992) and their career paths are boundary-less (Arthur and Rousseau, 1996), entrepreneurial (Kanter, 1989) and based on loose commitment to any one organization. As Barrett (2001: 2) comments, in this view, software workers:

> have joined the ranks of the young, upwardly mobile 'gold-collar professionals', who are said to earn high wages, work in modern workplaces for enlightened managers, and come and go from work as they please.

Far from being a quality confined to professional occupations, however, such enlightened images of knowledge work are thought to extend across the hierarchy of skills. Common to knowledge economy accounts is the notion that 'information technology has *empowered* the direct worker at the shopfloor level (be it in the process of testing chips or underwriting insurance policies)' (Castells, 1996: 257). Thus, whether in manufacturing or the office, the growth of empowerment, facilitated by information technologies, signifies the historical revival of work autonomy (Castells, 2001: 92) and the disappearance of routine, repetitive tasks. Relieved from repetitive, routinized and directed tasks, and imbued with greater skills, education and knowledge, the implication is that workers now derive greater satisfaction from their jobs. Reeve's (2000) panegyric to the new world of work is exceptional only by virtue of its uncritical enthusiasm, and many commentators depict knowledge work as a positive, optimistic and even liberating experience.

Many, often writing from the standpoint of core labour process theory, have challenged the view that old forms of control, bureaucratic and otherwise, have been rendered redundant in the new world of creative, committed, participative work (see Thompson and McHugh, 2002: 180–90; Warhurst and Thompson, 1998). Indeed a recurring theme is that, while recognizing that manifest changes have taken place and new forms of control have emerged, Taylorism has not only endured (e.g. Delbridge, 1998) but has penetrated new areas of work (Taylor and Bain, 1999), so that the 'shadow of scientific management continues to fall over contemporary work organization' (Smith and Thompson, 1998: 555). The contending claims regarding this paradigmatic shift will be evaluated in the context of our empirical investigation of nature of work organisation in call centres and software development in Chapter 3.

Organizational life and the role of management

The 'shock of Japan' of the early 1980s resulted in a paradigm shift in the approach of Western organizations to people management and, for the subsequent two decades, such catechisms of HRM as 'people are our greatest asset' have been dutifully recited as an essential component of the new management orthodoxy. This is, admittedly, what Storey calls the 'idealized and narrated model' and there has been a significant debate over the degree to which integrated and strategic HRM policies have actually been pursued in practice (Storey, 2005). However, whether formally pursued or not, the HRM model has become incorporated into the perspective and language about approaches to employment. The context for the reappraisal of the contribution of employees to organizational performance was the putative move in competition strategy from cost minimization to an emphasis on quality and flexibility. Whether this move away from cost minimization was ever as universal as was claimed is, again, debatable. What is important is that the goals of quality and flexibility have similarly become incorporated into the hegemonic management discourse.

Although quality models had their origins in manufacturing, by the 1990s this sector was employing a progressively smaller percentage of the workforce in the developed economies and, at the same time, in the service sector, quality of service and service delivery came to be perceived as the major way in which customers differentiated one service provider, such as a bank or insurance company, from another. Thus, at the same time as the diffusion of the HRM model of people management, a shift developed in the quality literature in the operational definition of quality away from Juran's 'fitness for use' towards the idea of meeting or exceeding the customer's expectations or 'delighting the customer' (Wilkinson et al., 1998: 10). As Legge has pointed out, these concepts of 'customer awareness and customer care', also serve as a legitimization of market forces as the parameters for social action (Legge, 1995: 192), and provide a useful, and powerful, underpinning rationale for intensified control practices in the workplace.

The 'differentiation of demand' which emerged from the new cult of the customer has helped to shape the nature of work relationships within contemporary organizations (du Gay and Salaman, 1992). In particular, the delivery of the two new iconic values of 'quality,' in both production and services, and 'flexibility' in just about everything, was perceived to depend on changing the subjective orientation of the employee to the organization through the manipulation of the concepts of commitment and the psychological contract. In a much-quoted, though essentially insubstantial, article in 1985, Walton (1985) transparently outlined the new project: to change the nature of the worker's engagement with the organization from one of grudging compliance, and a heavy focus on the employment cash-nexus, to one of ready commitment to the organization and its goals. Early 1980s prescriptions for HRM in the US stressed the need for mutuality and the building of high trust relationships (Beer and Spector, 1985; Walton, 1985) while in the UK commitment formed one of the four distinguishing features of HRM in Guest's model, along with flexibility, quality and strategic integration (Guest, 1987). Although the HR literature has been fairly vague about defining commitment, beyond seeing it as an internalized belief in the values of the organization, it is more specific in claiming which practices will enhance it and what behaviours can be expected from a state of high commitment. Whether such optimism can be justified has, however, been seriously questioned, in a number of critical accounts (see, for example, Legge, 2001; Ramsay *et al.*, 2000). Chapter 4 will contribute to these debates.

Nevertheless, 'high commitment work practices' have been identified as including team working, team briefing, multi-skilling, developmental appraisal and reward policies and culture management. It was perceived to be essential that the organizational culture promoted an individualistic high trust culture in which individual employees could feel 'empowered' to exert discretionary effort or 'constructive proactivity' (Legge, 1995: 174). To this end, the now familiar battery of performance related pay, individual appraisal and development plans (together with de-recognition or non-recognition of unions) provided the structural counterpoint to the new unitarist values based upon quality and the customer.

The implications for employee behaviour were to be significant: in the traditional orientation, workers had worked to contract in terms of the prevailing effort bargain (Baldamus, 1961), both in terms of working time and rate of work, so that extra effort (overtime, speed-up) was expected to be matched by extra remuneration. On the other hand, in the hoped-for new orientation workers would *willingly* (an important point) work 'beyond contract' (a phrase first suggested by Alan Fox (1974) in a much more humane vision of how employment could be). Such discretionary effort would, together with a lowered rate of employee turnover, be a key indication of a raised level of commitment to the organization.

It is managing the organizational culture which has probably most frequently been seen as the key to generating enhanced identification and attachment. Much of the importance attached to organizational culture derives from the much quoted, though methodologically dubious, work of Peters and Waterman in the early 1980s in which the two McKinsey consultants claimed to identify the possession of 'strong cultures' as the defining characteristic of successful companies (Peters and Waterman, 1982). While it was realized that this culture change would, in existing employment sectors, be akin to turning round an oil tanker, great hopes were held for the 'green' sectors of employment offered by the new knowledge intensive jobs. This view seemed to be given support by proponents of the information/knowledge society model, such as Zuboff (1988), who often seemed to see the technology itself, and its associated flatter post-bureaucratic and more open organizations, as engendering more integrated and committed employees. Similarly, Castells saw the emerging networked organization as *requiring* both discretionary effort and employment continuance. Much higher levels of employee involvement were needed 'so that they [employees] do not keep their tacit knowledge solely for their own benefit' and there must be stability of employment 'because only then does it become rational for the individual to transfer his/her knowledge to the company and for the company to diffuse explicit knowledge among its workers' (Castells 1996: 160).

Occupational life

Downsizing (or 'rightsizing'), de-layering, business re-engineering, offshoring, and other variations on the 'flexible firm' model imply a growing reliance on atypical employment practices, such as freelancing, subcontracting, teleworking and fixed-term contracts (Felstead and Jewson, 1999). These trends are associated with a transformation in the shape of employment which has important consequences for employees' experience of occupational life. According to new economy writers, the swelling ranks of symbolic analysts who make up the contingent workforce increasingly follow portfolio career paths (Cappelli, 1999; Handy, 1994; Reich, 1993), swapping the promise of secure employment for the acquisition of knowledge and skills which will enhance their employability (Arthur *et al.*, 1999; Cappelli, 1999). Occupational life, therefore, is shaped by the forces of supply and demand in the external market, even in sectors historically associated with 'jobs for life' employment, such as the civil service (Nolan and Slater, 2003).

The call centre and software sectors are often held to have embraced these structural transformations, but the notion of 'portfolio careers' based on marketability and employability may be more salient for software rather than call centre workers. The strong labour market position of software developers in both Europe and the US in recent years has encouraged a high level of inter-organizational mobility (Cappelli, 2001) with tenure in a single organization relatively short at an average of 18 to 36 months (ONS, 2000b). This high mobility implies less organizationally-bound work patterns and career paths, and is often thought to be fuelled by the personal preferences and efforts of the archetypal, self-motivated knowledge workers, dedicated to their work and career rather than to any one organization's mission (Kunda, 1992).

Call centres evoke quite a different occupational life. Much has been written about the ascendancy of management control through automation and scripting (Fernie and Metcalf, 1997) and the routine, deskilled and potentially stressful nature of the work. Counter to this image, though, is the portrayal of call centre agents as semi-professional, knowledge workers, who are valued, and hence rewarded, by employers for possessing strong social skills and competencies. Frenkel *et al.* (1999), for example, argued that employers involved in interactive service work are forced to pay attention to identifying and developing these competencies to meet the needs of their customers. In a detailed analysis of the components of service work, Hampson and Junor (2005) similarly emphasize the complex and 'invisible' interplay of intellectual skills, tacit knowledge, time management, negotiation, problem solving and emotional labour skills involved in call centre work which should form the foundation of training strategy.

Despite these claims, the reality in call centres is that training and development is determined largely by business need, and primarily conceived and operationalized as a means of performance management rather than a progressive approach to skill development. Some argue that the creation of strong cultures, based on sociability and a shared concern with customer service, may counterbalance the inescapably difficult working conditions and high turnover, engendering short-term commitment to organizational goals (cf. Belt *et al.*, 2002; Callaghan and Thompson, 2002; Deery and Kinnie, 2002; Thompson *et al.*, 2004). This leads us to question whether the notion of 'a career' as a progressive and developmental sequence of work experiences has any relevance in such a context.

Implicit in the supposed flexibilization of careers is the expectation that employees must now proactively manage these adjustments in a largely self-responsible manner. This has led some observers to identify a more profound transformation of work, employment and career underlying current trends towards flexibility and the fragmentation of production (e.g. Holtgrewe, 2001; Marchington *et al.*, 2005; Pongratz and Voß, 2003). Two aspects of this transformation are of relevance in this book. The first denotes a shift from adaptation to self-management of career (Chapter 5) and the second relates to a gradual erosion of the established frontiers between work and life (Chapter 6). With 'multi-employer relationships' (Rubery *et al.*, 2005) and the erosion of traditional career trajectories, employees are compelled towards sustaining their own marketability, or employability, through recurrent qualification and training, or geographical and occupational mobility. As already noted, the more highly skilled software developer is likely to be more readily able to adjust to these demands than the call centre employee (Saxenian, 1996).

Household and community life

A central theme of the present volume is an exploration of the interconnectedness between paid work and people's non-work lives, and the ways in which these can influence each other. Clearly, the contextual relationship between work and non-work will affect, and indeed be affected by, the meanings and significance which people attach to work. These in turn are influenced by other factors, such as level of pay, intrinsic satisfaction derived from work, career opportunities and so forth. There is no doubt, however, that tensions between the two domains have been exacerbated in recent years under pressure of spill-over from work in the form of extended working hours, longer and more flexible working days, and work intensification under the impact of new technology, performance indicators and target setting, work monitoring and tighter managerial controls over such employee behaviour as absenteeism (White et al., 2004). It is recognized that, in a more individualized employment climate, protections offered to workers through trade union membership and employment regulation have diminished, again with potential impacts on attitudes toward work and the workplace. Chapter 6 will provide a series of insights into the debates on the mutually conditioning relationships between the spheres of work and non-work.

From the domestic sphere, substantive changes have occurred with growing numbers of women in paid employment (EOC, 2005), aided by economic sanctions and political pressures applied to women with family and caring responsibilities to encourage re-entry to work (Taylor, 2002b). A further twist to patterns of working life is provided by the rise in dual-income households, either where both partners work full-time, or where there is some combination of full and part-time working (Bradley et al., 2000; McKie et al., 1999). In these situations, where either occupation may also be subject to shift-work and informal extensions to the working day, coping strategies need to be adopted to ensure both work continuity and effective care of children and other dependents, or simply in order to lead a reasonably fulfilled life. A further factor which may influence meanings attached to work is sense of community. On one hand, employers, in their aim of securing the holy grail of employee commitment, aim to inculcate a sense of community to their business activities. Historically, though, a sense of independent community based on combinations of occupation, industry and location, has emerged to provide significance as well as a protective barrier against the vicissitudes of work (Salaman, 1971). Industrial regions, such as those dominated by coalmining and shipbuilding, once prevalent in Scotland, have often provided a fruitful environment for occupational communities to flourish.

In this transformed economic and social context, it is not surprising that a family-friendly and later, work-life balance (WLB) emphasis, has dominated political and business discourse in recent years as employers, employee and social interests interact to attempt to ensure that effective economic activity can be maintained without undermining family and social relationships.

Women and men

Our analysis of the meaning of work takes place at a time of increasing female labour force participation and advancement, changing family structures, and increasing optimism in some quarters about the opportunities for equality. At the time of the study, women comprised 44 per cent of the

UK workforce, with 72 per cent of all women, and 65 per cent of women with dependent children, in paid employment; these figures have risen slightly (Twomey, 2002; EOC, 2005). Women made up nearly half of all university enrolments in the UK and were gaining ground in many skilled occupations.

In the last decades, there has also been a convergence in attitudes towards the sharing of work and family responsibilities, especially amongst those under thirty years of age (Walby, 1997). Moreover there has been a steady increase in voluntary childlessness, even in countries with egalitarian and family friendly social policies, although the highest percentage of childless women remains amongst those with higher qualifications (Coleman, 1996; McRae, 1997). With women able to make lifestyle choices about whether and when to have children, or whether to adopt the role of primary carer, it has been claimed that they steadily appear to be gaining control over their life course (Hakim, 2000).

Further optimism comes from the projections of the information age and opportunities for technological advancement which were assumed to bring equality to the workplace. As discussed in Chapter 1, the start of the nineteenth century marked a significant change in the relationship between life and work. Work was starting to develop into a time-bounded, paid activity which was located firstly in factories and then in other workplaces. Home, on the other hand was viewed as a retreat from work and the focus for women fulfilling roles associated with domestic activity, family time and emotional support. Moves towards micro-technological work, away from large manufacturing operations, eliminated the need for physical strength at work, bringing with it more opportunities for women, and promising to redress the gendering of jobs that followed the separation of work from home (Stanworth, 2000; Wacjman, 1991).

The ideal of equality, however, has been far from fully realized. Despite women's increased participation rates, there remains a significant pay gap between women and men overall (IDS, 2003) and in professions (Purcell, 2002; Smithson *et al.*, 2004). Much of the gain in female labour force participation can be accounted for by the increase in low status, part-time work – women still tend to be segregated into service, banking, clerical and hospitality jobs (Thiessen and Nickerson, 1999).

Moreover, lifestyle choice must be evaluated against the decline of the extended family and women increasingly being forced to adopt the 'provider role' in single earner households (Charles and James, 2003). Even in dual earner households, and despite the rhetoric of 'new men', there has not been a significant masculinization of the domestic division of labour (Bradley *et al.*, 2000), with few real changes in practice and attitudes with respect to women's role as homemaker and primary parent, even amongst female graduates (Hochschild, 1989; Charles and Kerr, 1999; Purcell, 2002). Hogarth *et al.* (2001) also comment on a potentially dysfunctional level of work-life spillover as work becomes more intensified, which is likely to impact more on women in the workforce with domestic responsibilities.

Class and status

Amongst academic and popular social theorists, several interlocking tendencies have dominated over the last thirty years; the perceived 'death' of the working class and of class as an organizing principle of capitalist society, and the related fragmentation and increasing complexity of social structuration and collective identity (Bauman, 1998; Bell, 1973; Castells, 1998; Drucker, 1993; Rifkin, 1995). These writers have been concerned not just with objective developments, but also with issues of subjectivity and, in recent years, have often been associated with theories of the information or network society. Central to all these theorists' perspectives has been the rejection, and claimed disintegration, of Marxist-inspired and social action-orientated class analysis.

More broadly, the Thatcherite mantra of 'there is no such thing as society' has been replaced under New Labour by the concept that 'we're all middle class now', notwithstanding rhetorical concerns for the socially-excluded. Such stances contain echoes of the earlier bourgeoisification – proletarianization debates, particularly concerning white-collar workers and the 'middle strata' (Braverman, 1974; Giddens, 1973; Goldthorpe *et al.*, 1969; Gorz, 1971; Wright Mills, 1951).

Variants of Weberian approaches, sometimes under the influence of post-modernism, have thus come to dominate where considerable (unexplained) distance has opened up between what Marxists call the base (economic imperative), and superstructure (the social and political structuration of society) (Bottero, 2004; Goldthorpe, 1996). Whether concerning workers in general, or white-collar and information or knowledge workers specifically, foci of identity based upon family, consumerism, gender, sexual orientation, career and popular culture are argued now to be dominant. Workers, it is claimed, no longer have a hegemonic class character, nor do they possess class consciousness. Consequently, working class collective social action, whether that be through its traditional political (the Labour Party) or economic (the trade unions) agency, is seen to be missing, presumed dead.

However, one of the most striking weaknesses of the recent Weberian approaches has been a failure to locate their arguments and theorizing in a grounded manner, through, for example, conducting primary research focused upon real workers, far less those employed in the knowledge economy (Webb, 2004). Others have argued that while perceptions of class do not serve to *unite* social groupings, class still has a *divisive* effect in society (Savage *et al.*, 2001). Chapter 8 integrates data on employee attitudes with these broader sociological and theoretical concerns.

The new political economy

Globalization

The networks underpinning the putative knowledge economy are held to be transnational, spanning the 'globalized' world. For some, all contemporary social phenomena are either evidence of, or are caused by, this globalization. In the version propounded by 'hyperglobalizers', the contemporary economy has become 'genuinely borderless' and 'information, capital, and innovation flow all over the world at top speed' (Ohmae, 1995). As nation-states are now obsolete, globalization has spelt the 'death of distance' (Cairncross, 1997). Even in circumspect accounts, it is accepted that the 'widening, deepening and speeding up of worldwide interconnectedness' (Held *et al.*, 1999), has exercised profound impacts on the worlds of work and employment. Ostensibly, the new ICTs permit knowledge work to be undertaken – to paraphrase the old Martini advertisement – 'any time, any place, any where'. Alternatively, as Castells (1996) has put it, the 'space of flows' replaces 'the space of places'.

The uncritical assumptions that have accompanied the term globalization, have been challenged by diverse writers including Hirst and Thompson (1999), Ruigrok and van Tulder (1995), Callinicos (2003), and a host of economic geographers (e.g. Castree *et al.*, 2004; Herod, 2001). Their critique does not dispel the significance of the growing interconnectedness of global economic activities, but serves to remind us that, at an economic level at least, globalization is a set of tendencies, rather than a single predetermined trajectory with inevitable outcomes (Dicken, 2003).

Nevertheless globalization exercises its influence both as discourse and material reality. At an ideological level, its assumptions permeate government policy so that economic success and prosperity, fundamentally, were and remain predicated upon the ability of the UK's knowledge-intensive industries to compete within global market places. More tangibly, the relocation of IT-services and business processes, from the developed to developing world had begun to impact upon both of our sectors. The outsourcing of various software processes to India had been a growing trend throughout the 1990s whilst, at the commencement of our research, call centre offshoring from the UK had yet to take off (Taylor and Bain, 2005).

Privatization, liberalization and the 'new economy'

We can see the utopian vista of de-alienated knowledge work, undertaken within non-hierarchical networks and information flows, not just as a positive grasping of the transformational potential of ICT, but also as being located in a distinct moment in contemporary political economy. Just as the early Industrial Society and Post-Capitalist models of Kerr *et al.* (1960), Bell (1974) and Dahrendorf (1959) were a product of the social theorizing that rationalized the quasi-corporatism of the post-war consensus, so the knowledge economy is closely associated, sometimes even synonymous, with the contemporary so-called new economy. Particularly in the US, but echoed in Britain, commentators in the 1990s hailed a productivity miracle, unleashed by computers and new information and communication technologies, and based mainly in the technology, media and telecommunications industries (Henwood, 2003). Undoubtedly, *the* symbol of the new economy was the dot.com company which in a wave of unbridled optimism, promised unending growth and gave sustenance to the view that society had indeed entered a new epoch of uninterrupted boom. The very fact that economic growth continued largely unabated throughout the 1990s reinforced the impression that e-commerce and the emergence of the new economy were the decisive causes of expansion.

At a macro-level, the policies constituting the 'Washington consensus' – privatization, de-regulation, liberalization, and adherence to fiscal and monetary stability – pioneered by the Reagan and Thatcher governments in the 1980s, provided the fertile conditions in which this knowledge-based economic activity could flourish. Significantly, subsequent governments, irrespective of their political hue, have remained committed to the core tenets of programmes, which have outlived their creators and are now accepted by erstwhile opponents (Anderson, 2000: 11). Most pertinent is the fact that, beginning in the late 1970s, and increasingly throughout the 1980s and 1990s, leading western governments embraced neo-liberal economic policies (Harvey, 2005), privatizing state-owned industries and de-regulating both financial markets and key sectors of their economies.

The claim of a permanent boom was, however, premature. Tarnishing the golden promise of the late-1990s, the collapse of the boom questioned the virility of the new economy and its alleged productivity miracle. As Brenner observes, it was the speculative stock market explosion which led to a significant disconnection in the underlying economy between the rise of 'paper' wealth and the growth of actual output, particularly of profits (2002: 188). The hype could not be sustained and, when the rate of profit began to fall, the crash was inevitable. In this sense, the collapse was the outcome of a particular phase in the boom-slump cycle, and of the recognizable tendencies to crisis within capitalism. It is notable that the new economy suffered particularly, since it was in technology, media and telecommunications that over-investment and over-capacity had been most profoundly experienced (Froud *et al.*, 2002).

The light regulation of employment

De-regulation and liberalization directly affect the lives of the majority of people through the dimension of the labour market. Evidently, the discrepancies in power within the employment relationship have been exacerbated by the erosion of constraints on management action, which have arisen from both the weakening of the labour movement and from social market political policy. The tensions, in the late 1990s, between the promotion by successive governments of deregulated labour market regimes, and the persistence of those pluralist values that had underpinned the postwar consensus may be seen in the mixed messages conveyed by UK employment legislation. At the time of the study, employees had recently obtained rights to statutory minimum pay (National Minimum Wage Act 1998), a maximum limit to working hours and a minimum entitlement to paid holidays (Working Time Regulations 1998), the right of trade unions to seek statutory recognition for collective bargaining, and the right to representation for disciplinary and grievance purposes (Employment Relations Act 1999). Furthermore, employees enjoyed extended rights to take parental leave (Maternity and Parental Leave Regulations 1999), to be informed and consulted (Transnational Information and Consultation of Employees Regulations 1999), while discrimination law had been extended through the Race Relations (Amendment) Act 2000, and the Part-time Workers (Prevention of Less Favourable Treatment) Regulations 2000. Notionally, therefore, employees seemed to be in a better position in terms of legal rights than they had been for twenty years.

However, many of the new entitlements have been described as unitarist and individualistic, with a paucity of sanction (Novitz, 2002). The 1997–2001 Blair government, once having acknowledged New Labour's increasingly fragile historical links to the union movement by awarding recognition rights and initiating minimum wage provision, essentially continued the Conservative policy of encouraging flexibility in the labour market and chose not to repeal any of the previous Conservative government's legal restrictions on taking industrial action. In the Foreword to the *Fairness at Work* White Paper of 1998, the Prime Minister was anxious to reassure the business community that,

> Even after the changes we propose, Britain will have the most lightly regulated labour market of any leading economy in the world.

At the same time, the government was committed to implementing a succession of EU labour market directives, most of which had originated in the essentially pluralist Social Charter of the mid-1980s. The resulting compromise has been typified by an approach which grants individual redress for collective problems, but avoids any extension of collective rights. This position is perhaps exemplified by Government reticence to give legal basis to the Draft EU Charter of Fundamental Rights adopted in October 2000, which recognizes key trade union collective rights such as the right to strike. EU-derived changes, such as the information and consultation directive, have been promulgated with a heavy emphasis on traditional British 'voluntarism' (which, in a time of reduced union activity, has always served as a euphemism for managerial prerogative), and which have not been accompanied by any continental-style references to the 'Social Partners'. In sum, the government's approach could aptly be described as 'minimalist' (McKay, 2001).

The Scottish economy and labour market

Turning to the specific Scottish economic contexts, the long-term decline of Scotland's traditional heavy industries, notably steelmaking, shipbuilding, mechanical engineering and mining, forms the broader historical backdrop to our project. Indeed, it is several decades since even half of Scottish employment was based in manufacturing industry (Scottish Enterprise, 1998). In order to regenerate Scotland's industrial base, an inward investment strategy (captured by the phrase 'from ships to chips') had, since the 1980s, increasingly focused on attracting to Scotland multinational electronics companies who would establish production facilities in order to penetrate European markets (Turok, 1992). The apparent success of this policy and the importance of electronics to the Scottish economy was seen in the fact that an estimated 80,000 were employed in the sector (Fraser of Allender, 1996), and no fewer than 35 per cent of Europe's personal computers and 11 per cent of semi-conductors, were produced in Scotland (EIRR, 1995).

However, several factors, including over-production and saturated markets, the emergence of globalized production in the developing world, and economic crisis in south-east Asia, led to contraction, symbolized by the mothballing of Hyundai's Dunfermline facility (1999) and the final closure of Motorola's massive Bathgate plant (April 2001). Thus, just at the moment when optimism was being engendered by the prospects for the ICT-enabled new economy, Scotland was experiencing the precipitate decline of an earlier wave of technologically-based industry. The broader Scottish context, then, was both the continued erosion of traditional manufacturing *and* the immediate crisis in the newer productive activity of electronics. Consequently, between 1994 and 2001, manufacturing employment fell by 35,000 while employment in services expanded by 161,000 (Scottish Enterprise, 2002: 19, 21).

What emerges from Table 2.1 is the salience of both the public sector, and of business services of various kinds, to the Scottish economy. However, the inflexibility and inexactness of the classifications employed have notoriously made it difficult to identify specific areas of business activity, notably in relation to the imprecise, all-embracing 'services' descriptor. Nevertheless, unpacking the categories, and using data from other sources enables us to highlight notable features of the economy. According to one study, more than 102,000 people were employed in Scottish financial services, and the industry was more significant to Edinburgh's economy than to London's, representing 10.4 per cent and 7.5 per cent of employment respectively (Financial Services Skills Council).

Table 2.1 Scottish employment by sector, 2000

Industry	Number employed	%
Public administration, education, health	721,000	32.3
Banking, finance and insurance, business services	375,000	16.8
Wholesale, retail, repair etc.	342,000	15.3
Manufacturing	302,000	13.6
Hotels and restaurants	164,000	7.4
Construction	132,000	5.9
Transport, storage and communication	118,000	5.3
Agriculture and fishing	38,000	1.7
Energy, water and mining	36,000	1.6
Total Employment	**2,229,000**	**100**

Source: Annual Business Inquiry, cited in Scottish Enterprise (2002: 21).

Further, financial services was growing at 5.4 per cent per annum, twice the rate of the economy overall.

From the mid-1990s, call centres, particularly in financial services, had been targeted by government and inward investment organizations as a source of high-skilled job creation. Typical of government pronouncements in this period was the then Scottish Secretary Michael Forsyth's statement at the opening of the TSB telebanking centre in Glasgow, that it was the 'skilled and flexible workforce together with one of the most advanced and comprehensive telecommunications networks anywhere in Europe' that made Scotland the 'obvious choice for such projects' (*Herald*, 6 September 1995). A few years later, the Department of Trade and Industry and the Call Centre Association could estimate that almost 40 per cent of all new jobs created were in call centres (cited in Taylor and Bain, 2003b: 1). The negative press that subsequently clouded the characterization of call centres should not make us forget that they had initially been widely welcomed as skilled, 'high-tech' enabled employment.

These policies were given added impetus by the developments that resulted in the devolved political settlement embodied in The Scotland Act 1998. This Act established areas of 'devolved' and 'reserved' business; the former, for example, covers health, housing, education and transport while the latter, retained under the control of the Westminster parliament covers, for example, employment law and matters of defence and foreign policy. However, it can be argued that devolution, in reality, represents more continuity than change. Despite this, the Scottish Executive – effectively the government of Scotland – has the power to influence employment and employment relations in a number of direct ways, through public policy, and through a number of indirect means such as the awarding of public contracts. To this extent, the Scottish Executive has continued to pursue a labour market policy aimed at attracting and retaining highly skilled labour, and directed the agency responsible for attracting inward investment to prioritize the achievement of 'critical mass' in call centres and knowledge industries.

By the time of our study, then, the New Economy, however imprecisely identified by the Scottish Executive as a 'complex range of economic activities', was increasingly being seen as capable of generating employment where jobs had been 'lost to automation and competition from lower wage economies' (2002: 70). Reflecting the UK government's recent championing (DTI, 1998) of the knowledge economy, was this devolved policy orientation towards an ICT-based enterprise economy and its attendant virtues.

> The New Economy has a high growth potential and is a key driver of productivity and, consequently, of improved standards of living. As a highly developed economy, Scotland can have a competitive advantage in attracting New Economy industries because of its highly regarded Higher Education sector, its infrastructure and the quality of its graduates (Scottish Executive, 2002: 70).

Despite some minor disparities between Scotland and the UK as a whole (e.g. a higher proportion employed in public services, hotels/restaurants, agriculture, forestry and fishing), no significant differences exist in employment structure. In fact, as much variation is perceptible *across* Scotland, encouraging us to think, not in terms of a single unified Scottish labour market, but of sub-markets, partly demarcated by occupation, industry and geography.

In respect of the overall composition of the workforce, too, Scotland largely paralleled the UK. Most people were in full-time, permanent employment, with almost one-in-four part-time, representing an increase of 11.6 per cent between 1994 and 2001 (Scottish Executive, 2002: 18). The proportion of the workforce in temporary employment at 6.6 per cent was slightly larger than that for the UK but, in common with wider trends, had fallen in recent years due to a tightening labour market. Women in 2001 accounted for 45.8 per cent of Scottish employees compared to the UK's 44.3 per cent. Several gender differences are discernible, including the fact that larger numbers of part-timers were to be found amongst women, and that women were disproportionately represented amongst new workforce entrants (ONS, 2001b).

In sum, the profiles of employment and occupation in Scotland were not dissimilar to those of the UK overall, although the comparison is more strictly apposite with regions of the UK with a similar industrial past. Nevertheless, given the contrasts with its previous industrial structure and the rapidity of change in recent decades, Scotland provides a particularly useful prism through which to explore the meaning of work in emergent sectors that are generalizable to the UK as a whole, and which might be regarded as emblematic of the new economy.

Sectoral trends

We now move to a consideration of the actual market and sectoral conditions faced by our chosen companies. Both employment sectors had grown around the informating properties of ICT and its application to the provision of services as the new economy had expanded. The fact that our study spanned the boom, and then the downturn in the new economy following the dot.com crash, provides an opportunity to consider some of these macro themes against the backdrop of economic and organizational turbulence.

Call centres

It is significant that, in different ways, all the case study companies were operating in conditions of intensified competition and market turbulence. In financial services, de-regulatory reforms in the 1980s had transformed the business environment, breaking down the barriers between bank, insurance company and building society, intensifying sectoral competition and leading to perpetual restructuring, downsizing, cost-cutting and widespread merger activity (Marshall and Richardson, 1996; Bain and Taylor, 2002a; Morris et al., 2001). Throughout the 1990s, our case study, Moneyflow, pursued an extremely aggressive acquisition strategy, attempting to transform itself from 'a newly converted bank into a diversified, international provider of financial services' (Moneyflow internal document, 2001). Yet, from 2000 this over-ambitious policy signally failed, generating intense intra-organizational flux and severe cost-cutting and leaving the company itself vulnerable to take-over.

Telecommunications, equally, has been subject to profound change, stemming as much from government de-regulatory liberalization policies and the growth of financial markets as from technological innovation (Cave et al., 2002; Fransman, 2002). Staggering levels of investment led to over-capitalization and merger, but sectoral crisis spectacularly followed as the vastly-inflated share prices collapsed in the wake of the dot.com crash. The Entcomm case study exemplified the generic weaknesses of new market entrants in the 1990s; exaggerated expectations of customer demand, revenues and profits, massive indebtedness and 'merge to grow strategies' (Trillas, 2002). The scale of corporate debt – $17.5 billion by late 2000 (*Financial Times*, 8 December 2000) – ushered in continuous capital and operational restructuring, including 7,300 redundancies in 2000 and 2001 through the euphemistically named 'Planning for Growth' strategy. Ultimately, given intractable difficulties in both telecoms and financial markets, and acute competition from its remaining UK rival, Entcomm was forced to seek bankruptcy protection in 2002.

The UK holidays sector was marked by the apparent paradox of oligopoly – the domination of the market at that time by four companies – and sharp competition which, during the 1990s, produced depreciation in real income and exerted sharp downward pressure on margins. These pressures led to three main responses: an increase in 'self-focus', merger and acquisition, and increased use of telephony and e-sales. Feverish acquisition activity, though, was halted due to shortages of surplus capital and the shock to long-haul sales following 9/11 which further squeezed profit margins. Our case study, Holstravel, reflected these trends, both acquiring subsidiaries and being itself subject to part buyout. Furthermore, indicative of a steep decline in business and sales, was the decision to contract operations, downsize its workforce and the threat, late in 2001, to postpone indefinitely all salary increases until market conditions revived.

Outsourcing, as a general phenomenon, is a relatively new occurrence in many areas of production, distribution and exchange and, in terms of back-office, or call centre services, it is an even more recent development (see Bain and Taylor, 2002b; Kinnie and Parsons, 2004). While outsourced operators may provide either dedicated services for a particular client, effectively substituting for in-house provision, or may undertake a variety of services for diverse clients, the underlying logics driving outsourcing remain similar. They offer the ability to concentrate sales and customer servicing functions, and promise to deliver substantial cost reductions to clients, who might be unable or unwilling to provide similar services in-house. Yet, as this particular sub-sector has grown even faster than the call centre sector as a whole,[1] competition between generalist outsourcers, such as Thejobshop case study, intensified. Competitive bidding emerged as market rivals vied for customers, fundamentally on the basis of cost (largely labour) and efficiency, notwithstanding claimed differentiation on quality grounds. Despite overall expansion, the process of matching supply to demand in this environment was, and remains, fragile and indeterminate and for Thejobshop led to financial performance problems, and pressures on costs and margins. Ultimately, and exacerbated by the bursting of the dot.com bubble, this culminated in dramatic slumps in share prices of, successively, 30 per cent and 90 per cent.

Software development

During the late 1990s, the rate of growth of the software industry in Scotland was calculated at 15 per cent per annum (Scottish Enterprise,

---

[1] In 2000 1-in-5 of the Scottish call centre workforce were employed by outsourcers, a proportion that had risen to 1-in-4 by 2003 (Taylor and Bain, 2001b: 11; 2003b: 18).

2001). Evidently, developments in Scotland were reflective of the rapid expansion of software and IT-related activity that was integral to the new economy (Henwood, 2003). According to the Labour Force Survey, the numbers of economically active core software occupations (including computer systems managers, software engineers and computer programmers/ analysts) in the UK as a whole rose by 39 per cent to 726,000 between 1996 and 2000 (ONS, 2000b). If anything, expansion was more marked in Scotland than in the UK as a whole (Scottish Enterprise, 2001). This prevailing trajectory of sustained growth created a generally tight labour market which, in turn, generated major government policy developments in an attempt to alleviate skilled shortages (ONS, 2000b).

At the commencement of our research project, software had undergone almost a decade of accelerating growth. However, by the conclusion of our field-work, sectoral conditions had changed remarkably following the bursting of the 'dot.com bubble' in the US in 2000, which presaged a decisive shift within technology-related sectors (Brenner, 2002; Henwood, 2003). The deflationary impact was not fully felt in the UK until 2001, when many IT start-ups had run out of the venture capital that had been keeping them afloat. Another reason for subsequent decline was the working through of the consequences of the large-scale investment cycle as businesses of all kinds prepared for the year 2000 computer switchover. The advent of the millenium without major incident produced a hiatus in demand, as many companies had only recently retooled their systems and upgraded their software.

Thus, the lifespan of our research in software is bounded by contrasting circumstances, in that the momentum generated by sustained business and employment growth was halted by the general effects of economic slowdown. Indeed, shortly after the commencement of our field-work one of the smaller operations, Kappa, collapsed. The longer-term consequences for the meaning of work would be realized, in part at least, through the medium and mechanisms of the labour market. Here the evidence suggests that, although a substantial dip occurred in the requirement for IT professionals after 2001, during the period of the field research the technology market in Scotland was in relatively good shape, with demand for IT professionals exceeding supply.

In conclusion, this chapter has offered some essential contextualization which prefigures the presentation and analysis of data from the research. First, we explored the broader conceptual underpinnings to the world of contemporary work and employment, focusing particularly on the paradigm shift popularly associated with the knowledge economy. We then outlined the key themes and issues of working life that parallel the concerns of the book's chapters, in which the knowledge economy and its critique appear as key themes. Second, we sketched the new economy, political-economic, regulatory, regional and sectoral contexts, within which our case studies are embedded, and which provide invaluable insights that inform the specific lines of inquiry of the empirically based chapters. These chapters now commence with an examination of the nature of work organisation.

3
Organizational Life: The Nature of Work

Introduction

In this, and the following chapter, we are concerned with the overarching and broadly-defined concept of organizational life, and focus on two core themes. In the present chapter we examine work organization, labour process and management control, and employee experiences and perceptions in relation to these, and explore the contrasts that exist between the sectors. On the basis of previous knowledge, although with important qualifications, we expected call centres to more approximate regimes of 'direct control', while software development would exhibit strong tendencies towards 'responsible autonomy'. In Chapter 4, we explore management strategy and, in particular, subject to critical scrutiny the extent to which the much-heralded agendas of human resource management deliver the promised, but elusive, outcomes of commitment and job satisfaction. This chapter includes discussion of pay and pay systems. A third related theme pertaining to organizational life, which considers worker attitudes, and principally investigates the claim that individualism has replaced collectivism as a new orthodoxy of employee relations, will be discussed in Chapter 8. We begin by outlining the work settings of our individual case studies.

Work settings: call centres

An understanding of historical context and legacy is critical for appreciating the profound consequences for work organization and the experience of work that have accompanied the emergence of the call centre. From the late 1980s, and accelerating rapidly through the 1990s, the call centre became an organizational imperative as companies recast their mode of interactive customer contact.

Undoubtedly, qualitative advances in information networking technologies were a pre-requisite for the call centre's emergence. These included digitilization, optical fibre developments, the dramatic increase in computing capacity and, later, connectionless architectures based on Internet protocols, which further facilitated voice and data integration (Cave et al., 2002; Miozzo and Ramirez, 2003). Yet, the call centre is defined fundamentally by the integration of telephonic and computer technologies (Taylor and Bain, 1999: 102), and the *key* innovation was the Automatic Call Distribution (ACD) system, which enables incoming calls to be routed in succession through headsets to available operators at workstations, who simultaneously enter or manipulate data on PCs. A 'predictive dialler' provides a similar facility for outbound calling. Since these technologies collapsed distance and permitted the location, and indeed re-location, of operations to regions, cities and towns characterized by the availability of suitably skilled labour at lower cost, there was always a spatial dynamic inherent in the call centre project (Richardson and Marshall, 1996). Once it was no longer essential that customer servicing loci were geographically proximate to customers, economies of scale could be realized through the concentration of functions that hitherto and otherwise would have been dispersed. From this perspective, then, the rationale for the call centre's existence lies in its promise to cut costs, slash overheads and maximize profits through the drawing together of customer servicing or sales channels. Rather than exemplifying the 'end of the gathered organization' (Handy, 1985), many call centres emerged as large-scale sites of mass service delivery; for example, in Scotland, almost three-quarters of the entire call centre workforce were employed in establishments of 250 or more employees (Taylor and Bain, 1997, 2001b).

Mindful of the temptation of a technological determinism which would privilege the advances in ICTs as the sole explanation for the rapid diffusion of the call centre model, we must acknowledge some of the environmental conditions that conditioned servicing companies to be receptive to its adoption. In broad terms, the wider political and economic environment of neo-liberalism, deregulation, restructuring and the financialization of markets are significant. For example, the 1986 Financial Services and Building Society Acts precipitated an accelerating sectoral transformation, in which competition rapidly intensified, producing instability, and extensive merger and acquisition activity. Inextricably intertwined with these developments was the increasing adoption of ICTs (Cressey and Scott, 1992) but the path-breaking innovation occurred when Direct Line and First Direct, in insurance and banking respectively, launched their 24-hour branchless remote sales and servicing operations (Bain and Taylor, 2002a; Taylor and Bain, 1999). By the early to mid-1990s, there was a competitive scramble to catch up with and overtake these patently successful innovators, and to capitalize on the cost reducing and profit maximizing opportunities offered by the call centre.

Imitation followed not just in financial services, but throughout the economy as call centre operations became established in telecommunications, retailing, entertainment, travel and holidays as well as in the public sector. Here was a lean, efficient and revenue-generating template for customer service and sales, whose attractions were to prove irresistible. In the final analysis, and integral to the call centre's appeal, was the promise that it would deliver its economic benefits through novel forms of labour utilization and control.

In the four case studies, a similar, although not identical, technological architecture was extant; not merely the ACD technologies, the work station turrets and branded PCs, and the screens and menus which facilitate the interface between agent and data but, additionally, the highly-visible electronic wallboards, which typically display the numbers of calls received, handled or abandoned, the longest call waiting times and the numbers of customers queuing. Acronyms, such as CHT (Call Handling Time), AHT (Average Handling Time), CW (Calls Waiting), CQ (Calls Queuing), QL (Queue Length), were commonly used in the four centres.

There was resemblance, too, in the workplace environment. Admittedly, variation existed in relation to building dimension, structure (number of floors, size of work rooms) and other architectural features. For example, operations at Thejobshop were housed in four separate square-shaped blocks, each with two floors and connected via a central courtyard, whilst Entcomm's were spread over two largely open plan floors, but with cordoned-off workspaces. Holstravel's building was exceptional in that it was uniquely and consciously designed to accommodate its user, the holiday and travel company, and will be described in more detail in Chapter 4 in the discussion of company culture.

Despite these differences, there was remarkable similarity in terms of the workspaces occupied by, and immediately surrounding, the call-handlers. Within open plan, 'deep' offices (Baldry et al., 1997), clusters of approximately a dozen workers were seated in recognizable formations (stars or diamonds, straight rows, 'L' shapes), and each call-handler was separated from her, or his, neighbour by shoulder-high partitions designed to act as noise buffers. Hot-desking and multiple shift working frequently prevented the personalization of workstations so that, apart from papers, documents and notepads, desks tended to the anonymous. Crucially, this physical landscape was also the spatial expression of an organizational feature, the universal practice of teamworking, as agents were collectivized around particular workflows. These, centred on market fractions or customer segments, could be either inbound or outbound functions, and related to sales, customer service or telemarketing specialisms. In essence, this is the tangible representation of a functional division of labour, in which call centre agents are grouped according to subdivided functions of the generic customer service (or sales) role. Typically, at the head of, or adjacent to, these clusters of agents sat one or more team leaders and, at a further remove, managers with responsibility for a number of teams. In the midst of these spaces, whose borders were defined by these discrete configurations, were white boards and flip charts, where updated summaries of individual and performance criteria were prominently displayed. Thus, statistics, hand-written by supervisors and specific to each team, complemented the universally visible overhead electronic data.

Similarity, though, does not entail uniformity or homogeneity and, inevitably, differences existed between the work performed at each of the call centre establishments, as a result of the industrial sectors in which these operations were embedded, the nature of the services provided, and the unique characteristics of the firms.

In Moneyflow, on the non-secured side, agents – known as Customer Advisers (CAs) – received incoming calls on a variety of 'unregulated' products on a near-continuous basis, with call cycle times averaging 5.5 minutes at the commencement of our research. On the secured side, employees were described as Financial Planning Advisers (FPAs) and Mortgage Advisers (MAs), whose quasi-professional titles indicate jobs of greater task complexity. The former served a relatively small number of clients (four per day in 1999). For these agents, lengthy document and paper work was interspersed with potentially protracted telephone discussion, lasting in some instances as long as one hour.

Within Thejobshop, as many as twenty distinct client services were operational, with our study concentrating on the six most significant businesses, and a further section which embraced seven small contracts. At *Energycom*, a utilities business, 75 Customer Service Advisers (CSAs) were employed on inbound sales and customer care, where calls averaged five minutes. On *Drinks Now* lines, a drinks and gifts delivery service was provided for a major UK brewer with call cycles of between three and five minutes. In *Genbusiness*, Thejobshop gathered together seven micro-volume businesses (including a baby clothes supplier and government agencies) into one operation, with the majority of calls averaging less than three minutes. Thejobshop delivered for *Bluechip*, a US multinational computer software company, all its UK telephone-based services, including pre-sales and technical support. CSAs were expected to deliver customized, 'quality' service to high-value customers, but those employed on 'core' and 'front-line' lines received a continuous flow of calls which necessitated relatively standardized knowledge of *Bluechip* products. *Carco* and *Carexec* supplied sales and service information for owners of executive automobiles. At *Gamesco* Thejobshop provided technical help and customer services for a games console manufacturer (see Taylor *et al.*, 2002).

A Scene from the Front-Line – A Morning in the Life of a Call Handler

8.30 am, Call 1 – Customer requesting supply of gas, scripted contract verbally agreed, and Danny begins the wrap, preparing the paper work, and is interrupted by a call following quickly. Call 2 – An existing gas customer wishing to transfer to electricity supply from Seboard to Energycom; Danny calculates the savings and informs the customer. Call 3 – Hydro-electric customer wishing to change to Energycom. Call 4 – A call that should have gone straight to Customer Service. Danny explains the reason why so many calls come through to Inbound Sales that really should be going somewhere else is because Inbound Sales is a freephone number, so knowledgeable customers will exploit this and expect/hope to be diverted. However not everyone will divert these calls through to Customer Care or Customer Service. 'I've heard agents giving out the proper number and telling the customer to ring it directly. I don't do that. It takes longer to look up the number and explain to the customer what they have to do than it does to divert the call. Also, it's about good customer service. They've rung an Energycom number and it's up to us to give a good impression of the company'. Call 5 – Another call re-routed to Customer Care. Danny attempts to complete the backlog of paper work. Danny refers back to Call 3, 'I could have pushed that one. I could have got a sale if I had really gone for it, but I didn't because there are 5 calls waiting (indicates the display on the turret) and I have got two wrap-ups to do from earlier calls.'

'Monday mornings are horrendous. Look around and see how many staff are on. There's not enough people on the phones and even then Nina (team leader) will come over and say, "You don't mind if I take someone off the phones to do administrative work". Basically what you have got on mornings like this is under-staffing. And then when the phones are not busy you've got loads of people on the phones so you're waiting 30 minutes for a call.'

Call 6 – Customer trying to arrange gas supply for their son. Call 7 – Elderly customer trying to contact a member of Customer Care staff. Call 8 – A woman trying to check details of her son's gas supply. Call 9 – Customer looking for Customer Care, Danny re-routes the call. Call 10 – Another customer looking for Customer Care. Call 11 – Hydro-electric customer requesting an information pack for electricity only. Call 12 – Call from Manweb call centre in Warrington re. customer in Liverpool and query. Call 13 – Very long call from Manweb customer wanting to be put on a quarterly bill for both gas and electric which leads to a contract. Danny begins wrap but is interrupted again by the ring in the headphones Call 14 – Check who supplies gas for a customer. Call 15 – Internal call. Call 16 – Customer still paying bill although they have left the supplier and property, call rerouted to appropriate section. Call 17 – Customer wishing to cancel. Call 18 – Hydro-electric customer wishes to have gas and electric together with Energycom. Call 19 – Customer wants account opened for business premises, call diverted to team responsible. Call 20 – Question regarding gas central heating, call passed to relevant number.

11.20 am, Danny takes 15-minute break almost three hours into his shift, having achieved only two of his daily target of 11 sales.

Observation and unstructured interview, Thejobshop

At Entcomm's site in the greater Glasgow hinterland, 530 mainly Customer Service Associates (CSAs) were employed on both inbound and outbound operations. Workflows were not uniform, with separate sections devoted to *inter alia* customer service (digital and analogue), customer retention, digital migration, installation and administration and 'moves and transfers'. However, despite some differences between sections, the fact that call cycle times overall at Entcomm averaged less than five minutes (Bain et al., 2002), provides insight into the limited extent of call complexity.

Within Holstravel, of the two inbound functions, customer help and sales, the latter comprised three distinct inbound workflows: main reservations, teletext business and bookings for a single brand. Again, some disparity existed in the average duration, complexity and content of the workflows, with the single brand and teletext lines generating more straightforward requests, standardized responses and shorter call cycle times.

Despite differing job appellations, and variation in task complexity, it is evident that certain essential commonalities existed in task performance. What united the CSAs, CAs and the TCs was the content of a call-handler's job which consisted of telemediated interactions with customers, and that these were structured, although not entirely determined, by the data-integrative capacities of information and communication technologies (Miozzo and Ramirez, 2003). Consequently, it is widely accepted that call centre work is imbued with two logics, the need to be both cost-efficient and to be customer oriented (Korczynski, 2002), a formulation which has been expressed, alternatively, as the perpetual tension between the competing managerial priorities of quantity and quality (Bain et al., 2002; Taylor and Bain, 1999; 2001a). How these contradictions were played out in practice, and how they affected organizational life and the experience of work, will be explored below.

Work settings: software development

As with call centres, some historical contextualization is essential for providing an understanding of the work settings of the software case studies. Early software work had seen little division of labour between the distinctive aspects of the process, so that individuals undertook system design, programme design, code writing, and testing and debugging, albeit often under the supervision of an experienced specialist (Kraft and Dubnoff, 1986). However, when the industry was subsumed into electrical engineering in the 1950s and 1960s, the separation of system design from the more mechanical conversion of design into lines of code occurred (Barrett, 1999). This hierarchical partition of work between analysis and design on the one hand, and code writing, testing, and writing documentation on the other has, if anything, become reinforced over time. Kraft's later study (1999) revealed a separation between some employees engaged in highly creative development work and others involved in lower-status support activities, including maintenance, testing and quality and service work. This technical and occupational division is closely related to disparity in educational qualifications and entry routes. As Kunda (1992) demonstrated, university graduates tended to be employed as engineers in the more creative, 'glamorous' work, whereas the self-taught and those lacking formal advanced qualifications were largely confined to lower level support work. As such, the use of the designation of engineer can denote both a professional title and an organizationally-defined employment category. In both respects it reflects differentiation from other software employees in terms of entry route to the profession and then work content.

Subsequent language evolution generated further complexities in the division of labour. The emergence of object-oriented (OO) or 4GL languages such as Java in the 1980s, and their application to more 'conventional' areas, such as programming, as well as the Internet, have rendered the third generation languages (3GL), such as FORTRAN and COBOL, largely obsolete for development purposes. Consequently, employees with 3GL language skills increasingly undertake routinized tasks, while OO developers possess the skills to programme on virtually all computer platforms. Some have argued that 4GL have vocabulary and syntax similar to natural language, which makes programming more accessible to a wide spectrum of people (Quintas, 1994). However, this overall division in language requirements is representative of, and contributes to, differences in organization and type of work undertaken at each of the software sites. Thus, an appreciation of the contrasts between the demands for older and emergent skill sets, which themselves reflect technological developments, will contribute to our analysis of the case study evidence. Similarly, issues of routinization (Ramsay, 1999) and deskilling (Barrett, 1999) have emerged as recurrent themes in the literature. Recently, Andrews et al. (2005) have argued that software development, generically, involves four stages, namely customer requirements, design, development and testing. Consistent with this segmentation, the most common methodological model adopted is the 'Rational Unified Process' (RUF) which is related to the authors' discussion of structuration and standardization of the labour process. They conclude that while structuration was widespread, essentially because of the creative character of the software development labour process, standardization was more difficult to achieve.

To summarize, there exists a division of labour – or more accurately divisions of labour – in software work, an understanding of which prefaces and informs the analysis of our data. That there is heterogeneity in task content and work experience is further suggested by the specific characteristics of the software case study work settings.

At the outset, however, it is necessary to appreciate the significance of a universal characteristic of work organization in software development. Teams, based upon discrete and stand-alone, or successive, projects are the fulcrum around which productive activity is organized. Unlike teamworking in call centres, where employees performing the same or very similar tasks were gathered together in tightly concentrated units, the software teams in our case studies tended to embrace diverse skills and specialisms, and their members were likely to be physically dispersed. However, contrary to the fanciful notions of the knowledge economy paradigm (cf Toffler, 1980) the dispersal of these cyber professionals was not to decentralized 'electronic cottages'. In common with the industry as a whole, the extent of home teleworking in our case studies was extremely limited, due largely to the intense demands placed upon developers by delivery dates at project end, and the value placed on expert information from colleagues which may be required at a moment's notice.

In Beta, although a formal policy existed to equip all employees with the technology to enable homeworking, management discouraged its adoption. Similarly, in Omega, management provided the technology to work from home, in part to conform to their family-friendly culture, but they actually discouraged its regular practice. The strong emphasis on project teams meant that some roles, such as testing equipment which was permanently located on-site, were regarded as inappropriate for homeworking. Equally significant was the perception that it would prevent interaction between members and thwart the development of a team culture. The only technical employees who were found to work regularly from home were a few itinerant Pi employees based in England.

These inhibitions did not apply to the same extent to offshoring, where the migration of software and IT work to India predated and prefigured that of call centre services. Driven by domestic labour shortages, and the attraction of available skills and much-reduced cost, programming and testing have been most susceptible to offshore outsourcing (Bott *et al.*, 1995; Carmel, 1999; Ramsay, 1999). Both Omega and Beta had developed relationships with Indian software organizations. At the latter's case study site, Indian developers would spend lengthy placements acquiring the requisite knowledge to ensure that work could be transferred successfully on their return. In this sense offshoring represents a form of indirect collaboration.

In the main, the dispersal of team members took place throughout or across their employer's, or on their client's, sites. In this respect, it is helpful to regard companies' various team arrangements as existing along a spectrum ranging from the 'virtual' to the 'actual', although these might co-exist or overlap within a particular company. At one extreme, at Gamma, the majority of the 70 coders and 14 team leaders in deployment teams, described as performing the high-skilled or 'high octane' work, were generally 'outplaced' for extended periods to client sites. Many of these

Some Contrasting Experiences of Software Professionals

The job's methodical and creative. There are days where I'm trying to solve. Sometimes I'll look at a problem, it can take three days. I don't work on it continuously but I'll try and write it down and look at it from one angle and then leave it and go and do something else and then come back to it, maybe the next day, and then suddenly it doesn't seem as hard any more because your subconscious works on it a bit. The software that I'm doing is a form generating thing, so you see little things on your screen, on the windows, little widgets, little text boxes and you want to be able to resize everything properly, so I look at it and it's not working, why isn't it resizing like that? You then have to go into the code and see – it's always been a bit of a puzzle so you see that it does this and then that, why is that, that over there that should be like rock steady. And then things like when you are thinking of how you want to put in new menus, how people are going to use them, if they are going to find it intuitive or not, that's the creative aspect of it, you've got to think of what these thousands of people that are using are going to be looking at on this screen, … and what is going to help them out kind of thing, but you don't actually get to see those people using it. So that's just something you've got to have at the back of your mind.

Gamma, female software developer; G-I-09 (describing development)

Someone phones up and says 'our call centre isn't working and the reason is that one of your programmes has stopped responding to messages' and so they will usually be on a telephone. So I'll ask them what they are trying to do to restart it, what the other messages they are sending do, what's in log files, talk it through with them and they usually have to send me some things on the e-mail as well. So look through the files, at the logs, what the programme thinks it's doing in the e-mails, looking through various ways they can figure it and set it up and try and talk them through to some sort of solution. Sometimes I might ask people for help on that.

Gamma, male IT support engineer; G-I-10 (describing support work)

A normal working day will start for her at about 7:00 until 16:30. First thing in the morning, she will log on to the computer, check the system, and 'get to any jobs that have been kicked off the day before'. She will normally work along the routines set out by her schedule, interrupted only occasionally by team meetings and the like. Hence, her work is rather routine-driven and sometimes even boring such as when she has to write documentation: 'A really boring task, but it has to be done'. Other tasks, however, such as solving complex technological problems are far more exiting, and represent one of the highlights of the job. Simultaneously, such problems may also become a major source of frustration once they cannot be resolved satisfactory.

Observation and unstructured interview, Beta

Once the contract has been negotiated by sales we establish a development group. This will deal firstly with risks, and estimates time and work required. The work goes through a number of stages: Analysis (the design phase) – defining what is necessary and how to be completed; Build phase – each component section is built and unit tested, there is the policy of build and test for each unit; Unit testing – each section and adjacent sections are tested using standard sets of data; System testing – running data through and testing the completed application.

Observation and unstructured interview, Omega (description of the project cycle) were situated overseas, with 12 seconded to both Sydney and Jakarta. By contrast, development teams totalling 35 employees were based at company headquarters.

At Omega, the preference was to have team members, whether permanent employees or contractors, situated in close proximity to each other since, in the words of one team leader, 'better productivity [results] from people overhearing other people's conversations'. In practice, though, unless prior notice of projects dictated seating arrangements, this objective was rarely realized as team composition and seating remained relatively fluid. In parallel, four Omega offsite teams were housed in dedicated rooms at three host organizations. There were also a few employees working contractually for a large insurance company.

As a consequence of Beta's matrix structure, which led to the functional and geographical diffusion of work, developers were attached to projects led by managers, who could be located within our case study site or externally in any one of the company's three other software centres. Thus, team members could be sub-contracted across UK locations and even relocated as the project work necessitated the use of NetMeeting teleconferencing technology and real-time on-line collaboration. Alongside these virtual teams where, in the words of senior management 'work was an activity, not a location', there existed more conventionally located teams, although membership of these tended to be scattered throughout the building. There were some synergies between the work undertaken here and the servicing work that prevailed at another Beta location in Scotland. At Pi, segmentation into discrete teams was prohibited by the scale of operations so that collaboration took place amongst the whole workforce of 11 developers and three quality analysts. In Lambda, project managers 'owned' the contract, and led a small team of developers.

The dominant trend, then, was to favour dispersed teams, whether on-site or between locations, although the specific permutations did vary greatly. Where geographic diffusion prevented the coming together of project teams, video- and tele-conferencing were the most common forms of communication. Where possible, face-to-face interaction took place at periodic (often weekly) team meetings, but these were supplemented by electronic consultation and information exchange. Further contact between on-site team members was less formal, evident in the small huddles at workstations or in discussions in staff kitchens and restrooms, which punctuated individuals' long periods of largely isolated interaction with the computer. This suggests a sensory contrast between the software house and the call centre; the noise level. Whereas a call centre is a relatively strident environment, for the most part, software operations function in relative silence. The general atmosphere was reminiscent of other locations of what might be called 'white-collar craft' work, such as the engineering drawing office (Baldry and Connolly, 1986).

The built working environment of the software case studies, notwithstanding differences in scale, bore some similarity with that of our call centres; modern, open-plan office spaces in which employees sat at individual workstations dominated by PCs. At Beta, software developers occupied an entire floor, one of the multiple levels which encircled a grand central atrium in a recently constructed 'high-tech' building. At the perimeter of the open workspace were glass-fronted, oval meeting rooms designed for team or customer meetings. Compounding the overall sense of lack of privacy was the near-complete absence of dividers between workstations on the main floor. Gamma's on-site operations were in two locations; first, a Baronial granite building just outside Glasgow, where internal refurbishment had created, albeit on a reduced scale, the familiar open-plan office and, second, an office on a modern industrial estate closer to the city. Pi differed only in that workstations were housed within refurbished warehouse offices. Omega shared similar characteristics but occupied a rather cramped two-storied modern office block, in which low dividers separated teams and functions. Senior managers occupied individual offices on the periphery of each floor, but generally, staff and managers were visible to each other. Team meetings were held in available managers' side-offices or, if booked in advance, a larger office utilized for more formal meetings and presentations, while the preferred location for informal meetings was the heavily-used adjacent kitchen/rest room. Lambda's premises were located on the ground floor of a new office building in a new town technology park. Their configuration was along 'traditional' lines, with no more than six people occupying functionally defined rooms, while directors enjoyed private offices.

Our case studies provide insight into the heterogeneity that characterizes the software industry, its projects and its work content. At Beta, a former public utility, there was a dichotomy in the work undertaken. On one side, the primary role of Beta's service department was to provide internal support to the company's other divisions such as customer services, finance or marketing. On the other, challenging developmental work ranged from creating bespoke telephonic systems (voice recognition, emergency and screen-based linkages) to robotic tools and the protection, modification and integration of database and financial systems. Omega specialized in IT services and solutions predominantly for the public sector, health services and some financial sector organizations, mainly in applications development, knowledge management, resourcing, testing and client support. Gamma's core product linked databases and hardware to enable manipulation between front and back end applications and was developed mainly for call centres, web-based digital providers and Web Access Protocol (WAP) for Psion organizers. Pi's main product was high quality practice management software for law firms, capable of being linked to other business applications. Lambda specialized in software on health and safety legislation and workplace systems.

These differences between software companies – scale of organization, nature of product, location of work, team arrangements – impact upon the organization, control and experience of work, as we discuss below. However, as these contrasting work settings suggest, despite heterogeneity in software development, in general, it is distinctive in key respects from call centre work.

Work organization, labour process and control

Working time and temporal flexibilities

In the more optimistic accounts of the new economy, issues surrounding working time are held to be largely non-problematic. It is assumed that the empowerment of the new professionals and the flexibility of working arrangements will ensure that task performance loses the temporal compulsion associated with regimented work. Illustrative of this is the significant omission in Frenkel et al.'s (1999) monograph of any mention of working time and its effects. In this paradigm, it is implied that if workers do work longer and harder it may be because work is now more intrinsically satisfying (Ichniowski et al., 1996). In contrast, recent accounts paint a bleaker picture, both of an extensification of working hours (Bunting, 2004) and/or an intensification of effort, as the gaps between tasks during which the body or mind rests – the 'porosity' of the working day (Green, 2001) – are filled. The evidence from both sectors, although in contrasting ways, concurs with this latter, less sanguine, scenario.

Considering contractual hours, a slightly larger proportion of software employees (95 per cent) compared to call centre workers (84 per cent) worked the 30 hours or more which may be seen to constitute full-time work. In terms of additional hours, call centre employees were more likely to undertake *paid* overtime than software workers, with 21 per cent and 14 per cent respectively working up to ten hours a week. There is, however, marked disparity in the extent of *unpaid* overtime worked. While the 53 per cent of software employees who worked up to ten hours on average each week was a substantial proportion, the 23 per cent of call centre agents who did likewise were not inconsiderable. The reasons given by respondents for working overtime, whether paid or unpaid, deliver insight into the contrasting character of work between the sectors (Table 3.1).

The picture that emerges from the data is of software developers working extensive unpaid overtime, but in concentrated bursts, as projects approach completion, as these developers from different organizations report.

[Although] it is relaxed I think it depends on which project you are on. I sit over in that corner and [in another] corner they seem to be working

Table 3.1 Most important reasons for working paid or unpaid overtime

	Software developers (n = 154)	Call centre agents (n = 369)
Project deadlines	40%	10%
To get work done	20%	2%
Don't want to let colleagues down	13%	13%
Don't want to let customers down	12%	8%
Enjoy work	3%	15%
Need money	1%	43%
Told to by boss	1%	1%

> all the hours God sends because they are going to hit a deadline...like the piece of work that I'm doing, when it gets close to deadlines, then I'll be working like 5 days instead of 4, that sort of thing. (Beta, female developer; B-I-14)

> At times it gets up tight just because we run up against deadlines particularly within the installation and project departments where the job is cyclical. They go through a quiet period and then around installation they are running up against deadlines and client pressures. (Pi, male developer; Pi-I-03)

This experience differed from call centre agents who reported working additional and, to a larger extent, paid hours on a continual basis, partly because of the effects of lean staffing and, as agents widely reported, due to financial necessity. For software workers, these periodic upswings in effort represent, despite superficial appearances, not so much a freely given commitment, but the obligation to meet deadlines, an integral aspect of the cyclical rhythm of software product development. In addition, a proportion of software workers were required to be on-call throughout the evenings and nights. Evidence of the compulsion to work unpaid hours comes from the employee handbooks of two case study companies, which lay out terms and conditions. Although Omega management stated that they 'did not intend to rely on overtime as a way of meeting product schedules/work targets' they simultaneously acknowledged that 'in our industry a rigid day may be inappropriate'. The implications of this position, that the onus was placed unequivocally on employees to work unpaid overtime in order to meet managerially-determined targets, are evident from this clause,

> Where extra hours are worked because of failure to meet agreed targets through poor performance or where work has to be redone to elim-

inate errors, no reimbursement should be expected or offered. (Omega Handbook)

At Pi, there was evidence of a similar compulsion. The written 'terms of employment' referred to the fact that 'flexibility in working hours is often required due to the nature of our business', but overtime would not be paid unless staff were engaged on specific projects which entailed out-of-hours support for clients (Pi Terms of Employment). In Lambda, most employees systematically worked in excess of the formal hours, thus falling into line with the managing director's explicit statement that he did not want people with a 'nine to five' mentality (unstructured interview, Lambda, male managing director). Some graduates, he continued, had not been able to keep up to pace with 'the steep learning curve'.

In practice, the demands and reasons for overtime varied. For those working on long-term projects as, for example, in the offsite Omega teams who were employed on maintenance projects of between two and ten years, there was very much a nine to five culture. However, for employees working on shorter-term projects, and on software installations, deadlines and overtime came thick and fast. At Pi there were no set shift patterns and no time sheets, and different departments worked contrasting hours. Most employees worked nine to five except those on implementations who worked longer days, particularly if they were located some considerable distance from head office, or if there was a new product release. They also tended to work weekends and travelled more than their colleagues in other departments.

Conversely, what determined working time patterns in call centres, more than any single factor, was the obligation to marry staffing levels to actual, or anticipated, levels of customer demand. The consequence was a mosaic of shift arrangements (Table 3.2) which extend well beyond what were once regarded as conventional clerical service working hours (Bain and Mulvey, 2002). Sixty-three per cent of agents reported working 'always' or 'frequently' on Saturdays and 42 per cent on Sundays, with as many as 76 per cent working evenings and 39 per cent nights. By contrast, apart from the pre-deadline intensive periods, only negligible numbers of software developers normally worked these 'anti-social' hours. The observable variation between the call centres is related to the nature of the sector, to product, and to the specific service provided, so that in the holiday/travel firm Holstravel, and in the entertainment/telecommunications organization Entcomm, shift diffusion is even more pronounced. For example, at Holstravel 79 per cent of agents 'frequently' or 'always' work Saturdays and 74 per cent Sundays while, at Entcomm, 77 per cent do likewise on Saturdays.

Invariably, staff shift patterns were calibrated with microscopic precision to correspond to volumes of incoming calls. For example, at Holstravel

Table 3.2 Call centre operating hours and extent of 'atypical' working

Call centre	Moneyflow	Thejobshop	Entcomm	Holstravel	
Operating hours:					
Mon–Fri	07.00–22.00	07.00–24.00	07.00–23.45	24 hours	
Sat	09.00–17.00	07.00–24.00	09.00–23.45	24 hours	
Sun	None	07.00–24.00	09.00–23.45	24 hours	
Week total	73 hours	119 hours	120 hours	168 hours	
Shift	% responding 'frequently'/'always'				Mean %
Weekday evenings	76	57	78	76	76
Weekday nights[a]	23	25	27	70	39
Saturday	49	35	77	79	63
Sunday	4	24	39	74	42

Note: [a]With the exception of Holstravel, a 24/7 operation, 'nights' are taken to mean employees working to the end of the last shift.

between 11 a.m. and 1 p.m. separate teams would commence work at 15 or 30 minute intervals and, later, part-time shifts would begin at 4 pm, enabling maximum agent availability to be attained during peak periods of customer demand, particularly in the evenings. The organization of shifts was often dictated by detailed, but questionably accurate, predictions of call volumes generated by management information systems such as the *'Blue Pumpkin'* software package. Managers and team leaders would 'read off' data from printouts, and plan shifts accordingly, often to the chagrin of employees:

> I do not like this *Blue Pumpkin*. They say it's going to be a lot better and you have got more time to organize your social life with *Blue Pumpkin*, because you get your rosters three months in advance. But we are getting next week's [rosters] today…there's not much opportunity to change shifts. (Holstravel, male travel consultant; H-I-10)

What generated these intricate arrangements were the simultaneous requirements to optimize active labour utilization and to reduce, as far as possible, the number of 'surplus' non-engaged agents, so that the underlying objectives of cost reduction and profit maximization could be achieved. These complex labour schedules appear as contemporary manifestations of 'time thrift', to apply the term that Thompson (1967) used to describe employers' imposition of temporal discipline in the early years of industrial capitalism.

Patently, these contrasting temporal work patterns produced differing outcomes and experiences for employees in the respective sectors. More than one in four call centre agents expressed dissatisfaction with their 'normal' working hours and shifts, compared to negligible numbers of software developers who, with the notable exception of the periods preceding project deadlines, largely expressed satisfaction with their working hours. Tellingly, the deepest discontent amongst employees of all sites in both sectors was to be found in those call centres, Entcomm and Holstravel, where shift variation was most pronounced.

> We had like focus meetings where so many of us from each group got sort of pulled in...the company [admitted] morale is really low and wanted our opinions, and at every meeting [we] brought up the shifts. It wasn't so much the amount of late shifts. In here you don't have a constant shift for one week. I mean, you could come in and start at 9 o'clock on a Monday, start at 11 on a Tuesday, off Wednesday, coming in to 12.45 in the morning Thursday, Friday, that's what was annoying us, because your body doesn't know when it's meant to be sleeping and when it's meant to be awake. (Entcomm, female customer services adviser; E-I-12)

Work organization and management control – call centres

Teamworking

As indicated above, teamworking, where the workforce was divided into distinct groupings, was widespread. As is well known, the presence of teamworking, in itself, tells us nothing about which of the particular forms are in place and the diverse range of managerial objectives, processes and outcomes that are implied (Procter and Mueller, 2000). Universally, in our call centre environments, teams represented a convenient way for management to disaggregate the workforce into groupings of between eight and 15, and thus exercise control over sizeable numbers of employees. Teams were mostly gathered around distinctive workflows, although several provided duplicate channels of customer service. Given the essentially individualized labour process, where sedentary call handlers were frequently engaged in near-continuous communication with customers, and were physically and audibly separated from colleagues, there are undoubted limitations to the degree to which inter-group communication and participation could occur. Inevitably, horizontal work organization, between agents, was constrained, particularly on those workflows where high call volumes were prioritized and agents were required to remain at their workstations for extended periods. Challenging the knowledge work stereotype, team productivity represented the aggregate of the individualized outputs of its members, rather than being the product of the creative and synergistic interaction of colleagues with variable and complementary skills (van den Broek *et al.*, 2004).

However, this does not mean that cooperative engagement between team members was non-existent. At Holstravel, for example, agents frequently interrupted calls, placing customers on hold, to check details with, or acquire information from, colleagues. This would happen when newer workers drew upon the experience of longer-serving colleagues and demonstrated, in this call centre at least, the importance of tacit knowledge. On occasions, customers presented agents with queries they could not answer, which also led to consultation with colleagues. The conclusion to be drawn is that the more complex the work, the greater the extent of inter-group communication. However, what tended to dominate was the individualization of tasks and the expectation that even the most thorny of customer questions could and should be resolved at first contact. Pull-down menus of frequently asked questions and step-by-step protocols were utilized increasingly to guide agents through problem resolution.

Interaction between team members could take oppositional forms. When the level of incoming calls was low, agents would often chat to each other or swap gossip, sometimes leaving their work stations during particularly quiet periods. At times, though, agents used the gaps between calls to subvert team leader authority and control, by engaging in diverse forms of misbehaviour (see Taylor and Bain, 2003a for examples from Thejobshop). At Holstravel, it was a widespread practice for agents to cover their microphones when talking to colleagues, mindful of the retribution that might follow comments critical of their supervisors, company or brand.

However, to re-iterate, horizontal exchange between agents was restricted by the need to be actively engaged on calls. As evidence of this, more than one in three respondents reported that they never had time to talk to their colleagues (compared to one in eight software developers). Further, a widespread complaint from agents and supervisors alike, and confirmed by observation, was that scheduled team meetings and team briefs were often cancelled because it was deemed impossible to organize time away from the phones. This is a further expression of the fact that call centres operate on lean production principles where working patterns closely correspond to levels of customer demand. Having anticipated the difficulty of physically separating agents from productive contact with customers, Holstravel ingeniously incorporated into the design of their workfloor small semi-circular areas, resembling baseball 'dugouts', directly adjacent to the workstations. Here, team leaders, like sporting coaches, could deliver short, sharp motivational messages to their team members, without losing valuable customer contact time that would have resulted from lengthier and more conventional team meetings that occurred at some distance from agents' workstations.

Monitoring

Tight surveillance and intensive monitoring were pervasive in all call centre case studies. Agent-customer calls were universally recorded, although in particular instances this was for legal or contractual reasons as, for example, in financial services at Moneyflow, or in Thejobshop-*Energycom* but, more generally was ostensibly for coaching or performance appraisal reasons. Monitoring took various forms, including retrospective sampling of a set number, or proportion, of calls, or supervisors listening to live calls either remotely, or openly whilst sitting alongside agents. Monitoring was so claustrophobic at Holstravel that team leaders would systematically listen in to agents' internal, as well as to external calls. On one occasion, a TC called a friend in another team to let her know that she had a job interview the following day and was going 'to pull a sickie'. Having listened into this conversation, the team leader phoned the agent's home several times the next day demanding to speak to her (unstructured interview).

Equally notable was the measurement of performance, whether of individual call handler or of a team. Quantitative statistics relating to call-handling (e.g. average call times, calls per hour, time between calls, 'wrap times', percentage of time on-switch etc.) were, despite differences in emphasis between and within call centres, a dominant feature of daily organizational life. Generated by the ICTs that are integral to the call centre, operational statistics were translated into spreadsheets which, in turn, became the habitual preoccupation of managers and team leaders. What mattered was not so much surveillance *per se*, but the supervisory interpretation of the system-generated statistics. These statistics acquired significance as performance indicators, when placed against the targets set for an individual agent, or team or section, or for an entire call centre or business. Typically, average times for call-handlers or teams would be calculated to one-hundredth part of a second and were displayed in the team areas.

Targets

Thus, a multifaceted array of *quantitative* targets were implemented, differentiated by degree and intensity rather than type, between distinct workflows of the same call centre and, given contrasts in market and sector, between centres. For example, at Entcomm, in the main customer service and retention teams, targets fluctuated between 13 and 14 calls per hour, with call handling times at between 250 and 270 seconds, while, at Moneyflow, the average time on loans was 5.5 minutes. At Thejobshop, in *Bluechip*, agents were required to handle 50–60 calls in a 7.5 hour shift on corporate lines, and 80 on more routine services for lower value customers. In three of the four centres, agents who exceeded stipulated call length could expect supervisory intervention in real time. At Entcomm, a dedicated service performance team continuously monitored the status of all call handlers, while, at Moneyflow loans, calls in excess of ten minutes would provoke managerial intervention. At Holstravel, 'Mission Control', a centrally-located, circular pen of PCs which, amongst its many functions, monitored performance, would detect irregular patterns of call activity, prompting internal phone calls to team leaders to alert them of their charges' deviation from prescribed norms.

In contrast to targets based on call volumes and duration, sales targets were composed of common elements – the value of total sales, conversion rates, leads or expressions of interest, or sales of particular products – which were related to bonus and/or individual pay awards. At Moneyflow each adviser was given a monetary figure to attain in new business for each year, and the extent to which this was achieved led to being graded in one of three categories; 'not met targets', 'met targets', 'exceeded targets'. At Thejobshop *Energycom* inbound sales, 11 sales per shift were expected, even when call volumes were low. Agents at Holstravel faced a bewildering mixture of targets leading to bonuses, based on monetary value ('base', 'stretch' and 'super-stretch') call conversion rates (CCR) and numerical criteria (calls handled per hour). At one time as much as 60 per cent of their salary could come from target-based bonuses.

In addition to these putatively objective numerical and sales targets, which reflect the cost-efficient, or quantitative, logic of the call centre, management implemented *qualitative* targets at three of our cases. For example, at Thejobshop, agents were evaluated on the quality of customer interaction according to 18 criteria, with marks on a 0–4 scale given for each. Not only were operators assessed on their conformity to prescribed call conventions ('opening' and 'closure'), but on the structure and style of diction ('pace', 'pitch', 'emphasis', 'inflection', 'construction', 'control'). Criteria making judgements on agents' attitude, manner and behaviour ('rapport', 'listening skills', etc.) were also applied, as well as those assessing success in engaging with customers with regard to a particular service ('product knowledge'), dealing with queries ('problem solving') and gauging customers' potential value to the business ('profiling'). At Entcomm, quality targets were even more extensive, involving 25 aspects, sub-divided into seven categories, with scores ranging from 1–4, thus giving an individual call-handler a total score out of a possible 100. The sheer range of these criteria employed to regulate, modify and improve, according to managerial prescription, agents' performance in customer interaction is quite staggering. What exacerbates the intensity of the process for agents is that their encounters were subject to evaluation on all these finely grained and discrete criteria, while simultaneously facing the inescapable pressure of tight quantitative targets.

Conformance to quantitative, or 'hard' targets, as they were frequently referred to by management in these centres, is patently redolent of scientific management with its infinitesimal measurement of work tasks (Braverman, 1974) and attendant worker compliance. However, the widespread utilization of qualitative, or 'soft', targets demonstrates the penetration of Taylorist techniques into new realms of the customer servicing relationship. In the managerial deconstruction of verbal communication, we are witnessing the concerted attempt to rationalize and standardize both agents' words and their emotional content. Several authors have applied Hochschild's (1983) insights into the performance of emotional labour to call centre work (Taylor, 1998; Belt *et al.*, 2002). Clearly normative control over emotion is important in the panoply of managerial controls over call handlers (Thompson *et al.*, 2004), and is integrated with the more explicit bureaucratic and explicitly Taylorist forms.

The evidence from these case studies powerfully refutes several of Frenkel *et al.*'s contentions, not least the claim that management's ability to measure call centre workers' outputs is limited 'insofar as service work encompasses aspects of quality in addition to productivity' (1999: 139). Even in the identifiable 'quality' workflows where the emphasis was placed upon developing personalized relationships with customers, agents still faced quantitative, qualitative and, where applicable, sales targets, to say nothing of the normative expectations placed upon them.

Similarly, the evidence from these case studies contradicts Frenkel *et al.*'s claims of 'management laxity' in taking 'behaviour measures' seriously and challenges their argument in relation to performance statistics.

> Although call centre managers did refer to these operational data regularly, they were rarely considered part of a call centre's key performance indicators...This meant that lower down the line, supervisors and workers paid attention to the data but did not ascribe overwhelming significance to them (*op cit*: 141).

As we argued in an earlier paper, target setting and systematically ensuring that agents meet them, lie at the heart of management's labour utilization strategy in the four centres (Bain *et al.*, 2002). The co-existence of *both* qualitative and quantitative targets demonstrates the managerial compulsion to resolve the inescapable contradiction permeating call centre work. How can managers ensure that agents provide quality customer interaction, whilst simultaneously delivering call volumes of a magnitude such that the cost reduction potential implicit in the call centre is fully realized? From this perspective, the systematic implementation of targets of all kinds should be seen as the central element in the attempt to solve the problem of the indeterminacy of labour that confronts call centre management.

Recalling our earlier injunction, it is clear that the real significance of targets emerges only in the context of an understanding of the broader political economy. Targets should be seen as a concrete representation of the competitive nature of markets and of the accumulation and profit-making strategies of firms. At corporate level, overall cost and revenue generation targets are grounded in recent performance, and are set in anticipation of market trends and the competitive positioning of the firm *vis-à-vis* its rivals. Targets are then translated downwards, from business unit to call centre level, from section to team, and then, finally, to individual agent. Sometimes, the targets established at corporate level were made explicit in order to encourage local performance. For example, at Holstravel in one particular month the centre-wide sales target was £16 million; progress towards that total was prominently displayed on the largest of the electronic wallboards. The evidence of widespread employee antipathy towards what were perceived as onerous, if not wholly, unachievable targets, is plentiful.

> At the moment morale is at a low...I'm told I'm too customer focused. If I see something wrong I try and fix any error [and] I get penalized for it, because of what they call AHT, 275 seconds per customer. Quantity instead of quality. Problem is many customers call back with repeat problems...numbers of calls rather than fixing first time (looks good on paper). Team leaders are told to clamp down on advisers. Stats, stats. Stress is at an all time high, and go home at night and can't sleep because of stats (numbers of calls per hour etc). (Entcomm, male customer service adviser, questionnaire comment)

Since targets are not the product of some disembodied internal logic, but the outcome of the externally-generated compulsion to benchmark perpetually against competitors' market share, performance and profits, they are susceptible to revision under the impact of external environment change. Thus, the sharpened competition and market turbulence evident in all the sectors in which our case studies were embedded, later exacerbated by the onset of generalized economic slowdown, could not but fail to generate a drive for improved efficiency (Taylor et al., 2005). Although the causal relationship between external shock and internal response was not always direct and immediate, the final outcome in all instances was the raising and tightening of agents' targets, and often additionally involved changes to shift patterns.

At Entcomm, in the words of one manager, the 'Planning for Growth' strategy of 2000 meant 'trying to squeeze out extra performance from each area'; for example, on retention calls, AHTs were reduced from 520 to 430 seconds in a three-month period. The policy aimed also at increasing the proportion of time agents talked with customers to 70:30, and then 80:20, as 'wrap' times were cut and clerical work was to be completed whilst the call was live. At Holstravel, tighter AHTs, meaning more calls per agent, and higher conversion rates, aimed to increase efficiencies as compensation for depressed sales prior to and in the wake of 9/11. Previous shift patterns were fractured, as the *Blue Pumpkin* automatically changed start times at short notice as working hours were allocated to call handlers without consultation. Moneyflow's Board announced the 'Year 2000 Challenge', which dramatically increased sales targets and produced for some agents a 12-hour day.

The arbitrary imposition of stricter targets, where their fulfilment was tied to bonus payments, entailed a loss of income, which, in Holstravel, could be considerable.

> At first when we started, like in October, November and December, they were offering you really good money...I was converting at 300 per cent. Now they [the targets] are unrealistic. Like 75 grand stretch [sales] target last month. They reduced it to 50 grand so that's a bit better...For your call conversion reaching, your stretch target they offer you eighty quid. For the same time last year for people in my team, they were offering six hundred quid. (Holstravel, female travel consultant; H-I-13)

Thus, upward target revision, a contemporary form of speed-up, became the principal means by which employers attempted to hike up the output of its workforce, in the circumstances of market uncertainty and concerns over levels of profitability. For agents this represented an intensification of effort, compounded by decreases in the 'porosity' of working time as shift and break times were further engineered. Of course, given existing technologies, and limits to the extent that intensification and extensification might be either feasible of desirable, employers' ability to raise productivity, reduce unit labour costs and restore profitability was inevitably constrained. In these circumstances, it is notable that both Holstravel and Moneyflow latterly offshored to India some of the most routinized of their services, in an attempt to drastically cut labour costs (Taylor and Bain, 2005).

Work organization and management control – software

Teamworking

Arguably, software work might be seen to provide a perfect example of contemporary teamwork. All projects are reliant on collaborative working between employees, who possess their own specific skills and the knowledge bases crucial for the creation of the final product. Unlike call centre work, where teams formed a convenient mechanism for disaggregating a workforce and exercising managerial control, those in software (although similarly sized at between eight and twenty employees) are more or less essential for the productive process. Nevertheless, while some have argued that co-worker relationships amongst knowledge workers require high degrees of interdependence (e.g. Tam *et al.*, 2002), we found that *formal* interaction between team members varied considerably as these conflicting quotes illustrate.

> Well, the whole project, I would say, hasn't been particularly good at teamwork, I don't think, and I don't know whether it's because we've been split into three distinct areas...another reason is maybe certain individuals who haven't worked in a big team before...they are maybe

used to smaller projects where they are pretty much kind of left to work on their own and there is less interaction by other people. (Omega, female developer; O-I-04)

The team I am in, the S team, it's sort of split into 3 or 4 smaller teams and yes we all help each other, everyone is excellent in that way. I can't have any complaints about that...The part of the S team I work in is four plus my team leader and, in the S team as a whole, there must be 25–30. (Beta, male developer; B-I-05)

Formal interaction was perhaps most obvious in relation to weekly team meetings, and in circumstances where an individual's expertise necessarily had to be supplemented by that of colleagues. Further, however, team members had often worked together previously on projects, so the appearance of limited daily interaction between individuals fails to capture fully the extent of collective engagement that develops over time. Nevertheless, although there is a high degree of interdependency between employees for the completion of the final product, day-to-day working is largely an isolated experience.

While teams in call centres could hardly be regarded as immutable bodies, given organizational flux and restructuring, the frequent movement of agents between teams, and the effects of attrition, they tended not to be time-bound to the same extent as those in the software sector where there was considerable variation in groups' longevity. Although not exclusively, longer-term projects tended to involve the maintenance of systems or work on updates. The shorter projects were more likely to be development projects. In Gamma and Pi, employees generally worked on two or three large projects each year and, in Lambda, the engineers and developers typically spent up to six months on each. In Omega, however, projects could vary in duration from three months to several years. Similarly, Beta projects tended to last for many years, each containing a number of related, but independent, sub-projects. Since employees in the smaller companies worked simultaneously on more than one project, they interacted more extensively with their colleagues. In Beta, and to a lesser extent Omega, where employees were assigned to one project only, this was based on individuals choosing from a central pool of projects, or on direct negotiation with the on-site resourcing managers. These projects were organized around a matrix structure and were made up of horizontal workgroups from across the organization. Projects would also include contractors, whether long-term (as in Beta) or short-term.

Beta and Omega both located teams to client or satellite offices for extended periods. A greater degree of *intra*-team interaction was observable within off-site teams (as compared to on-site teams) because of their remoteness. However, *inter*-team communication was almost non-existent, as the relative isolation led to resentment towards head office employees and, frequently, deliberate lack of co-operation between head office employees and offsite workers.

While competition *between* teams was commonly fostered by management in call centres, although to limited effect, engineered division took a contrasting and *internal* form in software. The latter was rooted in the fact that team members often learnt their trade by working on projects alongside experienced software workers, observing their programming and code writing. Employees used access to particular projects to learn new programming languages. In this manner, individual employees often used the team as a vehicle for knowledge acquisition and consequently engaged in political behaviour so that they might gain access to more desirable projects. These practices, though, generated a significant contradiction for organizations. On the one hand, ideally, they wished to keep their experts working on relevant projects but, on the other hand, they were aware of employees' desire to enhance skills by moving between teams and projects. At the time of the research, the labour market was sufficiently weighted in favour of employees, at least at the most skilled end of the spectrum, so that if organizations failed to meet developers' requirements, there were sufficient opportunities to move to other employers (for a fuller discussion of career paths see Chapter 5). In the most developed example of this tendency, Omega manipulated access to elite projects as a reward, using the team as a vehicle for regulating and controlling appropriate behaviours.

The weekly team meetings which monitored the progress of particular projects, or products, provided the opportunity for employees to access knowledge from other colleagues and from their team leaders. Importantly, it also afforded team leaders the occasion to assess the contributions of team members. Team leaders, particularly those in charge of more prestigious projects, were powerfully placed to determine who should be included in these programmes. For many employees these relationships impacted on their work opportunities, with the outcome of team leaders' decisions paralleling and reinforcing the major division in software work; between those who worked on 'cutting edge' projects and those involved in more routinized, lower level work. As we discuss in Chapters 4, 5 and 7, there is some evidence of a gender dimension to this.

Divergences in work content and control

As this discussion of teamworking suggests, forms of direct control in software are far less prevalent than in call centres, although explicit forms of surveillance and monitoring were not entirely absent. The fact that software work is not uniform, and that its employees are not an homogeneous group, is the key to understanding differentiation in the forms of control. To reiterate, our sample, which was largely representative of the broader software workforce, encompassed both highly skilled 'elite' professionals and the less skilled engaged in relatively mundane, repetitive tasks.

The latter category included those at Omega involved in testing, maintenance and implementation work, and a team at Pi responsible for documentation and technical authorship. At both Beta and Omega, dedicated teams were concerned with maintaining clients' outdated financial systems. Most lower skilled teams were familiar with the quantitative targets associated with bureaucratic modes of control as they tended to be presented with shorter deadlines, which were closely managed by team leaders. For example, failure to meet specific and tight deadlines by software implementation teams at Pi incurred pecuniary penalties such as the non-payment of quarterly bonuses.

However, the most extreme form of direct control in our software cases was to be found amongst servicing and support operations at Beta, where staff were responsible for solving the problems of both internal and external customers, and for testing systems and fixing faults. These processes, not uncommon in the software sector as a whole, resemble certain call centres insofar as they require staff to be available '24 hours a day, seven days a week and 365 days a year'. Furthermore, response times, of 'normally' 50 minutes, should be seen as strict. Frequently, though, the temporal constraints on workers were even tighter, as the section manager explained,

> I may have to hand over, let's say a fault, to another section. If I do this straight away, testing where the problem lies and handing it over to the responsible section or person, that's fine. However, at times, I may be too busy to deal with the fault immediately and get back to it after 45 minutes. If I discover that the problem lies somewhere else and hand over the fault after 45 minutes, the person receiving it has only 5 minutes left to fix it, and won't be too happy about that. (Unstructured interview, Beta, male manager)

Beta instituted mechanisms to enforce these temporal targets, where every fault was computer logged and the progress of resolution by a named employee monitored. Divergence from these required target times triggered intervention by members of one of the Major Incident Teams (MIT), who informed the appropriate manager of an employee's negligence. Given the intense pressure that MIT monitoring causes, it is hardly surprising that its members were 'not the most popular people'.

In contrast, highly skilled employees were engaged on more 'sexy' development projects, including specialized programming and analysis. For example, an Omega team was designing a payment system for a large government body. The development side of Beta embraced complex undertakings, such as high-level architecture design, which involved advanced technical roles. Formally, at least, in these more challenging projects, explicit targets were avoided. The absence of defined monitoring was premised on the belief that software employees' social distinctiveness was constructed on their practice as professionals and, consequently, a strong degree of self-supervision would be exercised. It has been argued that cultural-ideological control strategies which emphasize the values, ideas, beliefs, and emotions of employees as 'elite' professionals, working for 'elite' organizations, renders explicit control devices redundant (e.g. Kärreman and Alvesson, 2004). Correspondingly, the customary perspective regarding software developers is that management control has centred on the regulation of identity through a career mindset (Andrews *et al.*, 2005). In theory at least, in order to control employees, management strove to create forms of work and cultural environments appropriate to the image and rhetoric of an elite identity.

Although more complex projects had longer time-scales, skilled employees still had to meet specific deadlines. Clearly weekly team meetings provided some measure of progress, as did interim deadlines for sub-projects, and in confirmation of the argument developed above, organizations did depend on cultural-ideological controls to ensure productive activity for much of the duration of projects. Software respondents repeatedly echoed the perception that they were professional employees capable of making informed judgements on their own initiative. However, this powerful sense of professionalism was compromised as final deadlines approached when more bureaucratic controls, of both punitive and incentivizing kinds, were initiated.

Typically, there would be a rush to meet, or improve on, target dates, with software professionals as concerned as their lesser-skilled colleagues at the prospect of losing financial bonuses. Yet, arguably, failure to meet deadlines invoked even more stringent sanctions, which struck at the heart of professionals' social identity and damaged internal and external career aspirations (see Chapter 5). If team leaders could identify particular individual employees as having been responsible for the late completion of projects, then they would be penalized by being denied access to further prestigious projects. Conversely, potent inducements existed for meeting or exceeding deadlines, in terms of material rewards and the lure of expanded opportunity. Omega, notably, tended to bid for contracts within a narrow circle of clients, so that previously successful teams would be rewarded with additional elite projects.

A fuller understanding of the effectiveness of internal controls depends upon consideration of the external labour market. In this respect, as in so many others, the division of labour in software, and its associated skill and qualification stratification, are salient factors. The relative ease with which lower skilled workers could be replaced meant that organizations were less inhibited in using bureaucratic controls for these groups. Nevertheless, the general shortage of trained IT workers restricted the widespread implementation of direct controls, leading to a preference for quite subtle, normative forms related to the conscious encouragement of social relationships and inter-personal attachments (Fineman, 2003). While we discuss cultural issues more fully in Chapter 4, it is helpful to provide some illustration of these widespread activities; Pi organized pizza nights and a two-hour free bar for its employees every Friday evening, while Omega offered nights-out as a reward for its highly-performing teams. Evidently, initiatives such as these are contingent upon the particular conjuncture of demand for professional skills in a growing and competitive sector with a tight labour market. We can only speculate that the slackened labour market conditions that have prevailed since the period of our research may have seen the growth of direct, bureaucratic techniques at the expense of the carefully constructed cultural-ideological and normative control strategies which may no longer be essential.

Experiences of work – perceptions of control

Evidently (Table 3.3) call centre agents and software developers differ in the extent to which they see themselves exercising control over key aspects of task performance.

That a majority of the call centre agents across the four sites believed that they exercise no, or only a little, control over the pace of their work, is a reflection of the quintessential features of call centre work; the ACD system which, under conditions of continuous call flow, itself the consequence of managerial decision, erodes employee control over the tempo of work. Once agents are logged-on and 'ready', they are required to respond and exercise little choice over whether to take calls. Where call throughput is prioritized by management, cycle times are short, clerical and 'wrap' times minimized and call content standardized, the flow of calls can be experienced as relentless, like an 'assembly line in the head' to use Taylor and Bain's (1999) metaphor. While many examples could be cited from all four

Table 3.3 Perceptions of degree of control

To what extent do you...	Call centre agents		Software developers	
	'Not at all'/ 'Just a little'	'Quite a lot'/ 'A great deal'	'Not at all'/ 'Just a little'	'Quite a lot'/ 'A great deal'
...set your own pace of work	52%	25%	8%	64%
...decide when to take a break	60%	25%	3%	89%
...plan how to carry out your work	40%	32%	2%	82%
...set your own targets/ deadlines	69%	16%	19%	46%

case studies of call handlers this interview segment, parts of it in the local vernacular, provides most vivid testimony:

Q How much control would you say you have over your daily work?
A Nane.
Q None at all?
A No because you cannae have any control over the calls you get really.
Q In terms of volume or the actual....
A Well, you can have control over the volume–it's just dinnae answer the phone. (Laughs)
Q Do you do that? Say, for example, that call volume has been really high and you have been getting battered with all these annoying customers and you just want to have ten minutes to get your head together...
A I'll just sit on for a couple of minutes, because you are allowed to sit in wrap for, like not on the phone, for up to like 10 minutes. So basically we will just sit for a couple of minutes before we take another call.
Q You said that you had no control over your work. What other aspects would you say?
A You cannae control the calls...Basically, in main reservations you normally take all calls which is basically everybody just phoning in; [plus you] take overflow Teletext, Infinity calls, which are from banks that do special discounts, we get them; we get Othertravelco which we have just recently taken over, we get their calls which are totally different, like we are dealing with the customer totally different and everything, we get them. Plus we get overflow from the call centre in the south east of England which is the same as our calls...about eleven different kinds of calls. Sometimes it is like too much to cope with...some customers get discounts and some dinnae. Some get different deals than others, some get mair percent...Sometime you are like 'oh my god what is coming'. And it's just like 'I'll put you on hold for a second, aaaaahhhhhhhhh, what am I dae'en, I'm stuck!' (Holstravel, female travel consultant; H-I-13)

In these lean production regimes, the managerial compulsion to ensure that agents maximize their productive engagement with customers, the same underlying reason that causes team meetings to be cancelled, leads to minimal worker control over breaks. Invariably, breaks were staggered across and between teams and, frequently, team leaders would reschedule breaks at short notice because of unanticipated increases in call volume or employee absence.

Given the generally low levels of control reported by agents, it might seem surprising that as many as almost one in three respondents stated that they planned their work either 'a great deal' or 'quite a lot'. Yet, this is a reflection of the fact that some of the 'quality' call flows involve more complex work associated with longer cycle times, pre-arranging calls and off-phone task completion. This was certainly true of the regulated side of Moneyflow and sections of Thejobshop, where majorities reported exercising a relatively high degree of control over the planning of work. However, it should be noted that overall 40 per cent still believed that they exercised no, or only a little, control in this respect.

Further, in the light of our previous discussion of targets, it is not surprising that 69 per cent reported exercising little or no control over target setting. Indeed, targets remain one of the most unpopular aspects of call centre work. In response to an open question, almost one in five stated that it was the most disliked aspect of their job, and many longer-serving agents lamented the passing of a job that once had a powerful ethos of customer service, now replaced by strict sales and performance measures.

> Whereas before when I started it was more customer service orientated so you had to give good service to your customer, take time. But now you feel you have just got to get the customer off the phone. So again you are working harder, you are taking more calls, you feel you can't go for a break because you feel eyes are on you to be there on the phone taking calls. (Moneyflow, female customer adviser; M-I-15)

Analysis reveals differences in the pace, volume and, relatedly, the content of calls between the four call centres, and equally important, often between sections or 'workflows' within individual operations (Taylor *et al.*, 2002). The picture that emerges from the evidence is of two types of workflow. On the one hand, there are those that are the most volume-driven (e.g. Moneyflow-*non-secured*, Thejobshop-*Energycom*, Holstravel-*Teletext*, much of Entcomm), where agents exercise the least control and have the least discretion over task performance. On the other hand, there are those, less dominated by sheer quantitative criteria, where agents are able to employ greater discretion, but even here substantial minorities of agents report an experience of work, where they are driven by quantitative imperatives.

The overall position of the software employees was substantially different. To begin with, the overwhelming majority felt that they exercised considerable control over the pace of their work (Table 3.3). This finding is a reflection of the length of project cycles and some ability to determine working patterns. Indeed, as emphasized earlier in this chapter and reflected in other studies (e.g. Perrolle, 1986), despite the fact that software employees are differentiated by skill, qualifications and task complexity, many clearly do enjoy a significant degree of autonomy in the organization and completion of their work, albeit with the proviso that interim targets and project deadlines are met.

The extent of discretion over task performance is manifest also in the command over scheduling of breaks. Almost 90 per cent believed that they exercised 'a lot', or a 'great deal', of control over the timing of their breaks. This finding confirmed our on-site observations where employees, either in groups or individually, would regularly leave their workstations to make coffee in the kitchens or restrooms, or perhaps would leave their building at various points throughout the day to buy sandwiches. Things changed when deadlines were pressing, and breaks became shorter and less frequent. Towards the end of the project cycle, instead of going out for lunch or sitting in the coffee lounges, employees were more likely to be seen eating sandwiches at their computer terminals.

Similarly, it is unsurprising that over three-quarters of software respondents felt that they had 'quite a lot', or a 'great deal', of control over planning how to carry out their work. The lengthy duration of projects, and the importance attached to professional identity by organizations and employees alike, allowed for substantial autonomy *within* the overall parameters of any particular undertaking. However, the converse is visible in responses to the question on control over targets or deadlines. Indeed, this is the aspect of work over which software employees reported the least control. Less than half of respondents believed they exercised real command over targets. For the most part, this is a consequence of deadlines, determined by either clients or internal customers, and the pressure associated with achieving them.

One final observation regards the influence of customers on employee perceptions of control: the new orthodoxy ascribes to customers a benign impact, emphasizing that their wide-ranging demands constrain standardization and leads to both variation in task performance and an enrichment of the work experience. In both sectors, in different ways, although customer fulfilment was seen as a cherished ideal and a source of potential satisfaction, customers were more likely to be seen as an additional source of pressure, further eroding control over the job.

> ...the feeling I get very much here is because we have legal contracts and we supply to an outside supplier nobody wants to miss the deadline and not deliver...from my point very little manoeuvrability. The deadline was agreed months ago, nobody wants to let that slip. (Omega, male developer; O-I-07)

At Beta, the MPGs (Management and Professional Grades), dealing with customers 'on the frontline', face work pressures of varying intensity depending on the stages of the project (unstructured interview Beta).

In mass market call centres, the pressure deriving from customers is, at least in part, integrally connected to the performance of emotional labour.

> Yes, it's the repetitive nature of work that gets to you because you are constantly 'good afternoon' (adopts telephone voice), you have got to be cheery all the time, whether you are or aren't, because you could be having the crappiest day you have ever had in your life...(Holstravel, female travel consultant; questionnaire comment)

Sometimes, though, the pressure comes from simply having to contend with a level of abuse that in some centres seems inextricably bound up with customer expectations.

> You could have somebody that is ranting and raving at you and first thing in the morning it just sets you off on a bad day, you know, for the rest of the day. 'Why is she shouting at me, it's not my fault. During the summer you get people complaining about the holiday, people who haven't even booked with us. You feel like saying to them sometimes, 'Well if you bought something out of Marks & Spencer would you try to take it back to NEXT?' but you can't say that. (Holstravel, female travel consultant, questionnaire comment)

Conclusion

At the outset of the study, we suggested that significant contrasts would exist in the nature and extent of management control mechanisms between the two sectors. Allowing for differentiation within call centres and software at the levels of sub-sector, firm and workplace and, as we have repeatedly emphasized, important heterogeneity in work organization, it is possible to generalize from the data. Although, call centres do embody integrated combinations of technical, bureaucratic and normative controls (Callaghan and Thompson, 2001), what is most striking is the evidence of *direct control*, particularly through the universal implementation of targets. In contrast, and again with important qualifications, software work through the pervasiveness of normative and cultural-ideological controls (Kärreman and Alvesson, 2004) more approximates to *responsible autonomy* (Friedman, 1977).

This presentational schema (Figure 3.1) is useful as a heuristic device to explore the differences between call centres and software development. The closed rectangular boxes indicate that call centres and software development are distinct types of work and that also, *in the main*, the former tends towards direct control, while the latter tends towards responsible autonomy. Yet, within each category a differentiation exists, based upon identifiable and discrete workflows.

Organizational Life: The Nature of Work 81

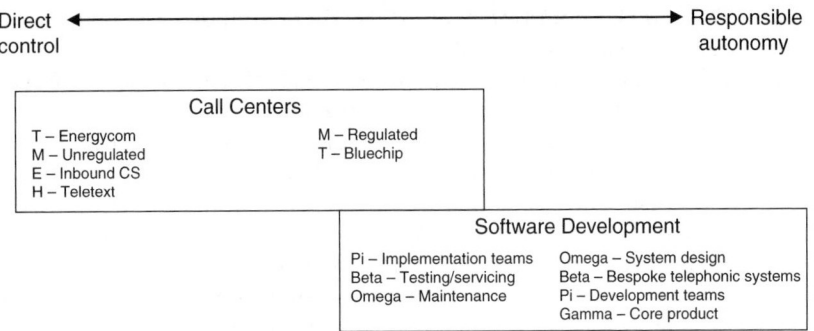

Figure 3.1 Spectrum of control

At the far left of the call centre box there are clustered a number of workflows with similar characteristics; quantitative imperatives and call volumes dominate managerial priorities, cycle times are short. The content of customer interaction is highly standardized, and targets are most stringent. Thejobshop-*Enerycom*, Moneyflow-*unregulated*, Entcomm-inbound customer service and Holstravel–*Teletext* are typical of call centre work where forms of direct control are most stringent. At the right side of the box, Moneyflow-*regulated* and Thejobshop-*Bluechip* are examples of more contradictory workflows. These comprise elements of direct control, in that targets and monitoring are certainly present, but because agents exercise wider judgement in task performance in their dealings with customers, these types of work should be seen as displaying some of the characteristics of responsible autonomy. The bifurcation in the software box reflects the division of labour in this work, discussed above. At the right side are examples of the elite projects, those highly-skilled, design-based and customized undertakings, while at the left side are the more Taylorized cases of the variable kinds of more repetitive work, of testing, maintenance, customer servicing and support. While monitoring and control never reach the intensity of the most standardized forms of call centre work, they are sufficiently pervasive as to enable us to suggest a shared location with the lesser – but still significantly – regulated forms of call centre work on this notional direct control-responsible autonomy continuum.

In the literature, there has been debate over how to categorize call centres. Batt and Moynihan (2002) propose three models; the mass production, mass customization and professional services models. The evidence from the case studies confirms the prevalence of the mass production model, notwithstanding the marginal existence of mass customization and professional services types of work. In this sense our findings resonate with diverse studies (Bain and Taylor, 2002a, b; Deery *et al*., 2002; Houlihan, 2002; Rose, 2002; Taylor and Bain, 2001a; Taylor *et al.*, 2002, 2003; Thompson *et al.*, 2004) that emphasize the managerial prioritization of call throughout.

What drove, and continues to drive, the establishment and diffusion of the call centre as a distinctive organizational form is not the desire to improve customer service, as the rhetoric surrounding the early call centres invoked and Korczynski (2002) and Frenkel *et al.*'s (1999) studies echo. Instead, the cost-reduction and profit-maximizing logics dominate, and are exacerbated by the inescapable competitive capitalist dynamics of the sectoral and market economies in which firms operate. Of course, there are a limited number of call centre workflows where companies emphasize service quality and satisfaction, and encourage agents to have relaxed and 'relational' exchanges, largely when they are dealing with higher-value customers in a segmented mass market. Yet, in the dominant mass markets the overriding requirement that customer service (or sales) delivers profitable outcomes, leads employers to privilege quantitative imperatives and economies of scale. Indeed, it is instructive that analysis reveals only limited evidence, in the quality workflows, that the varied demands of customers leads to challenging and varied call handling. Rather, customers appear as sources of tension and pressure. The problem with Korczynski's depiction of call centre work, as being imbued with the twin logics of cost-efficiency and customer-orientation, is that it is an idealized formulation, abstracted from the broader political economic contexts in which call centres are situated.

In the case of call centres, then, the paradigm of service work as empowered and non-regimented is hugely overdrawn. Rather than the informating properties of the ICTs facilitating creative encounters between agents and customers, the outcome is a labour process and an employee experience that challenges the nostrums of knowledge work. It is as if the more optimistic commentators of the phenomenon have neglected to consider the ways in which the call centre agent is at least in part the Taylorized successor to earlier generations of office worker (Huws, 1999), whether bank teller, ledger clerk, insurance salesperson, booking clerk or telephone operator. This is not to assert an unchanging, linear continuity with these occupations. Undoubtedly, the performance of emotional labour, and the importance attached to attitudinal, communication skills and the ability to control feelings towards the customer (Callaghan and Thompson, 2002), constitute important elements of change. Nevertheless, it is difficult to avoid the overall conclusion that the claustrophobic micromanagement of the call centre worker is quintessentially Gilbrethian.

Our findings on the nature of work in software help to bring into focus a literature that frequently appears contradictory. Certain accounts suggest that the software developer is becoming progressively deskilled, with work becoming more routinized and menu-driven (Ramsay, 1999). This perspective is reinforced by those who believe that the introduction of CASE (Computer Aided Software Engineering) tools, which automate tasks such as testing and debugging, have contributed further to the process of deskilling (Barrett, 1999). Contrary interpretations depict work organization as highly complex requiring the advanced skills of empowered professionals (Andrews et al., 2005).

The solution to this paradox is, as the evidence from the current study suggests (Figure 3.1), to recognize that there are distinct types of software work and worker, distinguishable by reference to a number of inter-related variables, including labour market position, education, skill level and work role. Although a simple deskilling is not evident, the rote work of the 'code monkey', debugger, tester and servicer certainly exists. This resonates with Andrews et al.'s (2005) distinction between the tendency towards structuration and a lesser tendency towards standardization. Despite predictions of increasing routinization, the evidence, to date, suggests that there are limitations to this process amongst the ranks of the software professional. As Ramsay argued,

> Their reservoirs of official and unofficial knowledge, often far less easily codified than textbooks would suggest, make management capacities for control limited (Ramsay, 1999: 9).

While the looseness of management controls in software (Alvesson, 1995; Kunda, 1992) can be exaggerated, the internalization of professional identity and self-control are powerful influences. The case study evidence would tend to support the argument of Kärreman and Alvesson (2004) and Andrews et al. (2005) that cultural-ideological modes of control, which use social identity and the corporatization of the self as a mechanism for managerial control, have purchase in the knowledge intensive firm, although even these authors, who are keen to conceptualize novel forms of control, acknowledge the enduring relevance of certain traditional, bureaucratic controls. Further, co-worker relationships amongst the elite of software workers are characterized by an interdependence within various team formations, resulting from the need for employees to supplement each other's expertise in order to analyse complex work problems (Tam et al., 2002).

Just as we were able to draw parallels between call centre agents and their historical antecedents, so the differentiation in software work is analogous to established distinctions between the elite design engineering role, draughting and technical authors in the Research and Development worksites of traditional electronics and aerospace companies (Barley and Orr, 1997; Perrolle, 1986; Smith, 1987). Allowing for the fact that the division of labour has become considerably more complex, with the emergence of diverse specialisms, the salience of a general bifurcation seems apposite. Advanced software workers could easily be seen to parallel traditional design engineering roles, or what Meiksins and Smith

(1996) call *managerial* and *craft* groups. That is, these elite cohorts or, to use the conventional contemporary terminology, knowledge workers, are distinguished by high levels of educational attainment, challenging design projects, significant autonomy and high labour market value. In contrast, there are the lower skilled groups who possess fewer conventional qualifications and generally work with older programming languages, or in support or testing roles.

Advocates of the knowledge work paradigm tend to make sweeping generalizations asserting, for example, that the work organization of *all* putative 'knowledge' or information industries is sharply demarcated from that of the past. The nature of work is now seen to be characterized by the absence of command and control, and by the pervasiveness of creative cooperation between networked and empowered colleagues. This is so, particularly because of the informating properties of ICTs and the variable demands generated by internal and external customers. Perhaps the most influential and sophisticated exponent of this perspective has been Manuel Castells who, for example, in a discussion of e-business and the new economy, makes references to 'self-programmable labour' being unable to 'deploy its capacity in a traditional, rigid, business environment', and the e-firm being based on 'a flat hierarchy, a teamworking system, and open, easy interaction between workers and managers, across departments and between levels of the firm' (2001: 91). Whether in factories, offices or service organizations, the technological revolution has generated 'the historical revival of work autonomy, after the bureaucratization of the industrial era' (2001: 92), and has led to the disappearance of 'the routine, repetitive tasks' as the 'Taylorist assembly line becomes an historical relic' (2000: 257–8). If this chapter has made any contribution to our understanding of work organization, hopefully it is to have demonstrated that universal prescriptions such as those of Castells are far removed from the weight of empirical evidence.

4
Organizational Life: The Management of Commitment

The context of managing

One of the research goals was to evaluate whether, after twenty years of the HRM agenda as the new orthodoxy, work had been elevated to a more central position in employees' lives, as measured by stated levels of organizational commitment. Despite the stated aim of integrating employment practice to company business strategy (Storey, 1992; Guest, 1989), HRM theory is often strangely de-contextualized, apart from token references to globalization and an enhanced competitive environment. For the purposes of HRM, the company is often treated as semi-autonomous capsule, isolated from the rest of society, and this narrow focus on the workplace is, ironically, mirrored in many critical studies of control in the work organization, whether undertaken from a labour process or Foucaultian perspective. Yet movements and changes in the operation of the capitalist economy, such as market turbulence and relations between units of capital (financial and industrial), often have a direct influence on all members of work organizations and on the employment relationship at the level of the firm (Hyman, 1987; Thompson, 2003). Thus we would argue that a major reason for the oft-observed disjunction between the HRM rhetoric and the experienced reality (Legge, 1995; Thompson, 2003) lies in the particular political-economic context within which organizations are located at any point in time and to which they must respond.

Kelly (1985) has reminded us that, in the 'full circuit of capital', the processes of employment relations within the workplace are influenced not only by the vertical relationship between the workplace and the market, but also by horizontal relationships between different units of capital, involving not just production but also the realization of surplus. There is a widespread belief that the market environment has become more turbulent since the early 1980s and, although difficult to quantify, there does seem to be evidence of shorter cycles of growth and recession, increasing rates of company birth, growth and death, an ever greater number of mergers and acquisitions. Our case study companies were far from immune from these external pressures and we have already discussed how their generalized effects and impacts were experienced at workplace level through disruption in structures, work design, work organization and process and patterns of management control.

In contrast, HRM prescriptive models frequently assume a stasis within the surrounding socio-economic context; a state of *ceteris paribus* is assumed to prevail, to allow the formation of proactive policies by HR Directors, integrating the resourcing, reward and involvement of the organization's human resources with its strategic objectives. However the actual situations in which our contemporary organizations found themselves were, as we have seen, characterized by volatility, uncertainty and fear, and management responses were frequently reactive fire-fighting exercises, with little evidence of joined-up thinking. Thus, in all our locations in both sectors, management responded to market turbulence with a series of frequently changing policy initiatives and *ad hoc* measures contributing to an atmosphere of permanent organizational churn and flux. As discussed in greater detail elsewhere (Taylor *et al.*, 2005), the immediate source of this was not market turbulence *per se* but senior management's assessment of the meaning and consequences of it for cost bases, revenue, profitability and share price.

Management structures

The combination of the changes in competition strategies at the end of the twentieth century and the organizational possibilities of electronic information flows, had suggested to many organizational analysts (such as Clegg, 1990) that we were witnessing a move towards the 'post-bureaucratic' organization through the adoption of policies of de-layering and the emergence of flatter, less hierarchical, matrix or networked structures (Grugulis, Vincent and Hebson, 2003). At first glance our two sectors would seem to exemplify such trends.

The call centres presented a typically flat organizational structure with, usually, one centre manager, a small number of operations or customer service managers (depending on the functional division of processes carried out by the centre), then a layer of team leaders or team managers (the terminology differed slightly) and then the customer service advisors; exceptionally, the multi-client nature of Thejobshop necessitated an additional layer of account managers above team leaders. There were also usually a small number of ancillary staff engaged in business support and call analysis. In our four call centres the modal ratio of team leader to team size was around one to twelve or one to fifteen, although some of the accounts at Thejobshop had teams as large as twenty, and in Moneyflow's specialized financial advisory side they could be smaller at 1:3 or 1:4

(although even these were increased during the research period to around 1:8).

One noticeable feature in several of our call centres was the high rate of turnover in management staff. A respondent in Entcomm reported that, in the two and half years she had been working in the building, the composition of the management team had completely changed, twice. This attrition at management level and the problems of retention at employee level, together with the constant re-forming and re-sizing of teams, are indicators of the high degree of organizational churn which characterized these workplaces, which itself reflected the turbulence of the external competitive environment.

Organizational structures in most of the software companies were again fairly flat with few functional specialisms but, at the same time, were more complex, with interlocking projects producing something much more akin to a matrix structure. At first sight this would appear to confirm why Burns and Stalker's (1961) classic 'organic' model of organization has taken on a new lease of life as a representation of the strategic organizational choice most appropriate to companies in a high-tech innovatory sector. The accompanying move away from hierarchy seemed to be echoed by Lambda's MD description of its 'relaxed atmosphere' and Pi's CEO who talked of a 'peer to peer oriented culture' with the values of 'camaraderie and close relationships'.

However, while this may have applied to the smaller companies, it contrasts with a much more hierarchical structure at Beta, possibly a legacy of its origins as a publicly-owned utility. There were a series of quite complex staff titles where entry level staff and others on the bottom of the pay scale were designated as MPG2 (management, professional grade 2) of which there were 75 members of staff. The slightly more senior MPG4 grade comprised 31 staff members. It appeared that those in the MPG4 category could be team leaders in some cases but might simply be more senior team members. There were three categories of staff that could fit into the project manager job title, amounting to 16 members of staff, in addition to which there were four senior managers.

Management practice

Call centres

Resourcing the call centre

As our call centres, with the exception of Thejobshop, were branches of larger national companies, it was unusual for them to have an HR function on site. For both Moneyflow and Holstravel, HR was located in the head office in the South-East of England, and visits to the Scottish sites by HR staff were infrequent. Thus, although the companies had formal policies on recruitment training and reward it was, in an almost HRM textbook approach, left to local line management to implement these. At Entcomm, for example, a recent take-over by another company had resulted in HR being moved off-site resulting in significant responsibility devolving to the team leaders:

> There are very few companies that team leaders are responsible for recruitment right through to dismissal – normally personnel take over at a certain point. Not in here – the team leaders do everything, with guidance from HR. So it is a very stressful job. (Entcomm, female team leader, E-I-06)

The takeover at Entcomm had also led to cut-backs in training, and to different sets of contracts for new and existing staff, so that new Entcomm staff were on a 40 hour week while those who still held the original contract were on 37 hours, a source of some friction. Training is discussed at greater length in Chapter 5 but, during the research period, Entcomm was not the only location to cut back its training period; at Moneyflow induction training was reduced from two weeks to a few days, reflecting pressure on operational management to get new starts out onto the floor as quickly as possible.

Recruitment practice varied widely. Moneyflow relied a lot on regular tranches of temporary recruits from agencies who could, after a period of satisfactory employment, be given an opportunity to become permanent employees. Entcomm and Holstravel both drew on the surrounding community, with Holstravel actually offering a 'friends and family' recruitment bonus to existing staff who could successfully recruit someone else. Recruitment in all companies often seemed entirely pragmatic and *ad hoc*, relying a great deal on contacting agencies to meet sudden fluctuations in labour requirements. New staff could be kept on agency contracts, with lower rates of pay and conditions, sometimes for months. The agency contracts were thus used both as a filter which screened out unsuitable employees before they were on the regular payroll and, in an illustration of the classic numerical flexibility model, as a flexible buffer against the volatility of customer demand. As pointed out in a contemporaneous study by Grimshaw, Ward, Rubery and Beynon (2001), pressure on management to show a 'lean headcount' to meet City expectations of company performance also served to limit the numbers recruited directly onto regular company contracts.

Pay and reward

While most of the centres possessed a formal pay structure, particularly in the two companies where there was a union or staff association (Holstravel and Moneyflow), actual earnings sometimes deviated markedly from the notional scale, mainly due to the weighting given to performance bonuses within monthly earnings and the fact that pay progression was universally based on management-evaluated individual performance. Thus, while Holstravel had retained annual collective bargaining with the union, agents reported that up to 60 per cent of their earnings could come from bonuses, although the vast majority of staff came nowhere near to reaching this figure. In Moneyflow, a team manager stated that few people had earned bonus under the previous incentive scheme while, in the new one, 'the targets are too high, I wouldn't use this to try to attract new workers' (unstructured interview, Moneyflow female team manager). Indeed, the disappointment expressed by a highly qualified financial planning advisor, when he received his first quarterly payment of £190 under the new scheme, was echoed throughout the call centre (unstructured interview, Moneyflow male financial planning advisor). Entcomm had a structure in which monthly pay was loosely linked to skill and competence levels, and examination of this revealed a number of complexities. Employees still on the contract initiated by the organization's previous owner got higher basic rates and, while the rate that each individual agent achieved was dependent on a performance review, it also varied with the number of days off sick. For most call handlers here, there were no monthly bonus payments and small variations in take-home pay were dependent on the award of prizes linked to product sales. Similar practices prevailed in Thejobshop, where bonus and incentive payments were related to sales and performance targets, which proved increasingly difficult to attain. Thus, while bonus and/or incentive schemes were in place in the call centres, in general they promised employees much more than they delivered.

Both Entcomm and Moneyflow had employee share-ownership saving schemes (mainly seen as a way of improving retention), and Holstravel paid a profit-related bonus in monthly instalments. While pay in Thejobshop could vary with target based bonuses and commission on individual and team sales performance, there was some variation between accounts, dependent partly on the client and partly on the grading awarded by team leaders. This was justified by the HR manager on the grounds that 'different teams have different motivational levels', which she felt was due to some team managers being 'better leaders'. It is not surprising that these variations in pay and in the perceived fairness of different managers fuelled a high level of what one call handler called 'Chinese whispers – where employees from different sections tell each other about bonuses and changes – there is a lot of rumour' (unstructured interview, Entcomm).

The result for the sector as a whole was what, in the days of shop-floor piecework bargaining, used to be called a 'decayed payment system', in which agreed basic rates were really only a floor or substructure on which a superstructure of different and varying *ad hoc* payments was built to give an actual level of earnings which could be considerably over the basic. The difference in the twenty-first century is that, while in the days of the Donovan Commission, such additional payments usually represented the results of collective bargaining by workplace union reps, here they were the result of management incentive initiatives and could therefore alter drastically, either with fluctuations in customer demand or on the frequent occasions when management redefined the targets upwards.

Communications, involvement and employee voice

The dilemma for the contemporary manager, in attempting to maintain a sense of 'belonging' on the part of employees in the face of the external commercial pressures dictating forms of work organization, was well expressed by the Centre Manager at Holstravel:

> [We need] somehow to make an individual feel as if they are an individual and not a number. That is easy said but very difficult when you have got 470 people on six different shifts working over seven days and twenty four hours. And, of course, it goes all the way down and it's the team managers, you know, they are the managers for those twelve and that team manager has got to make those twelve feel individuals. I can try, I can do a number of things but I have got to engender the right culture that means that team manager is treating those twelve as individuals. (Holstravel, male Centre Manager and Head of Operations, H-I-03).

Perhaps in response to this perceived problem, Holstravel had a very elaborate communications structure with a twice yearly staff satisfaction survey, quarterly staff updates, where the centre manager spoke to the workforce in groups of 40–50 on changes in the business, a monthly staff forum made up of representatives from each of the seven areas of the business, and also regular team managers' feedback which took a critical look at how the team managers had dealt with their staff. Each team had a monthly team brief lasting about an hour, and there were brief 'communication and motivation meetings' held in the 'dugouts' described in Chapter 3 five minutes before the start of shift and known as 'Five to Nines' 'Five to Fours' or 'Five to Sixes'.

At Entcomm a few of the team leaders did 'anonymous upward feedback', a variation on the suggestion box, in which team members could type out their comments anonymously and leave them on the team leader's desk, (s/he absenting themselves for this purpose). The leader we interviewed seemed genuinely surprised that this worked:

> You can actually pick up quite a few tips, I've never had anything too bad, touch wood, but I think it's important to do that, to give your guys

a chance to come at you, just to let you know what they're thinking (Entcomm, male team leader, E-I-04).

This may have been an exception however. Although the company held a number of specifically focused Forums, on for example facilities or retentions, which some call handlers regularly volunteered to attend to represent their section (and give them time off the phones), there seemed to be widespread ignorance by other CSAs that they even existed. As the same Entcomm team leader commented:

> For a communications company our communication is terrible... We rely entirely on e-mail ...and don't give the guys time to read their email. Team leaders are not good with time management... so they try to rush through everything. So you maybe have a team meeting and they only have half an hour to do it, with fifteen agenda points – it is just not going to happen. (Entcomm, male team leader, E-I-04).

At Thejobshop there was a clear disjunction between the rhetoric of team meetings and the financial reality. The contractual Service Level Agreements with the clients stipulated precise staffing levels and phone cover and this did not include any costing for CSAs being present but not on the phones; consequently team meetings simply did not happen. As discussed in the previous chapter, pressures at Moneyflow from ever higher targets led to a similar inability to hold team meetings and during our research period they were also sacrificed at Holstravel for the same reasons.

Software

Resourcing the software house

The differences in organizational structure in the software companies were reflected in their approach to HRM policies and practices. Beta displayed a sophisticated, highly centralized set of policies, including a formal training programme, appraisal linked to promotion/pay, profit-sharing via a share-save scheme, communication schemes, internal recruitment, and harmonization of pensions/sick leave. Probably due to the continued presence of a trade union, there was also a policy of no compulsory redundancy.

In contrast, the HR policies in the owner-managed companies such as Omega and Gamma, where they existed at all, were informal, unwritten, haphazard and rudimentary. Management language in these companies was closer to old-style entrepreneurial unitarism rather than contemporary HRM. The owner of Lambda explained that his graduate recruitment policy was to recruit people 'who want to join the club, not with a nine to five mentality'. Both Omega and Pi favoured recruiting former colleagues and close acquaintances so that, as the owner of Pi said, 'I knew them personally. I knew their families. I knew what they were capable of and I brought them into the business'. Formal systems of appraisal and training were either non-existent or inconsistently applied.

Pay and reward

Individualistic managerial orientations towards reward were even more marked in software. Apart from Beta, which had a clear pay structure, defined grades with shift allowances and unsocial hours' payments, pay levels and awards in software were secretive affairs. Omega claimed to have a spinal pay scale but none of the other owner-managed companies appeared to have any formal pay structure. The view of Gamma management was that the company had a 'natural pay scale' in which salaries were said to be based both on performance and market rates. This meant that salary reviews of team members were undertaken whenever someone new was appointed, a process which was inevitably strongly influenced by employees' awareness of their labour market position. The company claimed to be developing a flexi-benefit reward and remuneration package in partnership with a consultancy company which was likely to include incentives such as a company car or health care packages. Of the other smaller software houses, Lambda had a similar informal reward system to Gamma, with no formal appraisal plus some share-ownership incentives after five years service. Pi's reward policy was both blunt and vague:

> As a meritocracy, the Company aims to discriminate heavily in favour of employees whose performance is judged to be above merit. (Pi Terms of Employment, internal document 1997)

Pay at Pi was thus loosely tied to level of experience or qualification at entry and was then reviewed annually with individual performance taken into account. The company had recently appointed an HR officer on site who attended senior management meetings and, under her influence, the company was developing polices relating to performance related pay, appraisal, and benefits. However, we subsequently learned that, after our research period, she had left and that the post had not been filled.

Communications, involvement and employee voice

As might be expected, the more formalized organizational framework in Beta was associated with structured communication procedures based on participative team meetings and regular individual appraisal meetings. Each of the owner-managed SME companies, by contrast, was typified by charismatic leadership and unwritten codes of conduct in which communication from the top was a clear characteristic; in the words of Pi's owner 'the doors are kept open so that people can come and talk all the time ... I go to the pub every Friday night with them'. At Omega, formal communication consisted largely of evening meetings held about twice a year in a local hotel and addressed by the Chief Executive but which prompted little response from the assembled staff. As one manager subsequently commented to the research team, 'the managerial style is control', echoed by another manager who wistfully pointed out that 'the owners have had a problem letting go'.

Building the commitment culture

With a predominantly young workforce, with little likelihood of being socialized into an existing employment relations culture, such new employment sectors as our call centres and software development companies should present the ideal subjects for constructing the new organizational high-commitment culture. We were therefore interested to assess both the degree to which the case study organizations had introduced high-commitment, and the extent to which their employees manifested commitment related values. The mechanisms chosen by management to promote commitment values differed according to the work and market situations of our two sectors. In call centres the hoped-for lubricant of the wheels of commitment was often the promotion of 'fun', while in the software houses it was more likely to be the appeal to the professional values of the software developers.

The HRM project has always had as one of its strategies the attempt to replace workers' affective orientations to external collectivities, such as trade unions, with a re-orientation towards internal collective values. At the point of production this is via the now ubiquitous phenomenon of teamworking, while at the organizational level the focus is on the organizational culture. Where the latter is weak, the hope is that acceptance of its values can be strengthened through the promotion of after-work socializing or the creation of the idea that the company is a 'fun' place to work and/or that its members are the employee's friends of choice to socialize with after work.

While each organization had a distinctive culture or feel about it, the call centres displayed more evidence of attempts at culture-building, mainly focused around a commitment to the product or brand. At Moneyflow, a new management initiative exhorted staff to 'Live the Brand'. At Thejobshop, as an outfacing umbrella organization offering call-centre services for a variety of clients, each client was openly encouraged to impose their own 'signature' on the work:

> We try to replicate the culture of each client organization in their part of the operations. Thejobshop is a multi-cultural environment. (Unstructured interview, Thejobshop, male Operations Manager).

This was particularly true of the high-value accounts such as *Bluechip* where *Bluechip* corporate slogans, distinct email addresses (and even a separate telephone switchboard located, not in Thejobshop building, but in England) were in evidence. Agents here, while contractually employed by Thejobshop, tended to see themselves as belonging to *Bluechip*. Similar product-identification strategies where found at *CarExec* where employees got to drive the car as an incentive and to 'bond with the product'.

The prevalence of dress-codes in call centres was surprising in a personal service organization whose employees are never seen by the customer. At Moneyflow, the more professionalized financial advisers and mortgage agents tended to wear the smart clothes associated with employment in the finance sector. This helped to reinforce the divide already established by spatial separation from the speedily trained and relatively unqualified advisers dealing with customer loan requests. At Holstravel, all the agents wore coloured sports/polo shirts with the company logo. Such dress codes were usually rationalized by management as being justified in the event of 'client visits'; however, during our protracted immersion in each company, we never witnessed or were aware of any such visits and the expectations regarding dress appeared to be another dimension of the management control of the symbolic artefacts of organizational culture.

As described in Chapter 3, the spatial arrangement of the working environment was often part of the cultural manipulation. While most evident in the case of Holstravel, described below, in most of the call centres teams were located around clusters or pods of workstation desks (except in Moneyflow where loan advisers were in back-to back rows), while in Thejobshop the *Bluechip* client had requested a wall be built to divide its 'own' staff from other employees and used different coloured furniture to reinforce a stronger sense of organizational identity.

Dress codes in the software houses were surprisingly restrained, with an overall air reminiscent of an after-hours bank rather than the pony-tailed, kaftan-wearing geeks of legend. This decidedly reserved image was especially apparent in Beta, where public sector traditions of associating dress with status still apparently lingered.

In-house fun

It has been observed elsewhere that call centre managers have often seized on the promotion of a culture of 'fun' as a navigational route between the twin goals of maximizing employee commitment and controlling employee behaviour (Redman and Mathews, 2002; Kinnie *et al.*, 2000; Alferoff and Knights, 2003), and this was certainly the case in some of our organizations. The call centres frequently presented the paradox of tight and surveillant control structures existing alongside a continuous promotion of frequent spot prizes, raffles, quizzes, social evenings and themed dressing-up days. While, as Redman and Mathews' discussion shows, 'fun' is currently being used as a deliberate strategy in a variety of organizational sectors, it could be seen to be of special relevance to the provision of particular types of personal services, such as holidays and entertainment; here, the hope is that the positive emotions generated by a fun working environment will seep into the telephone conversation and be transmitted to the customer.

A good example is provided by our holiday call centre, Holstravel, where the travel consultants were expected to convey a mixture of friendly efficiency with a foretaste of the holiday spirit. To secure this emotion state, pop music was relayed over the PA system, there were frequent awards of small prizes, and the centre held regular dressing up days and social nights out culminating in the annual awards evening. The TV screens mounted on the interior roof pillars often screened promotional videos of different types of holidays, or details of coming themed 'fun days' such as James Bond Day:

> Wednesday 24th January is James Bond Day. The fun begins at 12.30. Prizes and Surprises. Get in the mood GUYS... come as James Bond. GALS are you a Bond Babe!? The World is Not Enough. Use Your Imagination. Dress to Kill. Have a Great Day.

All these activities took place in a deliberately constructed symbolic environment. The interior design of the Holstravel building had been outfitted in a conscious attempt to suggest the concept 'holiday'. A visitor, entering the building through a small corporate foyer, passes the reception desk and walls displaying Investors in People awards and the award for the building itself, to reach the main work space. The visitor would then cross a small bridge over an interior stream, where a 'sensorama' bathed the walls in pastel and sunshine colours, while holiday sounds (such as waves on a beach, a tropical rain forest, a jet taking off) and coconut scents provided a sensory backdrop. The main work-floor area was an open, warehouse-like space with a dark sky-blue ceiling and the walls painted in bright colours, with murals of exotic red and orange, while plastic palm trees were dotted about the floor amid the workstations.

As the Holstravel centre manager admitted, when describing the ideas behind the interior design:

> When they come to work we want to promote a happy atmosphere, where people are friendly, so that staff are then happy with the customer. ...So the idea was, 'Get people in the holiday mood and then they can talk to the customers...... It's designed to change peoples' minds. If people are coming in at 8 am on a dull day we want to change their mind set so that they are thinking, 'I am now ready to sell dreams'. (Holstravel, male Centre Manager).

Fun even extended to aspects of the work organization: while in all the call centres the teams were distinguished by names (for example, 'Thistle', 'Tartan', 'Piper' and other North Sea oil fields in Moneyflow), in those centres where a fun culture was being promoted, teams could choose their own names. Thus Holstravel sported 'Busty Bell's Buxom Bookers' and Entcomm had teams named after favourite TV themes ('The Simpsons', 'South Park Raiders'). Fun was thus often *competitive* fun, in which the constant exhortations to teams to raise call throughput and sales were disguised as monthly competitions in which prizes were awarded to the 'best'. The reactions of call handlers were ambivalent. They were well aware that the arbitrary nature of ACD routing of incoming calls could mean that teams, for instance in Holstravel, had no control over whether a call was an enquiry for five days in Benidorm or for a two month world cruise, and that therefore the total cash value of monthly holiday sales on the part of any team had little to do with their speed or commitment. On the other hand, the competitions, the prizes and the fun events were welcomed as making the job a 'little bit different'.

In several of the companies, much of the fun activity was left to the team leaders, who often seemed to double as entertainments officers. They were often given a packet of time by management to organize team-based fun, such as the example we were given at Entcomms of a team leader that had his team bouncing round the car park on 'space hoppers'. It was Entcomm that eventually went so far as officially to confer the accolade of 'Doctor Fun' to a member of the Communications Team. The Doctor Fun post was full-time and her duties involved attending team meetings and, after listening to the requests of team members, organizing theme days, similar to those in Holstravel, such as 'Funky Fridays', 'Mad Hair Day' and 'Pyjama Day'. While ostensibly linked to raising money for charity, they also served to promote the various products; so, for example, on 'Discovery Day' representatives from the Discovery Channel visited the centre with live animals and everyone in the centre was expected to come dressed as an animal. One of the difficulties faced by Doctor Fun, however, was that, at the very same time as her fun-promoting endeavours, the company was actually declaring significant redundancies, with a consequent plummeting of staff morale.

Fun in our call centres, therefore, can be seen both as an element in the promotion of a commitment culture and also as an attempt to overcome the intrinsic nature of profoundly alienated work. What is significant is that this latter aspect was often recognized and welcomed as such by the call handlers. However, what should also be recognized is the fact that the call handlers were by no means reliant on management's initiatives for humour as a release from tension and monotony. Agents' own humour (an account of which is given in Taylor and Bain, 2003a) was frequently directed against both customers and management and can thus be seen as evidence for a workplace counter-culture which had the power to subvert the meaning of 'official' cultural events.

It should be noted that fun was also used as a manipulative tool directed *towards* centre management by higher corporate management. At a national Moneyflow 'sales conference', attended by centre managers from all locations in the company, the evening was themed around the 'Starship Enterprise' with a lavish stage set and appropriate music as backdrop to a meal and drinks which were themselves a prelude to exhortatory addresses from senior executives to 'reach for the stars' and 'go boldly where no-one has gone before'. Soon the implicit meanings lurking behind these beyond-frontier images crystallized, as this was not a benign social occasion. Amid the peroration, came the dramatic announcement that targets for all products were to be revised upwards by an average of 30 per cent. Centre managers then had to return to their centres and reach for the stars by somehow 'selling' this idea to their team leaders and employees. In our case study location they did this, naturally, through an ostensibly fun event, a Moneyflow centre awards evening. This combined the announcement of 'gold' and 'silver' performance awards and star prizes, congratulations on engagements, weddings and babies born to team members, the revealing of new team structures, all interspersed with intervals of increasingly lewd jokes from the evening's compère (one of the managers). Buried among all this was a revelation of the new targets, which for some financial products were about to rise by 1,000 per cent (a more detailed discussion of the raising of targets can be found in Bain *et al.*, 2002). To illustrate the point made above concerning agency and peripheral workers, only full-time employees were invited to the Awards Evening, the part-timers only getting to hear of the new targets on their next shift. The raising of the targets was a direct consequence of the intensified and turbulent competitive environment which we have described earlier, and the management strategy was to dress up what was in effect a huge productivity drive in the trappings of entertainment (for a similar observation see Alferoff and Knights, 2003).

Fun, though rather subdued by comparison and pursued out of office, was also apparent in the owner-managed software companies. At Pi there was the regular Friday pub visit which the chief executive regularly attended. He had also created traditions such as a 'boys' golf outing' to which few outsiders were invited in order to maintain a 'family culture' – although one in which women were markedly absent. Similarly, at Lambda, the owner attempted to sustain a club-like atmosphere through days out, staff barbecues and raft races. Left to their own devices, however, most software social occasions consisted of occasional meals and drinks shared with selected present and past colleagues, and where the prime topic of conversation was software.

Formal and informal socializing

Anyone researching the call centre sector soon becomes aware of the apparently ubiquitous phenomenon of the 'nights out'. Although the majority of call centre workers say that they like to keep work and social life separate, there are, as in most workplaces, clearly defined occasions when work becomes social and it was clear that some of these were actively encouraged by management as a form of team bonding. We can therefore differentiate between formal centre social occasions (mainly at Christmas or other significant annual landmarks), formal team nights out (which in most centres seemed to occur about every two months) and the more employee-initiated occasions. The last of these seized on and made use of the many suitable opportunities that arose from the age and gender profile of the workforce such as 21st birthdays, engagements, hen/stag nights, or to celebrate a birth; the high turnover of centre staff also provided regular occasions for 'leaving dos'.

The call centre workers responded to these different types of social occasion in significantly different ways. The formal centre occasions, where management socialized with staff in a conscious attempt to create or contribute to some sort of unitary culture, were not rated very highly, mainly because there was usually little genuine socializing between the two groups.

> The last night out I went and there was like admin at the top...and then you have got Customer Advisors and sort of Mortgage Advisors and then at the very, very end is the management all standing kind of separate. You could see it. It was like a broken-down line – higher and higher level of staff as it went down the pub. I don't like that. (Moneyflow, male customer adviser; M-I-20).

The exception to this seemed to be Holstravel's annual national awards ceremony, organized on the lines of the Oscars, which everybody spoke of as being 'fun', particularly in terms of the considerable quantity of alcohol that seemed to fuel it.

Team nights, usually organized by the team leader or someone in the team she or he had deputed to take charge of socializing, were usually seen as a welcome, if semi-formal, opportunity for the team to get together. The events were often linked to the team winning a performance prize – either the prize was the night out, or a cash prize enabled a night out to go with less of a drain on personal finances. In Entcomm, under its previous owner, team leaders had been given about £20 per month by management to subsidize such 'team bonding'. The main organizational problem with these, and the informal nights out, was fitting them around shift patterns so that all the team were off at the same time and that no-one had to turn up for work the next morning. As one call handler commented, 'there is no way I could sit in here with a hangover, sitting listening to people for seven and a half hours with a hangover, no never. Just don't do it.' (unstructured interview, Entcomm, female call handler). In Holstravel, after Blue Pumpkin had changed the basis of working hours from team-based shifts to individual based shifts, team nights out became impossible and 'now you just seem to be ships in the night', as a Holstravel agent put it wistfully.

Informal nights based around 'leaving dos' or hen/stag nights were much more employee initiated and controlled, in which the team leader (if she or he was well-liked) might be invited along by the team. However, these events were mainly driven by the young and single; older employees or those with children tended to limit themselves to the organized team outings.

Evaluating these patterns of socializing is difficult and they are discussed in more detail in Chapter 6. The social events were largely welcomed as an opportunity to get to know fellow team members better and, like the 'fun' days, undoubtedly had a stress-release function. Yet most respondents in our call centres made a distinction between work associates and their own close friends and family, who remained their first choice with whom to spend their non-work time. Also, unlike regular friendship bonds, the nature of the socializing groups was inherently transient due to the rate of staff turnover in the centres, the regular churn in the organization of team structures and composition, and the frequently changing patterns of working time.

It is in this dimension of long and short-term bonds that work-based socializing in the software sector differed from that in call centres. There were some superficial similarities such as the formal annual company events such as Christmas and, in the case of Omega, a summer barbeque. Beta, perhaps displaying its public-sector origins, had a sports and social committee in its software engineering centre and events such as skiing and go-karting were subsidised by the company. Lambda had its barbecues and Pi its free beer and pizza nights and, being located in a newly renovated dockland area, was surrounded by a wine bar milieu which encouraged informal socializing. However, team nights out were referred to far less often and seemed to occur on a less regular basis. Nevertheless, as Chapter 6 indicates, informal socializing among software people was not uncommon and apart from its social benefits, was utilized as a forum for discussing the sector and its employment.

The limits to shared values

It would appear then that all of our case companies had introduced one or more of a variety of formal and informal commitment-related practices and, if hours worked beyond contract are to be taken as one index of discretionary effort, one might be tempted to conclude that there was a significant degree of organizational attachment in both sectors. However, when we examine the data from employee responses it becomes apparent that there are a number of conceptual and operational problems with the basic HRM commitment model.

The questionnaire measured Meyer and Allen's (1991) dimensions of affective and continuance organizational commitment, which reflect a value-based and cost evaluation notion of commitment respectively, as well as commitment to colleagues, customers and the occupation.

As can be seen in Tables 4.1 and 4.2, the evidence from both sectors does not support the internalization of shared values and suggests that more immediate groups have greater saliency for employees. In both sectors commitment to colleagues (agree/strongly agree = 69 per cent for call-centres and 67 per cent for software) and to customers (75 per cent call centres, 87 per cent software) scored much more highly than commitment to the organization. This was true even for managers in both sectors so that, while in an interview the Centre Manager at Moneyflow could say,

> My husband says I'm like a stick of rock. If you cut me through the middle it says 'Moneyflow'. (Moneyflow, female Call Centre Manager; M-I-08),

the responses to the questionnaires indicate that this stated level of commitment was far from universal (and we later learned, after the research period, that even this respondent had left the company).

The majority of respondents in both sectors saw the values of senior management and the company as different from their own. Software workers were more likely than call centre employees to demonstrate affective commitment to the company but were also less likely to show continuance commitment, a clear reflection of their enhanced labour market situation. The commitment focus particular to software workers was commitment to their professional grouping.

It is noticeable that, in both sectors, team/project leaders and management scored higher than employees on *all* commitment indices. There were also some differences between sections of respondents in the same organization, the reasons for which became clear in the interviews. For example, the financial services call centre, Moneyflow, had a subset of employees who felt a strong attachment to the organization. These were on the regulated side where status was higher, job content was more variable and which offered a more banking-style career trajectory and a perceived degree of job security:

> Q: Do you feel a sense of commitment to the job then and the company?
> A: ...I think when you come and work for a company like Moneyflow – good benefits, your share options, your salary, good salary for the job we

Table 4.1 Measures of commitment among call centre employees

	Total sample (N = 827)		Operators (N = 721)		Team leaders/managers (N = 106)	
	% D/SD	% A/SA	% D/SD	% A/SA	% D/SD	% A/SA
Organizational commitment						
I feel the company's problems are mine	50	20	52	17	35	37
I feel a strong sense of belonging to my company	36	34	38	30	24	56
Leaving this company just now would disrupt my life	39	46	40	46	36	48
I have too few options to consider leaving the company	50	31	49	31	57	27
I feel very little loyalty to this company	51	25	49	25	63	24
I feel that I have similar values as this company	32	29	33	26	21	46
I'd turn down a job with more pay to stay with the company	61	20	63	19	49	30
Commitment to employees and customers						
I feel a strong sense of loyalty to other employees	10	59	11	67	6	83
I hate to disappoint customers/clients	10	75	10	74	7	80
Occupational commitment						
If I could I would change occupations	29	47	27	49	42	35
I am proud to tell others of my occupation	32	30	33	28	22	40
I take interest in this employment sector	24	45	25	43	17	59

Note: Items were measured on a five point rating scale from 1 'strongly disagree' to 5 'strongly agree'. 'D' Disagree'; 'SD' Strongly disagree'; 'A' Agree; 'SA' Strongly agree.

Table 4.2 Measures of commitment among software employees

	Total sample (N = 307)		Developers (N = 221)		Project leaders/managers (N = 86)	
	% D/SD	% A/SA	% D/SD	% A/SA	% D/SD	% A/SA
Organizational commitment						
I feel the company's problems are mine	33	35	38	25	19	59
I feel a strong sense of belonging to my company	20	50	23	40	13	74
Leaving this company just now would disrupt my life	41	40	44	38	33	46
I have too few options to consider leaving the company	63	21	63	22	64	20
I feel very little loyalty to this company	57	20	53	23	68	13
I feel that I have the similar values as this company	24	30	23	27	26	38
I'd turn down a job with more pay to stay with the company	40	34	43	28	32	49
Commitment to employees and customers						
I feel a strong sense of loyalty to other employees	7	67	7	64	7	75
I hate to disappoint customers/clients	4	87	4	86	2	89
Occupational commitment						
If I could I would change occupations	60	21	61	22	57	17
I am proud to tell others of my occupation	8	63	9	63	7	63
I take interest in this employment sector	8	74	7	71	10	82

Note: Items were measured on a five point rating scale from 1 'strongly disagree' to 5 'strongly agree'. 'D' Disagree; 'SD' Strongly disagree'; 'A' Agree; 'SA' Strongly agree.

do – I'm happy. I am happy with the company and happy with the work. Yes, I have to say that. Definitely...if you have a bad day and things don't work...it's not a case of you know the company as a whole is bad. The company as a whole is great – great package'. (Moneyflow, male financial services adviser, regulated sector; M-I-2).

For many of the software developers we interviewed it was the job that drove their effort, rather than the organization:

...I think in development most of us are committed more to the job than to the company because we are all in it because we enjoy programming and that's the first thing. The second thing is what company you work for and what sort of work you get to do. (Pi, female software programmer; P-I-10).

The importance of colleagues and customers as groups with greater saliency is further demonstrated when we examine the responses to questions regarding such alleged behavioural outcomes of commitment as discretionary effort and staying with the company.

Discretionary effort

If one outcome of commitment is a willingness to expend discretionary rather than prescribed effort (Fox, 1974: 16), then the hours of paid and particularly unpaid overtime discussed in Chapter 3 would seem to suggest a high degree of commitment. However, both the survey responses and the interviews suggest that the primary motivational push for this came from loyalty to one's colleagues, commitment to the customers/clients, with software workers showing additional commitment to their professional occupation. This suggests that the notion of commitment is too crude a concept to be operationally useful. Particularly in software we can distinguish, first, the extra effort put in for the sake of the *organization,* mainly by managers (we can call this 'discretionary organization effort') as described by a sales manager at Pi:

[Commitment] from me to the company? Absolutely, yes.
How is this expressed?
Just my general attitude to work and what I'm prepared to do, when I'm prepared to do it. Whether that's working beyond standard hours or picking up on things for colleagues, getting involved in the social things we do, being involved in pretty much every element around Pi. (Pi, male director of sales; P-I-03,)

Secondly there were the long hours, working nights and weekends which were seen to be part of the *job* of software – you do the hours to get the project delivered because that is part of the identity of being a software professional – (we can call this 'discretionary job effort'). This is seen in the following extracts from interviews with a Beta developer and an Omega analyst, when asked about their commitment to their organization.

> If I have to, I'll work late. I'll work late every night for a month to get a release out. (Beta, female software engineer; B-I-03)

> At the beginning of the project I would say I was working maybe 50–52 hours a week…Weekends, not both days, normally a Saturday or something or I would take work home and do some work at home. (Omega, female software engineer and team leader O-I-04)

In the call centre companies, the graduated nature of commitment and its relation to effort was well expressed by an Entcomm team leader who admitted:

> My commitment is probably graded according to the area. I am very committed to my team, I am quite committed to my department, I am fairly committed to the call centre and 'kind of' committed to Entcomm. I don't know if that makes sense… The thing that makes my money or gives me my job satisfaction is my team. So they get the biggest part of me…. My commitment to Entcomm leaves when I walk out the door at night. (Entcomm, male team leader; E-I-04).

Staying with the company

Another commonly cited outcome of organizational commitment is a willingness to stay with the organization. The low level of such attachment among call centre employees is revealed most starkly in the companies' turnover figures during the research period. These were running at around 39 per cent in Holstravel, 37 per cent in Entcomm and Thejobshop and 29 per cent in Moneyflow (which figure did not include the release of agency staff). Available figures for the software houses indicate annual turnover averaging at a more moderate 15 per cent. However, in all the software organizations respondents indicated that decisions to stay or go hinged around their awareness of their positive labour market position rather than a positive desire to stay. A Beta developer, asked if he would leave for a pay increase elsewhere, replied:

> I would leave. If I stayed I guess it wouldn't be through commitment to the company, it would be because I enjoyed the work, which isn't the same thing. No, I don't think I would (stay). I'll defend them, but not to that extent, not where it's causing me personal injury. (Beta, male technical architect; B-I-19)

This orientation towards the profession or occupation on the part of the developers was recognized by some of the managers who, on the whole, were more likely to state a high commitment case for themselves. A male service manager in Pi compared his own commitment to what he saw as the more freewheeling style of the developers:

> I can see the young lads that come and go, the developers in the software side tend to come and go. There is very few of them will actually stay to be long term, but my approach is, if I'm happy in a job [then] I'm not looking in the papers for jobs. I think that's a sense of commitment. (Pi, male technical services manager; P-I-06).

In the call centres, where employees largely lacked this opportunity for occupational identification, answers to questions on staying with the company often reflected an instrumental version of what Becker (1960) called 'side bets' – those aspects of the company which you would not want to lose by moving. This aspect was certainly more evident on the unregulated side of Moneyflow:

> Basically, because I have been here for two years now I get profit-share, I get bonuses (but bonuses are negligible). I get good holidays and I can get cheap mortgages and cheap loans. It suits me to work here just now rather than go back and start with another company again. I'm actually studying with the Open University just now so I need some job obviously to get money. Me and my partner are buying a flat so obviously I need to pay the mortgage etc. So it's rather a case of I need to work here rather than I want to work here. (Moneyflow, female Customer Adviser, unregulated sector; M-I-15).

The same agent continued –

> I mean if I did stick in and 'live the brand' or whatever, yes, there are opportunities for the right sort of person. But I don't think I'm the right sort of person for Moneyflow.' *What do you think that person is?* 'Well someone who wouldn't sit and rubbish them. Somebody very enthusiastic and positive about the place, no matter how much you are getting paid or how much pressure is on you.

Job satisfaction

The often encountered assertion in the management literature that making quality a priority in service delivery will be automatically translated into an enhanced quality of working life finds a similar lack of support in the survey responses to questions about satisfaction with different facets of the

Table 4.3 Satisfaction ratings for different job facets: call centres

	Total sample (N = 806)		Operators (N = 721)		Team leaders/managers (N = 106)	
	% Dissatisfied	% Satisfied	% Dissatisfied	% Satisfied	% Dissatisfied	% Satisfied
Work conditions	10	85	11	85	6	86
Work colleagues	4	94	4	94	3	94
Customers	20	66	21	66	14	67
Supervisory guidance	18	71	17	71	25	70
Fair treatment	23	67	23	66	20	75
Pay	32	61	33	60	27	66
Pay-performance link	38	49	37	49	38	55
Management relations	29	58	31	57	21	70
Career prospects	35	41	37	38	25	59
Management effectiveness	32	48	32	47	33	55
Shifts	25	67	27	66	9	76
Job variety	36	51	40	47	16	75
Job security	17	64	18	62	11	72
Influence	33	45	36	40	10	75
Sense of achievement	29	61	32	58	14	81
Working hours	25	66	26	64	13	73
Performance assessment	27	57	28	57	25	58
Performance monitoring	32	52	28	46	18	31

Note: Items were measured on a seven point rating scale: 1 'Extremely dissatisfied', 2 'Very dissatisfied', 3 'Moderately dissatisfied', 4 'Not sure', 5 'Moderately satisfied', 6 'Very satisfied', 7 'Extremely satisfied'. Scores for 'dissatisfied' comprise responses for 1–3 and 'satisfied' 5–7.

job. On the seven point scale used for the questions shown in Tables 4.3 and 4.4 very few job facets elicited the mean score of 5 necessary to indicate 'moderately satisfied', either for call centre operators or software developers. The highest scoring job facet was 'work colleagues' for both call centre operators (94 per cent) and software workers (96 per cent), while the lowest scoring facets were 'career prospects' for call centre operators (41 per cent) and 'managerial effectiveness' for software developers (35 per cent).

Comparing the overall scores for both sectors call centre employees, as might be expected, were significantly more likely to express dissatisfaction in most aspects – in Table 4.3 the levels of satisfaction were significantly lower in the case of customers, shifts, job variety, job security, influence in the workplace, their sense of achievement from their jobs, and their working hours. Furthermore, in call centres, operators were significantly less satisfied than team leaders and other management with all of these job facets and several others such as work conditions, pay, relations with management, and career prospects.

Software employees reported lower satisfaction than call centre workers in the case of only five of the 14 job facets shown in Table 4.4 (work conditions, supervisory guidance, pay-performance link, management relations and management effectiveness), all aspects of their jobs over which software developers, arguably, have relatively less control compared to the other job facets. There was also less differentiation between the attitudes of software developers and their supervisors/project managers; non-management respondents were significantly less satisfied with their

Table 4.4 Satisfaction ratings for different job facets: software

	Total sample (N = 806)		Operators (N = 721)		Team leaders/managers (N = 106)	
	% Dissatisfied	% Satisfied	% Dissatisfied	% Satisfied	% Dissatisfied	% Satisfied
Work conditions	16	82	15	83	19	77
Work colleagues	3	96	3	94	1	99
Customers	10	66	10	64	10	72
Supervisory guidance	20	68	16	71	28	59
Fair treatment	20	69	20	69	17	69
Pay	32	63	34	61	27	67
Pay-performance link	36	48	37	46	32	54
Management relations	27	53	26	51	29	58
Career prospects	30	45	30	43	30	49
Management effectiveness	40	35	39	33	44	40
Shifts	4	83	4	83	2	83
Job variety	13	79	14	76	10	86
Job security	8	70	8	68	8	74
Influence	11	73	12	68	8	85
Sense of achievement	13	81	12	80	13	81
Working hours	5	88	4	89	8	86
Performance assessment	25	52	25	51	23	53
Performance monitoring	25	45	25	44	27	47

Note: Items were measured on a seven point rating scale: 1 'Extremely dissatisfied', 2 'Very dissatisfied', 3 'Moderately dissatisfied', 4 'Not sure', 5 'Moderately satisfied', 6 'Very satisfied', 7 'Extremely satisfied'. Scores for 'dissatisfied' comprise responses for 1–3 and 'satisfied' 5–7.

job variety and influence, while management were less satisfied with guidance provided by superiors. While at least 60 per cent of the software respondents overall reported being either moderately satisfied or extremely satisfied with pay, approximately a third reported dissatisfaction and this tended to be more marked among younger employees; this group also tended to express the willingness to move between companies.

Conclusion

The practices described in this chapter confirm the pervasiveness of the HRM discourse on the construction of management rationale, but confirms that supporting policies are being applied in a largely *ad hoc* and unformulated manner. The people management picture which emerges from both sectors is the relatively muted presence and influence of professionalized HR services, though many of the techniques associated with modern people management were clearly evident and practiced, albeit without too much finesse, by largely unschooled line managers, the same people charged with gaining the commitment of their charges.

The evidence illuminates the dilemma of maintaining the HRM discourse within a volatile socio-economic environment. There was little support for the HRM function in any of our organizations, HR issues usually appeared as marginal rather than central and, as we have seen, responses were reactive, piecemeal, pragmatic and frequently fairly chaotic. During our stay in the call centre companies, training programmes were cut back, communications channels attenuated, and the continued efforts to promote a fun culture increasingly grated when set against the reality of work intensification and economic uncertainty. The consequences for employees' resigned experience of these frequent changes were sometimes Orwellian in tone, such as the 'Planning for Growth' strategy in Entcomm which actually involved 10,000 job cuts across the company nation-wide.

While employees in both sectors saw the games and pizza nights as a bit of light relief from the stresses of the job, they were not so enamoured of their employing organization as to wish to take its values to their hearts. Indeed, most of our respondents seemed capable of creating that 'distance' which Fleming and Sewell (2002) see as one of the hallmarks of contemporary employee resistance. We can thus see from this analysis that the model of the highly committed knowledge worker lacks usefulness because it confuses commitment to the organization with commitment to the job and to more salient groups such as colleagues. A better understanding of the sources of social identity which our respondents did display is revealed in the next chapter through examination of their attitudes to their occupations and careers.

5
Occupational Life

Introduction

Of particular concern in this chapter is the shape of career trajectories within our exemplar areas of work and the extent to which employees are able, and choose, to identify over time with an organization or a single area of expertise. The chapter begins with a consideration of the institutional and organizational infrastructure of the two employment sectors, including the provision of skills, qualifications and career opportunities. These provide the 'objective' conditions for a career. From this, we consider the evidence for new forms of career in these two relatively young sectors of employment. We would expect limited opportunities for career progression in the relatively flat call centre structures, and the reverse in software firms. However, it is also possible that in the absence of traditional career patterns, plurality prevails and emerging patterns are as yet tentative.

Secondly, an analysis of career perceptions and attitudes provides the basis for understanding 'subjective' notions of what constitutes a career and the career expectations of these workers. We examine how individual aspirations and strategies develop *vis-à-vis* organizational demands for greater flexibility and in the face of fewer opportunities for steady career development. This addresses the evidence for strategic self-management which is often ascribed to these 'new' careers, as well as extending the notion of career identity to include both occupation and occupational community.

We conclude by proposing career typologies for each of the two sectors. Although there is greater evidence to support software development as the archetypal knowledge economy career, our evidence shows some diversity within each sector. Thus, despite more limited opportunities for development and progression within call centres, we can identify various organizational career routes, as well as more entrepreneurial occupational orientations, within both sectors.

The institutional and organizational infrastructure for careers

The purported trend in the structure of careers is a move away from fixed occupational, organizational, and hierarchical paths. As a result of these shifts and increasingly short-term organizational attachments, definitive career options no longer seem appropriate. Early models of vocational choice and career development aggregated across individual experiences to build general theories of occupational choice and development (Super, 1957). These laid out possible career paths and identified significant career anchors (for example, values, skills, lifestyle) (Schein, 1978). More recently, however, writers such as Kanter (1989), Pahl (1995), Thomas (1989) and Nicholson (1996) have all referred to the mythical elements of traditional careers characterized by a linear, vertical progression within one organization or even one occupation. In the 75 case studies examined by Arthur, Inkson and Pringle (1999), for example, the typical job-to-job moves were non-linear, involving 33 per cent to a new industry, 33 per cent to a new occupation and 29 per cent to a different geographic location.

Recent careers literature talks instead of 'career actors' who "spiral' around different activities so that some progression is apparent in terms of personal fulfilment, learning or earnings' (Arthur *et al.*, 1999: 35). Thus, careers may still involve the acquisition of greater expertise in the same specialization, but they may also be understood as a circular or spiral process, where qualifications and expertise are a reference point around which individuals move in order to acquire a wider range of knowledge.

In our relatively new sectors, formalized career paths, based, for example, on professional qualifications, may not yet have crystallized. Nevertheless, we might expect these sectors to represent model cases of new career forms which approximate 'spirals' rather than traditional linear progression. In examining this issue, we first consider the 'objective face' of career (Barley, 1989) which describes externally defined indicators of success. This may include issues of labour market structure and economic conditions (growth, unemployment), but here we focus on the occupational frameworks for qualifications and skill within each sector, and organizational indicators such as level and opportunities for advancement within the organizations.

Skills, training and qualifications

A knowledge-driven economy, with lifelong learning and the development of technical, scientific and professional workers at its core, is viewed by current policy makers as essential for both individual and national well-being (DTI, 1998; DfEE, 1998, 2000a, 2000b). Expansion in higher education and an effective vocational and training framework are essential vehicles for achieving this 'high skills society'. Interest has focused, most notably, on efforts to enhance the knowledge, skills and capabilities demanded by employers in the new economy (Keep and Mayhew, 1999; Brown, Hesketh and Williams, 2003), the causal factors leading to perceived skills mismatch (Handel, 2003), and the role which can be played by employers themselves in redressing these problems (Green, 2000).

In the UK, the responsibility for the development of standards for training has been encompassed within industry or occupational bodies initially known as Lead Bodies/National Training Organizations and now Learning and Skills Councils. This followed the establishment of the National Council for Vocational Qualifications (NCVQ) in 1986, which was responsible for developing a framework of NVQs that consisted of five levels and 11 occupational areas. In parallel, the government funded the Industry Training Organizations to develop the occupational standards on which NVQs were based. These were typically tripartite organizations, with employee representation in the form of trade union membership. By 1994 there were 500 NVQs covering 150 occupations, representing 80 per cent of all jobs. Also in parallel, SCOTVEC was responsible in Scotland for carrying out the implementation of the qualifications that were developed in the UK. On 1 July 1999, a new Scottish Parliament and Executive were established with legislative and executive responsibility for a wide range of devolved matters, including education and training, but the general occupational approach to the development of training and qualifications remained unchanged.

Both call centre and software work have been influenced by this move towards broad training frameworks. The Information Technology National Training Organization developed standards and qualifications for software work, ranging from levels one to five and covering all work involving the creation of software. It also included the investigation of customer requirements through to installation and testing of the completed project. The adoption of common skills' frameworks has also been endorsed on a European level (CEPIS, 2002; EU, 2001) as an alternative qualifications route to existing undergraduate and postgraduate degrees in software engineering and computing, and as a means of promoting a transparent common skills structure to encourage greater mobility across nations.

The diversity of operations within the call centre sector is evident in the analysis and mapping of the sector in the UK conducted by NTO tele.com (1999). It covered both call centres and other call handling operations and reported that its occupational standards on occasion reproduce units and elements from existing qualifications, but were generally a collection of diverse skills and qualifications. Although 92 per cent of companies were found to provide some form of induction training, it was confirmed that there were limited development paths for call centre agents. Legislative influences, such as the role of statutory bodies (for example, The Independent Committee for the Supervision of Standards of Telephone Information Services and OFTEL), already influenced database management, some outbound call agents and call monitoring, and were predicted to increase their influence over the occupation in the future.

Two of our call centre companies (Holstravel and Thejobshop) were involved in piloting the vocational qualifications for the SQA at the time of investigation, though in Holstravel, a CSA commented: 'It's a piece of nonsense' (unstructured interview, Holstravel, male operator). Thejobshop used existing customer service vocational qualifications and was involved in the development of new call centre qualifications but again, these were the focus of some ridicule. 'What they [operators] have to do is give examples of ways they have shown initiative. "You showed great initiative in the way you answered that phone"' (unstructured interview, Thejobshop, male operator).

The authority for the IT and call centre sectors merged in 2001 as part of a wider Government-led initiative and now rests with *e-skills UK*, the Sector Skills Council for IT, Telecoms and Contact Centres. *Connect*, the communications industry union for managers and professionals, represents employees' interests in these developments. The Sector Skills Council is responsible for developing the quantity and quality of professional skills, and brings together employers, educators and government to improve skills, designed to increase productivity and business performance in the UK. Within this framework, there are different Boards with responsibility for IT and Contact Centres, although the latter has yet to be constituted and at the time of writing, only one of the research locations has membership with *e-skills*. This body also produced the Contact Centre Career and Skills Framework, and instigated a comprehensive review of the National Occupational Standards for the industry that will dictate the content of all training provision eligible for public funding (*e-skills UK*, 28 June 2004). One of the largest software case studies offered Vocational Qualification routes to its members but this was in terms of project management rather than specifically software (Beta intranet).

In none of our companies could it be said that the vocational qualifications played a determinable role in creating an identifiable grouping within the occupation. In software, greater emphasis appears to have been placed on standard academic qualifications for entry and informal routes to learning in development, with occasional use of non-specific occupational qualifications which might lead it to be identified as an 'emerging' profession (Marks and Lockyer, 2005). In call centres, although it was probably too early in the development of these structures to draw firm conclusions, our observations provide little evidence that the new measures were taken seriously by staff covered by the standards.

Organizational provision for training and development – churn, change and company policy

In addition to the far-reaching changes in employment and work discussed earlier in this volume, particular trends within the two rapidly expanding sectors themselves could be identified. During the three years of the fieldwork (1999–2002), employment in Scottish call centres increased by around 60 per cent (Taylor and Bain, 2003b) and, in software, by 15 per cent in the year 2000 alone (Hyman *et al.*, 2004). Full-time staff constituted 86 per cent of the call centre and 91 per cent of the software workforces, respectively. Against a background of ambitious growth plans by each of the individual companies, a continuous process (or threat) of changes in ownership, structure and top management helped to create a volatile and turbulent business environment in which managerial thinking often appeared to be *ad hoc* and ephemeral in character (Taylor *et al.*, 2005).

As discussed in Chapter 4, under such circumstances, management's general approach to employee development and the employment relationship in both sectors tended to be short-termist or was perceived as emanating from a 'fire-fighting' reaction to concurrent shop-floor problems. This was particularly so for call centre employees who were relatively less independent from their current employers than software workers in terms of the acquisition of qualifications and skill.

Training and development in the call centres

In call centres, development efforts centred primarily around induction, some degree of coaching, and limited offerings of formal training opportunities. Induction programmes were of variable length and quality depending on recruitment patterns, but were believed to be essential by managers as poor induction contributed to high turnover. Nonetheless, the presence of induction was dependent on demand, as in Moneyflow, where the period was reduced to one week due to labour turnover. Usually, the induction period involved two weeks in the classroom, one week systems training and one week on the floor, and covered company procedures, keyboard skills, specific business unit information and sometimes role play exercises. In Moneyflow, high performing customer service advisers were seconded to this activity and then returned to their previous jobs. In Entcomm, several members of the dedicated Training Team focused only on induction training although in the later stages of our research period these staff were all made redundant and this role became the responsibility of selected customer advisers.

Continued support and coaching in the job and opportunities for development were less evident. There was a 'buddy' system in all call centres but only for the first few days or weeks, and sometimes this operated only informally. When training staff were made redundant in Entcomm, responsibility was allocated to 'superwalkers', experienced Customer Service

Advisers selected by team leaders (with no additional payment) to train part-time evening staff and engage in one to one coaching with trainees once they have gone 'live' on the floor. For those asked to act as 'buddies', call times doubled thus impacting on targets (Moneyflow, male financial adviser; M-I-05), and providing a significant disincentive to staff adopting this role.

Formal training tended to focus on technical skills rather than soft skills development, but, as mentioned in the previous section, there was some evidence of emerging cross-sectoral skills and qualifications frameworks relevant to call centre work, particularly in Holstravel and Thejobshop. In Moneyflow, a financial sector qualification was offered, with Financial Planning Advisers required to complete 12 month programmes leading to externally moderated examinations. In Entcomm, there was a range of qualifications offered: 'Explorer', awarded by the Institute of Customer Service (ICS), 'Fit for the Future' and the 'Team Leader Development Programme' which were aimed at team leaders, and the 'Customer Service Development Programme'. In Holstravel, when business was not so buoyant, they were piloting a call centre qualification in 'Personal Development' and employees could work towards a 'Certificate in Call Centre Operations' awarded by ABTA/SQA for the 18–25 age group.

These examples illustrate some attempts to establish an HR approach to personal development, but, invariably, in all organizations, there was less than consistent implementation and unfulfilled promise. Within Moneyflow, a 'Performance Development and Reward' system as well as the Financial Planning Advisers qualification was in place, while in Holstravel a 'Programme for Exceptional People (PEP)' provided a merit programme with four levels each defined by different success criteria. For example, PEP 3 was a combination of meeting targets for nine months out of 12 and business awareness. Entcomm's Explorer programme, as well as being difficult to access for some staff (for example, part-timers), held no promise of advancement on completion, as voiced by this CSA.

> It's allowed me to do my job better, but not allowed me to progress anywhere. I mean it's been done, it's been recognized, they took us for a meal and they gave us certificates which was very nice, but it doesn't let me go anywhere, it's left me again dangling (Entcomm, female customer service adviser; E-I-25, previously Training Co-ordinator at a major competitor).

Development of handbooks and guidelines on coaching and the piloting of 360 degree appraisal were discussed in all organizations. However, throughout the period of the research, there was little evidence of an embedded system of learning and development which was part of the culture of the organization and supported by formal policies and practice. As we described earlier, most companies had an HR presence at head office with part-time responsibility for call centres in Scotland; Entcomm made use of a part-time HR consultant reflecting its 'flavour of the month' approach to HR initiatives; and, increasingly, HR responsibilities seemed to devolve to team leaders. Some talked of having to abandon training because of high demand (unstructured interview, Holstravel, management) and even that mistakes made as a result of people being 'thrown in at the deep end' without training had led to one impending court case (work observation, Holstravel, management-employee meeting). Although an average of 70 per cent of survey respondents were generally content with the training provided by the company to allow them to do their job, 38 per cent across all companies also expressed a desire for further training in basic technical skills, mainly product knowledge (7 per cent) and IT skills (10 per cent).

The companies' approach to training seemed driven by changing business priorities, restructuring and the intake of new staff with different ideas on implementation of policy. In Entcomm, for example, there was high staff turnover and cutbacks affecting training managers as part of the national programme of staff reduction called 'Planning for Growth'. There was also poor communication between the separate HR function and the training managers who tended to be promoted from team leader positions, even though they sat next to each other. Also, while Moneyflow was generally perceived to be a good place to work, offering prospects of internal advancement, the external recruitment agency it subcontracted complained of the effects of recent changes in the company structure and of the increasing focus of team leaders on targets. Previous focus on an integrated training and placement programme was dependent on a manager who had moved on to another part of the business. His replacement – a more sales-driven, short-termist manager – encouraged rapid turnover and seemed content with a 'fire-fighting' approach to recruitment (unstructured interview, Moneyflow's recruitment consultants).

Training and development in the software firms

Of the software companies, only Beta represented a highly developed, formalized and centralized approach to training and personal development, embodied in the company's Investors in People recognition. The other four companies, all small to medium-sized indigenous firms, were examples of either informal *ad hoc* practice, inconsistent implementation of development plans, or emerging formalization driven by recently appointed, but still low status, HR officers. Almost 70 per cent of Beta survey respondents believed that the company gave them sufficient training to do their job well compared to around 50 per cent of other companies. Even in Beta, though, implementation of training and development lacked consistency: training needs were not linked to other HR practice, such as performance appraisals; there were instances of training being cancelled towards the end of the financial year; and there was no formal training provision for contractors or maternity returners.

In all cases, in fact, responsibility for identifying training needs largely lay with the employees. In Pi, employees chose which external courses they wished to attend within six months of starting, but the company was explicit about where the responsibility of career development lay and how these preferences would be considered. 'You are expected to take responsibility for your own career development and the direction in which it develops. The company will help you to realize your potential considering the objectives of the company as a whole' (Pi Employee Handbook).

Beta provided access to online preferred training providers whereby employees could choose relevant programmes. Omega encouraged employees to invest in the development of their technical skills, particularly as they were aligned to business objectives, through external training courses; and, in common with Gamma, Omega also had stated an objective to develop employees' soft skills (for example, interpersonal skills, teamworking, customer orientation).

Projects also assumed significance as a means of accumulating skills and experience. Again, Beta adopted a more formal approach. There was a policy of rotating people around projects every two years for the purposes of personal career development. Assignment to projects was based on personal choice from a central pool of projects, or by direct negotiation with one of the three personal development managers in the software centre. One of these managers commented:

> Once I have got someone into a project and they have been there two or three years, they start to become really productive. ...But from an individual's point of view this is not necessarily a good idea – particularly for graduates – to just sit in a project for five or six years (unstructured interview, Beta, Personal Development Manager).

In Omega, Gamma and Pi, there was acknowledgement of personal preferences – 'people wanting to work in new "sexy" areas' (unstructured interview, Omega, Business Manager, Resources) – but the business focus of these smaller companies was on supporting existing applications, and hence they could justify only a small number of employees being trained in relevant areas.

> Training must be in line with the company's business objective. There is a hard balancing act between ensuring this and allowing individual staff development. Almost all of the juniors want training in Java. However there is only enough business generated through using Java to justify a dozen people being trained in it. Only 20 per cent of the business is in pure new development (unstructured interview, Omega, Estimations Manager).

Opportunities for career progression and skill acquisition
The narrow road to career progression in call centres

The managerial emphasis placed upon teams as the basis of work organization was pervasive in both sectors, but for call centre workers, the role of team leader represented the only clear opportunity for advancement. This is visible from the job profile of call centre workers in our sample. Across the four call centre case study companies, 81 per cent of all employees were basic operators or call handlers who performed similar, individualized, highly monitored tasks within tightly defined temporal parameters; only 13 per cent of employees had a supervisory or management role. Workgroup size and composition was primarily determined by the number of operators who could be efficiently supervized by one team leader, rather than by any particular characteristics of the function(s) carried out by the team.

Clearly, the possibilities of operators being promoted within the call centre were extremely limited. In Thejobshop, there were six line managers out of 400 staff, and these were not necessarily appointed from within the company. A similar prospect was highlighted by an Entcomm CSA in his 20s:

> We were told – fast moving environment, room for change, great opportunities; but the amount of people that they bring from the outside while there's people here that have been here a long time that they could have promoted! (Entcomm, male customer service adviser; E-I-29).

Most call centre operators faced the often daunting prospect of having to conduct their basic call-handling duties indefinitely, while some hoped job opportunities might arise elsewhere within the company (for example, in high street branches or in IT). The lack of openings for those who completed any available team leader development training also was found to act as a de-motivator (unstructured interview with HR staff, Entcomm).

In some call centres, intermediary positions to which operators could aspire – such as deputy team leader, trainer, superwalkers (Entcomm), and call quality associates (Entcomm) – had been created. The question of extra payment for deputies while performing team leader duties had also arisen as an issue in Moneyflow, while the utilization of team leader applicants to 'act up' and manage teams on a temporary basis (which attracted no extra payment and could last for several months) was a bone of contention in Entcomm. Entcomm call handlers were only selected for team leader development if they had met 'all their objectives', 96 per cent attendance and no disciplinary record, and had been recommended by their line manager (unstructured interview with HR staff, Entcomm). In these situations, there was a feeling that employees' desire to get away from continuous, often repetitive call-handling, and attain team leader positions, was being exploited by the employer. The possibility of being accepted for training for higher-graded mortgage and financial adviser posts in Moneyflow provided an additional incentive for some operators, while the chance to transfer to certain more prestigious accounts within Thejobshop's outsourcing operations evoked similar responses. Management also drew upon call handlers, typically volunteers, to participate in short-term projects set up to examine particular aspects of the working environment (for example, new IT systems, skill census).

More generally, a plethora of team-based and individual employee 'best performer' prizes and competitions, as well as team and call centre-wide social events, offered other means by which workers might attract supervisory attention and subsequently be considered for promotion. However, uncertainty and worry about their prospects of continuing employment within a merged or competitively threatened company took precedence for many workers over career aspirations.

Software project teams as learning collectives

Software work was, intrinsically, collaborative and took place mainly in project teams. We have argued elsewhere that project teams are an essential vehicle for workers in the 'development of a portfolio of experience, new languages...skills, and added value in the labour market' (Marks and Lockyer, 2004: 2–3). This high degree of collaboration and interdisciplinarity suggests a more collective construction of skills development. Given that software workers cannot, and do not, rely exclusively on the employing organization to attend to their development needs (Foote, 2000), the role of teamworking assumes particular significance. Not only would software employees tend to be integrated into interdisciplinary teams but, in the interests of career development, they might seek to move between teams and projects.

In practice, people tended to stay on a project for two or three years before moving, or being moved, to another one. One team leader in Beta, not atypically, had worked on six projects during her ten years in employment, including three within her first year. In Beta, in particular, employees had a small portfolio of active projects at any point in time, and moved amongst these. On the other hand, an employee of one of the smaller organizations stated that two years was sufficient time to remain with a company. Outside contractors, who constituted 16 per cent of the total software workforce in our study, were perceived by managers as 'learning tools', important in updating employees skills. The ethos of sharing knowledge in the team setting was evident and acknowledged in all five case study companies, with the survey responses indicating that other colleagues provided the primary source of learning new skills for over half the respondents across all companies.

We indicated earlier in this chapter that projects or teams constituted the locus of skill formation, and thus potential marketability. Project teams become either arenas for the competitive acquisition of know-how or sites for collaborative learning in communities of practice (Wenger and Snyder, 2000). Clearly, whichever of these applies, membership within these communities is mainly instrumental, driven by the desire to increase one's own marketability. Thus, instrumentalizing and rationalizing their approach to skill acquisition and group work, software developers – consciously or not – may follow the self-managed approach to career development. However, only Beta had the capacity to formalize this aspect of career management in the form of personal development plans and enabled software engineers to express personal preferences. The smaller companies allocated project work according to business need, and even in Beta, access to high status, desirable projects was not always a matter of personal choice. Team membership was gained through 'career negotiation' between developers and their managers, or through informal networking. As we discuss further in the final section of this chapter, the successful employees tended to be the better qualified, younger and frequently male workers; for some female and older workers who had taken career breaks or had outdated skills, mobility and development opportunities were limited.

The subjective face of career and occupation

Our second area of inquiry focuses on the subjective accounts of career of call centre and software employees. We examine the extent to which employees have endorsed new notions of career, or whether there is still evidence that workers seek identity within an organizational context with longer-term commitment, promotion and advancement. In this section, we consider not only career attitudes, but go beyond the boundaries of the organization to establish the degree to which identification with an occupation and wider occupational community is present in the two sectors.

Arthur *et al.*'s depiction of careers as more than a linear path – 'the unfolding interaction between a person and society' (1989: 8) – is especially relevant for discontinuous forms of employment. Work or career sub-identity may be questioned more frequently as individuals shift jobs or occupations, and, as a consequence of this instability, may even play an increasingly minor role in shaping identity in comparison to other sub-identities (for example, identity derived from colleagues, family, friends or community) (Hall, Briscoe and Kram, 1997). Thus, patterns of commitment to company or to occupation (job as career) may be less relevant than commitment to family/leisure (job as convenient). Moreover, this instability and precariousness in work-related career identity leads us to question whether the notion of career, with its implicitly assumed stability of social relations and some degree of objective existence, can still adequately represent the contemporary employment condition.

Interpretivist approaches to understanding careers take their point of departure from an individual's experience of career – conceptualizing career as unfolding from recurrent acts of sensemaking that allow individuals to assign meaning to their employment biographies. Recent contributions to the career debate that have evolved around concepts such as Protean Career (Hall, 1996) or Intelligent Career (Parker and Arthur, 2000), have shifted from objective measurement towards the subjective experience of individuals' employment life. A growing number of authors (for example, Pongratz and Voß, 2003) present the new era of discontinuous employment and lateral careers as deriving not so much from a passive adaptation of individuals (for example, to the imperatives of flexibility), but rather as an active and strategic self-management process of their own marketability beyond the confines of a single job, organization or occupation.

This emphasis on self-management adopts a central position in new economy notions of a career. The 'new' psychological contract, with reduced job security and limited opportunities for internal promotions, holds employment relationships to be transactional (Rousseau and Parks, 1993) with little pretension of individual loyalty to a single employer. Individuals are expected to take responsibility for shaping their own careers, in a form of entrepreneurial self-management of career (du Gay, 1996), and the focus is on enhancing employability, gained through the gradual acquisition of a 'portfolio' of skills, knowledge and experience, rather than seeking secure employment (Heckscher, 1995; Herriot and Pemberton, 1996). Opportunities for career self-management and the ability to manage one's career effectively, making use of 'metacompetencies' of self-awareness and adaptability (Hall, 2002), seem to be a prerequisite for shaping this non-linear career path (Arthur and Rousseau, 1996).

The idea of self-managed boundaryless careers is relatively easy to envisage for professional workers (Hirsch and Stanley, 1996). The software industry which we examine in this book provides, perhaps, a close approximation to the high skilled, autonomous knowledge worker (Frenkel et al., 1999) for whom boundaryless careers have become the norm. This image is harder to conceptualize in other areas of work, however, such as call centres.

Career patterns and attitudes

The analysis thus far confirms that call centre and software employees experience starkly different work and organizational contexts as well as quite distinct employment and occupational conditions. There was, nevertheless, a considerable proportion in both sectors that identified with the prospect of a career, whether this was within their current organizations or within the sector generally.

Table 5.1 Perceptions of current job as career

	Call centres		Software	
	N	% within call centres	N	% within software
Long-term job	130	18	82	29
Career, same company	202	28	49	17
Career, different company	172	24	124	43
Short-term, not part of career	218	30	26	9

Note: Respondents were asked to choose only one statement which represented how they thought of their current job.

Whilst almost all software employees considered their current jobs as part of a longer-term career path, albeit in another company, call centre employees fragmented into three distinct orientations: 28 per cent overall, and in one organization (Moneyflow) 40 per cent, aspired towards career advancement in their current organizations; an average of 24 per cent foresaw a career in another company still within the call centre context; and another 30 per cent could not see their current jobs as part of a longer-term career at all (see Table 5.1). Thus, just under half of call centre workers still could relate to the prospect of a call centre career despite the restrictive and seemingly limited career opportunities within the sector. Later in this chapter, we elaborate on these groups as distinct call centre career typologies.

Contrasts between the two occupational groups are also evident in their career patterns and attitudes towards a career. Table 5.2 shows significant differences in the survey responses from the two employee groups with regard to average tenure with the company and in the average length of career path (i.e., the length of time spent in related work). The more professionally orientated and generally older, software workers had spent longer with the same company and in the software/IT labour force. Software workers had worked on average four more years in their current company (although the higher standard deviation for software shows wider variation amongst this group) and about a year more in their current section or project.

We also calculated the length of time they reported being in a related career from their descriptions of previous jobs. Software workers showed an average career life-span of about eight years compared to call centre workers' two years. In general, while a coherent progression around a software/IT career was evident, call centre workers possessed a more assorted career trajectory. One notable example of this variety was a key member of Entcomm's quality team who was seen as central to the success of the company's turn towards prioritization of call quality – a former civil

Table 5.2 Career patterns and attitudes

	Call centres			Software			
	N	Mean	SD	N	Mean	SD	t
Months worked for company	803	21.34	20.81	292	68.93	84.63	9.51***
Months worked for section	707	10.88	11.48	260	24.85	31.05	7.08***
Months in a career path[a]	806	26.07	31.63	298	63.17	79.10	7.87***
Importance of company career[b]	805	3.74	.97	299	3.47	.98	4.07***
Satisfaction, career prospects[c]	800	3.99	1.49	299	4.12	1.33	1.39
Occupational commitment[d]	806	2.92	.85	301	3.69	.70	15.16***

Notes: *** $p < .001$ (2-tailed, equal variances not assumed).
[a]Time in a career path was calculated as months in current job + months in previous job in same area of work.
[b]Importance of a company career was measured by one item scaled from '1' not at all important to '5' absolutely critical.
[c]Satisfaction with career prospects was measured by one item scaled from '1' extremely dissatisfied to '7' extremely satisfied.
[d]Occupational commitment was calculated as the mean of three items scaled from '1' strongly disagree to '5' strongly agree (*If I could, I would go into a different occupation; I take an interest in current developments in the call centre/software sector; I am proud to tell others that I am employed in the call centre/software sector*).

servant with a degree in brass band musicianship (unstructured interview, Entcomm, male Quality Analyst).

As might be expected, satisfaction with career prospects and occupational commitment also were higher for software workers; but a finding which is particularly notable in Table 5.2, especially given the limited organizational career support afforded call centre workers, is that an organizational career is significantly more important to them than software workers. By contrast, occupational commitment is significantly greater for software workers. Any commitment towards a call centre occupation was discernible in only 32 per cent of our call centre sample.

Thus, there seems to be an expectation, amongst some call centre workers at least, that their company can provide a traditional career path. This did vary across call centres, with the importance of an organizational career considerably higher in Moneyflow than the other three call centres (the mean for this variable in Moneyflow was 4.15 (n = 94) compared to the overall mean of 3.74). Moneyflow was notable in its more organizationally orientated careerists and its financial advisers with a sense of career progression – a distinct career cluster which we expand on further below. There were no significant differences across software companies in this respect, confirming the more homogenous nature of career and occupational orientation for this emerging profession.

Occupational identity

Further analysis within each sector was carried out to determine the influence of demographic factors on career and occupational attitudes. The results of stepwise regression analyses for call centre and software employees, separately, are shown in Table 5.3 for the three career/occupational attitudes examined above – perceived importance of a career in the present company, satisfaction with career prospects in the company, and occupational commitment. It is notable that for call centres, a career in the company was more important for men and older employees; satisfaction with career was higher for those with lower qualifications and for managers; and occupational commitment was higher for all these groups – men, older workers, those with less qualifications and managers. We might speculate that the greater the perceived opportunities for a career in their present companies, the more likely call centre employees were to identify with being call centre workers and identify with this emerging occupation.

For software, importance of an organizationally-bound career was greater for older workers, for managers, and for those with longer tenure – arguably those with the greatest investment in the company or with less marketability. Demographic predictors were not able to explain satisfaction with career prospects (the model in Table 5.3 for software was not significant), and our findings suggested that men tended to have greater occupational commitment than women. This latter finding is explored further in Chapter 7's treatment of gender issues where several potential explanations of women's lower occupational orientation are offered. Here, we focus on further conceptualizing the construct of call centre and software occupational identity.

Some call centre employees felt able to identify opportunities for upward occupational mobility in their employment. Nevertheless, distinctive patterns of career and occupational orientation were clearly more apparent for software workers, whilst a broader, more ephemeral range of aspirational dispersions were noted for call centre employees.

We saw that a third of call centre employees feel a strong sense of belonging to their occupation, compared with half of software respondents (see Table 5.2). Presented differently, whilst nearly half of call centre employees would willingly change occupations, this figure subsides to a fifth for the software sample. More than twice as many software employees (63 per cent) take pride in telling others of their occupation than do call centre employees (30 per cent).

Table 5.3 Prediction of career attitudes

	Importance of career in company		Satisfaction with career		Occupational commitment	
	Call centres	Software	Call centres	Software	Call centres	Software
Female	−.16*	−.08	.06	.04	.08*	−.15*
Age	−.11**	−.26***	.51	.11	.12**	−.01
Qualifications	.04	−.02	−.15***	−.05	−.23***	.01
Management position	.05	.21**	.16***	.08	.17***	.05
Tenure	.01	.15*	.05	−.15	.03	−.08
F	6.10**	8.28***	17.25***	1.58	22.67***	5.95***
Adj. R^2	.02	.08	.05	.03	.11	.02
N	737	280	734	280	743	280

Notes: *p < .05 **p < .01 ***p < .001

These patterns were confirmed in both workplace and home interviews. Very few of our call centre interviewees identified themselves specifically or primarily as call centre workers, though realistically many saw that for the immediate future their working lives would be associated with this kind of work. Moneyflow presents an interesting case here as many of our respondents referred to themselves as financial advisers rather than call centre employees, and through this association, as many as 40 per cent had ambitions to remain with the company in anticipation of occupational advancement through the financial advising route. Generally, though, two particular directions can be identified: first, few call centre people envisaged staying with the same employer (a finding reinforced by the high degree of mobility, an attrition rate of about one-third of employees annually), and whilst many respondents expected to stay in call centres in the immediate future, ideally, longer-term aspirations were directed toward 'getting off the phones', as indicated by several operators in interviews:

> I would like a job that didn't have to speak to customers all day long … more administration wise … my ideal job would be a bit of both, I suppose (Entcomm, female customer service adviser; E-I-02).

A temporary team leader stressed the strictly contractual nature of the relationship between her and the company:

> I do have an obligation to the company and I do realise the opportunity that I've been given, but I'll be quite honest I don't think call centres are for me and my intention when I get through this development course is

to say thank you very much, Entcomm, I'll take my knowledge and my learning and my tools and I'll go somewhere else and apply them there (Entcomm, female team leader; E-I-06)

I've got my future well planned out. I've got it planned out where I'm going to go. Now whether it will be within Moneyflow or another financial sector, but I won't be sitting in a call centre asking customers the same questions for seven hours in the day (Moneyflow, female customer adviser; M-I-14).

We can contrast the detached perspectives of call centre respondents with those of software workers, whose values as software workers are very much tied up with their self-image as providers of a professional service and the necessity to perform well on behalf of both the customer and the company. This point was cogently expressed by a software engineer at Gamma:

I don't mind doing the long hours because I know that ultimately it's going to be worth doing. Just the sort of person I am – I like to see at the end of the day, well, we did a good job and we got it done. It's part of the job and you just accept that if you are out on customer sites, generally you do work long hours (Gamma, female software developer; G-I-05).

The pivotal role of work for software people was stressed repeatedly by respondents as these two quotes from Pi and Lambda indicate:

(Work) is important in my life – it is just that I still like to do really well in my job. I like to have people around me that are happy with the work I am doing and I like to feel like our customers are happy with it as well (Pi, male development team leader; P-I-11).

(Work) is actually quite central. Possibly more than a lot of people would like it to be, but I don't see it as a chore, or don't sort of not look forward to coming in the next day because there is a free rein there and it is a challenge and every day is different. I do quite enjoy it to be honest because of that free rein which I think is quite fortunate (Lambda, male business development manager; L-I-02).

Occupational community

Conceptualizing career as 'the unfolding interaction between a person and society' (Arthur *et al.*, 1989: 8) highlights also its significance as a symbol of occupational specificity and expertise, and as a badge indicating both occupational and geographical identity. Software workers demonstrate many of the characteristics of an occupational community (see, for example,

Salaman, 1971), including intrinsic satisfaction with the job, satisfaction from deploying and extending their software skills, and a professional orientation derived from serving both clients and company. Identifiable career orientations founded on acquisition of specific skills and accumulated experience were also apparent, as shown earlier in this chapter.

Given this, and the strong sense of commitment to the work rather than the organization, we might argue there is a strong and identifiable culture of software work based on norms of attachment to the work and a typical software profile. Moreover, relationships, located in both work and social networks, provide a basis for occupational bonding. The majority of software workers reported socializing at least occasionally with former work colleagues (65 per cent) and others working in similar jobs (60 per cent), while socializing with team-mates and others in the organization was even more common (i.e., several times a month, weekly or daily) for 25 to 30 per cent of our survey respondents.

The professional or quasi-professional sentiments and attachments of software workers can be contrasted to the very different occupational and career perspectives of the majority of call centre employees. Value of the work in terms of the satisfaction of undertaking it was limited to a general enjoyment in dealing with customers, albeit telephonically, and from the support of colleagues. The routine of work, its intensity, lack of individual control and organizational target pressures combined to provide little obvious intrinsic satisfaction, and orientations to work were expressed largely in instrumental terms, as a 'necessary evil' or a means to paying the bills. There was little accepted fusion between work and non-work life and manifestations of negative spillover from work to home were evident and difficult for employees to avoid or to combat. As might be expected, far fewer call centre workers identified with either employer, career or occupation than did software employees.

Career strategies and typologies

Call centres

Based on the evidence presented thus far, we propose that, in call centres, we can identify four clusters of individuals with different aspirations and strategies towards career. Contrary to what might be expected, the first three are represented by employees who held clear career aspirations and pursued an explicit strategy of social mobility, progressing either within their company or within their occupation/sector. For these individuals, career was a central feature of their work life and seemed to mark a trajectory in terms of either vertical or horizontal mobility. Training was valued either as a means to a career in the company or elsewhere, and linked to general career satisfaction, as well as some degree of either organizational or occupational commitment.

The first cluster, organizational careerists, conforms most closely to traditional notions of a career. Of all the call centre companies, Moneyflow had the most visible internal hierarchy both within the call centre and in the wider company. In Moneyflow, the following sentiments were repeated by several staff.

> I think the company is trying to give more, for example, Mortgage Advisors are going to FPAs [Financial Planning Advisers]. I think they are trying to do that a bit more because for a while they just wouldn't promote any internal staff. ....I think they have to do that. I think after two or three years of being on the phone they will lose the staff if they don't promote them (Moneyflow, female financial adviser; M-I-07).

The two other explicit clusters of career orientations, which we call horizontal-bounded and horizontal-boundaryless, were apparent in some areas of Thejobshop and the secured loans section of Moneyflow. These employees perceived that they were gaining valuable skills which would contribute to their general employability either within the company or the occupational area generally. Training, both on and off the job, was relatively high and employees in these sections were more likely than other call centre employees to respond that training received in their job would make them more employable elsewhere.

For the high proportion of Moneyflow secured employees who also stated that they saw themselves staying in the same industry (finance) or in call centre management, a career within the larger company of which the call centre was a part, seemed a realistic aspiration. Forty-four per cent of the secured loans side employees saw their future career in Moneyflow. These horizontal-bounded career orientations, then, were defined in terms of the company or industry.

Some, though, also saw the accreditation by an external financial regulation body as an objective career indicator (the financial planning qualification) with relevance outwith call centres. Similarly, for Thejobshop's *Bluechip* employees, off-the-job training and certification provided by the client business (not Thejobshop itself) resulted in a qualification and experience recognized by employers other than call centre. One section of *Bluechip* employees in particular who dealt with enquiries from 'VIP corporate' customers (those with between 500 and 5,000 PCs in their organization) tended to be more involved in business events organized by *Bluechip* (unstructured interview, Thejobshop, male agent).

Such horizontal-boundaryless career paths reflected those who recognized their marketability in other occupations and industries. These individuals were actively and strategically pursuing their self-marketization and perhaps most closely resemble the proposed new economy career model. They proactively seized employment opportunities that offered career advancement and their investments were primarily directed toward developing formal qualifications and specialist know-how to be exchanged at a special (high-skill) segment of the labour market. For this group of call centre workers, identification with a particular occupation and a career is clearly possible.

The fourth identifiable cluster of individuals from this data was one whose experiences to date and aspirations did not simply fit either vertical or horizontal definitions of career. They seemed to drift between a number of jobs during their working life with neither a clear sense of direction nor concrete aspirations to progress within particular companies or occupations. Work was adapted instrumentally to fit their needs and interests in other spheres of life. Our interviews revealed different examples of how circumstance resulted in drift towards a permanency in call centre work. To illustrate, the following variety of 'drifters' could be identified in Thejobshop:

- a computer science student who dropped out of study due to debts and family commitments, and now has a house and young family and cannot afford to go back to study (unstructured interview, Thejobshop, male CSA);
- an agent who had entered Thejobshop short-term after having lost his own business, but stayed because he thought he liked his colleagues and thought he could progress (unstructured interview, Thejobshop, male team manager);
- a coordinator of Thejobshop *Bluechip* corporate team who had worked in museums, but because of the lack of stable funding and job insecurity 'baled out', and moved to a temporary contract call centre job with Thejobshop *Energyco*, which then led to her present *Bluechip* position (unstructured interview, Thejobshop, female agent);
- a French agent who had come to Britain to improve her English, stayed because she met her boyfriend, and expected to stay with Thejobshop two years as this was the length of time she felt was necessary to get a good reference (unstructured interview, Thejobshop, female operator).

A significant subset of this fourth cluster were graduates on permanent contracts and with over a year's tenure with the companies. The case study companies were atypical from the national profile of employees in comparable occupations in this respect because of the higher proportion of university graduates employed (38 per cent of the sample overall). The large student population in the Glasgow area provides a pool of labour seeking flexible work and higher salaries than retailing and other service sector jobs, but the salary differentials with other graduates' starting salaries are less favourable.

Certainly, few of the graduates we interviewed considered their present job as part of a career in call centre work. One Thejobshop *Bluechip* graduate commented that 'this was not a graduate job' and did not 'see any real career progression' (unstructured interview, Thejobshop, male agent). Another section leader in Thejobshop was a chemistry graduate and had a postgraduate degree but was unable to find a job so 'had to do something'. Although he had been with the company five years he commented 'I don't see it as much of a job, not much future to it, not much of a career' (unstructured interview, Thejobshop, male section leader). A media technologies graduate had consciously joined Entcomm in the hope of opportunities for internal promotion in the area of database development in the larger company (unstructured interview, Entcomm, male CSA). Ambitions beyond the call centre also were expressed by a Moneyflow employee who was a graduate, but this agent's response also revealed a draw to progress within the call centre or the company.

> I probably could have a career in here if I wanted to but it's not what I want to do at the end of the day. But it is convenient. It fits round my life outside work – if I knew what my shifts were going to be. [Laughs] Organize my study plan, you know! Everyone I went to university with who even went on to do honours didn't end up working in their field, you know, because it was science they did. It was silly. I should have stayed on and done an honours degree in genetics or something. Then a PhD. Yes, I definitely want to increase my skills and then see where that takes me (Moneyflow, female customer adviser; M-I-15).

In general, the survey findings showed that a significant proportion of employees could not see themselves in the same call centre job in five years time. This does not necessarily imply that individuals working in these conditions would always want to leave the company, but it reinforces a sense of career uncertainty. Some employees thought of career as movement within the company which would improve their working conditions or general satisfaction, for example, working their way out of the 'worst' sections in terms of the intensity and repetitiveness of the work (such as the Teletext section of Holstravel). Others thought of career as mobility into recognized 'better' sections which provided more challenging jobs or status (for example, the secured loans section of Moneyflow and *Gamesco* in Thejobshop) and maybe opportunities for management progression. Attraction to team leader roles, where it was possible to expand one's portfolio of skills, was evident in all the call centres. Others showed some inertia in looking for different jobs. They preferred the unloved but familiar situation of their present job or viewed it as a transitory stage into a completely different area of employment, enjoying the relative flexibility the job offers to upgrade their skill and, eventually, to move on. This career direction, albeit uncertain, is shown in the following quotation.

> I don't really want to start again and go to another company. I would rather stay with what I know and maybe move departments (Moneyflow, female mortgage adviser; M-I-17).

Software

In the spirit of 'new economy' writers, we began the chapter by presenting software developers as exemplar, skilled knowledge workers for whom the concept of self-managed and boundaryless careers have become the norm. The evidence presented from our data indeed shows that the emphasis on academic qualifications for entry into this emerging profession provides considerably more autonomy and employee leverage than the contrast case of call centres. Career and occupational orientation amongst these new professionals is stronger and more uniform, and less likely to be confined within the boundaries of a single organization. This group of workers also displayed a strong sense of occupational community, with the acquisition of specific skills and accumulated experience assuming significance as a symbol of success in the profession, and an identifiable culture of software work based on norms of attachment to the work and customer. The necessary conditions for the flexible, self-managed career appear to have been met.

Underlying this apparently coherent occupational profile, though, we were also able to discern diversity. As in call centres, there was a core of software workers for whom an organizational career assumed greater importance – again, we might label this group the organizational careerists. In software, this appeared to consist of those who were less employable – those considered to be less qualified – in the external market. Our evidence points to several subgroups who displayed these orientations – older workers, those who had transitioned from a technical to a managerial, business or support role, those with non-academic qualifications, and women returners who had chosen to shift to part-time contracts.

Employability in the software sector was defined by the accumulation of skills and experiences which kept pace with changing technological and business requirements. Outdated skills were a consequence of remaining on the same projects for long periods of time, being confined to older programming languages or in support or testing roles rather than creative development work, or as a result of management's short-termist, business-driven approach to training and development. The smaller, independent companies seemed to provide a much more constrained career development context than the larger Beta, where access to training was, at least on paper, driven by employee preference. This finding is consistent with the well-documented, wider concerns of small- and medium-sized enterprises, where research shows a reluctance to invest in the professional development of a skilled workforce which would make them more marketable, and an inability to recognize or predict future skill gaps unless driven by immediate business needs (for example, Barrett and Rainnie, 2005; Cappelli, 2001; Hendry et al., 1995; Hill and Stewart, 1999). In the more supportive and resource-rich environment of Beta too, however, access to creative work, training or other learning communities (experienced colleagues or mentors) required some element of negotiation and tended to be directed towards the younger, technically qualified, and, most often male, graduates. Thus, it seems that for some groups of software workers, development and career mobility were limited by their inability to negotiate access to appropriate opportunities (see also Marks and Lockyer, 2004).

Those who conformed to the horizontal-boundaryless career, as with the smaller subgroup identified in call centres, proactively pursued their self-marketization through the acquisition of qualifications and skills. In software, these were the individuals who successfully accessed the opportunities and resources in their companies, and in the wider occupation. A visible and salient occupational community also played a role in sustaining this external, market-driven orientation, as in this example from an experienced developer whose role had become increasingly specialized.

> Some of the stuff I've worked on is quite niche – you tend to bump into them [software developers in other companies] dealing on the technology side but socially as well....if the technology keeps going the way it's going just now the skills we'll have in six months, other companies will pay more than Beta for them – because Beta aren't the best payers in the world when it comes to this (Beta, male software developer; B-I-02).

Thus, in software, there were two identifiable career types. In one, we can detect the flexible, self-managed career assumed to be characteristic of knowledge workers. This was associated with high levels of educational attainment, access to interesting design projects, high labour market value, and high career autonomy. In the other type, more traditional forms of organizational career were evident and seemed to represent lower skilled employees with fewer conventional qualifications. This group were often relegated to less cutting-edge projects, or non-technical roles which restricted career opportunities externally and led to a more organizationally-determined progression.

Each of these merits further interrogation, although this is beyond the scope of the present chapter. Of particular interest is whether, for any of these subgroups, an organizational career path and orientation is determined by preference or workplace conditions, including for example, an ageist work culture, or institutional and informal barriers facing women in IT professions. Some of these possibilities are touched upon in other chapters of this book and elsewhere (see, for example, Barrett, 2005; Boerlijst *et al.*, 1998; DTI, 2005; Kraft, 1999; Weinberg, 1998). Recognizing also career, in an interpretative sense, as the active and strategic choices of individuals, career decisions are likely to interact with IT employers' attempts to retain highly skilled professionals against the lure of higher paying competitors (Alvesson, 2000; Cappelli, 2001; Walton, 1985). We did not directly explore this possibility here; however, elsewhere, in one example of this, we showed that the provision of greater personal flexibility and work-life balance was related to higher organizational commitment and intention to remain with the company for the software workers in our case study companies (Scholarios and Marks, 2004).

Conclusions

Both software engineers and call centre employees have been identified as occupants of the knowledge economy, with its flatter organizational forms and increasing individual mobility. As such, we might expect to find evidence of new career patterns which deviate from traditional forms based on hierarchical progression in a single organization.

Software workers especially are often regarded as the consummate knowledge workers. In contrast to the call centre workforce, these more highly qualified workers enjoyed greater labour market leverage, status and flexibility in determining the course of a career within a chosen field of expertise, and indeed a high proportion of these employees tended to regard their software careers as 'boundaryless', taking them to other organizations. Despite some efforts to formalize training and skill development in our call centre case studies, these efforts generally decreased in importance for the companies as business pressures arose. Call centre workers were less likely to acquire occupationally relevant qualifications and skills, and as a result, we found less evidence of a coherent boundaryless career in terms of accumulated skill and status.

Perhaps the most significant finding for the call centres was that there was still a sense of a company career for many, supporting the idea that the traditional career ladder still exists in the aspirations of workers (Guest and MacKenzie-Davey, 1996). These aspirations, however, are not accommodated by the institutional or organizational infrastructure. Given the call centres' flat structures, opportunities for hierarchical organizational advancement (for example, to team leader) were restricted, with many workers focusing on the potential for acquiring skills through horizontal moves into different areas of the business. Moreover, companies appeared to be paying no more than lip service to personal development, with induction, training and other efforts towards developing personal competencies sacrificed to business demand. These findings are consistent with writers who have identified barriers to a career in call centres for this predominantly female workforce (Belt *et al.*, 2002), and who have suggested that employers may even prefer to recruit women with no career aspirations (for example, those with dependents) in order to maintain stability in the face of limited opportunities and high turnover (Belt, 2002). Similar arguments have been made with respect to call centre employers' training strategies, which Thompson *et al.* (2004: 131) described as a 'springboard for normative control' rather than progressive efforts to enhance social or technical skill.

Software, although closer to the knowledge worker career ideal, is not uniform. We found evidence of a division between high-level intellectual work and lower-level work performed by those without specific technical skills. Only the former group could be said to resemble the upwardly mobile knowledge worker in the nature of their work and their career flexibility. Thus, for software too, we found barriers to career progression which confirmed others' accounts of this emerging profession (see Barrett's (2001) commentary on the ageist nature of software work).

As expected, the findings from this chapter reveal many differences between the two groups of workers in terms of the meanings they attribute to their work, career aspirations and their sources and expressions of occupational identity. Intriguingly, though, we also identified similar forces within both sectors despite the apparent extremes. These included the continuing importance for some of a company career; in software, this tended to be workers whose skills held lower external market value, while in call centres, these were individuals who sought to migrate to more skilled areas of work or management. Training and personal development, although more apparent for the software workers, was not guaranteed or equally accessible in any of the case study companies, making the reality of a self-managed, proactive approach to career development more difficult for some workers. In sum, the evidence for a knowledge economy career ideal, with the promise of flexibility, control and status for aspiring, skilled professionals, is confined to some groups within these two sectors.

6
Household and Community Life

Introduction

As previous chapters demonstrate, much contemporary management rhetoric is geared toward engaging the commitment of employees, exhorting them to co-operate with management demands to extend and flex working hours, to require availability to customers through call-outs, evening and weekend working and to take work home to meet required schedules.

Messages to metaphorically 'live the brand', to act as the human embodiment of the employing organization and its values, threaten to squeeze work even further into the domain of everyday living. Yet, clearly, as the title of this volume suggests, there are potentially other demands, other interests, which can occupy employees' lives and by doing so, question both the meaning and centrality of paid work and present challenges to managerial prescriptions and priorities. In order to better understand the meanings attached to work by those who undertake and supervise it, we also need to know about other life and leisure interests which might be compatible with work, compete with work or in contrast to management ambitions, even take priority over paid work. In other words, in contemporary socio-economic contexts, employment and household cannot be treated as separate dimensions but as 'two different worlds' (Campbell Clark, 2000) that can influence and impact upon each other. This chapter intends to examine these issues.

In order to more fully understand interrelations and dynamics between work and home, we first present the domestic and family circumstance profiles of employees in the two sectors. The contours and patterns of work are considered, the influences upon these (for example, decisions to work part-time) and the ways and extent to which these spill over into domestic life. We also examine the extent to which employees experience different levels of control over work life (enjoyed, for example, by some hard-to-replace software workers) and control over home life. Especially relevant factors are, on one hand, company policies and practices for work-life balance set against relatively inflexible shift and call-out patterns, paid and unpaid overtime arrangements, and informal extensions into domestic life through taking work home. Less tangible and more qualitative extensions into home life through the effects of work are also considered. In some cases, these extensions into domestic life may be experienced by employees as negative intrusions if they contribute to work-life tension, occupational stress or deterioration to other aspects of domestic life. In these circumstances, intrusion can be expressed in manifestations of post-work exhaustion, stress and sickness. The various strategies adopted by employees in order to cope with these spillovers are also considered in this chapter. The potential for spillover from home to work will also be reviewed. This exploration will also embrace the role of close and extended family and neighbours in supporting household employment strategies.

The relative importance of work is also examined through accounts of socializing and leisure. We assess the propensity by people to form attachments with their co-workers, and whether work relationships dominate people's leisure activities, suggesting more profound attachments to their employment and occupation. An alternative position to be considered is one of voluntary detachment from work and co-workers. On the basis of the accumulated evidence, we consider the extent to which work is indeed a central life interest in these new sectors of work.

Domestic and family circumstances

One of the major socio-economic changes to have occurred in recent years has been the growth of women in paid employment. In Britain, women now represent 46 per cent of the working population and over half (52 per cent) of women with children aged under five are at work, mostly in part-time jobs (EOC, 2005). If we consider that most households still tend to be made up of people related by marriage, partnership and kinship (McKie *et al.*, 1999), the relationship between household and paid work is clearly an important, and potentially delicate, one, especially as over three-quarters of men aged between 16 and 64 are also in employment. At the same time it appears that women's attachment (in a time sense, see Baldry *et al.*, 2005) to work is growing. Studies show that, in Britain, hours worked by women have tended to expand. Bunting (2004: 221) reports that numbers of women who work more than 48 hours grew by more than 50 per cent in the ten years to 2002, whilst numbers working more than 60 hours more than doubled to 13 per cent. The average working week for women also grew by 3.5 hours between 1998 and 2003. Clearly the potential for spillover from work to home life is apparent from these trends.

The greatest increase in women's employment has occurred among married women (particularly educated women) in households where the male partner was already in work, resulting in a growing economic polarization between two-earner and no-earner households (McRae, 1999: 6). These trends have presented two areas of potential social adjustment: the care of children and other dependents, and the division of and responsibility for domestic labour in general. Within the EU the European Foundation's survey showed that in 2000, 70 per cent of working couples had children still living at home, 24 per cent of whom were under six years old. Among working-age families in the UK with dependent children the proportion with two earners had risen to over 60 per cent by 1998 (McRae, 1999: 7). In practice there has usually been a prioritization of the male partner's career and earnings potential; women are still expected to give a lower priority to their own career interests and 'invest more resource in the collective project called "family"' (Hardill and Watson, 2004: 21). Findings from the recent EU-funded project *Household, Work, and Flexibility* that compared employment situations within the UK, Sweden, and the Netherlands has confirmed a strongly gendered division of labour between employment and household and caring responsibilities. In the UK, excessively long hours prevail for male employees (on average 43.5 hours per week); while women work much shorter hours than the EU average (Cousins and Tang, 2004: 535).

Hence, the culture of long hours that prevails in Britain remains largely confined to males working exceptionally long hours – one third of British men work more than the 48-hours threshold stipulated by the EU Working Time Directive – while their female partners work correspondingly less. Most mothers 'have already accommodated to the demands of family life by reducing the number of working hours and are therefore less likely to experience work and family conflict', with the result that only one in three mothers reports difficulties in balancing work and domestic responsibilities (Cousins and Tang, 2004: 541).

This does not indicate that all is necessarily well within British families. While balancing work and care demands quite well, women are less satisfied with their social life, as recent data show. Part-time employment may help women to juggle temporal aspects of their domestic responsibilities, but it also comes with low income and potentially reduced employment and career opportunities. In the *Household, Work and Flexibility* study cited above, British part-time employees worked an average of 17 hours per week and 72 per cent of these are in the lowest income quartile. It seems, then, that the traditional model of family – with males as main breadwinners and women taking over most of the domestic responsibilities – still prevails in Britain. Previous findings, such as those by Cousins and Tang (2004), suggest that working hours are not the main issue to British women and mothers, at least those in family units where a primary full-time wage is available. The present sample, of course, may not be representative of all sectors, in that most women in both occupations worked full-time. In order, therefore, to contextualise the strategies for balancing work and domestic life, an examination of working time in call centres and software will help provide a framework for analysing accommodations or tensions with domestic time.

Working time

In terms of working hours and provision of organizational flexibility, there were notable differences between the call centres and software houses. The call centre's integration of computer and telephonic technologies and the requirement to be engaged continuously in call-handling activities generates a unique work design. Most call centre operations prioritize call volumes, continuity of service, and measurement of operator performance, frequently combined with monitoring to ensure qualitative standards are maintained (Bain *et al.*, 2002; Taylor *et al.*, 2002). Though practice varied in the formal terms and provisions of working hours for their employees, a common characteristic in our case-studies was expansion of working time and a management expectation that operatives should be flexible in order to staff required shifts. Hence, at Moneyflow, during the research period, staff core hours were expanded from 8 am to 9 pm to 7 am to 11 pm for new staff. Saturdays were included as regular shifts. Existing staff worked 140 hours over a four-week period, with standard eight-hour shifts, though these could be adjusted either way by a maximum of two hours to 'meet business needs'. New staff had revised contracts with maximum ten hour shifts and management had discretion to vary start and finish times by up to two hours with 48 hours' notice. For all staff, there was a requirement to work additional hours, again in accordance with 'business needs'.

Shifts at the outsourcing company Thejobshop varied according to requirements of individual accounts, so that hours could fluctuate according to which account an employee was located and transfer between accounts was both expected and practiced. At Entcomm, contracts stated that staff were required to work a flexible 24-hour shift pattern over a seven day period and that shifts could be changed by management with 'reasonable notice'. Shift patterns at this company could be complex. Employees were hired at Holstravel on the basis of a 37.5 hour week over a five day period which 'may contain a provision for Sunday working'. In addition, in some areas of the call centre, a continuous four days on – four days off 12-hour shift system was implemented. A more detailed account of the frequent changes to shift patterns, even during the relatively short research period, can be found in Taylor *et al.* (2005).

By contrast, in the software houses, there was evidence of considerably more variability and reciprocal flexibility in work arrangements. This possibly reflected both the heavy demand for and limited supply of software specialists at the time of the research and the nature of the work, typified by project deadlines and speedy responses to client system emergencies. At

Omega, actual working hours operated in a 'peaks and troughs' system, with longer hours expected to meet project deadlines or to iron out operating problems. Part-time working to conform to family demands was encouraged, and a number of women voluntarily worked on a part-time basis. Opportunities for buying and selling holidays, again aimed at working parents, but open to all staff, was also introduced in the company. Beta operated a more formalized standard 42 hour week, inclusive of meal breaks. Beta, the only unionized software house, had an agreement with the union on formal flexitime systems, parental and dependant leave, and paid shift and unsocial hours allowances. Workshops on managing work and family were provided and the company was supportive toward teleworking arrangements. Pi employed staff on a standard five day 37.5 hour contractual basis, though flexibility was expected when required. A flexitime system had been introduced following a staff survey. No overtime was paid, but an 'on-call' allowance was payable. About four-fifths of software survey respondents reported that they were either moderately or extremely satisfied with intrinsic aspects of the job, hours of work and shifts.

It is not just the specified contractual hours which are relevant here. It is both the *actual* number of hours worked and, particularly, their *predictability* and *timing*, which are important in terms of compatibility with domestic life. In fact, both sectors show evidence of temporal extensions of work into the household, particularly for women. Table B1 in Appendix B summarizes these tangible extensions of work separately for men and women in call centres and software work, respectively. Focusing first on sectoral differences, shiftwork was much more common in call centres, with 29 per cent of respondents overall stating that they frequently or always work nights and 57 per cent that they frequently or always work Saturdays and Sundays. This contrasts with two and three per cent respectively amongst software employees. Paid overtime was relatively uncommon in both sectors, with only about a fifth of respondents in call centres and software firms stating that they worked paid overtime at all, and the majority of these working up to ten hours a week only. Qualitative answers in the questionnaire indicated differences in the reasons given for overtime, though. Of the call centre employees who did take paid overtime, over three-quarters did so because they needed the money, with some also suggesting that overtime was required for training purposes and to cover for staff shortages. The most common reason cited by the few software employees taking paid overtime was to meet project deadlines.

In common with other recent studies (for example, Hogarth *et al.*, 2000: 9), unpaid overtime was quite frequently reported, especially among software respondents (two-thirds of software employees compared to one-third of call centre employees). For those employees who reported working unpaid overtime, the main reason given in both call centres and software work by 43 per cent and 51 per cent respectively was to meet deadlines. Thirty per cent of software workers also responded that they wanted to get all their work done compared to only 14 per cent of call centre workers, which seems to imply an element of choice amongst the former not present for call centre workers. Instead, call centre employees were more likely to reply that they did not want to let down colleagues or clients. Other reasons for unpaid overtime cited by respondents also reflect the contrasting nature of work and degrees of worker autonomy in the two samples. Software employees mentioned that 'the work is cyclical and can't always be planned', '[the need] to keep organised', 'to ensure I don't lose my train of thought' and 'travelling from site or outside normal hours'. Call centre employees mentioned instead: 'to cover calls on busy lines', 'to show that I am interested in working', 'to get a permanent contract', 'asked by boss to lead by example', 'can't leave in the middle of customer interaction', and 'to show commitment'.

Over two-thirds of software employees reported having to take work home at least 'occasionally' compared to less than one-third of call centre employees. Although 68 per cent of the total call centre sample reported never having to take work home, when team leaders were examined separately, over 70 per cent, a similar percentage to software managers, reported having to do so at least occasionally.

Turning to gender differences for each sector, the first point to note is the reversal in gender distribution across the two sectors, with our survey respondents in call centres comprising 70 per cent women and in software companies 72 per cent men. Despite their relatively lower numbers within their workplaces, though, the software women differed little in terms of their working patterns (that is, in shift work and job status) from their male counterparts. In both sectors, however, women were significantly more likely to have care responsibilities and to work part-time and less likely to work unpaid overtime, all three of which are most likely related. The burden of domestic labour also was significantly more likely to fall on women regardless of type of work (see Table 6.1).

Additionally, in call centres women were more likely to have dependent children (there was no difference between men and women in software with respect to the latter), more likely to work weekends, and less likely, proportionately to their numbers, to occupy management positions. These differences are explored further in Chapter 7 and detailed in Table 7.1.

Disaggregated data on other characteristics indicate additional substantive differences. In call centres, older employees and those with dependents were more likely to take work home with them; and managers/supervisors were less likely to work weekends, though more likely to work unpaid overtime and to take work home. In software, as before, there was less differentiation, although again managers were more likely to work unpaid overtime and take work home. Thus, there is some evidence for work demands

Table 6.1 Household life: sample characteristics for men and women

	Call centres (N = 806)					Software (N = 303)				
	Men		Women			Men		Women		
	N	%	N	%	χ^2	N	%	N	%	χ^2
Care responsibilities										
Has dependents	58	25	178	32	4.06*	75	34	29	38	.410
Has care responsibilities	50	22	163	30	5.24*	42	19	26	34	7.31**
Contributes more than half or all to household income	103	45	166	30	14.95*	175	80	35	46	30.74***
Prime responsibility for:										
Children	58	22	163	30	5.24	42	19	26	34	7.31**
Cooking	73	32	300	55	34.98***	82	38	49	65	16.2***
Shopping	68	30	301	56	42.82***	73	34	46	62	17.7***
Cleaning	53	23	313	58	77.46***	59	28	45	59	24.41***
Washing/ironing	71	31	312	59	48.51***	64	30	49	65	28.36***
Total	231	30	550	70		220	74	76	26	

Note: *p < .05 **p < .01 ***p < .001

increasing for women, older employees, those with dependents, and managers, particularly in call centres. An example was offered by a call centre team leader who described the level of expectation associated with supervisory jobs:

> You have got to take some work with us and do extra work at home ... so it doesn't bother me that much ... I don't feel resentful. I knew that when I took the job on. It's not a 9–5, you have to take work home and finish it off the next day (Moneyflow, female team manager; M-I-09).

Such acceptance of an open-ended commitment to work may surprise at first glance. Perhaps less surprising is the case of software developers, who may interpret the long hours, temporal and functional flexibility as part of an investment into developing their own set of competencies and skills. For call centre operators, however, the situation is somewhat more diverse. While a large proportion of these rather reluctantly concede to work long hours or unpaid overtime, others, particularly at supervisory and management level, seem less resentful. Here, as in the case of most software developers, concessions to organizational demands for flexibility and extra work are accepted as part of the job and point to different attitudes towards the elastic demands of the contemporary employment contract. Given that less than a third of call centre workers envisage a long-term career within their current job or company, it seems, therefore, that extra contractual commitments and duties are accepted, albeit reluctantly, as part of a 'vocational' attitude to work at least as far as supervisors and managers are concerned.

Inter-role conflict and control over work and home life

Following Campbell Clark, we define balance 'as satisfaction and good functioning at work and at home, with a *minimum of role conflict*' (2000: 751, emphasis added). In order to better understand inter-relations between work and home, further analysis of potential impositions from either domain is necessary. From both directions there will be a fluidity of demands which can impinge upon the other. Domestically, there can be family circumstances, especially involving care provision for children and other dependants, which have the potential to change at short notice and which demand immediate attention. Formally, the relative certainty associated with earlier models of fairly static contractual temporal working arrangements has remained unchanged. The full-time employment rates in both sectors (86 per cent call centres; 93 per cent software) are significantly higher than the UK-average of 62 per cent (European Commission, 2004). Informally, however, this apparent stasis has conceded ground to more flexible conditions of work and employment, though these were manifested rather differently in the two sectors.

These distinctive labour process patterns were accompanied by different employee perspectives on the extent to which work impinged upon domestic lives and *vice versa*. The time-flexible regimes and shift patterns in the four call centres was perceived by employees to be more of a hindrance than a help in organizing their domestic affairs. An instance of interference with family life was illustrated by an employee at Moneyflow as follows:

> [the shift pattern] gets in the way quite a lot. It's not very flexible at the moment. Just really because I've moved into the new team and find I'm doing an awful lot of late shifts like one to nine. Which really I don't find it very convenient because I get the bus now and I don't get home until after ten at night ... I don't like my mum to be alone until that time herself ... (Moneyflow, female customer adviser; M-HI-03)

In Moneyflow, another operative complained that:

> They have sent a message can we stay and do overtime and take half an hour for our lunch. Just leave a bit of paper on your desk...They want you to take half an hour for your lunch and stay and do a couple of hours overtime. That would be a 12 hour day... They want us to be

100% flexible but they are not flexible in return (Moneyflow, female customer adviser; M-I-13).

Shortness of notice was also a problem at Holstravel:

> We get our shifts out once a month and you usually get it like two days before they are about to start the next month which is pretty annoying ... because you don't know what shift you are working...You can't sort of plan your life, you know (Holstravel, male sales consultant; H-I-23).

It seems, however, that while working commitments are extensive and while work assumes priority in instances of imminent conflict it may only occasionally severely impact upon the work-life-balance of most employees in our software and call centre companies. As Table 6.2 illustrates, only 'less than occasionally' does work get in their way of spending enough time with partners and friends. Yet this does not necessarily imply that work arrangements allow for a smooth accommodation of caring responsibilities or the absence of any frictions between work and household duties. Inter-role conflict, such as that experienced between parenting and paid employment (Barling & Sorensen, 1997), does indeed exist, as one junior manager in Entcomm testified:

> I've been on secondment for two months to do this constant backshift ... and they pay me quite a lot more money to do it but the money's not enough, because my son was saying to me the other day, a couple of weeks ago, Daddy, I don't like these shifts you are working because I never see you...(Entcomm, male team leader; E-HI-04).

While the above narratives indicate that company work regimes that combine flexible shift patterns and weekend working at short notice with tight staffing and high labour turnover can indeed cause practical as well as emotional problems for call centre staff with caring responsibilities, this does not necessarily give rise to severe concerns across the whole sample of respondents, as the rather moderate responses represented in Table 6.2 indicate.

So, while workers can feel exhausted and stressed as a result of their job, this is unlikely to solely arise from inter-role conflict with caring responsibilities – particularly since only about a third of the workforce surveyed in both sectors have such responsibilities. At least as far as call centre operators are concerned, Taylor *et al.* (2003: 449) have convincingly argued that much of the stress caused is rather work-induced and results from a combination of 'targets, call volumes, repetitiveness, and lack of breaks'. Yet this raises the question as to what causes the appreciable levels of stress and exhaustion found in the sample. Drawing on the data, it appears that extra-

Table 6.2 Work-life interface

	Call centres (N = 806)				Software (N = 303)			
	'Never'/ 'Occasionally'		'Quite often'/ 'All of the time'		'Never'/ 'Occasionally'		'Quite often'/ 'All of the time'	
	N	%	N	%	N	%	N	%
I have to take work home with me	767	96	34	4	266	88	37	12
I think about work when not there	525	65	281	35	138	46	164	54
I feel exhausted after work	480	59	328	41	177	59	124	41
Work problems keep me awake at night	687	85	118	15	264	87	39	13
My job prevents me spending enough time with family/partner	611	76	190	24	246	81	56	19
My work prevents me from spending enough time with my friends	598	74	208	26	260	86	43	14
Household responsibilities interfere with the time I can devote to work	784	97	23	3	285	95	16	5
Frequency with which I feel stressed in my job	208	26	361	44	93	31	99	33

work commitments and tangible as well as intangible 'spillover' of work into the life-world seems significant in this context.

Expectations of unpaid overtime, for example, were pervasive in call centres, although they were not identified as being as disruptive as shift working. When asked for confirmation of whether people working beyond their contractual working time could not claim time back in lieu, one respondent replied:

> That's right. Sometimes I have been an hour and a half over my time. I have still to get home. I have kids to look after [Holstravel, female sales consultant; H-HI-29].

It seems, then, that there is a normative organizational expectation for an attendance commitment by employees, who at least to some extent concede, albeit reluctantly, to this organizational expectation, notwithstanding the potential feelings of guilt and tensions aroused.

In contrast, the main distinguishing disruptive features for software workers were the long or uneven hours; expectation to undertake work when necessary; and the need to be on call for at least some engineers. At Beta, customer support required '24-hours a day, seven days a week and 365 days a year' operation and support services were guaranteed around the clock, using a rota system of on-calls, with the result that, for the staff affected, there may be as many as 20–40 call-outs per month. A Pi engineer commented that 'he certainly has no nine to five job' and often had to travel to client sites, leaving for an early morning flight and returning late. Employees usually took laptops and pagers home with them for use on call-outs and emergencies. One Beta newcomer pointed out that while electrical engineers (her previous experience) tended to be 'nine to five' people, software engineers seemed to be working all the time. Initially she felt embarrassed and irritated when, at about five p.m., she was the only one who wanted to leave the office. When asked whether work interferes with private life, a married male engineer pointed out that:

> I'm on call 24 hours, so I can get paged in the middle of the night and I have to get up and work ... but that will finish in June which is just nice timing for us with our family starting ... (Beta, male software engineer; B-HI-04).

A software engineer, in his description of being on call, offered further insights into the potential for work to disturb domestic life:

> ...I have nights like I had last night where I was actually paged six times in the course of the night although I only had to respond to two of those but it still disrupts your sleep...I was paged at midnight and again at three and that really wakes you up especially if you are going to try and then get up at a reasonable hour to be in early in the morning (Beta, male applications support analyst; B-HI-10).

The same engineer recalled the disruptive effect of call outs on his marriage: 'I was married for a brief period, eleven months it lasted, and yes, it (call-out) had a fairly notable effect on the marriage at the time'.

Thus, around-the-clock operations in conjunction with a call-out system can indeed cause inter-role conflict, as the case of Beta demonstrates. More positively, though, in all software houses, part-time working was readily accommodated and staff often had discretion, within the parameters of their projects, to work informal flexible hours or if practicable to work at home:

> I think Beta are actually quite good at being flexible and allowing people to work part-time if they want to. I know it's certainly not a problem for

returning mothers to actually dictate pretty much the hours they want to work (Beta, male team leader; B-HI-08).

At Omega, one engineer commented:

> There is a sort of unofficial flexitime. As long as you make the 37 hours, it's usually alright, although people don't tend to start too late. We have 90 minute lunches and nobody says anything. I decide when I take my lunch (Omega, female software engineer; O-I-04).

From these comments, there was a greater feeling of both working long hours as a concomitant feature of a professionalized life coupled with an ability to adjust flexibility to the individual requirements of employees when the need arose. Flexibility could be applied both to cope with temporary domestic demands but more systematically by arranging work to adjust to changes in family circumstances, for example, by working part-time following maternity leave.

'There really wasn't a life': Intangible intrusions into domestic life

One quality of contemporary working life, alongside the sometimes long and changing working times, is its intensity (Green, 2001), accompanied by experiences which though less tangible than working hours are clearly linked with them and can also impact upon people's domestic lives. Table 6.2 shows mean ratings of employee perceptions of the work-life interface for each sector, and indicates some notable consequences of work-to-home spillover in both sectors – relatively frequent feelings of exhaustion and not being able to 'switch off' after work, and, more seriously, frequent feelings of stress and, occasionally, even adverse health consequences. Nearly half the respondents in call centres and about a third in software experienced feelings of stress quite often or all the time. Additionally, over a third of call centres employees and more than half of those working in software firms reported thinking about the job quite often or all the time when away from the work-place. Further analysis of this data reported elsewhere and controlling for multiple possible influences (see Hyman *et al.*, 2003) indicated that levels of reported stress rose for managers in software, to 46 per cent, and for those with care responsibilities in call centres, to 52 per cent. For both sectors, respondents who reported taking work home and working weekends were also more likely to report feeling exhausted or stressed. In all cases, it was clear that being in management positions was likely to lead to increased feelings of stress and exhaustion and as well, managers were more likely to take work home.

In summary, the quantitative data demonstrate that work and home are not separate domains but sustain fluid and dynamic boundaries for which establishing normative balance can present considerable conceptual and practical difficulties in different work settings. The findings also suggest that hours of working are becoming more elastic and employees often take work home or think about work whilst away from the workplace. Worry and stress over work are commonplace. These factors collectively help to blur demarcations – at least the temporal and emotional – between work and home, and not only in the case of the software worker, where greater work-life overlap may be expected.

Interviews offered further significant insights into the potential of intangible elements of work to compromise the frontiers between work and domestic life. A team leader in a call centre expressed her concerns:

> Worry about work? Sometimes I do, yes... It's always at the back of my mind, have I done everything before I left, that sort of thing (Moneyflow, female team leader; M-I-09).

Software developers reported similar experiences, citing problems in 'switching off':

> I think if you're a developer it can be a bit difficult to suddenly switch off because once you start the wheels turning on a problem and you're trying to figure out how you're going to fix it, it just stays there (Pi, female software programmer; P-I-10).

This quote is revealing in another sense, as it points towards the process character of much knowledge work. Analogous to production in process industries (e.g. the chemical industry) knowledge creation seems to follow its own logic and thus largely eschews attempts of direct intervention or manipulation. This implies that the processes cannot be suspended or terminated nor easily resumed at will. It implies, further, that the very nature of knowledge work helps to determine the boundaries and that it is less susceptible to temporal or spatial manipulation. Consequently, part of the spillover generated in software is process induced instead of organizationally imposed or self-determined.

With approximately 40 per cent of both call centre and software employees reporting quite often or always feeling exhausted after work these manifestations of physical and mental spillover from work were frequently raised in interviews:

> I know if I do two long 12 hour days in a row then my brain is mince for the rest of the week because I'm just exhausted. I don't like that. It's not on. It's not healthy (Beta, female software engineer, B-I-03).

One way in which stress might express itself was demonstrated in an interview with a call centre customer adviser, whose all day telephone use appeared to have affected his social life:

> I used to go home at night and didn't want to speak for a couple of hours, you know. I had been talking all day on the phone, you know. If the phone went at home I didn't want to answer, you know, because you had been speaking all day (Moneyflow, male financial adviser; M-I-02).

As workplace pressures grow the stressful effects can accumulate:

> It's got more difficult as the years in Beta have gone on. It reached a point about a year ago when there wasn't really a life, the mobile was left on the whole time... (Beta, male technical architect; B-I-19).

Coping with the demands

From the above accounts, distinguishing factors derived from technology and labour market differences between the sectors are plainly apparent. Software workers enjoyed more autonomy over hours and patterns of work, with voluntary and temporary part-time options and teleworking available. The majority of software employees were men and long hours were treated by them more as a physical challenge and occupational expectation rather than domestic issue. In this context, long-hours, exhaustion and stress are not so much imposed by the employing organization but embedded as part of its sectoral working culture. Pushing body and mind beyond limits seems part of a response that seeks recognition from peers and employers as a means for securing self-identity.

Employees in call centres were subject to stringent management and organizational controls, which meant that balancing domestic with work obligations was a more sensitive and complex process with little scope for employees to make adjustments through work to help meet domestic contingencies. Indeed, work-based approaches for flexibility *for* employees (rather than *by* them) in call centres enjoyed little company support and in consequence tended to be fragmentary and informal. There was some informal shift swapping among operatives, though finding a 'partner' at weekends could be difficult, for example at Entcomm, where a formal process for nominating individual shifts was not recognized by the company.

A more formal workplace approach could be job sharing, though little evidence for this practice was found in any of the four call centres. Where it had been attempted, it has been either through the direct initiative of individual members of staff, or encouraged by management in order to cover awkward shifts, as explained by an Entcomm operative:

> ...it's job sharing that suits them ... If you are prepared to work one to nine they will give you job share. (Entcomm, female customer service adviser; E-HI-02).

Other, more individual, approaches to deal with work pressures include informal absence or more rarely, a simple refusal to take on extra responsibilities. After being told by his son that he never sees his father, the operator at Entcomm refused to continue with the better paid but disruptive backshift, despite the pleas of his manager that he should continue. There were no instances in any of the interviews of staff working at home instead of working in the office, a not unexpected finding for call centres. As we have seen, there was evidence, however, of team leaders and more senior managers taking extra work home after their regular work hours.

For software workers, longer-term workplace coping strategies include part-time working whilst for more short-term demands, flexible workpatterns, involving either home working or manipulating working hours, were utilized and accepted by management in return for employee commitment to work flexibly when required.

A team leader at Beta pointed out that:

> I guess the phrase I would use is you are responsible for your own hours ... There is nobody looking over your shoulder ... so you are trusted to work your own hours and I think that is probably better (Beta, male team leader; B-I-08).

A Beta software engineer also demonstrated the choices available to him when asked how he uses the home terminal provided by the company:

> I work from home now and again depending on the circumstances. I use it to suit me. I don't want to work from home full time, because it suits me coming in here (Beta, male software developer; B-I-02).

At Omega, similar flexibility was offered:

> ...their full week is $37\frac{1}{4}$ I think it is. When I started with them I said that I couldn't – you see I live in Dunblane and I have a family, so 35 hours was all that I could manage to work so that's what I'm contracted to do (Omega, female senior systems builder; O-I-13).

With little scope or encouragement for workplace support for coping with domestic responsibilities, most call centre employees with dependents relied on a combination of domestic strategies involving the immediate household, support from neighbours and extended family, and more rarely institutional arrangements, for example, for childcare. Male partners, where part of the household, provided some support:

> There is an equal share. Basically my husband and I are both sort of taxi drivers for the kids now ... we both share whatever's to be done in the house. The mornings that I'm off will normally be my sort of housework mornings. G does all the ironing. I never ever iron (Moneyflow, female financial planning adviser; M-HI-18).

Nevertheless, the most common and consistently applied coping strategy for respondents with care responsibilities was reliance upon extended family, with about half of survey respondents pointing to family as a source of care provision. The interviews confirm the key role of the grandmother within the family network:

> Well, my Mum takes the kids for me. She knows when he (partner) is on standby ... so normally she will say bring them down the night before to save them getting up in the morning (Entcomm, female customer service adviser, E-HI-02).

The same employee also confirmed that 'Mum' takes the children if there is an in-service day at school or a similar event, but also confirmed her husband's role in taking the children to school in the morning, though 'that's one of the things that annoys me in winter because [her son] is really in school at about 8.25, so he is there quite a bit before the school goes in but...'

A call centre sales assistant at Moneyflow made a similar point:

> My Mum gets the girls three days a week for me and watches them from three till five until my husband comes in from work. My mother in law gets them two days a week. So the two grans are widows, live on their own and it means that they enjoy... (Moneyflow, female, customer service adviser; M-HI-18).

The extensive use of family, neighbourhood or friends for dealing with the demands of homework and caring are quite consistent with findings in other EU countries that caution against dismissing a model of family as a cellular microcosm of society too hastily (Cousins and Tang, 2004). Very little use was made by interviewees of institutional childcare which was often rejected on the grounds of expense, or less often, because childcare times did not conform with shift working times. When used, it tended to be adopted as a temporary solution to immediate child caring problems.

In this context, we might conclude that new versus traditional forms of life and family ties are represented respectively by software and call centre work. The rigidity of the work regime within call centres suggests more reliance and dependence upon family and other support networks; whereas the flexibility of software employment opens up greater chances for self-realization. In the face of imposed work patterns and lack of institutional support call centre operators construct their domestic lives as a form of basic network that allows for sustaining (an industrial) life, as it was in the past. Yet the 'freedom' that software workers enjoy may be illusory and comes at a price: the price of increased levels of stress and self-exploitation; the price of having to progress in a demanding and fluctuating occupational culture.

Compared with call centre employees, there were two key differences for software workers. First, the availability of workplace provision, formal or informal, meant that less reliance was needed in seeking domestic remedies. Second, three-quarters of software workers were men, who unlike the women in the call centres, rarely, if ever in our interviews raised the question of coping with domestic chores or emergency caring demands. Children, where they existed, were scarcely mentioned by (male) respondents. For women, however, the second shift (Hochschild, 1989) was in evidence:

> I seem to have to do most of the washing up and the ironing, all these household chores.... It is certainly difficult even if you consider yourself quite liberated. I think the onus is always back on the women if the man isn't going to do it then the woman is going to do it. The buck stops here if you like (Omega, female business manager; O-I-09).

A part-time engineer at Omega described the reality of her ostensibly attractive long weekends:

> I work four days a week. "Long" weekends. Friday morning is taken up with the weekly shopping, children home from school at midday and I look after other people's children on a Friday afternoon so it's not a day off as such (Omega, female senior software analyst; O-I-14).

Organizational provisions

A key question for this chapter concerns the ways in which coping strategies are identified and developed by employees to deal with work-home responsibilities and tensions. Negative spillover from work to home was evident in both tangible (e.g. shiftworking) and intangible (e.g. exhaustion) ways, though spillover can be experienced differently according to sectoral or organizational context, where the nature of the product and associated labour processes are key factors. Call centres are typified by overt organizational controls complemented by rigid (though expanding) shift systems and rotas, often involving evening and weekend working. The dominant management imperative was to staff phones to ensure maintenance of an efficient service to clients, sometimes on a 24 hour basis.

Notwithstanding stated employer policy commitment to family-friendly employment, in some cases responses from employees indicated that these operational demands were accompanied with few practical concessions from their companies to employees' domestic demands or pressures. Table 6.3 shows this especially in the case of call centres, where employees were afforded significantly less influence and control than software workers in managing their non-work commitments. Software workers were more likely to report supervisors who were supportive of personal demands, time flexibility, not being expected to put job before family in order to advance in the company, and personal influence over their work-family arrangements. The analysis reported in Hyman *et al.* (2003) also shows that having such control is related to lower reported adverse effects of the job on health and feelings of exhaustion, even when employees work shifts.

Thus, the problem of lack of control over the work-life boundary is acute for call centre workers. Here, there is little obvious permeability between work and home, with each domain treated as segmented (and potentially competing). We saw in Chapter 4 that call centre respondents infrequently chose to socialize with work colleagues out of work, and, in interviews frequent reference was made to attempts at 'shutting off' on leaving work, though in practice, the intrusive nature of call centre work often made this difficult to achieve. Call centre work is generally low paid, low status with few opportunities for development or career advancement (Belt, 2002; Belt *et al.*, 1999) and of course, the majority of employees in the present study

Table 6.3 Family-friendly culture

	Call centres (N = 806)		Software (N = 303)	
	N	%	N	%
	'Strongly agree'/'Agree'			
My immediate boss is quite sympathetic about personal matters	538	66%	239	79%
It is hard to get time off during work to take care of personal or family matters	189	23%	7	2%
To get ahead in the company employees are expected to put their jobs before family	264	33%	53	18%
	'Quite a lot'/'A great deal'			
Influence over workplace family friendly arrangements	88	11%	50	18%

were women, as is commonly the case in call or contact centres. Employees were expected to work shifts, often on a rotating basis and sometimes changed at short notice. Whilst individual supervisors may be sympathetic to employees' domestic demands, the nature of the work and their subordinated status provided employees with little control over work and domestic boundaries, and coupled with high labour turnover, this ensured that there was little organizational scope for employees to construct or manipulate work-derived strategies to combat spillover. For employees with caring responsibilities in particular, this lack of organizational provision required the development of coping mechanisms as best they could from their domestic base.

Interestingly, though three-quarters of call-centre workers in our sample were women, several with caring responsibilities, the lack of practical organizational support seems to run counter to studies which suggests a positive association between proportions of women workers and employer provision of family-friendly policies (Goodstein, 1995). Rather, our findings are consistent with the argument that employers' perceptions of a link with productivity provide a more likely predictor of provision of family-friendly practices (Morgan and Milliken, 1993; Osterman, 1995).

In contrast, the majority of software workers were men, whose professional status was reflected in their pay, work autonomy and elevated status, assisted by working in an expanding and developing sector. These workers were able to exercise a measure of control over work-domestic boundaries, both through formal provision in terms of part-time contracts and informally, through adjusting working times. Software production does not impose the same spatial and temporal demands on labour. Whilst teamworking is common and project deadlines need to be met, the execution of knowledge work was far less constrained than in call centres. For software workers, the work environment was more open to manipulation and boundary flexibility by employees. Though spillover was evident in long and sometimes intense working hours, work regimes were flexible. Further, the software market was growing at about 15 per cent annually at the time of the study and markets for software workers were tight. Flexible working arrangements such as part-time working were formally accommodated by employers and working times could often be informally adjusted by employees to comply with domestic demands. Even so, this partial control is exerted within a broader context which allows workers to decide on when they work, but rather less on the quantity of work or the conditions under which it is undertaken, suggesting that this control may be less substantial than is sometimes associated with professionalized knowledge workers.

From these observations, it is apparent that formal and informal organizational accommodation to domestic demands differs according to sectoral and product requirements. For employees, this has obvious implications. In call centres, where work is routine and largely unskilled, we found little evidence of practical organizational support. A related factor in the development of coping strategies was clearly gender. From both surveys and interviews it is clear that irrespective of sector or working hours, women take responsibility for more routine domestic responsibilities regardless of their occupation (see Table 6.1) and hence work spillover compounds the demands placed upon them. Women in call centres, with little employer support, often had to rely upon a combination of family and social networks to deal with childcare, which usually excluded institutional provision on grounds of cost. Men in the software companies had fewer difficulties in organizing their work-home environment, both because of the informal and formal organizational mechanisms available to them but also because of supportive domestic circumstances in many cases. Despite these more favourable work contexts, the situation for women in organizing their domestic lives could be problematic. We saw from interviews above, that shortened paid working weeks were often burdened with additional caring responsibilities. Further, as we show in the following chapter, the prospects for part-time women in a male-dominated occupation were not always favourable.

Centrality of work

Central to contemporary management and knowledge economy debates is the priority assigned to the role of human capital. Similarly, much HRM rhetoric is directed toward the metaphorical capture of the whole person in terms of demonstrable commitment to the employing organization. But this begs an important question which needs to be confronted empirically: how central to people's lives is the actual work that they do? The discussion above indicates that many employees, especially in call centres, reluctantly rather than voluntarily, accede to the demands of their workplace, suggesting that orientations toward work may be more complex than desired by employers or anticipated from management prescriptions.

Mean ratings on work value items from the employee survey are shown in Table 6.4. These help confirm that work is not the most important aspect in these employees' lives. Respondents in both sectors indicated that their major satisfactions in life come from their families or their leisure rather than work, although, perhaps not surprisingly, this was more the case for call centre employees than software. Software employees were comparatively more likely than call centre workers to agree that they were so involved in their work that it was often hard for them to distinguish the boundaries between work and non-work, a finding which is probably reflective of the contrasting nature of the work in the two sectors.

Table 6.4 Work values (percentage responding 'agree'/'strongly agree')

	Call centres (N = 806)		Software (N = 303)	
	N	%	N	%
I'm so involved in my work it is often hard to say where work ends & leisure begins	91	11	46	15
Most of my personal life goals are connected to work	126	16	57	19
If you have enough money there's no reason to work	218	27	69	23
The main reason I work is to afford a good social life	284	35	96	32
My leisure time matters to me more than work	449	56	139	46
The major satisfactions in my life come from my family	611	76	193	64

The qualitative dimension to the study provides valuable support to the survey findings. A call centre Customer Adviser perhaps best summed up this position when she said:

> The job is just a means of getting money... just now my main things are my boyfriend, my house, my family, my hobbies, my [OU] studying, you know. The work probably comes underneath all of that (Moneyflow, female customer adviser; M-I-15).

While workers might take work home, stay the extra hours, even think about work when not there, workers in both sectors made a clear distinction between their personal goals and the work-related goals of the organization. Even a team leader, the new level of first line management in many workplaces, maintained:

> I think you work at a career to make sure you get the things in life that you want to get. But I have a family to think about, you know, and I have got a lot of friends. My working life has got its place in my life and that's where it lies (Moneyflow, female team leader; M-I-06).

Social networks and occupational community

A central theme of this book has been to examine the significance of work to people's broader experience of life, and this significance has been explored from a number of directions. One further aspect of this examination is the extent of integration or distance, whether emotional or spatial, of work from other significant aspects of living. These linkages are based on the 'notoriously open-ended concept' of community (Salaman, 1971: 389). Salaman identified a number of potential community relationships. The first entails a deliberate separation between work and domestic lives, founded on work which holds primarily instrumental and little intrinsic value to participants. Community in this case is primarily *domestically* focused around family, friends and locality.

On the other hand, specific factors can serve to integrate work with life to form the basis of an *occupational* community in which 'the worlds of work and non-work are closely inter-dependent, each world permeating and affecting the other' (Salaman, 1974: 45). In an earlier analysis, Salaman (1971) identified these integrating factors as self-image, values and relationships. Self image applies when people identify themselves strongly or primarily through their occupation or profession, for example as a miner, steel worker or doctor. Values are represented through codes of behaviour in terms of supporting colleagues, acknowledging occupational standards, observing solidarity and performing rituals. Relationships refer to the extent to which out-of work linkages and friendships are founded upon work-based ties and occupational inclusiveness. The more potent each of these elements, the greater the sense and cohesiveness of the occupational community.

Nevertheless, under specific circumstances of high degrees of mutual employee support between workplace and local community, reinforced perhaps by spatial or occupational isolation, workplace risk and hardship and where employers can exert control over the supply of labour, a deeper and possibly more oppositional sense of identity and community, drawing from both work and location may be experienced, as described in a number of classical accounts of industrial work (see e.g. Dennis *et al.*, 1956; Brown and Brannen, 1970; Salaman, 1974). Many areas of industrial Scotland, for example, shipbuilding (Clydeside) and steelmaking (Motherwell) had identifiable patterns of interlocking domestic and work community based on location, collectivism and political radicalism. As we have seen, the industries which supported these traditional communities have declined and in some cases been extinguished: does this mean that these configurations of community have also been changed?

Taking Salaman's analysis further, occupational community can be subdivided into employer-derived and profession-derived, though sometimes distinctions between the two become blurred (e.g. accountants employed in large companies). Basically, work elements can be overlaid with more binding factors which aim to reinforce workplace cohesiveness and community spirit. As discussed earlier, contemporary business emphases on service quality and product specificity encourage employers to cultivate high levels of occupational identification and work-based community through techniques such as team-working. This is not a new approach. Part of Elton Mayo's rationale to encourage positive social relationships at work was based on his interpretation of the decline of traditional community and its values with the ascendancy of mass industrialization. His prescription was to instil compliant employer-facing normative values through managerially-induced workplace communities (Rose, 1988). As we saw in Chapter 4, part of the HRM 'mission' is to develop work-based community through commitment and promoting a sense of common endeavour to the occupation, job, team and employer. Overall satisfaction derives from both performing the job well as a member of the work community and the emotional rewards associated with membership and these serve to influence the meaningfulness of the work experience. The degree of control over the job will also be relevant. Where these are positively experienced, we can anticipate high degrees of work attachment.

Chapter 5 demonstrated that an alternative source for occupational community derives from internal membership of a specified occupation itself and draws strongly upon the same components of self-image, values and relationships. However, these are constructed, interpreted, and in some cases, policed by the members of the community themselves rather than by employers, from whom the members will maintain a degree of independence in constructing and progressing both occupation and career. Professions offer the clearest example of internally-developed community.

Our initial thoughts were that call-centre employees would be more likely to be orientated toward membership of a more domestically focused community, based on desired separation of home and leisure from work and in consequence employees would tend to seek and find contingent work convenient for and in close proximity to their community. Conversely, we expected software workers to be more professionally orientated, as indicated in Chapter 4, where software commitment was clearly directed toward the task, team and customer rather than to the employer. For software workers, there would also be a weaker orientation and fewer membership attachments to domestic community and they would be likely to demonstrate more mobility in relation to employer or location. They would therefore be more likely to move residence according to the attractiveness of the work and its prospects, motivated by expectations of occupational advancement and helped by their favourable labour market position, relative youth and fewer non-work attachments. Similarly, we also expected a higher incidence of travel independence and car ownership among software workers. Also, there may be low interest in out-of-work activities; on the other hand, more control over the timing of and personal access to work may offer opportunities to pursue leisure interests.

We first looked at travel to work times and modes of transport. We expected call centre workers to be more closely embedded in their local communities and therefore have shorter travel to work times and possibly greater reliance on communal or public transport. Conversely, requirements of shift-working and inconvenient working hours may make call centre employees more reliant on personal means of transport, even if their travel distances would be shorter. In fact, though there were differences between the sectors, these were not especially marked: mean travel to work times for call centre employees were 32 minutes compared with 37 minutes for software workers. Nevertheless, twice as many call centre employees used the bus (17 per cent) as did software workers, and there were considerable variations in car use among different call centres, For example, at Moneyflow, located centrally in Glasgow, over two-thirds of respondents relied on public transport, compared with ten per cent or less at the relatively isolated Entcomm and Holstravel call centres, where four-fifths of respondents used their own transport. Shared car use was 13 per cent for call centre workers, double that of software respondents, which may hint at a more collective use of resources.

Another indicator of local community attachment is provided by experience of earlier jobs. Previous jobs in the locality might suggest closer attachment, whilst evidence of greater mobility could be related to willingness and capacity to pursue a greater spread of occupational opportunities irrespective of location. For call centre workers, 91 per cent of the 798 respondents who had worked elsewhere had worked previously in the Glasgow/Edinburgh areas, with little variation between companies. This figure dropped to 71 per cent for the 299 software workers, though with a considerable spread between companies. These figures would suggest that call centre workers are more likely to restrict their occupational sights to narrower, more familiar geographical territory than do software workers.

Domestic and family configurations also differed. Only 14 per cent of call centre workers lived alone compared with 21 per cent of software respondents, another two-thirds of whom lived with a partner. A quarter of call centre respondents lived with parents, reflecting both numbers of students as well as possibly income and traditions of staying in the family home for Scottish young people from working-class backgrounds. Only six per cent of software workers lived with their parents. About one-third of respondents in both sectors have dependents for which they claim prime responsibility. Socializing patterns tended to reflect the family orientations of both sets of workers. Most frequent socializing in both sectors with immediate family (81 per cent call centres and 86 per cent software) and other family was reported than with colleagues from work. Non-work friends were also a frequent reported source of social contact. Frequency of contact does not of course imply intensity, and potential social contact could undoubtedly be constrained by work obligations (shifts etc) and family responsibilities.

Almost invariably, call centre work was expressed in transactional or instrumental terms, as a prime source of income, a 'necessary evil', rather than as a source or expression of more binding social or emotional relationships or of occupational identity. When asked her order of priorities, a call centre worker at Entcomm responded:

> My family comes first, then my friends, then my work... it is a necessity (Entcomm, female customer service adviser; E-I-01).

An operator at Entcomm emphasized the essentially economic, though somewhat joyless, nature of his relationship to work:

> It just pays the bills to be honest. In an ideal world obviously it would be something that you would really like doing, that you really enjoy doing, but in respect of work I don't know what I would enjoy...(Entcomm, male customer service adviser; E-I-18).

This sense of alienation was expressed in even starker terms by another telesales operator at Entcomm:

> Probably everything in my life means more to me than my work, you know (Entcomm, female, retentions adviser; E-HI-19).

In terms of social relationships, there was little evidence of voluntary socializing among fellow call-centre workers, with the possible exceptions of prior acquaintances working as colleagues or in some cases where team members live in the same locality. Further, some interviews suggest that where work is perceived negatively, as we have seen with call centres, the prospect of co-worker contact may even act as a disincentive to follow social and leisure activities. One adviser rapidly terminated her membership of a fitness club when she discovered that:

> ....it was just full of people from work which spoilt the whole idea of going there really; you wanted to get away from people that you are working with and just go somewhere that you could just either work out on your own or relax on your own or meet new people but it was everybody from work (Entcomm, female service adviser; E-HI-03).

When questioned about socializing with colleagues, a male team leader at the same company responded with familiar feelings of detachment and dissociation:

> Unless it's a works do or my team's won something I don't socialize with the work ... as soon as I walk out of there I've got my mind onto

something else... When I walk out of that door they are not paying me any more (Entcomm, male team leader; E-I-04).

This approach of 'keeping work just a wee bit separate' was commonly reported among call centre respondents, confirming our earlier finding that such work is perceived largely in extrinsic or instrumental terms.

For software workers, in contrast, a feeling of centrality of work was pronounced, also finding expression in choice of home. With these workers our impression of choosing home to integrate with work and of relatively sparse links with domestic community was confirmed in a number of interviews:

> We'd a big list of this kind of area. I wanted to be this side of Glasgow. I was working in Glasgow, so I wanted to be fairly close to there. We just kind of mapped things on transport and how nice the area was (Beta, male software engineer; B-HI-09).

Any involvement outside of work was limited. After six years in a city-centre apartment another software developer at the same company still has not made any links outside of work:

> I hardly ever see my neighbours...Most of them are working. So they are all like me. They come home in the evening, they've got a limited amount of time ... they haven't idle time to just sit and chit chat (Beta, male services manager; B-HI-01).

By contrast with call-centre employees, voluntary *work-related* social networks and a sense of occupational cohesion or distinctiveness among software workers appear to extend beyond the immediate boundaries of the workplace, as shown by these comments from Omega and Gamma. In the latter case, realization of the potential implications of these relations was noted:

> I am quite happy to spend my home time researching stuff, because I'm interested in it... Social life? Yes, I got a lot of friends as I say from University and friends from high school and I have a social life with people from here, but whether they are friends or colleagues or somewhere in between. I don't sort of group them altogether in different categories (Omega, male software engineer; O-I-05).

> I think what's kept people in is the kind of atmosphere that they have with friends in the company...you do eventually kind of sit back and think I've given months in total of my own personal time over the years and got zero back for it. That's actually not very bright (Gamma, male IT consultant/team leader; G-I-11).

Other respondents also felt that the relationship between work and non-work was closely integrated:

> [Work life and home life] are far too much linked. That's probably wrong. I think because I moved from Glasgow to Edinburgh and I didn't know anyone in Edinburgh, so everyone I know in Edinburgh pretty well comes from my work environment, so the two are absolutely dependent on each other. If I left the job I'd really be struggling in Edinburgh (Pi, male pre-sales consultant; P-I-21).

A husband and wife, who both work at Beta, reviewed their inter-related social lives in the following terms:

> (Wife) Both of us have friends at work...there is a sort of group of us... I go out with them outside of work and see them, plus we've had parties and things when we've had folk from work to our house. We do have like team nights out with the people that we work with that we go on every now and then.

> (Husband) I've got one really good friend at Beta and I've got other friends that we go to the football and go out for lunch and things like that and there are other people that have left Beta and now working for different companies. We meet up with them regularly, go for lunch and things like this...(Beta, male software engineer; B-HI-04).

Separation of work and non-work

Our evidence indicates that there is clearly no fixed boundary between the domains of work and domesticity. This, in turn, suggests that attempts to conceptualize and apply a balance between work and life are doomed to failure. With time being a limited and contested resource, social processes are clearly significant factors in negotiating its sharing and allocation (Thorne, 2001). Work, family, the broader community and its context provide the foundations from which these processes and their negotiation arise. Greater control over one or more domains allows for wider employee discretion over domestic coping strategies and for maintaining permeability between work and home.

Hence, in line with their instrumental orientations, call centre staff would like to keep work and home as separate entities but interviews with staff demonstrated that it is not always possible to exercise either physical or emotional control over the two domains, especially by those on the junior rungs of management:

> I don't think I take customer issues home with me, I kind of cut off from them. If something's happened like maybe in the team, if somebody'd

been upset over something, I tend to take them home with me...it's something I've learned to do. I remember taking books home from work and sitting at 10 o'clock at night trying to catch up (Entcomm, female, customer service adviser; E-I-25).

Work, I try to keep out of my head when I can but I'm not the type of person who can. I usually do take my work home with me. You will go home, you cannae help it, you will go home to your partner and you will be like "you will never guess who I had on the phone today, this guy and this and that" and Joe sitting there listening to it for an hour when I come in from work. I cannae help it but then I do try and block it out (Holstravel, female, sales manager; H-I-22).

For software workers, as indicated in interviews above, blurred boundaries between work and non-work were both common and warmly embraced:

... the job I do nine to five is very much focussed around Gamma; however, even at weekends I still discuss, obviously with colleagues... we still discuss Gamma and how best to improve and acknowledge the good things, what would you say bump up on the name Gamma outside the company. It's very difficult when you are talking to friends in social circles, talking about Gamma is a very boring subject, but I do see Gamma as – I mean they pay my wages, they pay my mortgage – that's important, people should realise that. I'm very keen to make sure this company moves from being a £20 million turnover company to £100 million to £150 million company. It has to be done... My partner works in Gamma – so it's every day of the week (Gamma, male business development officer; G-I-03).

The opportunity to discuss software issues in social settings was readily utilized, as described by one software engineer:

I mean I guess I can talk shop with other software engineers and my boyfriend's a software engineer – that is just by chance we ended up doing the same thing. Our closest friends that are another couple are both software engineers ... I'm not friends with them because we have the same kind of job or even the same interests, no it's just other things you have in common (Beta, female software engineer, B-I-03).

For software workers, socialization with both current and previous work colleagues may not be the most frequent activity, but its occurrence was common, generally welcomed and appreciated. With these workers, conversation at social events centred on work, which usually represents 'the main topic of conversation' (Beta, male software engineer; B-HI-07). From our development of Salaman's typology, it does appear that a form of professionalized occupational and work-based community is beginning to take shape, largely independent of employer efforts to secure worker integration to organizational interests.

Finally, if people are less inclined to surrender sovereignty over their lives to their employers as some might wish, we need to enquire into the presence of spillover from home to work. Table 6.2 confirms that only rarely do family and household responsibilities intrude into people's capacity to undertake their paid work. Even here, there are perceptible differences between software and call centre workers, with the former more inclined to report spillover, though from a low base. These differences can be explained by the requirement of call centre workers to adapt their domestic arrangements to suit the generally inflexible demands of their work. Software workers show deeper attachment both to work and to colleagues, but those with family responsibilities may well resent perceived constraints imposed by the latter over their ability to devote time to their work.

Conclusions

Both software engineers and call centre employees have been identified as occupants of the new knowledge economy, though the findings from this section reveal many differences between the two groups in terms of the meanings they attach to their work and domestic lives and their sources and expressions of occupational and personal identity. In contrast to the call centre workers, apart from spatial proximity, software workers demonstrate many of the characteristics of an occupational community, including intrinsic satisfaction and a professional orientation derived from serving clients, colleagues and company; occupational bonding, located in both work and social networks; and a transparent dedication to and satisfaction from deploying and extending their software skills. Blurring between work and non-work boundaries was also common and largely accommodated without question. Perhaps another factor associated with occupational community should not be overlooked: the occupation is strongly masculinized, with about three-quarters of our company employees being men, an aspect which is developed in greater detail in Chapter 7.

For call centre employees, for many of the women living and employed in and around urban central Scottish cities with strong associations with now mainly redundant industries, the picture is more complex. They do tend to seek and be employed in jobs in workplaces recently established close to their homes and families. Nevertheless, the frequently alienating character of their work and instrumental orientation of the workers themselves to it make them little disposed to associate with colleagues once work finishes. In this sense, community based on Salaman's integration of work and home is little evident. However, evidence of persistence of local community based on shared background, past occupational experience and family interests could still be traced among some call centre workers:

> I mean Motherwell is basically steel and they've either worked at or been involved with Ravenscraig and they've just gone on since then. A lot of them have never worked since Ravenscraig closed, no other skills... when you walk into any pub about here, oh I remember him from the 'Craig. Him, he was a fitter or something... the 'Craig was about 5,000 strong or something like that, huge, absolutely huge, but no, I don't think the community has broken up...'(Entcomm- male team leader, E-HI-04)

The extent to which a lingering sense of community informed call centres workers' attitudes and actions at work is uncertain. From the employers' perspective, of course, the prospects of a ready supply of local potential employees with obsolete skills and close community and family recruitment links served their interests quite nicely.

A second major point to note is that spillover from work to home, in whatever form it takes, is a consistent outcome of work in the contemporary economy. This presents particular problems for all employees and particularly for those with caring responsibilities. The analysis indicates different employee coping strategies in the two sectors, largely driven by contrasting labour processes and labour market positions. The professionalized software workers, aided by responsive organizational provisions for family-friendly policies, enjoy some flexibility in managing potential work-family conflict. Although negative work-life spillover, such as long hours, is still detectable the work-life boundary is more permeable and flexible. With call centre operations driven more obviously by cost and volume imperatives, the burden of managing work-family conflict is placed on individual employees, the majority of whom are women, but without the flexibility offered to the generally 'higher value' software workers. This appears to result in coping strategies which reflect a more fragmented work-life boundary. From these findings it is clear that, in contrast to some expectations for new forms of work and the associated policy rhetoric, establishing balance between the demands of work and home can be complex and contested, especially for those women with little work autonomy or status.

At the policy level, potential tensions between work and domestic demands are being recognized and receiving governmental, employer and media attention, though there was little evidence that these pressures had impacted noticeably upon the practices of the employers. Software managers accommodated part-time and flexible work because they had no wish to lose valuable and difficult to replace employees. Call centre employers were not facing these constraints and could tolerate high staff attrition levels. These employees had little opportunity to adjust their working lives (indeed their working lives were being adjusted around them), and so were faced either with leaving or organizing their domestic arrangements to accommodate work.

This suggests that the higher relative levels of job control and autonomy displayed by software workers are reflected in a greater ability to maintain some control over the work-home boundary. From the above discussion it is clear that this is partly a function of gender but it also reflects a more flexible labour process and strong labour market situation. Call centre workers are in a weaker labour market and working under much tighter and more direct managerial direction. With only limited (or informal) scope for job control they have also fewer possibilities for work-life adjustments. 'Flexible' working time patterns were flexible for the employers primarily and actually undermined workers' own coping arrangements. Those that could do so utilized a mixture of informal strategies (for instance, shift swapping) at work and recourse to family and kinship networks at home; those for whom these were not available tended to leave. Thus boundaries between work and household are not static but the result of a continuous process of social negotiation in which the differential power and resources available to employer and employees are critical to the outcome. Where the employee has workplace resources available, such as the union at Beta, then negotiated workplace adjustments are possible; where there are no equivalent workplace resources then employees will fall back on what kinship and community resources they may have. In particular, these constraints raise significant questions about the range of life-style choices available to women performing routinized jobs (see Hakim, 2002).

The negotiation of the boundary between work and household involves not only function (who does what? who is breadwinner? who is carer?) but also time (when are these forms of social action carried out?) and space (where are they performed?). As we have seen, the work-household boundary is thus not a single time-defined border but composed of several interpenetrating dimensions. While most of the attention has been given to the temporal impositions of work on home, as in the case of our call centre shift workers, contemporary technology such as ICT makes possible an increasing spatial overlap between work and domestic life (as the literature on teleworking demonstrates, see Hardill (ed.), 2003) and, in addition, means that the 'private' sphere of the household can be invaded at any time by the 'public' sphere of work, as was the case with our software workers on call. In either case, the coping and collaborative processes identified, *inter alia*, by Pahl (1984), Anderson *et al.* (1994) and Thorne (2001), through which workers and their families attempt to structure their work and domestic lives, become increasingly sensitive to organizational shifts and priorities, demanding constant renegotiation of domestic obligations and concessions and in the process, reinforcing doubts about the conceptual and practical value of notions concerning work-life balance.

7
Women and Men

Introduction

A little-discussed component of the knowledge society model has been the predicted eradication of the gendered inequalities that have been a feature of industrial capitalism. Castells (1996), for example, claimed that information and communication technologies would reverse the relegation of women to deskilled or menial jobs as historical stereotypes were replaced by the demand for an autonomous, skilled labour force. As relatively new employment sectors, we might expect call centre and software work to demonstrate this convergence between men and women. Yet, they already represent horizontally segregated occupations with female-dominated (call centres) and male-dominated (software) workforces, and are often presented as examples of distinctively women's and men's work. Our data is also suggestive of vertical segregation: women were underrepresented at management levels in call centres despite their numerical dominance within the occupation, and in software, our findings showed a tendency for women to be located in less technical, lower-level roles.

In this chapter, our aim is to understand and identify those factors that contribute to this segregation and what these mean to the people concerned. We consider the experiences of men and women, their attitudes towards gender roles, and practice with respect to equality of opportunity and treatment in these new workplaces. We also seek to provide some explanation for any observed women's disadvantage. Theoretical accounts range from an emphasis on social stratification, institutionalized and reproduced by societal and organizational norms, to more individualized perspectives. Individualization, generally, has been a dominant theme of contemporary writers who claim that the absence of universal certainties in the new economy is more empowering for both men and women who have the freedom to choose their own values and lifestyle (for example, Giddens, 1991). Perhaps the most notable and controversial of these arguments is offered by Hakim (2000), who proposes that women's own preferences and choices are the primary source of any inequality with respect to employment opportunities. This view, in turn, has been widely criticized for not acknowledging constraints on women's choices produced by financial and family situations (Fagan, 2001). Other explanations, such as those of human capital theory (Becker, 1964, 1985) also focus on individual characteristics, including age, qualifications and career stage. For example, lower qualifications, along with the higher priority given to family have been used to explain women's inferior position in the IT industry (Igbaria and Chidambaram, 1997).

This chapter focuses on three sources of potential disadvantage – domestic circumstances, work preferences and values, and organizational conditions. Through these, we explore the tensions between individual characteristics and choice on the one hand, and the constraints of situation on the other. Although other potential explanations of inequality exist – the interaction of gender with ethnicity or social class, for instance – we focus on these three areas to capture the interface between work and home life consistent with the themes discussed so far in this book, and to show how structural constraints as well as individual agency shape the choices and experiences of women at home and at work. Before presenting the evidence for gender differences and disadvantage from our data, we set the context with a brief consideration of the issue of gender in the two sectors.

Women in call centres and IT

Recent trends in the gender composition of the UK labour force were broadly outlined in Chapter 2, where we commented on the continuing concentration of female employment in services, banking, clerical and hospitality work. Our own chosen sectors confirm this occupational segregation, with women comprising 70 per cent of the generally low paid, low skilled call centre workforce, and men 72 per cent of those in the skilled software jobs (Table 7.1).

For some, this profile runs counter to the expectations of the information age. Computing and software work were expected to be gender neutral (Knights and Murray, 1994; Panteli *et al.*, 1999), but only 19 per cent of students on computer science degrees are women (Wilson, 2004) and there has even been a decrease in female participation in the UK IT industry to less than 20 per cent of all employees (Panteli *et al.*, 1999). Moreover, it has been shown that women in IT and computing tend to be segregated into more peripheral roles such as sales, help desks and customer service work, whereas men are more ubiquitous in technical roles, such as systems analysis and programming (Wilson, 2004). DiDio (1997) found that women are overlooked for elite project work and are less likely to be in management posts, as well as having lower salaries (see also Adam, 2002; and Baroudi and Igbaria, 1995). Some explain this in terms of qualifications, with

Table 7.1 Sample characteristics for men and women (survey respondents)

	Call centres					Software			
	Men N	%	Women N	%		Men N	%	Women N	%
Survey responses: Total	241	30	567	70	Total	230	72	90	28
M	24	25	73	75	Omega	79	68	37	32
T	104	48	114	52	Beta	92	81	21	19
E	62	26	175	74	Pi	25	66	13	34
H	41	18	188	82	Lambda	10	71	4	29
					Gamma	16	89	2	11
Age									
16–20	18	8	47	9		0	0	2	3
21–30	114	50	271	50		80	36	27	36
31–40	64	28	136	25		78	36	29	38
41–50	23	10	72	13		46	21	14	18
Over 50	7	3	17	3		15	7	4	5
Qualifications									
No qualifications	11	5	19	4		2	1	2	3
School/vocational	130	56	371	68		51	23	22	29
FE college/HNC	36	16	51	9		16	7	7	9
Undergraduate	42	18	94	17		101	46	26	34
Postgraduate	12	5	15	3		52	23	20	26
Contractual status									
Permanent	208	90	501	92		185	84	62	82
Contractor/temp.	37	16	63	12		34	15	12	16
Full-time	212	92	451	83		216	99	58	76
Job status									
Non-management	189	82	488	89		157	71	58	75
Team leader/management	42	18	62	11		65	29	1	25
Shifts									
Frequently nights	74	32	151	28		4	2	2	3
Frequently Sat/Sun	112	49	341	62		7	3	3	4
Contracted hours/week									
Less than 30	16	7	88	16		1	1	11	14
30 or more	215	93	460	84		218	99	66	86
Paid overtime									
Up to 10 hours/week	33	14	83	15		17	8	5	7
More than 10	6	3	8	2		5	2	2	3
Unpaid overtime									
Up to 10 hours/week	61	27	106	19		97	44	37	49
More than 10	11	5	9	2		38	17	1	1

women less likely to possess relevant degree qualifications in software engineering or computing (Igbaria and Chidambaram, 1997). Our own survey sample of software workers, indeed, confirms the lower level of qualifications, overall, amongst women. As several feminist writers have repeatedly claimed (Wacjman, 1991; Henwood, 2000), the interaction between gender and technology is difficult to avoid.

Women's numbers in IT and computing may be static or even decreasing, but the same cannot be said for those engaged in interactive service work. Some suggest that female labour is increasingly in demand because women are perceived as possessing the social skills required for service based work. Bradley *et al.* (2000: 78), for instance, argued that the mounting importance in modern organizations of 'good' customer service, means that clichéd female traits, such as, 'caring, communicating and making people feel good' are now viewed as essential assets. Whereas technological work is culturally masculine, interactive service work, such as call centre employment, is seen as essentially feminine, and stresses and markets a variant of femininity which emphasizes 'passivity, servicing and generous attention to customers' needs' (McDowell and Courts, 1994: 733). Hebson and Grugulis (2005), more pessimistically, highlight the new risks to equality posed by this expansion in customer service work in newer, less bureaucratic organizational forms; for example, the less visible nature of gendered power relations, and the stereotyping and downgrading of skills associated with female-dominated sectors.

These trends raise the issue of gender disadvantage in both sectors. Call centres have been described as a 'female ghetto', comprising low skilled service work and limited career prospects (Belt, 2002). Despite some writers' (Frenkel *et al.*, 1999) optimistic portrayal of call centre work as knowledge-intensive, employing skilled, semi-professional workers, recruited because of their impressive interpersonal skills, the reality for most, as we established in Chapters 4 and 6, is a routinized, monotonous, Taylorized working environment with few prospects for advancement. For women in IT, the issues are no less significant, with possible barriers both to entry and progress in this emerging profession. The remainder of the chapter presents the evidence from our case studies in order to explore the potential sources of this disadvantage.

The evidence for gender difference and disadvantage

Domestic circumstances

Paid hours and contribution to household income

It is certainly true that women now make a significant contribution to both the labour market and to household incomes. It has been proposed that the dual-income household model is overtaking the 'traditional' family breadwinner model (Bradley *et al.*, 2000; Crompton, 1999; Hogarth *et al.*, 2001). As we saw in Chapter 6 though, having a family does appear to affect women more than men in terms of labour force participation and overall career prospects. Mothers in full-time employment work 4.6 hours a week less than childless married women (Harpaz, 2001), and even short breaks from employment to attend to child rearing and childcare can result in discontinuous careers which lead to low paid or unchallenging jobs, and lower overall lifetime earnings than men (Bonney and Love 1991; Rake, 2000).

In our data, over 80 per cent of men and women in both sectors worked more than 30 hours per week; however, women were still more likely than men to work fewer than 30 hours (16 per cent versus seven per cent in call centres, and 14 per cent versus one per cent in software) (see Table 7.1). While the numbers are relatively small (104 call handlers and 12 software workers), working less than 30 hours per week was confined almost entirely in both sectors to those with children or care responsibilities, and, in call centres at least, this was mainly women.

Similarly, men contributed a larger proportion to household income, especially in software. In the call centres, this was strongly associated with the relationship between gender and the presence or absence of dependants. As Table 7.2 shows, 68 per cent of women in call centres with dependants contributed half or less of household income, compared to 30 per cent of men with dependants. These differences were absent amongst call centre employees without dependants, i.e. the younger under 30s. In software, however, there was a persistent divide between men and women irrespective of the presence of dependants, with women more likely to be the minor contributor in both cases.

Table 7.2 Contribution to household income

	Call centres					Software				
	Men		Women			Men		Women		
	N	%	N	%	χ^2	N	%	N	%	χ^2
No dependents										
Less than half or none	66	39	158	44	2.38	14	10	9	20	21.49***
About half	41	24	94	26		17	12	17	37	
More than half or all	63	37	110	30		114	79	20	44	
Has dependents										
Less than half or none	11	19	82	47	25.90***	5	7	11	38	16.23***
About half	6	11	37	21		6	8	3	10	
More than half or all	40	70	56	32		63	85	15	52	

Note: Numbers with dependents: call centre men N = 58; call centre women N = 178; software men N = 75; software women N = 29.

Women's role in the dual-income model is often viewed as being related to the type of work in which they are engaged. In a review of evidence from several countries, Hakim (2000) reported that of the 16 per cent of working women with children under the age of three in the UK, a high proportion were middle class professionals. Among our survey respondents though, the proportion of working mothers in the software industry (38 per cent) was similar to the proportion in call centres (32 per cent), and, as we have seen, software women regardless of dependants, were still more likely to be secondary contributors to family income despite their higher qualifications.

Unpaid domestic work

A second area of domestic life which may impact on the relative positions of men and women in employment, is the extent of change with respect to women's domestic role. With increasing harmonization in the qualifications of young men and women (Walby, 1997; Kirton and Greene, 2000) we might also expect convergence with respect to attitudes towards gender roles at home and work.

Using six questions from the British Social Attitudes Survey, we compared the attitudes of men and women in each sector with respect to women's work and family roles. The mean ratings of agreement shown in Table 7.3 indicate that employees showed strongest agreement with those statements supporting equality, such as women working full-time and the desirability of shared household responsibilities. Nevertheless, in both sectors, women were more likely to express these attitudes than men, even after controlling for age and the existence of dependants. The analysis of variance (F) tests reported in Table 7.3 show persistent gender differences for all age groups and for all domestic circumstances. The statements reflecting approval with gendered roles (men as primary breadwinners and more suited to management; women as childcarers) received lower levels of agreement, although again, men were more likely to reflect these stereotyped attitudes than the women in our sample.

Our findings overall provide support for some convergence in men and women's attitudes towards more egalitarian views of domestic and work roles. This is perhaps unsurprising given that our case studies represent a relatively young workforce. Proctor and Padfield (1999) found that young single women and young mothers rejected the absolute homemaker role and were committed to employment, while Pilcher's (1998) study of three generations of women identified the differing attitudes and values with the emphasis for young women on individualism, independence and choice. Nevertheless, while our own evidence might indicate that traditional attitudes are shrinking, men were still more likely to view women as having to take responsibility for family rather than progress their own careers, even in a dual career household.

Table 7.3 Attitudes to equality and women's roles for men and women (mean ratings)[a]

	Call centres			Software		
	Men	Women	F[b]	Men	Women	F[b]
'Equality' statements						
There is no reason why family life should suffer if the woman has a full time job	3.65	3.82	.67*	3.21	3.69	6.00*
Nowadays men and women should share household tasks equally	4.07	4.29	6.06*	3.88	4.30	7.46**
'Different values/roles' statements						
On the whole women are not as ambitious as men in their jobs	2.13	2.05	.02	2.35	2.27	.06
I'm not against women working but men should be main breadwinners for a family	2.03	1.99	.33	2.08	1.69	4.81**
Men are more suitable than women for positions of responsibility at work	2.00	1.65	8.68**	1.98	1.55	8.88**
If a child is ill and both parents are working it should be the mother who takes time off to look after the child	2.38	2.63	6.79**	2.55	2.34	.13

Notes: *p < .05 **p < .01 ***p < .001 [a]Respondents were asked to indicate agreement with each statement on a scale of '1' strongly disagree to '5' strongly agree [b]F statistics represent tests for main effects of gender controlling for age.

Additionally, despite men and women reporting opinions which, in principle, approve of egalitarian attitudes to work and non-work roles, actual role division and behaviour is very different, reflecting the constraints placed on individual choices in the domestic sphere. In Chapter 6, we showed that in both call centre and software work, and despite the status of the latter, women continued to bear the prime responsibility for most domestic chores. In call centres, women were more likely to hold prime responsibility for care of an elderly/sick relative, cooking, shopping, cleaning and washing/ironing, despite working full-time; only prime responsibility for children did not differ between men and women. In software, women were more likely to bear prime responsibility for all household chores, even though both groups were equally likely to have dependant children. As demonstrated in the previous chapters, we also found that those working part-time hours tended to hold more of the responsibility for household chores than their partners.

This was clearly illustrated in our interviews. As one male participant in our research (whose wife works two days a week) confessed,

> ... I do nothing. It's as simple as that. It's not a proud thing but I do sometimes have to work long hours, if there is a job comes up, well to be fair maybe at the weekend I'll make a meal or something like that, but the general intensive housework etc, shopping is done by Lorraine (Entcomm, male team leader; E-HI-04).

When asked who took responsibility for most of the housework, many female participants responded without hesitation 'me'.

> Me ...... Me for the general cleaning and all that, and washing. Not me as far as ironing is concerned, because I don't like it, but as far as the general cleaning and that is concerned I would say, as a rule, it's me that does that and my husband would help out. He does other things like washing windows and stuff that I don't do, he does that and he does all the DIY. So that's the balance (Moneyflow, female team manager; M-HI-21).

This pattern confirms large scale surveys and previous research (for example, Biernat and Wortman, 1991; Dex, 1999, 2003; Hochschild, 1989; Hakim, 2000) which shows that the division of household labour remains less than equal. Women still perform the bulk of domestic tasks, with men participating at their discretion. Such behaviour has been described by Hochschild (1989) as the 'stalled revolution', wherein women's influx into the workplace has yet to be accompanied by cultural changes, both at home and at work, that would make the transition achievable. She found that in its place, women work, on average, an extra month a year to perform the 'second shift' of domestic labour, over and above their paid employment, and irrespective of their employment status.

Work-life boundaries

The third aspect of household life we investigated, was whether women were more likely to experience work-life tensions than men. Whilst women still appear to accept their prime role in domestic chores, men's contribution has started to grow (Wise, 2005) and some have shown related increases in male domestic stress, particularly amongst higher status workers (Kirchmeyer, 1993; Stroh, Brett and Reilly, 1996). Equally though, others have found no gender differences in work/non-work conflict (Wallace, 1997) or preoccupation between work and family (Frone et al., 1992), whilst others continue to find that women report more interference from work to family than men (Cinamon and Rich, 2002).

In our own study, we found rather equivocal results regarding the stress and exhaustion experienced by employees as a result of spillover from work commitments to the home. The majority of our men and women experienced potential work-home or home-work spillover, as represented by the statements in Table 6.2, only occasionally. As noted in Chapter 6, however, while exhaustion and stress were evident as a result of work-induced pressures, employees appeared to employ coping strategies to manage possible work-life spillover. In both the call centre and software sample, there was relatively little evidence of family responsibilities interfering with work commitments, and no significant gender differences in this respect. Only in response to two statements – 'Household responsibilities interfere with the time I can devote to work' and 'My job prevents me spending enough time with family/partner' – did employees with dependants give higher ratings than those without dependants, irrespective of gender. Men and women appeared to react similarly to the potential spillover from work to non-work life.

Our findings so far suggest that aspects of the traditional male 'bread winner' model have been sustained in our two sectors of new work – women still appear to make the sacrifices in terms of hours in paid and unpaid work in order to sustain domestic order whether they are in software or customer service roles. Although attitudes are changing, men still appear to hold more defined views of women's domestic duties.

The implication of these domestic circumstances for women's working life is clear. High status and well-paid careers are predominantly full-time, demanding and competitive (Evetts, 2000), and so it is not surprising that career breaks for child rearing and household migration have been found to lead to career stagnation for married women (Hardill and Watson, 2004). Part-time workers, and those who take significant career breaks for maternity leave, may also be viewed as less dedicated and less professional by employers (Epstein et al., 1999). Hence, childcare responsibilities limit full labour market participation and women's ability to develop their careers.

Furthermore, our own interviews provide evidence that even women in dual-career households without childcare responsibilities are likely to give precedence to the male career; this was particularly the case in software, where the importance of a career was greater. As a woman developer in Gamma explained, she had decided to work part-time despite having no children:

> In a relationship you have got to decide, it's very difficult for two people to have full on careers, quite often one person has got to give a bit and, in our relationship, it happens to be me and I don't mind doing that. So that's why I would have to go part time, because as soon as you do go part-time I'm sure that your career isn't going to go forward in the same way as it would have (Gamma, female software developer; G-HI-9).

In the same company, a senior software engineer recounted the difficulties faced by his wife, as a professional woman trying to return to her career following a migration for his job and a period of child-rearing:

> I've played the role of provider for the family ...since we moved, my wife gradually (she is a professional) went part-time after the first child and then to nothing after the second. Then went back to do some part-time work ...... she has been unable to get into that again so I'm sole breadwinner ... it's a bit of a strain (Gamma, male senior software engineer; G-I-07).

The female partner often emerged as the holder of a secondary career who followed her partner round the country, depending on his work needs (see also Bruegel, 1996). Femlee (1995) also found that women had four times as many inter- as intra-organizational job shifts and that this was significantly related to marriage.

Where women had chosen part-time contracts to accommodate family demands, these decisions were experienced somewhat ambivalently. In the following examples, the satisfaction with the flexibility of part-time hours offered by the software companies was more than tempered by the awareness of the sacrifice in terms of internal career progression and intensity of work pressure.

> The flexibility that I have as a mum with two children is to me a big bonus. I work two full days, and I work on a Wednesday until 2.30, and I work till 12.30 on a Thursday and Friday, which is basically 4 days. The equivalent of four days over five days which I have chosen to do and the company has accommodated that. However the company pays you *pro rata* to do that and I have exactly the same revenue targets, the same responsibilities as the other business managers who work full-time (Omega, female business manager; O-I-09).

I've got three children, so I've been off quite a bit between the three of them. So every time you come back you feel as if, it's a long time before you feel, oh I've caught up now. The last time I came back it was quite difficult in that I came back to a different project, there was a whole new sort of technology, it was technology I hadn't used before and I wasn't familiar with it, and also I'd come back on a part-time basis. So it was hard going, the learning curve seemed to go on for ever. .... If you wanted promotion or anything I don't think it would be looked upon favourably. ....It suits me because my main driving force is my family; I'm not here to climb the career ladder at the moment (Beta, female software engineer; B-I-14).

Our evidence suggests therefore, that in a professional career-oriented sector such as software, there may be a price to pay when women opt for fewer working hours, career breaks, or part-time contracts. Such patterns might seem to reflect little more than a continuation of patriarchal values, which see women as fulfilling the traditional childrearing and homemaking role and as having a career which is secondary to her husband. Yet some women themselves, seemed to consider promotion as less important than accommodating family needs, and their companies were praised, particularly the software companies, for the flexibility they had offered them in managing personal demands. This suggests an alternative source for this personal choice, driven by a different set of personal values for men and women. This is the focus of the analysis in the next section.

Work preferences

It has been argued that women's decisions to work part-time or take career breaks may be the result of genuinely different values attached to work, which make them more likely than men to prioritize childrearing, homebuilding and other domestic tasks over paid work (Hakim, 2000). Attempts to show these differences in orientation, however, are largely inconclusive. For example, whilst Mannheim (1983, 1993) claimed to show that women are less work-centred than men, others have found no gender difference (Rabinowitz and Hall, 1977) or that professional women, even those with children, are as work-centred as men (Kaufman and Fetters, 1980).

Hakim's (2000) argument suggests that differences in women's attachment to, and attainment in, employment persists because many prioritize family commitments. Preferring 'low-commitment' employment, they may also accept lower rewards from paid work (Hakim, 2002). However, other conceptions of women's domestic role have focused on the constraints which this places on women's choices about work – for example, the potential role conflict between career commitment and family demands (Crompton, 2002), the accessibility of childcare (McRae, 2003), or the practical difficulties of combining work and family responsibilities, especially with respect to the hours demanded in management roles (Harkness, 1999; Grimshaw and Rubery, 2001).

Moreover, the reality of today's working and home life means that families more often have to balance two careers in a culture of long hours and work intensification. Something has to give and, as we have noted above, the point of compromise is frequently the woman's career. Women's choices to work fewer hours or take career breaks may be because they have no other option – or for short-term convenience – although this has longer-term implications for their working life. As Hardill and Watson (2004) note, the large and frequently disproportionate drop in income for women when they become mothers disadvantages women even further given the unequal distribution of domestic, particularly child rearing, duties within dual-career households. Our own second area of enquiry, whether there are gender differences in work preferences and values, allows us to examine this interplay between individual preference and situational factors, such as family constraints and employment opportunities.

Work centrality

The notion that values may be converging is one implication of the 'reflexive modernization' thesis (Beck *et al.*, 1997). This holds that men's and women's identities and experiences with respect to work and family life are now less susceptible to rigid societal norms and institutions which dictate gender roles. Hochschild (1997) also proposed that men and women increasingly seek the same rewards from work and that, in the US, at least, work has become the location for emotional support and personal satisfaction, while home forms the source of stress and boredom. Today's dominant work ideology, she argued, is the same for men and women (Hochschild, 2003).

We explored the issue of convergence, first, by examining the values attached to work, leisure and family. Our survey data showed that for both call centre and software workers, *and* for men and women, family was rated significantly more important than leisure, which in turn was rated significantly more important than work (see Table 7.4). No differences in the priorities of men and women were found for software workers; here, ratings of work, leisure and family were essentially identical for men and women. In call centres, leisure was rated higher by men, while family was rated higher by women. This is unsurprising given the higher proportion of women with children and other dependants, as well as the apparent burden on women of being responsible for the household. In software, the proportions of men and women with children were relatively evenly balanced, which may account for the equal levels of importance attached to family.

Testing further for the effects of gender and children together in a two-way analysis of variance, neither of these was predictive of the importance attached to work in the two sectors. We cannot conclude, therefore, that gender in itself accounts for differences in work centrality in these areas of work. Gender and having children, however, accounted significantly for differences in the importance of both leisure and family in call centres and, in the case of family orientation, the interaction between gender and children also was significant ($F(1,771) = 11.81$, $p < .001$). Although women tended overall to rate the importance of family higher than men did (see Table 7.3), men with children rated it even higher (mean = 4.49) than women with children (mean = 4.38).

These findings illustrate the complexities of gender differences with respect to work priorities and the inappropriateness of oversimplifying the orientations of men, as well as women, with respect to family. In software, there was no such contrast between men and women with children. Instead, software men and women were more similar, and whether or not employees had children was the only predictor of high family orientation.

To some degree, this supports the idea of convergence between male and female preferences and values. There remains, however, some suggestion of an imbalance in terms of the values and expected gender roles in handling work and family obligations. Notably, our findings with respect to number of hours of overtime may indicate that women were less willing to sacrifice their family responsibilities for work demands. Earlier, we reported that women with children worked fewer hours – over 30 per cent of this group in both sectors reported working less than 30 hours, compared to seven per cent of call centre fathers, one per cent of software fathers, and almost none of the employees in either sector with no dependants. In addition, the call centre mothers amongst our survey respondents were also less

Table 7.4 Importance of work, leisure and family for men and women (mean ratings)[a]

	Call centres			Software		
	Men	Women	F	Men	Women	F
Work	2.19	2.08	2.93	2.28	2.12	1.45
Leisure	3.22	2.98	11.49**	2.93	2.80	2.76
Family	3.89	4.15	13.37***	3.72	3.88	2.75
Paired-samples t-tests						
Family-Leisure	8.36**	23.88***		9.77***	7.81***	
Leisure-Work	11.85***	16.47***		7.13***	5.08***	

Notes: **$p < .01$ ***$p < .001$
[a]'Importance of work' was measured with a 2-item scale, 'importance of leisure' with a 3-item scale, and 'importance of family' with one item. Respondents were asked to indicate agreement with statements on a scale of '1' strongly disagree to '5' strongly agree.

likely to work any paid overtime. In software, the picture was slightly different as there was no difference in the paid overtime hours reported by men, women, or women with children.[1]

With respect to unpaid overtime, 32 per cent of men and 21 per cent of women in call centres reported working at least some unpaid hours (see Table 7.1). However, unpaid overtime was less likely among mothers (26 per cent) compared to fathers (52 per cent). In software, unpaid overtime was more common, with 61 per cent of men and 50 per cent of women reporting regular unpaid hours each week. Among mothers, 42 per cent still reported some unpaid overtime compared to 70 per cent of women without children, but consistent with earlier research (Hogarth et al., 2001) men with children were the group with the highest levels of reported unpaid overtime hours each week. Overall, 70 per cent of this group reported some unpaid overtime, with 28 per cent suggesting that they regularly worked more than 10 hours unpaid extra hours each week.

Thus, in both sectors, but especially in software, mothers seemed more likely to sacrifice their work for their family, while the opposite appears to be the case for fathers. Ahmavaara and Houston (2005) also found that despite having very positive views towards fatherhood (50 per cent of the men surveyed felt more involved with their children's upbringing than their own fathers were), 66 per cent reported working more overtime since the birth of their child. Considering that the majority of fathers had felt that they would like to spend more time with their children – therefore work was not an escape from home life – we can only assume that for these men and the men in our own research, additional overtime hours are viewed, in some way, as fulfilling a traditional role in providing for their family. This, however, was not justified in terms of the immediate provision of extra income, as the hours were unpaid. Rather we have to understand it partly, in terms of a long-term calculation of the positive effects on job security and promotion prospects of showing a commitment to the job in hand, plus in the case of software, the absorption of the values of this particular occupational community. Working the hours and delivering the project in software enhanced individual chances of getting a better project next time and thus overall marketability.

For women, we found some evidence of accommodating their own career for their partners due to lower work centrality. Again, we can refer to the married Gamma software developer in her 30s with no childrearing

---

1 This itself suggests an additional source of pressure for software workers with children, whether male or female, as these workers may be required to work the necessary extra hours to meet project deadlines (see Chapter 6's discussion of reasons for overtime, and Chapter 3's discussion of the pressures of deadlines for software workers).

responsibilities, who had decided to work part-time to accommodate her husband's career:

> When I was full-time it [responsibility for household chores] was very much split 50/50 but now I tend to do more of the housework. Yes, one of my days off is pretty much spent just tidying up and doing washing and all the rubbishy things that you do.....I can't imagine him ever going part-time. I think he really does enjoy his job and probably doesn't have the same sort of drive for free time as I do. I can happily amuse myself trying out different things from one week to another, and feeling more like a balanced human being, but he doesn't seem to need that. He gets more out of his work (Gamma, female software developer; G-HI-09).

In the call centres, many women workers (such as this married woman over 50 years of age and with no children) also enjoyed the social dimension of work, regarding her work as the secondary income to the household:

> Mine's [salary] is pocket money. He earns enough for us to live a very good lifestyle. At this stage in my life I am now working to keep some company, I've got lots of friends…I couldn't be at home full-time right now. That would be too boring. I don't have any family you see (Holstravel, female sales consultant; H-I-28).

Finally, in partial support of Hochschild (1997), we also found a small number of part-time women who regarded work as an escape from the pressures and stresses of children and home, an attitude-set that some employers were well aware of. A whole evening shift at Entcomm was comprised of women with daytime family responsibilities. Their feelings are exemplified in the following quotation:

> I like to come to work because, I know this sounds terrible, but I get a break from my family. You get to be with other people, you get to have a chat to others, you get away from the children. I've got two very young children, one child of one and one of three, and my partner's got two young children from a previous marriage, also four and seven. Four children under the age of seven. I've got the other children at the weekend and on the Wednesday so, at times, I could just be pulling my hair out my head. I just want to go to work. I think I'm just going to go full time………Well I love my children, of course, they matter more than anything in the whole world but there is only so much that you can take of the crying and moaning, screaming (Entcomm, female customer service advisor; E-I-28).

Castells (2000) has argued that women's own desires for working flexibility, in terms of time, entry and exit to and from the labour market, is well matched to the needs of new economy service sector work, of which call centres are a part. Moreover, as call centre operations are frequently located in suburban areas, this is more likely to attract a local workforce; in many cases this may be married women with dependants seeking flexible shiftwork and convenient travel to work times (see, for example, Belt *et al.*, 2002).

Preferences and career orientation

The final aspect of work preference examined here is career orientation. Our survey asked respondents to indicate the reasons for taking their present jobs, and again we did not detect any significant differences between men and women in the reasons cited. While call centre women were more likely than men to cite 'convenience' as a reason – as indicated in the previous sections of this chapter this was mainly the view of women with dependants – an equal proportion of women (41 per cent) also cited 'career decision' (see Table 7.5). In software, career decision was the dominant reason for both men and women.

Career orientation, however, could be directed towards a career in the present company, a career in other companies, or simply to keeping the present job in the long-term for financial or domestic reasons. As shown in Chapter 5, there was a significant subgroup of the call centre workforce, primarily women, who sought to progress within their present call centre to team leader levels or to higher skilled sections. Another group, mainly women with dependants or older women, saw their current jobs as long-term but not necessarily as part of a company career. Call centre women with dependants were less likely to consider moving to another company, and a small proportion (23 per cent), similar to women with no dependants, considered the job part of a career in their present company. A similar pattern was clear for software women – the job was viewed as long-term by 55 per cent of those with dependants compared to 24 per cent of those without. The latter (younger women with no children) were more

Table 7.5 Reasons for current job choice

	Call centres				Software			
	Men		Women		Men		Women	
	N	%	N	%	N	%	N	%
No choice	12	5	8	2	14	6	1	1
Convenience	77	34	224	41	62	28	21	28
Only one available	28	12	49	9	18	8	6	8
Career decision	99	44	224	41	117	53	45	60
Better pay	7	3	19	4	2	1	0	0

likely to consider their long-term career as taking them beyond the present company and job, as were men with dependants.

These contrasting perspectives are illustrated by the mean ratings of the importance of a company career for men and women with and without children in Table 7.6. Women in call centres with children, were less career-orientated than men with children, perhaps viewing their jobs simply as a source of income. For those without children, there was still a prospect that the job could afford a career in the company as shown by the almost identical ratings for men and women. Clearly, this group of women with no children, similar to their male equivalents, fell into the group of call centre careerists we identified in Chapter 5. Comparing the ratings for call centre women with and without children, though, we can see that a career for mothers is less important than for non-mothers ($F(2,552) = 4.03$, $p < .05$). In software, again, there is less evident difference in the career orientations of men and women *per se*. There were no significant differences between men and women in their ratings of a company career. Once more, though, there are differences in the orientations of different groups of women; those with children rated a company career as less important than those with no children ($F(2,86) = 4.53$, $p < .05$).

As we saw earlier in our analysis of domestic circumstance, call centre work for women was convenient for the accommodation of domestic responsibilities. Remaining in one organization, particularly one that was geographically convenient was preferable for working mothers, as illustrated by this call centre agent, who framed her job as one of convenience and ease rather than career development.

> I am happy with the people that I work with and in general the job is quite a simple job to do for the money that we are getting. Plus it's only five minutes up the road as well (Entcomm, female customer service adviser; E-I-02).

Table 7.6 Importance of company career for men and women, with and without children (mean ratings)[a]

	Call centres			Software		
	Men	Women	F	Men	Women	F
Overall	3.84	3.68	4.51**	3.53	3.42	.83
No children	3.77	3.76	.02	3.53	3.57	.06
Children	4.07	3.51	14.32***	3.51	3.13	3.46

Note: **$p < .01$ ***$p < .001$ Call centre men N = 239; call centre women N = 555; software men N = 224; software women N = 89.
[a]Importance of company career was measured on a scale of '1' not at all important to '5' absolutely critical.

Organizational conditions

Our final focus of attention is the nature of the organizations to which these employees belong. We begin with a consideration of pay and the position adopted by each company with respect to equal opportunities polices, before evaluating employee perceptions of fair treatment. We then consider the nature of the work within each sector separately, and the degree to which management of emotional labour in call centres, and technical skill in software, renders these inexorably gendered areas of work.

Pay equity

While the extent of pay equity was impossible to determine from our data, we can see that there was little attempt by some of the organizations to follow the Equal Pay Code of Practice (EOC 2003), for example, by having a transparent pay system. As outlined in Chapter 4, the most sophisticated formal pay structure from our case studies existed in Beta, the larger software organization, where pay was tied to formal grading and included shift allowances and unsocial hours payments. Again, as far as we know, there had been no equality audit of the pay structure, but the view was that the pay system treated people fairly and equally, and for one manager this was not gender related:

> We don't aim to treat every person equally, but we do aim to treat them fairly and fairly is then with respect to a number of things, not just with respect to each other. It's also with respect to the external market (Beta, male personal development manager; B-I-15).

Certainly, there did not appear to be a concern regarding gender differences from the union representative (Beta, female software developer; B-HI-09). Of our interviewees, only one employee expressed reservations about the pay system, a male team leader, who commented that there was a perception that pay was not linked to the annual performance reviews.

Although there was no explicit evidence to suggest pay discrimination in the companies studied, the informality of the payment systems in the owner-managed software companies, and the complexity and ephemerality of the bonus systems in the call centres, resulted in a general lack of openness and transparency for most of the case study companies which made it difficult to assess the evidence for equal treatment. Monitoring for discrimination was given little prominence in these companies. For software workers at least, perceived inequalities with respect to pay and the need for greater transparency have been reinforced in other research conducted by the IT trade body (*Intellect*, 2006).

Equal opportunities policies

Throughout the last decade, government policy and legislation has been introduced to promote equality of opportunity and the adoption of flexible, child friendly working practices. However, implementation of such policies, especially within private sector organizations, is generally voluntary and variable (Noon and Hoque, 2004). It has also been proposed that the implementation and regulation of formal anti-discrimination practices may become even harder in the more fluid structures and working relations typified by newer organizational forms, thus introducing a more invisible threat to gender equality than was present in the bureaucratic structures of the past (Hebson and Grugulis, 2005).

Our case studies ranged from having no or few documented formal policies on equal opportunities and diversity (Entcomm, Gamma, and the smaller software companies), to a statement of intended equal treatment (Omega), to a well-developed, documented set of policies (Beta, Holstravel, Moneyflow and Thejobshop). Where documented policies existed, this was, for the most part, linked to the pressure exerted from unions or staff associations within the companies (the exception here was Thejobshop where there was no representative body).

Beta and Moneyflow could be held to most closely resemble the liberal approach as identified by Jewson and Mason (1986), with a plethora of handbooks and policies on equality of opportunities and diversity intended to affect all aspects of organizational life. Beta promoted itself as one of the 'leading equal opportunities employers'. It possessed an equal opportunities champion and steering group, measures of diversity performance, an internal website on equality reflecting 'internal initiatives and best practice', and continuous efforts to 'mainstream equality and diversity into HR practices' (for example through the introduction of an equal pay statement agreed with the union). In addition, it provided 'a women's network for managing work and family' and, in a review of its employment statistics for a range of groups, highlighted a small upward trend in the proportion of female managers. These initiatives were summed up by the equal opportunities statement set out on the employee intranet:

> [We are] committed to developing a working culture that is fair and 'inclusive' – enabling all employees, to make their distinctive contributions to the benefit of the business. ... We expect our managers to exercise leadership in this field by discouraging prejudice and role modelling appropriate behaviour. A positive attitude towards equality and diversity is right for society, right for Beta, right for our employees and right for our customers. This means that we shall regularly review our policies and practices to make sure that they are appropriate and operating effectively (Beta, company intranet).

Moneyflow was a founding member of 'Opportunity 2000', an initiative aimed at improving the representation of women at management levels and increasing the responsibility of line managers for ensuring equality. This focused attention on providing open access to training and development, objective selection processes based on a competency system free from sex bias, 'career break' schemes which held positions open for employees, and flexible working arrangements to allow women to balance work and family commitments (for example, enhanced maternity leave, and a returner's bonus for mothers who had been employed two years). The company claimed that over 75 per cent of women now returned to work following maternity leave, and our own findings, showing Moneyflow as the most organizationally career-orientated workforce amongst our call centres (Chapter 5), may provide some support for the success of these initiatives. The female call centre manager of Moneyflow spoke at length of the opportunities she had been given by the company:

> I think I have always been judged on my ability to do my job. I have never been made conscious of the fact that I'm a female. …..I joined Moneyflow in the 1970s where there was certainly opportunity around for discrimination, or for you to be made feel that you maybe were going to be judged in a different way, or there was a ceiling on the opportunities that were going to be made available to you (Moneyflow, female call centre manager; M-HI-08).

Holstravel, where there was both a union recognition agreement and a number of workplace representatives, had a written sexual harassment policy which stated – 'it is the duty of all employees to comply with this policy and ensure that their colleagues are treated with respect and dignity. In addition, managers are responsible for implementing the policy and taking corrective action to ensure compliance.' This was supplemented by a 14 page disciplinary policy and four page grievance policy. Formal policies also provided for flexitime, absence, maternity/parental leave, time off for dependants, and a career break scheme (particularly designed for rearing children and caring for the elderly) which stated – 'every effort will be made to provide a job in a convenient location with similar responsibilities, hours and salary to the time of the employee joining the scheme'.

Thejobshop's 'Fairness at Work' document stated – 'we believe in maximizing the potential of staff and will strive to provide equal access to recruitment, career development, training reward and all other aspects of employment'. The remit of the document was broad, covering: 'age, colour, disability, ethnic or national origin, marital status, nationality, race, religion, sexual orientation or other considerations not justified in law which are irrelevant to the performance of a job … for treatment of staff in all situations.' Despite these formal policies, however, women made up approximately 40 per cent of Thejobshop workforce, substantially less than in our other call centres.

The female-owned and managed Omega omitted any explicit references to equal opportunities or diversity in its handbook, but there was a general reference at aiming to meet both business and personal objectives. Consideration of personal commitments was delegated to individual managers; for example, with respect to flexible working arrangements: 'You do not have the right to work on a 'flexitime' basis but a manager may authorize an individual to work flexible hours on a temporary basis in special circumstances' (Omega Handbook).

Employee perceptions of fair treatment

Our survey and interviews provided evidence of women's perceptions of fair treatment by their companies. In all call centres, over 90 per cent of women agreed that they were treated the same as men. In the male-dominated software houses, though, women were more divided. Of the 60 women in the software sample, 19 per cent felt they were treated worse than men, 68 per cent the same, and 13 per cent better. Most significantly, in the most highly developed diversity employer Beta, 38 per cent felt they were actually treated worse. By contrast, in the female-owned Omega, none felt worse off compared to men, and 21 per cent felt they were treated better. For all Beta's formal company-level efforts towards equality, therefore, female software developers in the company still perceived themselves as disadvantaged, while the more female-orientated culture of Omega seemed to remove some of these barriers for women.

These mixed perceptions are reflected in interview comments, particularly in relation to the promotion of women. For example, one woman believed it was not easy to make a career in Beta although she did not attribute this to gender bias as such.

> Until within the last months I was the only female project leader. We've now got one other – just promoted. So, we are still very much a minority (unstructured interview, Beta, female team leader).

Most software women commented that being in a male-dominated field was a feature throughout their careers, starting at university where there may be as few as four women out of eighty in a class (Gamma, female software developer; G-I-09). Male domination was certainly visible but these women did not appear to feel constrained in terms of career advancement.

The formal benefits offered by Beta, including maternity leave, job sharing and flexible contracts, were acknowledged and increasingly accepted by management:

> You can change your own contract – you state how many hours you want to do and you decide weekly how many days you will do and what

the arrangement is going to be. So they are fairly good...basically you say to your team leader these are the days I'm coming in, it's not going to bother the project leader if you are in for three days, you are in for three days' (Beta, female software developer; B-I-17).

Yet, there was also recognition that these disruptions to women's careers were in the longer-term harmful to progression, as we noted earlier in this chapter and Chapter 5. The software developer with three children and working part-time described her return to work and prospects for promotion in Beta as follows:

> It can be quite daunting if you've been off a long time...... I didn't feel as though, oh gosh I'm not coping here, there was no pressure put on me from the team to say, you need to do that a bit quicker – nothing like that. People understand if you've been away for over a year.......They're an understanding employer, very much so. [However] I feel it is a disadvantage within the Centre. If you wanted promotion or anything I don't think it would be looked upon favourably. Not at all (Beta, female software developer; B-I-14).

In the other software companies there was also a perception of differences in the levels of achievement for women. In Pi, for example, the male finance director commented: 'You've only got to look at this company at the Board level, there are seven of us and we are all men' (P-I-05).

These differences in advancement though, did not seem to stem from unequal treatment of women, as we saw in our survey responses. This is borne out by comments made by our interviewees. One women project manager in Beta appeared to believe, if anything, she was treated more politely because she was a woman (unstructured interview, Beta, project manager) and, in the same company, one male commented, referring to Beta's formalized and visible HR and equal opportunities policies, that 'they do take an active role in trying to promote women in the company' (Beta, male technical architect; B-I-19). Omega was acknowledged as having a large number of women in management positions – 33 per cent of female survey respondents described themselves as managers, the highest proportion of our software companies. Even in the smaller companies, which lacked formalized equal opportunity or diversity policies, there was no apparent feeling of disparate treatment towards women. Some women also contrasted the more egalitarian attitudes of the younger IT industry and workforce to other sectors in which they had worked; for example:

> A stockbroker I worked at was a 99 per cent male partnership, very old fashioned attitudes ...they'd only just allowed women to wear trousers (Omega, female software engineer; O-I-6).

Table 7.7 Family friendly cultures (percentage responding 'agree'/'strongly agree')

	Call centres				Software				
	Moneyflow	Thejobshop	Entcomm	Holstravel	Omega	Beta	Pi	Lambda	Gamma
My immediate boss is quite sympathetic about personal matters									
Men	88%	54%	56%	59%	73%	76%	80%	100%	75%
Women	59%	75%	70%	67%	89%	90%	83%	100%	0%
It is hard to get time off during work to take care of personal or family matters									
Men	4%	14%	23%	32%	5%	3%	0%	0%	0%
Women	25%	11%	28%	32%	0%	0%	0%	0%	0%
To get ahead in the company employees are expected to put their jobs before family									
Men	13%	21%	43%	44%	16%	20%	24%	0%	19%
Women	37%	12%	36%	43%	78%	81%	92%	0%	0%
Total number of women	73	112	174	185	36	21	12	4	1
Total number of men	24	103	62	41	77	92	25	10	16

[The bank] was a very male dominated man's world and ... it was the men who still made it, or single women I suppose, but I would say here and if you think about all the other software houses as well, I really don't think that is an issue (Omega, female business manager; O-I-09).

Finally, questions targeting the role of line managers in balancing personal demands and the potential conflict between career and family demands indicated more sharply the conflicting forces which may be operating in these organizations against women's advancement. Table 7.7 – which shows the percentages of men and women in each of our case study companies agreeing with statements about balancing work and home life – confirms the finding, reported in Chapter 6, that software employees have considerable flexibility in managing their own time with respect to personal commitments. The majority also viewed their supervisors as supportive in this respect, and this applied equally to software men and women. For call centre employees, though, supervisors were less universally supportive of personal demands, particularly for women in Moneyflow, which had presented itself as encouraging greater flexibility to promote opportunity for women. Most notable from this table, is that the majority of software women (but not men) in Omega, Beta and Pi, and at least one third of call centre women in all companies, except the Thejobshop, felt that advancement depended on putting one's job before family. Not only is this finding antithetical to many of the claims of the equality policies and initiatives in many of our companies (for example, Beta, Moneyflow, and Holstravel), but it shows some divergence in the perceptions of men and women, with women apparently more attuned to the tradeoffs required in order to progress within their companies.

The nature of the work

Emotion work, women's work

Historically, women have been associated with occupations which involve helping people or artistic expression (England, 2005) but, more recently, it is the low skill service jobs dominating the contemporary economy which are increasingly regarded as feminized in terms of numbers and in the attributes required of the workforce (Liedner, 1991; Filby, 1992; Tyler and Taylor, 2001). A gendered notion of desired skill is also evident in call centres. The delivery of personal services requires employees with 'soft' interpersonal skills and management may see women as better suited than men for what is often called 'emotion work'. Belt et al. (2002), for example, illustrated how female customer service agents consciously used feminine qualities to calm down angry customers or persuade men to buy their products using what one of their team leaders called 'a flirty way of selling' (2002: 26). Women may also be better equipped to go beyond prescribed organizational scripts to deal with unexpected situations, reflecting the attainment of the multidimensional skilled emotion managers described by Boyd and Bolton (2003).

The issue of interest here, is whether management target this quality and so contribute to the concentration of women in low status and stressful areas of call centre work. There is inevitable variation in how agents manage the emotional demands of the job, for example, in their abilities to suppress their own emotions when dealing with difficult customers. Management's aim may be to recruit and promote individuals who are best able to handle these situations; perhaps women with suitable domestic circumstances or the 'right attitude' to accommodate these demands (see also Callaghan and Thompson, 2002). More subtly, gendered assumptions reflected in hiring decisions may then be reinforced by responses from employees to the cues of management, thereafter, evolving into shared gender norms associated with new posts (see, for example, Davis and Hunter's (2004) illustration of this in a bank re-organization).

The consequence of these processes, however, may be to amplify any consequent disadvantage for women. In Chapter 6, we showed, as have others (Deery, Iverson and Walsh, 2002), the negative consequences of the emotional demands of call centre work in terms of spillover to non-work life, while other writers have suggested the perceived low skill and status often attached to emotion work (Bolton, 2004).

Entcomm provides a useful illustration of three different individuals' reactions to the demands of emotion work. A single female in her 20s, describing the events which resulted in her taking a fortnight's sick leave, identified a single customer as the trigger:

> I never admitted to the work that it was stress, but it was – I actually got up off the seat one day and I threw a booklet. I was so happy I lifted a soft folder, because the force I threw the booklet at the computer screen it would have went right through the screen... I had to go. I couldn't stay any longer .....I put it down to the fact that I had been really stressed with that customer... screaming customers I can cope with...it was a really patronising customer and it just threw me completely,..... it was just the straw that broke the camel's back (Entcomm, female customer service adviser; E-HI-02).

By contrast, a female agent in her 50s confidently described her more resilient approach, attributing this to her experience in different departments and in self-employment. She also continued to describe one young male customer service adviser in the company who was unable to suppress his feelings towards customers, resulting in what she described as an inappropriate response.

> I can let a customer scream away and let them rattle on until they are finished and then say now I'll help you.... I do know that that's not

everybody, but it is just [my] past experience and that's why I can cope with it...... there was one boy in one of the teams I was in, he took everything that was said personally, and he was so stressed out and we used to try and calm him down and say it is not you they are getting at, but he felt ...he wasn't doing his job ....he would eventually lose the rag with a customer as well and start shouting back at them (Entcomm, female customer service adviser; E-I-01).

In none of our call centres was there any attempt by management to deal with the emotional strain inherent in these customer service roles by helping employees or providing relevant training. Instead, it was left to individual employees to adapt, either by modifying their own behaviour in order to avoid being disciplined or by withdrawing, perhaps in exhaustion, sickness or absence, as in the case of the young woman above. Another coping strategy was to transfer calls to operators who could 'go beyond the script'. We observed one difficult call in Thejobshop which was transferred to an older, more experienced woman who was able to 'pacify the customer' (work observation, Thejobshop).

Thus, management strategy seemed to be directed towards selecting individuals who could cope with the emotional demands of the work, and we could argue that this is more likely to target women with particular qualities. A (female) HR manager wished to attract more women returners (unstructured interview, Thejobshop), providing additional evidence that older, experienced women were regarded as especially suited to the work. All the call centres used role play and the assessment of personal skills as part of their selection procedures, downplaying the importance of formal qualifications or technical/office skills which could be trained. One company, for example, assessed individual telephone manner in a role play with a difficult customer who may 'shout and scream to some degree' (work observation, Entcomm).

One of the consequences of these management strategies would be to find greater concentrations of women in customer service roles, and men in more technical or non-customer facing roles. The distribution of our survey sample between team leaders and non-managerial agents indeed shows that men were more strongly represented in management positions in all except Holstravel (see Table 7.8). In Thejobshop, which employed the greatest proportion of males of all our call centres, most accounts were evenly balanced in terms of gender. However, in the more 'prestige' accounts (for example, *Bluechip, Netco*), team leader and technical IT helpline roles were held predominantly by men (over 70 per cent), while *Genbusiness*, which required short duration, more intensive general customer service calls, was dominated by women (73 per cent). Elsewhere, there was evidence that men were more likely to be selected for high status roles, as in the Quality Team at Entcomm. These positions required an

Table 7.8 Managers and non-managers in call centres, by gender

	Managers (N = 104)		Non-managers (N = 677)	
	Men	Women	Men	Women
Moneyflow (N = 97)	46%	54%	22%	78%
Thejobshop (N = 218)	54%	46%	46%	54%
Entcomm (N = 237)	39%	62%	25%	75%
Holstravel (N = 229)	19%	81%	18%	82%

aptitude for operating IT systems and analyzing error, efficiency and quality data, rather than customer service skills, and there was 'healthy competition' to be selected into this team of 'experts' (unstructured interview, Entcomm, quality manager). Although women dominated overall in call centres, therefore, there is some evidence that men were more likely to move away from the customer facing roles, and this often implied promoted or higher status posts.

This partly reflects the profile, and hence preferences, of the female workforce – either young and transient, seeking convenience rather than a career track, or older with dependants seeking flexibility. However, this division may also be reinforced by management assumptions which hold women as best suited to particular roles, as well as cultures and strategies which associate women with the operator role or reinforce gendered patterns of behaviour. We can identify several examples of how this may emerge. In this chapter, we described recruitment and selection procedures, in all our call centres which target and hire particular gendered qualities. In Chapter 4, we also noted the macho senior management culture at Moneyflow, and the gendered flavour to team socializing in all call centres, which tended to use the occasions of engagements, weddings, and births for nights out. Finally, in Chapter 3, we saw the inflexibility of shift patterns and overtime requirements designed to accommodate call volumes, which, we can argue, adversely impact women's flexibility and choices because of domestic constraints and even raise concerns about safety when working at night.

Technical work as man's work

For software, we examined the possibility that women were prevented from moving out of lower-level work which offered less challenge, fewer opportunities for skill development, and hence fewer possibilities for career advancement. Using two indicators of job complexity and skill level required – the degree of autonomy and cognitive complexity – we asked survey respondents to rate the frequency with which they experienced a range of features related to these two dimensions. The overall ratings for men and women in software are summarized in Table 7.9 separating out those with and without people or project management responsibility.

As noted already in Chapter 3, software workers had considerable control in how they carried out their work; here, we can see that this pattern did not differ for men and women. Both men and women, and particularly management, also reported their jobs as high in cognitive complexity, requiring, for example, close attention to the work and the application of problem-solving skills. For non-management, though, there also was a significant gender difference in this respect, with men performing the more demanding work.

In additional survey questions aimed solely at software respondents, we asked the importance of six software functions to the job – programming, systems analysis, business analysis, testing, software design and user/application support. As shown in Table 7.9, software programming and design, arguably the higher-end functions of software work excluding management roles, tended to be dominated by men. For all other tasks, and for all management respondents, men and women were equally balanced across the range of tasks representing software work.

The distinctively male character of pure development work was clear; for instance, the 11 developers in Pi, were mostly male, young and single, and Omega's technical services team, consisting of science and computing specialists, comprised two women out of a total of 15. Our interviews also reflected the relegation of women to low status support, testing or customer-facing roles:

> This is sexist, sorry I apologize for this but you tend to find more women in the support roles, which is what we've actually got. Both girls we have do primarily support. So I guess if anything that's putting women down again, sorry (Gamma, male senior software developer; G-I-08).

> Support has a bit of a bad name .. it tends to tie you to a single role and it tends not to kind of carry the same recognition as a development role.... there are not the same opportunities for movement....you tend to go into support and never come back out again (Beta, male applications support analyst; B-I-10).

Differences in entry qualifications may partially explain why women tended to hold less highly-skilled non-technical roles; testing in Omega, for example, was carried out only by those without technical qualifications. Women in software were less likely than their male counterparts to have an undergraduate degree qualification, but more likely to have completed a postgraduate degree (see Table 7.1) – in most cases an IT conversion course. This may have restricted their opportunities for high profile, challenging work. One male employee saw it as only a matter of time before females caught up in terms of appropriate degree qualifications.

> You see the amount of girls that are doing Masters in IT after doing their degree in something else, and I think it's just a matter of time, if not already, that they'll just go straight in and do the full computing science degree in the first instance... maybe it's just that girls don't do maths as much at high school (Gamma, male graphic applications developer; G-I-14).

In addition to entry qualifications, though, the ability to network within the organization and negotiate access to more elite work was important. As discussed in Chapter 5, some groups of software workers enjoyed easier access to high status, technical projects, and our evidence suggested that these employees tended to be the better qualified, younger, and frequently male, employees. For the older, female or less qualified employees, who had remained on projects for long periods of time, or had not progressed in terms of skills, mobility and development, opportunities were limited. The Beta engineer who had had three maternity leaves described coming back each time to new technology requiring new skills, and the impact this had on her familiarity with the projects (B-I-14). By contrast, a young developer with no children, even lacking an undergraduate computing degree, showed the importance of assertiveness in gaining access to all the technical training she wanted, and the prestige project work which would enhance her employability.

> Part of it is just chance you speak to the right people at the right time. My personal development manager was driving the external ventures project so I was able to go right to him and say ok I'm interested so ... "either move me or I'll move myself"' (Beta, female software engineer; B-I-03).

Gamma's business development manager described this need for assertiveness in managing one's access to relevant work – for both men and women – as follows.

> There is a certain amount of freedom within the organization to actually develop your own skills which I think is good – but ... if people are not on a project or not visible they tend to get left behind (Gamma, male business development manager; G-I-03).

The implications of this are clear for women contemplating or returning from career breaks, particularly in a culture, as we have seen, which demands putting the job before family in order to progress. Moreover, the

Table 7.9 Perception of job characteristics in software, by gender

	Men	Women	F/χ^2	Men	Women	F/χ^2
Method control (mean rating)	3.64	3.69	.38	4.21	4.28	.17
Cognitive complexity (mean rating)	3.66	3.89	10.73**	4.22	4.28	.23
Importance of skills: (% rating skill 'important'/'essential')						
software programming	74%	51%	9.95**	38%	16%	3.15
systems analysis	65%	53%	2.56	50%	37%	1.02
business analysis	40%	37%	.22	63%	63%	.01
testing	68%	67%	.03	39%	37%	.03
software design	67%	50%	5.11**	47%	32%	1.41
user support	62%	55%	.84	52%	32%	2.35

Notes: *p < .05 **p < .01
'Method control' is the mean of eight items from the Perceived Intrinsic Job Characteristics Scale (Warr, Cook & Wall, 1979) which asked respondents to rate the degree to which jobs required task repetition, personal initiative/judgement, and provided control over various aspects of their jobs (e.g. planning work, setting targets, deciding breaks, when to work overtime). 'Cognitive complexity' is the mean of four items adapted from Jackson *et al.*'s (1993) concepts of monitoring demand (the requirement to pay close and constant attention) and problem-solving demand (the requirement to diagnose and solve problems). All items were measured on a scale of 1 'none at all' to 5 'a great deal'.

maleness of the workforce was reflected in 'blokey' activities such as raft racing, beer and pizza nights, and golf weekends, all of which in turn reinforced conventional attitudes connecting men and technology. The distinct identity of the single 'lads' in development was mentioned in all our companies, as in the following example from a female developer in her 20s:

> I'm the only married person in [development], most of them are single men so in terms of things in common, I think *they* have – there's a lot of sporting interests but I don't really get involved in that sort of stuff ...because most of them are guys, sometimes I think I don't have anything in common with them at all – the Sun newspaper, looking at page 3 when you come in in the morning, discussing Kylie Minogue on MTV the night before, it gets a bit silly at times (Pi, female software programmer; P-I-10).

Conclusions

The new capitalism portrayed by, amongst others, Sennett (1998) and Beck (2000), would propose a convergence in male and female domestic and working identities, but as Wacjman and Martin (2002) argue, research findings reveal the endurance of gender structuring of choices about career and family. Our evidence confirms competing realities for women. Although there was some convergence with male colleagues in attitudes and employment preferences, especially amongst the software workforce, women's choices remained constrained within both their domestic and working lives.

Women in both sectors contributed a lower proportion of household income, and assumed responsibility for the majority of domestic work regardless of position and hours worked. Consistent with Dex and Joshi (1999), we also showed that any gender division of roles intensified with parenthood or the ontake of care responsibilities. Although our male and female workers demonstrated fairly egalitarian attitudes in their opinions of appropriate gender roles in the home and the workplace, these were more a declaration of a desired state, perhaps, rather than their lived experience. These experiences were just as much the case for the more career-orientated software women as the generally younger less qualified women and older women returners in call centres seeking primarily 'low commitment' work, flexible shifts and convenient work location. This, perhaps, suggests that women's expressed preferences are not always consistent with their actual employment choices, as implied by Hakim (2000). Women were still more likely than men to prioritize their family and partner's demands over their own career, despite expressed preference, all of which suggests that notions of the male breadwinner role have yet to be fully eroded.

In considering why these employees' lives were more gendered than their attitudes, we cannot ignore the organizational structures and cultures which constrain choice, and over which individuals have little control. Women did not perceive themselves to be treated unfairly in their organizations and, in some of the software companies, women explicitly acknowledged the flexibility offered for accommodating personal demands. In many of our case studies, but not the smaller software companies, there also was formal and widespread recognition of equality and diversity goals. Despite these positive indicators, in both sectors, there was evidence of masculine sub-cultures and a reality which deviated from stated equal opportunities policies, resulting in some barriers to women's progression to higher status or promoted posts. Shared assumptions about the work in which women excelled (customer-facing in call centres or support-based in software) were reinforced through hiring and promotion practices, or social relations in the workplace. This resonates with Hebson and Grugulis' (2005) findings of restricted opportunities for women in both low paid and managerial occupations within new and more fragmented organizational forms.

In sum, while there is clear convergence between men and women in their work preferences and career orientations, a combination of domestic circumstance, continuing patriarchal attitudes, and organizational context presents this as a constrained convergence. As in more traditional employment areas, these constrained choices lead to continuing disadvantage for women, with limits to progression in their careers and in the workplace.

8
Class and Status

Introduction: farewell to class?

This chapter examines whether the influential analyses of the changing patterns of social class and perceptions of class identity amongst employees, symbolized by the 'death of the working class' thesis, are verified in our two leading new economy sectors, namely, software and call centres. These analyses concern the assumed disintegration of Marxist-inspired class analysis, the fragmentation of class structure and their replacement by other organizing criteria of social groups, such as voluntarily chosen identities. The claimed emergence of the information or network society has added a further dimension to the extant sociological debates concerning the existence and basis of class.

Drawing upon evidence from our nine case study organizations, a rich and complex picture is presented of the attitudes of the respective workforces – with their widely varying task content, sectoral, contractual, educational, gender and age characteristics – towards their occupational and social status, to management and trade unions, as well as their more general perceptions of class. Intra- and inter-sectoral comparisons are also explored in order to investigate the presence or absence of collectivist/solidaristic and individualist/instrumental outlooks and behaviours amongst these representatives of what some see as the increasingly dominant knowledge worker (Castells, 1998; Drucker, 1993). We objectively locate both call centre and software workers as wage-labourers under capitalism as a result of deploying a perspective of radical political economy. However, where software workers are accorded higher remuneration, greater autonomy and social status, leading the majority of them to subjectively determine themselves as 'middle class professionals', relatively inferior terms and conditions of employment, and their perceived subordinate status, suggested that the majority of call centre workers identified themselves as 'working class'. We also explore whether collective attitudes are more prevalent in call centres than in software. The chapter begins with a brief survey of the extant literature to provide a conceptual and theoretical foundation for discussing and evaluating the research findings.

Marx was the first to argue that class antagonism was the fundamental principle of social theory, and that capitalism created a polarization between the working class (proletariat) and the owners of capital (bourgeoisie), resulting in the formation of 'two great hostile camps' (Hyman, R., 1980). Three propositions underpin Marx's conception of class:

(a) social relations within production are the most important determinant of class structure – the capitalists own the means of production, distribution and exchange, while the workers do not;
(b) classes are defined and identified by the exploitative relationship between them – under capitalism, this takes the form of the extraction of surplus value from workers by employers;
(c) class antagonism – the class struggle – is the most important motor of social transformation, under which class-consciousness develops 'subjectively' and the working class becomes the social agent of human emancipation, because it has not only a vested interest in seizing control of society and remaking it in its own image, but also the collective means to do so.

While such theory has long informed, influenced and underpinned intellectual endeavours in many fields, it has not gone uncontested. At the close of the twentieth century, the view that the concept of the working class was anachronistic attracted support from a growing band of writers in western industrialized countries, drawn from a diverse range of academic disciplines and theoretical perspectives. Bell (1974), Blackburn (1967), Drucker (1970, 1993), Prandy (1965) and Stonier (1983) represented the first wave of 'revisionists' here, while Rifkin (1995), Pakulski and Waters (1996), Castells (1996, 1997) and Bauman (1998) represented the second. While they analysed and conceptualized developments at societal level in vastly differing ways, two contentions united them; a) that the working class had no potential as a transformative agent of social change, and b) that widespread, rapid, indeed paradigmic, changes in the industrial, occupational and social structures had taken place, facilitated and driven by unprecedented levels of uptake of new information and communication technologies (ICTs) within a globalized economy. These developments had not only transformed the socio-economic landscape, it was argued, but also definitively signalled the passing into history of (primarily) Marxian theories concerning both the existence of class and class conflict. However, some recent contributions have re-stated the commitment to Weberian approaches to class analysis (Goldthorpe, 1996; Marshall, 1997), while others proposed 'an expanded and transformed class theory' (Crompton and Scott, 2000; Devine and Savage, 2000). These latter new accounts,

> question the centrality and distinctiveness of the 'economic', inflate 'class' to include social and cultural formations, and reconfigure the causal model that historically underpinned class analysis (class position leads to consciousness and action)...such approaches abandon the notion of distinct or cohesive class identities or groups, focusing instead on individualized hierarchical differentiation. (Bottero, 2004: 986)

What is also noticeable about more recent sociological debate on the existence and nature of class is that it continues to orient on a societal or general level, rather than upon any research-based analyses of developments in the so-called knowledge economy or those which examine the attitudes of information workers *per se*. We aim to help fill this substantive and theoretical gap.

White-collar workers and class

Although most participants in the class debate recognized that the post-war western workforce was now demonstrably more white-collar, and that these employees were increasingly female, service-based, educationally qualified and unionized, disagreements existed over the significance of this phenomenon, particularly in regard of precisely how this strata was affected by changes in capitalism, and how these developments influenced broader analyses of class itself. Nonetheless, Weberian-based criteria of work and market situation dominated this thinking, leading to categorization predicated on occupational grading and status (e.g. Lockwood, 1958; Giddens, 1973).

One of the main threads of debate concerned relative differences in white-collar workers' circumstances (remuneration, job autonomy, occupational mobility, status) *vis-à-vis* those of other workers, primarily manual workers. Two trajectories, often held to be polar opposites, were identified; the embourgeoizification of the (manual) working class (Dahrendorf, 1959; Giddens, 1973) and the proletarianization of the white-collar workforce (Braverman, 1974; Callinicos, 1983; Crompton and Jones, 1984; Klingender, 1935; Mallet, 1975). Meanwhile, Poulantzas (1975) posited that all white-collar employees and all 'non-productive' manual workers were not part of the 'productive' working class, but were the new petty bourgeoisie, and Gorz (1971) argued that certain scientific and technical workers should not be considered an integral part of the working class. Allied to this, Wright Mills (1951) termed a host of white-collar occupations as 'the new middle class', and Ehrenreich and Ehrenreich (1977) defined certain white-collar workers as comprising the 'professional-managerial class', similar to Goldthorpe's

(1982) later formulation of 'the service class'. Arguments that organizations and occupations were too diverse to yield a generalized condition of class subordination were rebutted by Parkin (1979: 182), while Marx himself had observed that claims of such fragmentation suggested there existed an 'infinity of classes' (Hyman R. and Price, 1983: 20). For our concerns in this chapter, the range of writing on white-collar workers collectively suggests we might expect call centre employees to exhibit certain similarities in attitude and behaviour to those analysed in earlier studies of clerical workers (Crompton and Jones, 1984; Klingender, 1935), namely, being subject to the control of managers, not exercising (formal) control over other workers, having little autonomy at work and experiencing relatively unrewarding wages and conditions. However, the origin of these practices lies not in some general trends towards immizeration, proletarianization or deskilling, but in the conscious design of such work and jobs at the outset by call centre employers. Similarly, software workers might be expected to approximate to those characteristics and views reported in research which had focused upon various technical/professional strata (Gorz, 1971; Hyman R. and Price, 1983; Mallet, 1975; Smith, 1987), namely, job and professional autonomy, superior wages and conditions, and higher social standing.

Whilst in Marxian analysis, class *per se* is defined by its relationship to the economic structure, class-consciousness can nevertheless be influenced and shaped by a range of factors leading, for example, to a diversity of views on self-ascription to emerge as a result of political conviction or social aspiration. In this vein, Lockwood (1958) and Giddens (1973) argued respectively that clerks' and white-collar workers' material and status circumstances led them to distinguish themselves as socially superior to manual workers. By contrast, Mallet (1975) suggested that in resisting the objective conditions of modern capitalism, technical workers might develop a consciousness which pushed them to become the combative vanguard of 'the new working class' while Gorz (1971: 87) argued that these workers would collectively 'rebel not *as* proletarians, but *against* being *treated* as proletarians' (emphasis in original). Smith (1987: 67) posited that most technical workers did not have any supervisory function and, in fact, were employed 'within social and institutional practices that foster a working class identity'.

In presenting the research findings, we consider a wide range of factors which are perceived to be important in defining and locating both the existence of class and individuals' self-ascribed class location. These factors include consideration of the basic nature of the tasks carried out by call centre and software employees, the contractual relationship with their employer, as well as analysis of questionnaire and interview responses concerning the existence of class and class identity, workplace attitudes and behaviours, and towards forms of collectivism. We then relate the interpretation of our findings to the debates set out earlier on the objective, class character of white-collar workers and their subjective class-consciousness, by extrapolating from them to higher, societal units of analysis, before presenting our conclusions.

Work tasks and contractual relationships

The vast majority of the people who worked in both the call centres and software were employed on full-time, permanent contracts. Contrary to what we expected to find – as well as in marked contrast to the assumed defining characteristics of the knowledge economy – only 9 per cent of the total workforce in call centres, and 12 per cent in software, were contractors, agency or temporary workers. Furthermore, 86 per cent of call centre employees were on full-time contracts, as were 93 per cent in software. The employing organizations were all private sector, capitalist firms, who operated and competed on a commercial, profit-seeking basis in what were often turbulent business and market environments (Taylor et al., 2005).

Call centres

In the case of the call centre operations, the services on offer to customers were clearly differentiated, but generally intangible in nature. Call handlers were employed to respond to customer inquiries over the telephone, and/or to sell services such as loans, mortgages and financial planning advice (Moneyflow), holiday and travel packages (Holstravel), television channel rentals and telephonic equipment installation (Entcomm), and everything from arranging the delivery of drinks to servicing luxury cars in the dedicated outsourcing organization, Thejobshop. The call handlers' assigned role was to act as the front-line representative of their employer (or, in Thejobshop's case, the client organization), and to deal with customers in accordance with how management defined the company's best interests. However, staff were employed, not to act as 'mediators' between customer and company during these telephonic transactions (cf. Korczynski, 2002) but, literally, to be the firm's mouth-piece, *albeit* one which was often scripted and invariably tightly monitored.

Sometimes, the initial call could resolve matters (e.g. notification of a customer's change of address) and no further action was required but, on other occasions, the call handler might have to arrange for a letter or contract to be posted to the customer from another section in the call centre. Furthermore, in response to customers' needs and/or company protocol, call handlers often had to contact other departments of the parent organization, such as installation engineers (Entcomm), 'high street' branches (Moneyflow), or the client firm who had outsourced work (Thejobshop). Thus, in terms of the process of the production, distribution and exchange of goods, from the holistic perspective of the 'total social organization of labour' (Glucksman, 2004) or Marx's 'collective labourer' (1976), the call handler's function generically can be seen as clearly contributing to the *realization* – and not the *production* – of value.

While many call centres offered financial bonuses based upon individual or team performance, profit-related schemes and other inducements, as discussed in general terms in Chapter 4, the basic wage (and related premium payments) undoubtedly constituted the most important element in employee reward systems. During the period when the workplace-based research was being conducted, basic pay for Moneyflow's customer service agents (most staff were on this grade) ranged from a minimum of £9,950 per annum to a maximum £17,880 and, for customer advisors, from £13,620 to £25,680 (IDS, 1999). Moneyflow did not pay a premium for shift-working, but all four call centres paid enhanced rates of time-and-half for working overtime on Saturdays, and double time for Sundays. In Holstravel, service representatives received a minimum of £10,200 per annum and a maximum of £12,750, while team leaders' pay ranged from £14,000 to £16,800 (IDS, 2000); shift premium varied from 9–30 per cent of basic pay, depending upon the patterns worked by individual employees. In Thejobshop, most staff were on the customer service grade, with minimum and maximum annual salaries of £10,000 and £14,500 respectively, while team managers' pay was between £15,500 and £20,000 (IDS, 2000); staff available to work 24/7 received a shift premium of ten per cent. The starting salaries at Entcomm ranged from £11,500 for customer service advisors to £19,500 for team leaders, with no shift premium (unstructured interview, Entcomm, female customer service advisor).

By way of comparison, the mean annual gross pay for all UK employees stood at £18,939, or £354.50 per week (ONS, 2001a). As can be seen, this was significantly higher than the basic pay for call handlers in all four call centres, as well as above the team leaders' rate in Holstravel; it was only slightly below the team leader and manager rate in Thejobshop and Entcomm, and only those in the upper bracket of the highly qualified advisors in Moneyflow were paid substantially more. Therefore, in order to gain parity with the UK average gross wage, most call handlers would have had to work extensive shift patterns and/or put in overtime hours.

In summary, in terms of their contractual relationship to the employer, the nature of the tasks they undertake, and the level of their remuneration, it is difficult not to perceive the vast majority of call centre staff as having a close, socio-economic, class affinity to not only a wide range of other, lower status, contemporary service and office jobs (Huws, 1999), but to many semi-skilled manual occupations as well (Head, 2003).

Software

In contrast to the intangible nature of the output of call centres, software firms usually sold a physical product but, sometimes, also the maintenance of, or changes to applications programmes to their corporate customers, while those software employees in Beta produced for their own operational requirements. The product typically took the form of a disc containing a dedicated bespoke (e.g. health and safety, the law) or systems applications programme, but could also involve maintaining or amending the latter. Thus, in those software companies whose contractual relationship with their clients was based upon the exchange of their products for money (i.e. with the aim of making a profit), the collective workforce can be regarded as directly contributing to *the production of value*. In Beta's case, where the software was specifically designed for, and would be applied in the company's internal operations in pursuit of commercial gain in the outside world, the employees' output can be seen as being related to *the realization of value*.

As we discussed in Chapter 3, the most common method of organizing production favoured by management was to group employees in teams, dedicated to the completion of projects within a stipulated time-frame, and to specified and attested quality criteria. The project teams were placed under the direct control of managers or senior members of staff – and, in some instances, they worked in the client's office for considerable periods of time. Generally, clients would be consulted or engaged in regular discussion and negotiation for the duration of their project, so there was a perceived need for communicative as well as technical skills among staff. The range of job titles utilized in software establishments is listed elsewhere (see Appendix B, notes to Table B1).

Beta was unusual among the software companies in that staff pay and conditions were the subject of annual negotiations with the appropriate union and, so, were in the public domain. This approach clearly reflected the company's ex-public sector, heavily unionized, historical background. The entry level for the 'managerial and professional' grade in which the majority of the workforce was concentrated, was £19,500 per annum, rising to a top rate of £35,000; the grade rate covering senior staff and team leaders started at £23,000 and increased to £41,000. Those required to work continuous, rotating shifts were paid a monthly allowance ranging between £280 and £700, dependent upon employee grade and pattern of shifts worked. Normally, non-managerial employees received time off in lieu when they worked overtime, but double time was paid for Sundays and a premium of time-and-quarter to time-and-half for other periods.

Of the smaller software firms, Gamma said they had no formal pay structure but, based upon prevailing market rates, they paid what was necessary to attract staff. Pi's 'Terms of Employment' set out their wages policy as follows, 'As a meritocracy, the company aims to discriminate heavily in favour of employees whose performance is thought to be above average'. Only in rare circumstances were overtime payments made to employees. Apart from Beta, only Omega had a formal grading structure, under which technical grade staff started at £12–13,000 per annum if they did not possess a degree, while graduates' starting salary was £16,000 (unstructured interview, Omega, female HR manager). There were two intermediate grades, with a top rate of £22,000, before the scale leaped to the two top technical rates – paid to senior developers and project managers – between £35,000 and £40,000. The company's Employee Handbook took a firm line against relying on overtime to meet deadlines or targets.

Again, using the mean annual gross pay for all UK employees as a basis of comparison, this stood at £18,939 per annum (ONS, 2001a). If we take Omega management's statement, that their pay policy was 'competitive but not brilliant', as an approximate measure of what the smaller software companies were offering, then the lower technical grades were below the UK average figure, while intermediate groups were slightly above. Furthermore, there were few opportunities to boost earnings by means of overtime or shift payments. Thus, in the smaller software firms, only a small minority of the most senior developers and project managers were paid substantially above average earnings. While pay scales and overtime and shift payments in Beta were clearly superior to those in the other organizations, new employees and those at the bottom of the 'managerial and professional' grading structure were not paid significantly more than those on the UK average wage.

In terms of the fundamental aspects of their relationship with the employer – i.e. demonstrably based upon wage-labour – and noting the level of their actual earnings, the class situation of the majority of the software workforce can be regarded as not being qualitatively different from that of their call centre counterparts. In other words, objectively, these sections of software employees can be considered to be members of the working class. The question of whether or not the upper echelons of the software workforce are more fittingly categorized as part of 'the new working class' (Mallet, 1975), 'middle strata' (Callinicos, 1983), 'the new petty bourgeoisie' (Poulantzas, 1975) or members of a 'professional-managerial class' (Ehrenreich and Ehrenreich, 1977), will be discussed below.

Class: attitudes and behaviours

In presenting the rest of the research findings, and in order to begin generating insights into the threads of the broader debates, we follow the structure of setting out and examining our respondents' perceptions of: (i) the objective existence of class; (ii) their own class identity; (iii) their 'workplace' attitudes; (iv) their 'workplace' behaviour; and (v) collectivism and individualism.

The existence of class

Around two-thirds of respondents to the employee questionnaire in both call centres (63 per cent) and software (68 per cent) rejected the proposition that there were no important class divisions in Britain today, with only 9 and 10 per cent respectively agreeing with this statement. These views were broadly in line with those expressed in the individual workplace interviews which were conducted, where the researchers were able to probe further to find out how class was defined by respondents. Following Goldthorpe et al.'s (1969) formulation, few people perceived class in terms of a 'power' model, in which there were two major classes differentiated by the extent of the power and authority which each possessed. While there were many respondents who identified huge differences between what they saw as a rich elite and 'the poor' or other subordinate classes, this was rarely related to the privileged minority's *ownership* of the means of production, distribution and exchange as the source of their wealth and power.

However, just over half of those interviewed in both sectors held what Goldthorpe et al. (1969) characterised as a 'money' model perspective, in which there was perceived to be one large class alongside one or more smaller and/or elite classes, who were differentiated by wealth, income and consumption. Of the respondents who took this position, most used the terminology of 'class' in setting out their views, revealing a widespread sentiment that some kind of a distinct upper class was still identifiable in the social structure. Evidence of the existence of this elite was evoked by reference to the royal family, the aristocracy and – by one call handler – to what she saw as the obviously non-working class credentials of the rich socialite, Tara Palmer-Tomkinson. Examples were:

> I think what you might call the upper class is still different, because I think the difference in jump between middle and upper class is so big that you don't often get a step between them ... So I guess it's the middle and bottom that are coming together, but I view the top still as a different world almost. (Gamma, male product development manager; G-I-11)

> All the footballers with obscene amounts of money ... Things like that, you know that's where you see the divide. All these big bosses of those companies who are paid a fortune, then get all these bonuses. If it wasn't for us people down on the front lines they wouldn't be getting a profit. I don't think that's fair. (Holstravel, female sales consultant; H-I-27)

However, some proponents of a 'money' model of social group or class structure placed more emphasis upon divisions based upon money and wealth *per se*, rather than upon identification with any concept of systemic factors determining class location. These views were sometimes accompanied by a belief that 'class' was in decline, and more egalitarian processes were at work:

> I don't think class has relevance. I just think it's rich and poor ... So I don't think that class has anything to do with it anymore. (Pi, female support consultant; P-I-18)

> You can't deny divisions that there are between groups in society, but I think that the implication that there is an inherent part of people that puts them in whatever category...is a false notion ... I think that people are divided by the money that they have, (and) divided by the opportunities they have. (Thejobshop, male customer service adviser; T-I-08)

> There is still that dividing line – oh, we've got money and you haven't, and you can see it in every day life. Don't get me wrong, I don't think it's as bad as it was years ago, I definitely don't, because there are more opportunities now for people. (Entcomm, female customer service adviser; E-I-3)

> I think over time, [Britain is] probably less [class divided]...there is more distribution of wealth. I mean Britain still has a class society. What I'm not sure is whether that matters any more. Yes, there are rich people, there are poor people, but there is a growing amount of people who are quite happy with the amount of wealth that they have, and...people who can afford more expensive cars and bigger houses. (Gamma, male product development manager; G-I-01)

Other influences which were seen by respondents as contributing to determining or defining class included people's social roots, accent, education and leisure activities, as well as their attitude to home ownership:

> If you are from the right social group, then you will get on a lot quicker. If someone came here looking for a job and she was from the wrong side of town, if she comes over with a very rough accent, then I don't think we would take her. (Pi, male financial director; P-I-05)

> Private schooling compared to like your council schools. All these debutante balls, coming out parties...if you look at 'Hello' and things like that, all these events they have been at – and Ascot with their hats. (Holstravel, female sales consultant; H-I-29)

Although our data suggests that class divisions are widely recognized, it does not suggest, as yet, that these divisions were seen by respondents as necessarily socially divisive or abhorrent. Class was seen primarily as a financial and consumerist hierarchy, where symptomatic aspects of the reproduction of class were focused upon, and not as a relationship of power or (economic) resources between two large and universal social groups. However, Savage (2005), in an analysis of Goldthorpe *et al.*'s data (1969), makes the point that the extent to which the 'affluent workers' actually differentiated between the existence of a distinct rich upper class and 'money' models of society was exaggerated. Thus, he argues that 'talking about money is in part a way of talking about power and in particular about the prominence of the upper class' (Savage, 2005: 935), and this may account for much of the manner in which our respondents viewed class.

Class identity

Those employed in call centres were of little doubt that, both in terms of their occupational status and as individuals, they were of the working class. By this, they meant that they identified themselves economically, financially and culturally as part of an 'impoverished', subordinate social group. Notwithstanding the fact that perhaps more socially aspirant team-leaders and part-time university students were included in the survey, of those interviewed, only ten per cent described their workgroup's class location as middle class, and 15 per cent perceived their own class identity in this way.

> The majority of call centre staff would be kind of at the bottom end of middle class, I would suggest. Obviously rising the higher through the organization due to level of income, but the majority of them bottom middle ... Due to a fairly large inheritance I got a good few years ago, I would probably put myself at middle middle. (Entcomm, female team leader; E-I-04)

However, around 80 per cent of respondents said call centre employees were working class (with some attributing a middle class element), and two-thirds described their own social status in similar manner (17 per cent provided no response):

> Q. So what sort of class would you put people working in call centres – I mean could you do that, or is it irrelevant?
> A. No. Just normal working class people.
> Q. And what class would you say you are?
> A. Me? I'm just working class.
> (Entcomm, female team leader; E-I-17)

> Q. If you had to put yourself into a social class, where would you put yourself?
> A. Well, I am working class.
> Q. Why?

A. Well, there's no inheritance to fall back on. There's no capital. In terms of the family structure...There's no long line of brothers and sisters and cousins that go back. I mean, I was born in an industrial part of London. Basically, I have no pension. I have got to work to survive – and that's what I think it's about.
(Holstravel, male booking clerk; H-I-30)

On the other hand, the responses from software employees were much more complex. While a number of respondents experienced difficulties in locating their occupation in class terms, of those who did, the vast majority used the appellation 'middle class/professional', with very few suggesting that software employment was working class in character. However, as can be seen from Table 8.1, when asked to identify their own class identity, a very different picture emerged.

Three-quarters of those who designated themselves working class, referred to family background, upbringing and/or community to give this grounding. The following quotes also illustrate that some respondents were conscious of perceptions of possible tensions between their current material wealth and their class origins and self-identity:

People tell me I'm middle class because I own my own home, and I have two cars, and I go abroad on holiday every year ... but my grandfather was a socialist. My uncle was a trade union spokesman. My husband's father was a coal miner and my mother-in-law was a cleaner in the pit. You can't have people so close to you who were definitely working class and still not be a bit of that yourself. (Beta, female services manager; B-I-01)

I'm definitely working class...My wife doesn't agree but ... that's where I come from. My father was a miner and my mother worked in a shop, so I'm very definitely working class...and I have to work for a living, I've got no choice...I own my own home, I've got two cars, my wife's a professional and my son goes to one of those top schools...we both went to university and got degrees, we are probably in the top salary earners, so we are middle class. But I personally don't believe that. I believe I'm working class. It's the background that I have – I'm true to the politics of the working class. (Pi, male chief operating officer; P-I-02)

In contrast, software employees who identified themselves as middle class tended to refer to education, income and/or lifestyle as the defining features of their background and experience.

I suppose I went to a good school and got university education and now work in a professional job, so I'd have to go in at that level, compared to somebody who say didn't get any qualifications and maybe they went to college. (Gamma, male graphics applications developer; G-HI-14)

> That would be middle class I think ... because I am married to an [IT] sales consultant as well so we live in a nice house in Edinburgh...so I couldn't say working class anymore even though I would like to be still. (Pi, male software programmer; P-I-10)

However, there were other software workers, numbering some 14 per cent of those interviewed who, when asked to state their class location, regarded it as unimportant or irrelevant in their own lives. While the existence of class was often acknowledged, its perceived effects were regarded as undesirable or neutral.

> I don't think [class] relates [to me]. I don't actually feel I have to touch my forelock or bow down to anybody above me. (Pi, male technical sales manager; P-I-06)

> To me personally it doesn't make any odds. Obviously to some people it does. I really just don't care about the class issue and stuff like that. (Pi, male installations analyst; P-I-19)

This declared non-interest in the existence of class may relate to having enjoyed a reasonably comfortable standard of living while not encountering, and thus possibly being troubled by, aspects or evidence of class divisions with regard to, for example, poverty and deprivation within working class communities.

Hence, in subjective and self-ascriptive terms, call centre workers view themselves as predominantly 'working class', while most software workers view themselves predominantly as 'middle class' and/or 'middle class

Table 8.1 Positive self-location of class identity for software workers

Class identity	Percentage
Working class	38
Middle class	31
Professional	28
Upper middle class	8
'No class'	10

Note: N = 72. As some respondents used more than one term to describe their identity, e.g. 'middle class' and 'professional', the percentage total is greater than 100 per cent.
Source: Fieldwork interviews.

professionals' (although more than a third thought they were working class) (see also discussion of careers in Chapter 5). This self-ascription is an important part of the dynamic social processes by which subjective notions of 'class' are constructed and reified.

Workplace attitudes

There is no mechanical relationship between the degree of employee-employer conflict or antagonism in the workplace and class identification or attitude. Nevertheless, when considered in combination with other known employee behaviours, analysis of the nature and extent of these consensual/adversarial stances can contribute towards a greater understanding of the complex broader issues related to work, employment and class.

Questionnaire respondents in both sectors, were generally less than enchanted with their own management's attitudes and performance (Table 8.2), but were even more sharply critical when asked to assess managerial performance and policies in Britain generally (Table 8.3).

In their own workplaces, more respondents in both sectors agreed than disagreed that management was only interested in profits and efficiency, although those in call centres displayed a considerably more critical approach to management. With very little inter-sectoral difference, around half agreed that day-to-day policy-making was too remote, with only one in seven disagreeing. Software employees were notably more satisfied with the respect they received than were their call centre counterparts, probably indicating the impact of a greater degree of job autonomy in their work. Perhaps surprisingly, in software, more respondents (just over a third) disagreed than agreed with the proposition that they and senior management shared common aims – a stance which was supported by a margin of 40–30 per cent in the call centres. As expected, because of a closer and relatively more empathic relationship, shared common aims with team leaders received greater support in both sectors, although around one in five opposed this notion (see also Chapter 4). Just over a third in both sectors agreed that management had the welfare of employees at heart – slightly outnumbering those who disagreed.

The majority of respondents in both sectors agreed that management generally was only interested in profits and efficiency (fewer than one in seven disagreed), and similar numbers disagreed with the suggestion that management had the welfare of their employees at heart (less than one in six agreed). In both sectors also – but more strongly in software – more disagreed than agreed with the proposition that management and employees had common aims (see also Chapter 4). Similarly, more agreed than disagreed that management would always try to get the better of employees.

To briefly summarize and compare the findings of Tables 8.2 and 8.3, it is evident that while respondents were critical of management over most

Table 8.2 Attitudes to management in respondents' own workplace

	Call centres		Software	
	% D/SD	% A/SA	% D/SD	% A/SA
Only interested in profits and efficiency	20	50	25	39
Policy-making is too remote	14	46	15	53
Employees are never treated with respect they deserve	43	27	50	19
Senior management and employees have common aims	30	40	35	29
Team leaders and employees have common aims	19	58	24	41
Has the welfare of employees at heart	32	35	27	34

Source: N = 827 in call centres; N = 281 in software. 'D' Disagree; 'SD' Strongly disagree; 'A' Agree; 'SA' Strongly agree.

Table 8.3 Attitudes to management in Britain generally

	Call centres		Software	
	% D/SD	% A/SA	% D/SD	% A/SA
Only interested in profits and efficiency	11	62	14	55
Managers and employees have common aims	40	29	47	22
Management has the welfare of employees at heart	56	16	56	16
Management will always try to get the better of employees	25	39	28	32

Source: N = 827 in call centres; N = 281 in software. 'D' Disagree; 'SD' Strongly disagree; 'A' Agree; 'SA' Strongly agree.

issues, this attitude was expressed much more strongly at a generalized societal level, compared to how they felt about management in their own workplace. Both call centre and software workers displayed significant evidence of critical and oppositional attitudes towards management – whether or not these are transmuted and actualized into action and behaviour results from, *inter alia*, the development of grievances and the availability of other organizational and attitudinal resources like shadow stewards and opinion formers (Bain *et al.*, 2004: 79–81; Kelly, 1998).

Workplace behaviour

Our concern here was to try to identify employee workplace behaviours which might indicate an orientation towards – or rejection of – the adoption of a class-based approach to resolving issues and problems. Towards this end, we consider responses to questions related to how the role of employees was perceived, not least in terms of support for, or membership of, a trade union. Whilst trade unionism may display sectional and competitive worldviews, membership of unions is most likely to be predicated on an implicit notion of 'them and us' at both workplace and societal level – a rudimentary form of understanding class dynamics. This is not to imply that it is possible to 'read' off class attitudes based upon whether or not someone is a member of a union, but it is to recognize, as Lockwood (1958: 137) put it, while 'there is no inevitable connection between unionization and class-consciousness...(nevertheless) the trade union movement is a working class movement.'

As far as the role of employees was concerned, questionnaire responses clearly indicated that acquiescence and passivity towards management, their functions and their actions were not perceived to be desirable. For example, while less than a quarter agreed (call centres 19 per cent and software 24 per cent) that management generally had the right to manage their organization without interference, almost half (49 per cent in call centres, 47 per cent in software) disagreed. The right of employees to take industrial action in order to get a fair deal was supported by 69 per cent of call centre respondents, and by 57 per cent in software – those disagreeing amounted to nine and 18 per cent respectively.

With regard to the importance of independent employee representation in any job, while 30 per cent of call centre respondents described this as very important or absolutely critical, 41 per cent said it was not very, or not at all, important. However, when those who believed it was 'quite important' are taken into consideration, the percentage who attached some degree of importance to independent employee representation increased to 59 per cent; perhaps not surprisingly, the corresponding software figures were only eight per cent who said it was very important or absolutely critical, 71 per cent thought it not very or not at all important, while 29 per cent attached some degree of importance.

These findings on the importance respondents attached to independent employee representation stand in sharp contrast to the actual levels of union membership in the workplaces. Only three companies recognized unions for bargaining and representational purposes (call centres Holstravel and Moneyflow, and software house, Beta) and, outwith these, there was a mere smattering of individual union members. Even in the 'unionized' offices, while membership was just over 50 per cent in Holstravel and Beta, for reasons related to the company's organizational structure, it was below ten per cent in the Moneyflow call centre (see Bain *et al.*, 2004: 72–4). According to the 2004 *Labour Force Survey* (as cited in Grainger and Holt, 2005: 18–19), professional occupations were 48.6 per cent aggregate unionized, with transport and communication at 41.3, financial intermediation 26.6, and business services 10.5 per cent. Thus, our case study organizations are below their respective sectoral medians.

The disjunction between the expressed demand or support for independent employee representation and the actual levels of unionization indicates that, although such attitudinal and ideological characteristics are necessary to set in train a process of class-based collectivism and action, they are insufficient in themselves. The 'missing' components needed to attain such an outcome include a range of behavioural and institutional constructs, like oppositional ideology and union organizing presence (Bain et al., 2004: 81).

Collectivism and individualism

In recent years, it has been argued that fundamental changes have taken place in the relationship between contending collectivist and individualist influences, policies, attitudes and behaviours in the workplace (Bacon and Storey, 1996). In particular, it has been claimed that the adoption of HRM strategies by many organizations was a key factor in significantly shifting the balance towards a much more individualistic approach to the employment relationship (see also Chapter 4). More generally, some writers believe that individualized cultures and 'life politics' now predominate at a societal level, and that these developments mark a distinct break from past notions of collectivism and class (see the review in Savage, 2001).

Leaving aside for the moment the question of the veracity of these claims, it remains the case generally that no organization can operate without the collective effort and mutual co-operation of those whom they employ. As we have seen in both the call centres and software firms, on the surface, some jobs could be viewed as being essentially individualistic in character. In fact, the provision of these services and products required workers to co-operate with each other inside each company, and these operations, in turn, were embedded in wider processes of production, distribution and exchange. Thus, some form of collective endeavour can be seen as being intrinsic to the successful operation of both the capitalist labour process and related product markets (Marx, 1976).

In reporting our research findings in this area, we will identify and differentiate between, three forms of collectivism: first, new or unitaristic collectivism, consciously instigated by management in the company's interests, and often associated with the posited rise of HRM through practices such as the promotion of team-working, profit sharing and employee consultative bodies (Bacon and Storey, 1996); second, instrumental collectivism, by means of which groups of employees unite in order to defend and/or pursue their perceived sectional interests (for example, the formation of restricted membership professional bodies and trade unions) (Goldthorpe et al., 1968); third, class-based collectivism, an expression of broader political and cultural considerations which transcend sectional concerns and foci, and which identifies with a range of oppressed or fellow combatant groupings (Kelly, 1998: 39–40).

However, this formulation does not mean that these different forms of collectivism are mutually exclusive, as employees may adopt overlapping, or even seemingly contradictory stances simultaneously – as Savage (2001: 98) put it, 'individualistic cultures need not be inimical to class cultures'. Further, according to social identity theory, everyone has a personal identity and a social identity, and 'this suggests each person can think and act individually *and* collectively depending on which facet of their identity is currently dominant or 'salient'' (Kelly, 1998: 31, emphasis in original). The possibility of such duality is illustrated in the discussion which follows.

Our respondents' attitudes towards group working could be interpreted as an identification with, or acceptance of unitaristic collectivism and the employer's agenda. Around two-thirds of call centre employees, and three-quarters of those in software, expressed agreement with the general proposition that members of workplace groups should both subordinate their wishes to those of the collective in the interests of productivity, and be prepared to make sacrifices in the group's interests. However, this response could also be seen as an example of employee instrumental collectivism, intended to preserve group solidarity and ethos, or even as an adversarial 'restrictive practice' – for example, respecting an overtime ban in support of a sectional claim for enhanced conditions. Further, if we assume that the extent to which respondents perceived employees sharing common aims with management as an expression of their support for unitarist collectivism then, as the findings in Tables 8.2 and 8.3 show, within the individual firm, this is strongest regarding team leader level (albeit with significant numbers of dissidents), weaker concerning senior management (with more opposed in software than agreeing), and rejected by majorities in both sectors in relation to 'management in Britain generally'.

A clear preference for organizing work on a team/collective basis was reflected in the fact that fewer than ten per cent of questionnaire respondents said that they would rather work alone than with other employees. This finding may be a further indication of the generally favourable attitudes already expressed towards work colleagues, and/or of a greater commitment to them than to the employer (see also Chapter 4). At the same time, a strong individualistic attitude was evident in the survey responses, as fewer than one in twenty software employees, and only one in seven in call centres believed that people doing the same job should be paid the same, regardless of performance. Some respondents' attitudes towards union membership also displayed individualistic rather than instrumental collectivist tendencies.

> If I had something to say, then I would stand up for myself and say it...if I felt I couldn't sort out my differences on a personal level, then I probably wouldn't want to stay here. (Moneyflow, female customer adviser; M-I-12)

[This] is a growing industry – everyone I know who has been made redundant in this business...have always had a job which is as good, or nearly as good, or occasionally better, very quickly...[While] the industry is growing so much...as an employee you have a lot more leverage, a lot more bargaining power. Just as an individual, you can go in and say well, if you don't give me another £5,000, I'm going to go, and then they sort of argue you down to £3,000. (Gamma, male IT support engineer; G-HI-10)

However, as already discussed, more than half (59 per cent) of call centre employees and more than a quarter (29 per cent) of those in software, stated that they attached some degree of importance to the right to independent representation, and instrumental collectivist approaches to union membership are evident in the following quotations. Indeed, one respondent argued that workers needed unions,

I'd never have advocated unions in the past ... I have actually made inquiries about the communications union because I was a bit concerned about my contract...they are kind of shoving it out the door now and changing bits of it, and we are scared to sign things away ... I would take a union line now and I can't believe I'm saying this, because I was never like that. (Entcomm, female customer service advisor; E-HI-02)

[T]here is still a place for union representation. [T]he union were taking a very active role in [a voluntary redundancy exercise]. They've not done so much since then but, at the time, it was good to know that they were behind you and that they were there if you needed them, and it was one of the first things I did when I joined Beta was join the union ... [T]hey do take a minimal role in our pay but I think they should take a more active role. (Beta, male software engineer; B-HI-07)

Again, as discussed above, such indications of respondents' support for *the principle* of the right to independent representation, were not reflected in *actual* union membership figures in either sector. For example, even in the only unionized software company, one interviewee commented,

[If I had a grievance] I think I would tend to talk to my colleagues first to see what they thought and to gather the general feeling, and then I would go to my boss after that...[W]e are in the sort of job that gets reasonably well treated anyway, unions are more effective where employers are causing their employees a lot of problems ... I think it's [union membership] not a great necessity in the sort of job I'm in. If things got bad, and conditions got bad or something, then people would just leave. Whereas, there are a lot of jobs where people are kind of stuck where they are, and their employer could screw them down and cause them all sorts of hassle, and there unions are very effective. (Beta, male software engineer; B-HI-09)

In considering the broader perspective of the influence of collectivist and individualist cultures at a societal/political level, one respondent recounted her feeling of social isolation whilst living in 'better-off' suburban neighbourhoods,

> Everybody kept themselves to themselves, very much so ... I used to get the train every day into Glasgow and you would see the same faces...and everybody sat in the same seats ... people were friendly on the train, but once you got home you didn't see anybody ... There were a couple of neighbours that were certainly very friendly, and you could approach them if you were going on holiday, or invite them in for a chat and a drink ... but I don't know about community. (Entcomm, female customer adviser; E-HI-03)

Radically differing views to the above, on how the basis and role of 'the community' and collectivity was envisaged, were emphasized by other employees. For example,

> I would like to think that everybody was the same, there's probably a bit of a communist in me ... but you've got to be realistic – there are 'haves and have nots', and probably in the last few years the 'haves' are getting more and the 'have nots' are getting less...(a single tax based on income) would give more money to distribute to the lower earners. I mean it's a form of madness – people desperate to work, but collecting 'broo' money (i.e. unemployment benefit). (Entcomm, male team leader; E-HI-04)

In software, some respondents emphasized their sense of a professional community (see also chapters 6 and 7),

> I think it's one big community almost. If I was to meet someone else who was a software engineer you've automatically got something in common with them, but there is still a certain snobbery as well within that culture. (Beta, male software engineer; B-HI-07)

Both the call centre and software respondents' recognition of class structures, and their self-ascribed class location, are broadly in line with the comparable regional data from British and Scottish Social Attitudes surveys over the same period (for a summary, see Gall, 2005). The most salient feature here, is that attitudes towards class and social justice are more pronounced in Scotland than in England (although this relationship breaks down when intra-England regions are used as comparators); within Scotland, such attitudes are more strongly adhered to in the west and central belt compared to elsewhere. Given the location of our case studies, this influence can be detected in the subjective identification with the working class, when the objective circumstances of respondents might suggest a middle class orientation.

Discussion

Having presented our research findings, we now consider their relationship to two issues of central interest in this chapter, namely, the formulation of overall judgements concerning the class character, and the class-consciousness, of our two groups of sectoral respondents.

The class character of call centre and software workers

We started from the premise that class is most productively defined as an underlying *relationship* between dominant social groups, resultant from the ownership and control of capital. Recognition that ownership of the means of production, distribution and exchange, by one group rather than another, and the necessity of the then property-less class to sell their capacity to labour to the owners of capital, leads us to locate the embedded dynamics and rationale of capitalism as the basis of the method of analysis. Henceforth, issues related to the strategic function, interests and power of sub-class groups (for example, based in industrial sectors such as call centres and software) can be situated *within* this larger compass. Consequently, the starting point for attempting to analyse the class position and situation of white-collar workers cannot begin, or end, merely with either an assessment of the changes in their material economic position, or their job grading and characteristics, and whatever status is accorded to these (cf. Dahrendorf, 1959; Giddens, 1973; Lockwood, 1958). Whilst these characteristics flow organically from wider societal processes, they do so in a mediated manner, subject to an array of intersecting forces that leads to complex social outcomes, including the different experiences of occupational groupings.

At the outset, we can venture that both our call centre and software respondents are workers by virtue of engaging in waged labour because they manifestly do not own capital. Limited opportunities for share ownership by workers in the individual companies, amongst both groups of respondents, appeared to have little bearing on their attitudes. Neither does either group perform a function that accords to it control of capital, either for its own benefit or on behalf of another socio-economic grouping. Both workforce groups are in subordinate positions *vis-à-vis* the employing class – call centre workers are the direct or indirect providers of services that facilitate the distribution and exchange of goods and services, whilst those in software engage in work which is intended to augment the provision of either the production of goods and services, or their distribution and exchange. In performing these functions, the vast majority of the workforce is clearly not located in managerial strata, deployed by the employing class to oversee their profit-driven and accumulative activities. Indeed, respondents in both sectors strongly supported propositions concerning management in their workplace, that policy-making was too remote, and that they were only interested in profits and efficiency (Table 8.2).

Nonetheless, because of variations in the functional roles that these two groups of workers play within this overall framework set out above, considerable differences in job autonomy, remuneration, and status are accorded to them. One particularly salient aspect of the dynamics of capitalism which influences the relative degree of autonomy, remuneration and status is the strategic and innovative role of their respective productive functions (cf. Poulantzas, 1975). Call centre workers are accorded lower and software workers higher overall rewards, because of the mass servicing facility which the former provide, compared to the more specialized, bespoke production in which the latter are engaged. Moreover, call centre work, by and large, was designed and constructed *from the outset* as an 'assembly line in the head' (Taylor and Bain, 1999). This work, and these workers, cannot be proletarianized, because they have few material or status possessions to lose (cf. Klingender, 1935; Lockwood, 1958). On the other hand, software workers enjoy a status perhaps akin to the occupationally respected clerk of old, yet approximate more to the characteristics identified by Giddens (1973) as synonymous with the professional and technical strata of the white-collar middle-class. Yet, even in software, many employees are paid at, or below, the level of the UK average wage.

Put another way, call centre operations are primarily concerned with the execution of work and its related tasks, and software with its conception. The necessarily sequential order of these functions – in a situation where capitalism has yet to totally standardize and commodify the creative process of conception (and development) – leads to the granting of a measure of responsible autonomy, rather than use of the direct control which is deployed for call centre workers (see Chapter 3 for fuller discussion). This differentiation in *lower* order functions *within capitalism* is a main reason for the difference in the self-ascription of class position between these groups. It is thus, the starting point, and the particular direction of attribution and causation, that separates this analysis from those of Dahrendorf, Giddens and Lockwood. The fulcrum of their Weberian analysis necessarily leads to a picture of social differentiation, because it is predicated on particularism, not universality.

As a result of this ordered method, the analysis applied here to twenty-first century call centre and software workers has some similarity to both that of Wright Mills (1951: 71), who argued that the 'new middle class...are in exactly the same property-class position as the wage-workers'. Ehrenreich and Ehrenreich (1977: 107) also defined their 'professional-managerial class' as 'consisting of salaried mental workers who do not own the means of production, and whose main function in the social division of labour may be broadly described as the reproduction of capitalist culture and capitalist class relations'. But there is greater common ground with the overall thrust of the analyses of Braverman (1974), Callinicos (1983), Crompton and Jones (1984), Klingender (1935), Mallet (1975) and Smith (1987). A commonality of starting points, however, does not necessarily lead to a similarity of conclusions, because these writers examined different phenomena, and at different points in time. Nonetheless, Braverman's and Callinicos' analyses seem to provide the most convincing general outlines which can be applied today. These writers create broad theoretical frameworks which seek to explain both the proletarianization of white-collar workers and the emergence of middle class occupations. Furthermore, within these analyses, there is recognition of dynamic processes at play, which lead to different outcomes based on disparate functions and roles.

The class-consciousness of call centre and software workers

Whilst in a Marxist analytical framework class is defined by the social group's relationship to the ownership and control of capital, class-consciousness is more indeterminate, being influenced and shaped by subjective interpretation of a range of factors, and so intra-class differences exist. The process by which working class-consciousness is formed is a complex and dynamic social process, whether generated by immizeration, deskilling and/or social struggles.

Three problems have emerged in the way in which the process of forming class-consciousness has been conceived. First, the *sine qua non* in the formation of working class-consciousness should not be seen as being synonymous with replicating the characteristics of the traditional, blue-collar, manual working class (Smith, 1987), because studies of those workers tended not to recognize the historical specificity and functions of these workers within that period. Second, there have been, and continue to exist, significant differences within the manual working class *vis-à-vis* levels of class-consciousness (Goldthorpe *et al.*, 1969). Third, class-consciousness is a contingent process, which ebbs and flows, rather than being uni-linear and cumulative (Callinicos, 1983). This is all the more so amongst subordinate classes because of the difficulties in creating a mass consciousness that challenges the *status quo* (Hoare, 1977).

With these points in mind, the levels of class-consciousness of both the call centre and software workers studied, as well as the differences within and between the two groups, can be interpreted as evidence of the interaction of the impact of differences in how capitalism structures different groups of wage workers with regard to their specific sub-functions, mechanisms of control, and in generating acquiescence as part of profit-seeking strategies. One reflection of the effects of these processes may be identified in employee responses to the broad proposition that they were 'never treated with the respect they deserve'. While 27 per cent of call centre workers agreed, only 19 per cent did so in software, and 50 per cent of the latter disagreed, compared to 43 per cent of call centre employees (Table 8.2). Moreover, it is worth emphasizing that the two groups of workers were being studied within a period of overall low levels of working class action compared to the late 1960s/early 1970s (Darlington and Lyddon, 2001). Thus, perceived labour market advantages can encourage the development of internal differences and dominant states of consciousness. However, these differences do not alter the *fundamental* position and function of individual social groupings, as these remain subject to change as a result of the dynamics of capitalism and attendant accumulation and control strategies. Such an analysis is thus at variance with Lockwood (1958) and Giddens (1973), but has some measure of agreement with the studies by Mallet (1975), Gorz (1971) and Smith (1987).

It should also be noted that although there is, as yet, little evidence of software workers taking collective action, whether union based or via professionalization, to protect their 'privileges' (cf. Gorz, 1971), neither is there evidence of them having an intrinsically antagonistic relationship with the working class (cf. Ehrenreich and Ehrenreich, 1977). Indeed, in comparison to their call centre counterparts, software workers displayed a more adversarial attitude towards sharing common aims with both senior management and team leaders (Table 8.2). This may result from a clash between their own notion of their expert, professional authority and that of the firms' owners' hierarchical authority, that is, managerial prerogative. Table 8.3 provides additional evidence of software workers' anti-management sentiments at a more general level. However, because of the physical separation of software from other workers, unlike the kind of technical employees whom Smith (1987) studied, there is little prospect of an osmosis of collective values and beliefs being transmitted to them through close contact with a unionized manual workforce. This, and their strategic location in a relatively new and expanding occupation, suggests that, in the short-term at least, software workers are unlikely to see themselves as either an 'aristocracy of labour or a poor relation of capital' (Smith, 1987: 69).

While the low levels of unionization and union activity amongst both call centre and software workers is marked, this is all the more noticeable amongst the former. In addition to recognizing class divisions (only 9 per cent of survey respondents thought there were none), and predominantly identifying themselves as 'working class' (around 80 per cent of those interviewed did so), overall, call centre workers displayed more oppositional attitudes towards their own management, and management *per se*, than software workers. Almost a third of questionnaire respondents (30 per cent) also stated that 'independent employee representation' was very important or absolutely critical to them. It can be suggested that the absence of recourse, or proximity, to robust trade unionism, meant that these relatively favourable attitudes found no means by which to translate or develop into widespread unionization and workplace organization. The gap between call centre workers and trade unionism was too wide to be bridged by the workforce's own volition in the period under study (Bain *et al.*, 2004).

Although union membership reflects a collectivized approach by workers to the employment relationship, the bounds of this collectivism are contextualized, and thus often influenced and delimited by an array of factors. These can range from traditional membership territories of particular unions and their respective organizing approaches, to the way in which unions are perceived by workers (for example, as outdated, ineffectual or self-interested), and the terrain set by the dominant models of employment. For example, in Denmark and Sweden, ICT professionals are highly unionized in comparison to those in Norway (Dolvik and Waddington, 2003: 360). Furthermore, the struggle to create or maintain job autonomy can also take the form of an endeavour to generate occupational identity via attempts to forge a profession (see also Chapter 5). These factors, and the implications for work and employment because of the over-arching dynamic and volatile nature of capitalism (Taylor *et al.*, 2005), mean that the development of (particularly) working class-consciousness, is a contingent and uneven process across space and time.

Conclusions

In this final section, we consider how our findings relate to three key areas of contemporary theoretical and practical interest; our original research formulation concerning collectivism and individualism; knowledge economy/network society perspectives on class and class-consciousness, and the sociological debate on these issues.

We postulated that there would be significant sectoral differences in respondents' perceptions of, and attitudes towards, collectivism and individualism, whereby call centre workers would generally display greater propensity to adopting more oppositional positions than those employed in software. While, in overall terms, this was confirmed, the picture was much more complex, with certain differences notably narrower than anticipated (or even reversed). In some instances of oppositional stances to managerial prerogative, the more adversarial position of software respondents is likely to be related to their stronger individually based expectations of job autonomy, participation in workplace governance, and professional status, based upon a discrete and quasi-exclusive base of knowledge and skills (see also Smith, 1987: 235–6, 301). However, on other measures, like the rights to take industrial action, to independent employee representation, and to criticize the motives of managers, call centre respondents evinced relatively higher levels of support. This, together with their higher levels of self-ascription of being working class, suggests a more collectivist worldview, whether of an instrumental and/or ideological nature, which rejects HRM-inspired unitaristic collectivism. But, alongside these intersectoral differences, it is also striking that more than half of both call centre and software workers agreed that class still existed and supported oppositional stances towards management. Given our expectations, the relative proximity of the views of software respondents to those of call centre respondents is also marked, reflecting, *inter alia*, the influence of social values in Scotland as discussed above.

Whilst many futurologist and post-modernist proponents of the network society or knowledge economy heralded the death of disappearance of class (Castells being a notable exception), this alleged momentous historical development also meant that, on *a priori* grounds, these writers did not concern themselves with issues of class-consciousness. As class no longer existed (or was in terminal decline), class-consciousness must have also disappeared (or be increasingly irrelevant). To the extent that any other macro-identity has been perceived to be a substitute for class, it was represented by attempts, at varying levels of theoretical sophistication, to categorize diverse groups of employees as information or knowledge workers, consequent upon their use of ICTs. *De facto*, Weberian criteria, based upon perceptions of occupational grading and status, not class, dominated such thinking – and hence a focus upon the use of qualitative terminology, such as professional, empowered, creative, symbolic analyst, autonomous, routinized, and standardized, which was employed to allocate rank and status within the informationalized workforce's perceived hierarchy. However, the validity of these *déclassé* approaches does not stand up well to the interrogation of our data on workers in the two 'leading edge sectors by a perspective grounded in the totality and universality of the political economy of capitalism. Both call centre and software workforces studied have been shown to be employed, universally, by capitalist organizations as wage-labourers. This, combined with the nature of the tasks performed in the production process, and their remuneration, clearly places the vast majority of our respondents squarely in the ranks of a mass subordinate class. Indeed, very few of them could be located in putative higher social echelons, such as the Ehrenreichs' (1977) formulation, a 'professional-managerial class'. Endorsement of the objective existence of class by both sectoral groups, and the strong self-identification of call centre respondents as working class (and by almost two in five software employees), lends further weight to the conclusion that – albeit often imprecisely – many of these representatives of the new economy attribute their subordinate position in society to factors which are structured and systemic. The absence of evidence of 'class-for-itself' actions does not negate the existence of evidence that points towards the presence of 'class-in-itself'.

As we noted earlier, a surprising aspect of current and recent sociological debates concerning class and class-consciousness has been the absence of contributions based upon research into the rapidly expanding, high-tech industrial sectors which are often portrayed as indicative of future patterns of work and employment. To the extent that writers like Giddens and Sennett have addressed issues related to the new economy, they have tended to do so at high levels of abstraction, reflected in a focus upon the defining characteristics of the new era – deregulation, privatization and globalization – and in sweeping generalizations about the claimed effects of these processes, rather than drawing upon primary research which focused on the workforce (Webb, 2004: 725). By way of contrast, the findings and conclusions of this chapter – focused upon the class character and consciousness of the 1,000-plus call centre and software workers studied over prolonged periods of time – are based not only upon locating them firmly within wider political economy, but also upon our utilization of a rigorous, multi-faceted methodology, designed to establish, assess and test their validity. On the basis of this research, it can be stated that employee accounts of 'contemporary selfhood' still retain strong and unmistakable elements of class identification and awareness.

9
Back to the Future? Change and Continuity at Work

The original title for this book was *'Should life all labour be?'* Tennyson's evocative summation of the duality that work has always represented in our lives: recognized for its sustaining necessity but at the same time resented for its dominance. It could be argued that, historically, the prevailing work ethic in society has striven to enhance the former meaning and diminish the latter and, in the introduction to this book we noted that, in recent government economic and social policy, we can discern the constituents of a new work ethic for our time. The repeated theme that full citizenship and personal fulfilment are only attainable through participation in paid work has elevated the concept of work centrality, the philosophical importance in people's lives of the work they do, beyond the somewhat confined circles of academic discourse and into the area of policy.

Policy makers are not alone in raising the profile of contemporary work. In the period marked by the closing years of the last century and the first years of the new there has been, for Britain, an unusual amount of popular discussion and discourse concerning work and the workplace, a discussion which, like that surrounding the 'new technology' of the early 1980s, has tended to polarize around predictions of either dystopia or utopia. Critical voices, particularly from the labour movement, have pointed to epidemic levels of occupationally-induced stress, a potential for greatly enhanced surveillance and control in the workplace and an increase in economic and social insecurity. At the same time, and more influentially, positive claims have been made of observed changes and innovations such as the near ubiquity of ICTs as the vehicle for both manufacturing and service delivery, the perceived increase in non-standard forms of employment, individualized initiatives in people management and the decline in the profile of such previously established features of the employment landscape as trade unions and collective forms of industrial action. These trends, and many others which have been examined in this book, have been seized upon and elided together to provide a claimed evidence platform for assertions about a paradigmatic change in nature of work and the role which work plays in our lives. Furthermore, as debates about the nature of work almost inevitably involve debates about the nature of society, these new images of work have usually been contextualized within a new societal paradigm.

Regrettably, these claims were seldom based on, or substantiated by, any body of rigorous research. Policy makers in both Government and the economy seemed more willing to pay attention to dramatic blue-sky scenarios produced by consultancies and think tanks than the more measured and grounded observations of social scientists. And even those were thin on the ground; as Richard Brown commented, just when work was becoming more problematic and unsure for people than at any time in a generation, the scientific study of work seemed to have gone out of fashion, to be replaced by a focus on consumption and cultural change (Brown, 1997). It was to rectify these shortcomings that the ESRC's *Future of Work* programme, of which this study formed a part, was established in the late 1990s (Nolan, 2002).

Our starting premise, therefore, was that, by examining the daily experiences and attitudes of employees and managers in two relatively new knowledge and information based employment sectors, it might be possible to identify any emerging trends in work organization and experience and in the mutual interactions between work and non-work life. We would also be able to question the validity of those assertions about the changing nature of work for which no evidence was forthcoming, on the grounds that, if evidence for a new work centrality was not to be found in such areas of employment, it was unlikely to be encountered elsewhere in the economy.

We began this book by noting the difficulties inherent in talking generically about the meaning of work. Work has many different meanings for any given individual and these are mediated through a variety of social contexts, at both the organizational and societal levels and it was hoped that these particular processes would be illuminated through study of two quite distinct areas of employment. At the same time, we hoped to be able to draw wider generic conclusions about work in the new century, if only to hold up to scrutiny many of the assertions and predictions that have been made about work in general. For this reason we felt it necessary to revisit the principal social dimensions, such as home, community, class and status, which the researchers of forty years ago saw as being intrinsically attached to, or surrounding, work but which have all too often been omitted from most contemporary treatments of employment. We also wanted to include such important aspects as gender which many of the classic studies either ignored or took as given. Above all, we felt it important to subject to renewed enquiry the observation that we evaluate work as much through the social processes of the non-work part of our lives as those of the work context itself.

The recurring theme of this book, the contrast between radical break or transformationalist theories and those explanatory models which stress continuity in social structures and relationships, is of course only the latest instalment of the 150-year old debate on the nature of capitalism. It will be evident by now that the writers of this book (although we come from very different academic and philosophical backgrounds) generally favour an approach which is inclusive of continuity. While the findings detailed in the preceding chapters do indicate the scope and variety of changes to the contemporary workplace, rather than interpreting these as indicative of a disjunction with the past, we have argued that it is crucial to understand the factors making for both social change and the persistence of patterns of social action. The major reason for rejecting the idea of the knowledge economy as a new evolutionary stage (along with a similar rejection of most of the associated 'post-' models and Castells' claims for a new 'mode of development') is the simple one that there is no evidence that capitalism has yet evolved into a new socio-economic form; indeed capitalism has seldom been so unreluctant to speak its own name. Several things follow from this.

Work, or more strictly speaking employment, is still essentially the exchange of effort for money. Our call centre workers and software developers enter the labour market and sell their labour power to the owners of the customer service centres and software houses (at a price which, as we have seen, will currently be largely fixed by management rather than the outcome of collective negotiation). Employment is thus first and foremost a monetary exchange relationship with reward, the cash nexus, as the hinge around which all other aspects of the relationship turn. It is, however, just these other aspects of the exchange that form the basis for debate.

We saw in our introductory discussion that by the end of the nineteenth century the classical social analysts were coming to very different conclusions about the inevitability of the nature of work and its outcomes, with Marx having asserted the inexorable and unavoidable alienation of labour under capitalism while Durkheim saw the possibility for redemption of such a situation through a shared moral order.

This dialogue, between the assertion that capitalist work is inevitably alienating and the claims that it need not be so, is still essentially with us in the prediction of the informationalists that work in the knowledge economy will be intrinsically more satisfying than the admitted alienation of past 'industrial' work. This is of course not a new argument, being proposed most notably in the 1960s by Blauner (1964) who saw the emergent high tech process industries as being less alienating than the prevailing mass production paradigm. In addition to yet another version of this 'new work equals happier work' scenario however, we have also witnessed, from the 1980s onwards, an influential attempt at gaining Durkheim's shared moral order in the workplace though the diffusion of the HRM agenda. We have examined both these claims in detail in the preceding chapters and we can now draw on this analysis to make some general observations about change and continuity at work.

In accounts of the changing workplace, technology is frequently portrayed as the major change agent. As we have discussed in the introductory chapters of this book, the informationalist argument as propounded by Castells is, like that of Blauner before him, essentially one of technological determinism, in which the use of ICT is seen not only to liberate work, but actually to require particular changes in the behaviours, attitudes and expectations of the new knowledge workers. While the attitudes expressed by employees and managers in our two information sectors provide no evidence for this, in rejecting the knowledge society scenario we do not want, as Ramsay put it, to throw out the technological baby with the determinist bathwater (Beirne and Ramsay, 1992). It is very clear from our study, that information and communication technologies have enabled a number of significant innovations in the way work is organized.

One that has received a lot of speculative attention is the potential which ICT bestows for the dispersal of economic activity. In looking for evidence of organizational decentralization and the end of the gathered organization, our evidence suggests that the conclusion depends on what level and from what perspective observations are taken. Three of our call centres were part of multi-site service provision by their respective organizations, in which an ACD system routed customer calls to whichever site currently had agents available. From the viewpoint of the customer the experience could be seen as an interaction with a dispersed organization in which their needs and queries might be handled by a different location each time they phoned. For the several hundred employees gathered under one roof at workplace level however the experience was of being in a fairly traditional organizational structure. They had virtually no contact with fellow employees in other centres, although the product of their collective labour was accessible as an on-screen customer file. Furthermore, at the level of the organization, of which the call centre was typically only a part, the structure was very much that of traditional bureaucracy with tight central control of the targets, budgets and job design within all the organization's sites. In this sector, the appearance of geographical dispersal actually masks a trend towards increasing processual centralization.

Virtual team working was more likely to be a feature of software work, particularly in the larger companies such as Beta and Omega, where members of the same project team could be located on different sites. Beta however was very far from being a virtual or dispersed organization and was probably the one company out of all our cases that most resembled a classic bureaucracy. In all cases the majority of employees worked in a central location.

Secondly, it is important that the organizational changes which have accompanied technological development should be understood holistically.

It is significant, to take our call centres as an example, that the same technology which is the new vehicle for service delivery is also the means of measuring, monitoring, and controlling the performance of those delivering the service and that, in this process, the customer is thus unwittingly drawn in to become an integral part of the managerial control system. This, incidentally, seems a significant refutation of the thrust of recent customer oriented literature which has argued that organizational customer focus and the role of customer as agent is bound to result in upskilling, empowerment and an increase in employee responsibility.

The mention of management control reminds us, if reminder were needed, that in addition to a monetary relationship employment is also an authority relationship. Management, whether managing production, the delivery of services or the processing of information, has a continuing necessity to control the labour process, using whatever means are appropriate to the situation, and the wealth of post-Braverman research has thrown up myriad examples of direct, bureaucratic, technological, normative and responsible autonomy control strategies. We saw that one prediction for the knowledge economy was that the new information workers would be characterized by a high level of autonomy and empowerment with a decreasing reliance on Taylorism as a control model. We expected to, and did, find some support for this in the software sector as some developers, like manufacturing craft workers, retain a high degree of personal knowledge and skill. However, this should not necessarily be interpreted as supporting the emergence of the free-floating autonomous knowledge worker, for our observations may be conditioned by the prevailing tight state of the software labour market. More fundamentally, the developers' affirmations of professional identity were indulged by senior management and/or the owners as a subtle form of performance management *because* of the way in which developers' professional values were expressed through the desire to do a good job, desire to acquire new skills and the desire to work hard to deliver the project on time.

In contrast, in our call centres we were surprised at the degree of persistence of quite traditional forms of direct control, now enhanced and refined by a powerful technology, such that the reality of the call centre agents' day places them as the historical heirs to previous generations of routinized white-collar work, now qualified by the addition of varying forms of emotion labour. As we stressed in Chapter 3 however, differences between the sectors must be seen as strong tendencies rather than concrete distinctions, on account of the differentiation *within* each sector based on identifiably different workflows. There was, for example, also a strong degree of normative control in call centres deriving from team membership and the customer facing nature of the work, both of which provided pressures on performance levels which were at times more salient and immediate than senior management or the company. One reason for the general *increase* in managerial pressure experienced by both sets of employees lies in the wider economic context. We have seen in earlier chapters how the economic and organizational turbulence created by the contemporary drive for accumulation, was responsible for cascading pressures on each subsidiary unit and sub-unit of operation or profit centre, from corporate management to centre manager, to operational manager, to team leader and, ultimately, to employee.

If there are new frontiers of control in the contemporary workplace one of the more important is perhaps focused on aspects of working time. The length of the working day has been contested for over a hundred years in the struggle for shorter hours that most people would assume had been won. Yet, despite the fact that Britain had recently finally achieved the legal possibility of a maximum working week, we found significant proportions of our respondents working more than their contractual hours, often in the case of software workers on an unpaid basis and usually reflecting the strong normative pressures referred to above. In addition, what was new about all our workplaces was the degree to which managerial control has been extended to when and to what patterns those hours are to be worked. The popular image of white collar work being characterized by a contractual nine to five time pattern is certainly no longer reflected in employees' experience which can now include working permanent night shifts, shift patterns which vary on daily basis, or being on permanent call when not at work. Whereas, in software, hours worked were more likely to be determined by developers' own professional standards of getting the job done and delivering the project to time, in call centres sophisticated software systems assisted management to squeeze the porosity of the working day by micro-adjustments of headcount to match call flow, so that the utilization of the centres' human resources was kept as lean as possible. Although the time pressures on employees in our two sectors were reflected in different patterns of working time, the experience of time compulsion was common to both. The reality of work today, as graphically documented in the popular account by Madeleine Bunting (2004), delivers to the employer both relative and absolute increases in productivity through a combination of an intensification of work during contractual time *and* an extension of hours worked.

We noted, above, that the claims for the transformation of work in the knowledge based workplace were based on the twin track of technological change and the goal of a new shared performance ethic, provided through the now dominant discourse of HRM. Historically, management ideologies have had two functions: they have provided or sustained a general ideology of work (Anthony, 1977) and secondly they have provided a justification or rationale for management action. The rhetoric of HRM is an attempt to do both of these in that it conveys the message that, unlike past industrial work, work today, and particularly knowledge work, can be *good* work because of the opportunities it offers for individual empowerment, personal development and a commitment to a set of higher level goals that will be of benefit to everyone. At the same time, if management take decisions which employees experience as negative (raising targets, altering shift patterns, downsizing, relocating) it is in everyone's best interest, an approach encapsulated in Peters and Waterman's Orwellian term 'tough love' (1982).

Like all ideologies it does not of course always correlate with the experienced reality. The evidence in this study illuminates the dilemma of maintaining this HRM discourse within a volatile surrounding environment. There was little support for the formal HRM function in any of our organizations, HR issues usually appeared as marginal rather than central and, as we have seen, responses were reactive, piecemeal, pragmatic and frequently fairly chaotic. Much of the inconsistency in management practice that we encountered in our case study organizations must be seen in the context of the continuous organizational restructuring that occurred in both sectors. Furthermore, and on a wider note, these findings offer endorsement to the repeated observations of the large scale UK workplace industrial relations and employment relations surveys (see for example Cully *et al.*, 1999: 295), and a recent ESRC study by Guest and colleagues (Guest, 2000), that the development and diffusion of high-commitment management practices in general remains extremely sparse. We would suggest that their absence from the very sectors where it has been widely hypothesized that such practices would be most appropriate does not lend support to the view that we are witnessing the gestation of a new high-trust, high commitment knowledge economy.

What was in evidence however was the widespread diffusion among management in both sectors of the *idea* of the organizational culture as a vehicle for enhanced commitment, even if the practices promoting this were *ad hoc* and unconvincing. Perhaps for this latter reason, the critical literatures which see the commitment offensive heralding the capture of the whole worker (Casey, 1995; Flecker and Hofbauer, 1998) are not supported by our evidence. Like the predictions of total surveillance, similarly unsupported, they give employees no credit for perception and distancing. The employees in our two knowledge using sectors retained a capacity to distance themselves from the cultural rhetoric and the affective demands made on them. They went along with the fun days and the social evenings because they made the job 'a bit different', but did not accord these occasions the same qualitative weighting as their chosen socializing with friends and family. Similarly, while it is true that our call centre respondents were expected to control the affective content of their interaction with customers, even in the face of customer rudeness and aggression, such emotion work, while frequently stressful, did not result in the surrender of self or identity but often in the development of collective ways of covertly extracting humour from the situation, at the expense of both customer and organization. Most of the time these workers seemed capable of co-inhabiting two different mental worlds.

The major limitations on the success of all commitment-inducing work practices however lie not just in the practices themselves but in the poorly thought-out theoretical underpinning. Our study shows that organizational identification is not the same as organizational commitment, as it does not necessarily imply an internalization of company values. Thus, our respondents could identify themselves with the organization in the sense that this identification provided a label for a significant part of who they were ('I work for Beta') but this does not necessarily mean they took its values as their own. Our respondents did in fact display high levels of commitment but this was to other foci, such as customers, work colleagues and the values of their profession.

In a sense, this provides a clue to the debate between the Marx and Blauner models of alienation; both are in different ways true. Over twenty years ago Fox reminded us that work is designed exclusively to meet such criteria as profits, output, fulfilment of targets or effective performance, and not in the light of the profoundly rival conception that work should ideally provide a humane, balanced and fulfilling life for those engaged in it (Fox, 1980). In this sense, says Fox, it is work design that is exclusively 'instrumental' as the emphasis is on the practical outcome of work rather than the value of the experience itself for those who do it. Yet, as workers have always done, our respondents *did* get additional satisfactions from many aspects of the work situation, whether it was the work-based fun (official and unofficial), the idea of helping customers, or a sense of autonomy and control and professional identity. On the other hand a majority of call centre workers saw their jobs as repetitive and a significant minority of respondents in each sector reported feeling stressed at work quite often or all the time. In both sectors lower job control was linked to greater perceived health problems, stress and exhaustion. Baldamus (1961) suggested that it is the mix of satisfactions, together with the monetary reward for the job, which are weighed against the dissatisfactions and unpleasant aspects of work to form the subjective equation of the wage-effort bargain. Baldamus' point however was, in contrast to the organizational behaviour orthodoxy, that most people *expect* employed work to be fairly unpleasant and that satisfactions in work are always relative satisfactions, the things about the job which make the daily grind of earning a living more tolerable.

It was Goldthorpe and his Luton collaborators (Goldthorpe *et al.*, 1968) who pointed out that there is no direct and immediate relationship between the objective nature of a particular job situation and the attitudes towards the job of its occupant. As we have seen in this book, rather than a mechanical response to the objective features of the job, how employees perceive those features and the meaning they give to them will be mediated through their membership of a range of other social contexts, such as profession, family, community and their perceptions of class and status position.

One social dimension which was under-examined in the predominantly male Luton studies is gender. Despite the predictions of 'new economy' writers, that we will witness increasing convergence in the positions of men and women at work, we found that women are still potentially disadvantaged in these new employment sectors. Women in call centres, despite their numerical dominance, were under-represented at management level and in some of the prestige areas of work, particularly technical/analytical roles. We have mentioned the emotion work content of much call centre service delivery, and there is some evidence that women, particularly those who chose call centre work to accommodate domestic demands (such as women returners), were targeted by organizations for their perceived greater ability to deal with front-line, customer facing roles. In software, as well as being in the minority, women were often found in support roles rather than the more high-end technical work and elite teams. While career breaks and part-time working were offered as options by all companies they were seen as restricting career advancement.

We concluded that it is unlikely that attitudinal or value differences can explain the continuation of such gendered differences in life-chances, but that they reflected structural and cultural conditions within organizations. Despite the existence of formal equal opportunities policies and activities and the perception of fair treatment overall, experiences at work still mitigated against total equality; examples from the previous chapters include the expectations by supervisors that job would be put before family, a lack of any genuine flexibility particularly in call centres, and the persistence of assumptions about women's and men's work built into the predominantly male culture of software.

Another filter, between the objective nature of the work and the meaning the individual might attach to it, is the degree to which it is expected to form part of a personal career trajectory. We found that while organizational structures were flatter this did not seem to have changed how work and careers were perceived. One might expect that it would have cut off expectations of career progressions but our findings show that this does not seem to have happened. In both sectors employees still spoke of their current job in career terms even where, as in most call centres, there was little realistic chance of this. Following speculation about the role and pattern of gendered attitudes towards work and career, we found strong evidence for some convergence in work preferences, values and attitudes between men and women. Expressed attitudes towards domestic roles were essentially the same, as were career orientations, and both men and women rated family as more important to them than leisure (second) and work (last). Having children did make this picture more complicated, as men with children were even more committed to family than women with children yet, paradoxically, worked longer hours than those without, while women with children rated career as less important in both sectors. Yet, despite this attitudinal similarity, when it came to actual practice women were still more likely to make different choices. In both sectors they were less likely to work paid or unpaid overtime and more likely to sacrifice career progression for the sake of accommodating domestic and family responsibilities, or their partner's career. Similarly they were more likely to choose 'low commitment', flexible, part-time work and express a preference for this.

Again, our evidence on domestic and organizational conditions suggests that the reasons for these observed differences in practice and career progression are to be found in the lived realities of their domestic situation, as women in both sectors were still more likely to bear the burden of responsibility for domestic labour and childcare, despite male and female respondents holding fairly egalitarian views about domestic roles. Overall, then, women did appear to be making lifestyle choices which affected their experiences at work, but these were still affected by structural constraints at home and in the workplaces which acted to limit the span of discretion in decision-making.

Management's enhanced control of working time in both our sectors was one of the major reasons for what we can call the increased permeability of the work-life boundary. Extended working hours or fluctuating shift patterns inevitably frequently impinged upon the rhythms of social and domestic life, although the form taken by such spillover varied in form and intensity. As we remarked in an earlier chapter, to understand the extent to which this is now a fundamental characteristic of the contemporary workplace we need to move beyond the usual work-life balance nostrums of flexible hours and family friendly policies. While it is true that those employees with caring responsibilities did face extra problems in juggling work and home, it was clear from our data that most employees felt there was a degree of work-life imbalance in their lives and this was not only composed of quantitative time intrusions but, for a significant minority, of intrusions into the quality of non-work life in the form of work-induced fatigue and stress.

The permeability of the work-life boundary produced different coping strategies in the two sectors, deriving substantially from the different labour processes and labour market position. In the absence of any widely available government or employer provision, in the call centres the burden of managing work-family conflict was placed on employees, resulting in coping strategies which included shift swapping (official and unofficial), complex articulation with partners' work timetables and reliance on close family for childcare. The result was constant compromise rather than balance, and establishing this could be complex and contested, particularly for women with little work autonomy or status. In the more professionalized, and predominantly male, software sector, it seemed that higher relative levels of job control were reflected in a greater ability to maintain some control over work-home boundary. This was aided by responsive organizational practices and a tight labour market at the time of the study, but was nevertheless still constrained by internalized values and client requirements.

Whereas in the classical studies of single-industry communities such as coal and shipbuilding, the high profile which work-related matters enjoyed in non-work activity was taken as an index of work centrality and as the supposed cement of proletarian solidarity (Lockwood, 1966), we should not infer that the increased permeability of the work-life boundary today is reproducing such historical social patterns. Just because work takes up a lot of someone's waking hours, and often interferes with how the other hours can be spent, does not imply that work has qualitative centrality in that person's life such that it becomes a central life *interest*. We have shown that the meaning, role and importance which work has will be mediated through other commitments, demands, interests and community orientations, and our findings indicate substantive differences between workers in the two sectors in the meanings they attached to work and the sources and expressions of occupational and personal identity. The professional values of our software workers were, for many, manifested in the sense of belonging to an occupational community which, while geographically dispersed, did often permeate aspects of social life. Our call centre respondents on the other hand, despite the location of several of the centres in the ex-industrial heartland of central Scotland, expressed little wish to meet with colleagues after work, and work itself was largely seen in instrumental terms.

The major social dimension which both mediates workers' perception of work and its meanings, and is itself a reflection of the different life-chances bestowed by the labour market under capitalism, is of course class and social stratification. As Fox put it, 'how the individual looks at work depends to a considerable extent upon his or her location in that complex social layering that we think of as the class structure' (Fox, 1980: 167).

What we can say quite clearly is that those information/network society and post-modern/futurology perspectives which have suggested that class has disappeared remain unsupported by our data. We found evidence for a widespread perception of social class stratification, which was seen to be embedded in work and extra-work processes and outcomes. A large majority of respondents in both sectors disagreed with the idea that there remained no important class divisions in Britain with, surprisingly, software employees more likely to disagree and indeed, in some regards, to express more socially dichotomous views and attitudes than their call centre counterparts. Both groups saw employment relations in general in adversarial and pluralistic terms, and a majority in both sectors saw management being more concerned with profit than employees' welfare, although this was seen to be more true at societal than organizational level.

It has to be admitted that the attitudes and perceptions of class and collective values in our findings contain as many ambiguities and contradictions as those of previous studies. Our call centre workers could legitimately be described as members of a contemporary white-collar proletariat in terms of their wage labour status, their function and the over-arching power/control relationships in which their work is situated. Yet as many as 40 per cent of them agreed that senior management and workforce shared the same aims although, as indicated above, the idea of shared attitudes did not extend to stratification at societal level. In contrast, among the quasi-professional software workers less than a third agreed with the 'sharing the same aims' statement, despite the 'family atmosphere' encouraged by most of the owner/employers; indeed, the co-existence in our software developers of dichotomous views with high levels of job autonomy was reminiscent of nineteenth century engineering craft workers or mid-twentieth century technical workers (Smith, 1987). Respondents from both groups expressed a strong belief in the importance of independent trade union representation and in the right to take industrial action, despite the fact that the vast majority were not union members. Yet, in those sites that were unionized the union was perceived as generally ineffective.

It is perhaps the absence of any effective agency for worker voice in our locations that explains some of these apparent contradictions. Despite the evidence of relatively widespread workplace and extra-workplace oppositional attitudes to management found amongst both groups, this was not reflected in any structured or observable patterns of collective behaviour. The generally positive attitudes towards trade unionism show that this lack of collective action was not due to any post-Thatcher attitudinal shift towards individualism or the adoption of individualist values but was perhaps more a reflection of the consequences of two decades of the deliberate dismantling of the structures and processes of employee representation in the British workplace.

Should life all labour be?

This book has attempted to reconnect the many facets of work – its context, the way men and women experience it, how it is organized and controlled, how it relates to family life, gender and class and status – and the size of our sample and the three-year duration of the study makes it, we hope, a significant contribution to understanding the trajectories and processes within contemporary work. Although located in Scotland this study should not be interpreted as narrowly Scottish in scope. Because of its recent industrial, economic and political experience, Scotland and its economy presented a particularly apposite context for exploring the consequences of the shift from industrial to information based work. However, we hope our conclusions may be recognized as observations on the nature of work in all market economies at the start of the twenty-first century. Without wishing to diminish the importance of 'place' and the influence of particular national factors, similar, though not identical, pressures of tight management control and organizational instability are, after all, experienced by call centre workers in Mumbai, Memphis or Motherwell.

Although we have been interested both in continuities with the past and emergent trends for the future, the timing of our study proved to be significant as during the research period many of the predictions of the knowledge economy were themselves undermined by the puncturing of the dot.com bubble. This reinforces the point made above that working life today is characterized by more uncertainty and impermanence, even in the daily organization of work, than has been the case for half a century. This has served to seriously undermine the promise of job security which authors such as Castells and Walton saw as underpinning the new commitment contract.

While this book is about futures, it is not about making specific predictions. However, in so far as we can detect trends in the present, our evidence suggests that contemporary knowledge work, far from becoming more pleasant and satisfying, is actually becoming more intensified. Critical readers might accuse us of taking too small a time frame in which to judge something with as broad a sweep as the emergence of a knowledge economy. To which we would reply, not only that we found no evidence of even the green shoots of a new society but that in some cases trends in work organization seemed to be retrogressive: all our call centres had started out with an explicit focus on the quality of customer service but became *more* instrumental and target driven even during our research period.

The conclusions of this book serve to reinforce Richard Brown's warning against the acceptance of over-determined accounts of what work might 'mean' to people (Brown, 1984). As we have shown, the meanings of work will not be exclusively determined by single factors such as technology or management strategy, or even by the prevailing socio-economic structure, whether that is capitalism or some notional information society. To claim such automatic relationships ignores the possibility of individual or group agency, and thus of human intervention in the processes of social change, even at the micro level of the workplace. Nobody wants their job to have no meaning, even if the primary or indeed only meaning is its economic support for home and family. Wherever possible people at work look for something beyond that, a sense of purpose or redemption, a source of challenge or enjoyment, or the ability of the work to confer or reinforce social identity or identities. These relative additional meanings, which are overlain on top of the underlying economic necessity to work, have to be retained in the face of monotony, stress, insecurity, and managerial discipline. Within the structures and social contexts in which men and women find themselves they will seek to find relative satisfactions and the opportunities, however small, to ameliorate dissatisfactions. They will seek them from what is on offer, even if it is something as transitory as a Fun Day in the centre or a beer and pizza evening with the lads from the Java project. More importantly they will collectively create their own sources of meaning, independently of the formal organizational culture.

What then can we say of the contemporary work ethic? To what degree do employees today see work in terms of Fox's 'two great alternative meanings': that work is of central importance to our personality development and life fulfilment, or work is little more than a tiresome necessity in acquiring the resources for survival (Fox, 1980). The attitudes towards their work, and the role of work in our respondents' lives, show many similarities with studies done forty years ago in that, while work is still an unavoidable compulsion, it has not become central to life but remains subsidiary to family and non-work interests. At the workplace there is no heightened sense of commitment to the employing organization although there is a degree of conscientiousness and concern for colleagues and customers. While people still work for the money, employees today do not base their behaviour while at work on values of materialist individualism, but rather we find a continuation of work based sociability and collegiality which, as personal work ethics, serve to counter official work cultures and normative controls.

Over a thousand men and women willingly completed our questionnaires and many of these took time out from work and home to talk honestly and in some detail about their work, their lives, their likes and dislikes and their hopes for the future. What is noticeable from these accounts is the number of instances where positive attitudes and perceptions by our respondents diverged from what might seem an unpromising objective reality; what is remarkable, in other words, is their frequent optimism. Call centre agents still hoped for a career in their organizations, despite the flat organizational structure, the high turnover and the general lack of recognition given to their skills in handling emotional work. CSAs and software developers alike said they prioritized home and family before work, despite their jobs' increasing incursions across the work-home boundary. Men and women each professed egalitarian attitudes towards domestic work and the importance of career, yet their actual domestic labour responsibilities continued to follow traditional patterns. Respondents in both sectors expressed a firm belief in collective representation and the right to take industrial action even though few of them were union members.

This suggests that any discussion of the meaning of work has to include the additional dimension that its meaning is not only a reflection of what is but also what we might hope for, of the world as it could be.

Appendix A Research methods and data collection

Table A.1 Description of data and research methods

Data/research method	Description
Company data (e.g. history, work organization, employment relations)	Company documents, observation of work activities, focused interviews with key informants (managers, supervisors, trade union representatives, call centre operators, software developers), observation of management meetings, and guided conversation, focused discussion, with key groups (e.g., call centre operators, call centre inductees, team managers, union representatives).
Employee profiles and attitudes[1]	Self-report questionnaire on: biographical information, employee perceptions and attitudes towards the organization, management, representation and communication, and work-life linkages
Workplace Interviews[2]	Semi-structured interview schedule on: (a) work and educational histories and their influence on present job (b) experiences of working in the present company, and (c) work-life linkages and perceptions of society, class and status.
Home/Community Interviews[3]	Semi-structured interview schedule on: (a) immediate location/household (e.g. experiences of current/past locales; nature of household; family background/role, neighbours and social networks) (b) family/community background (e.g. social mobility, influences on career) (c) leisure/social time (e.g. interests and overlap with work) (d) involvement in community activities and (e) society (e.g. perceptions of local community and social structure).

Notes:
1 The questionnaire was distributed to all workers and management over several weeks to account for different shifts, sick/holiday leave, and variable work patterns. Sections were standardized to allow cross-company comparability and questions constructed from developed scales where appropriate (e.g. job control, satisfaction) or designed for the project (e.g. on social and family networks and obligations, open-ended questions on career expectations). A total of 1,163 questionnaires were returned reflecting a mean response rate of 62% and median rate of 72% (see Table A.2 for response rates by company).
2 Representative groups of employees (by gender, age, job type and grade) were interviewed for 1.5 hours in their workplaces (see Table A.3 for sample breakdown).
3 Home/community interviews were conducted in four case studies (two in each sector in city and non-city locations) for selected employees who had agreed to follow-up interviews.

Table A.2 Survey response rates and sample

	N	Response rate	% total sample	% within sector
Call centres				
E	258	48%	22	30
H	256	58%	22	30
M	109	85%	9	13
T	232	63%	20	27
Total	855	60%	72	100
Software				
Beta	117	72%	10	36
Gamma	22	24%	2	7
Lambda	17	85%	1	5
Omega	129	76%	11	39
Pi	43	88%	4	13
Total	328	69%	28	100
Total sample	1183	65%	100	

Table A.3 Interviewee profile

	Call centres		Software	
	Work Interviews	Home Interviews	Work Interviews	Home Interviews
Gender				
Male	27	2	51	11
Female	50	12	24	1
Age				
16–20	7	2	0	0
21–30	40	14	30	5
31–40	13	2	18	3
41–50	7	4	15	3
Over 50	2	3	2	0
Marital status				
Married/cohabiting	38	7	42	8
Single	28	3	17	6
Other[a]	8	1	6	2
Job status				
CSA/non-management	51	7	42	3
Team leader/senior management	18	5	23	9
Consultant supplier	NA	NA	6	0
Total number of interviews[b]	77	14	75	12

Notes: Missing data on age, marital status and job is a result of incomplete self-report questionnaires distributed at the beginning of the interview process.
[a] Includes separated, divorced or widowed.
[b] Two software home interviews were conducted with husband/wife couples both working in the same company.

Appendix B Survey respondent characteristics

Table B.1 Call centre and software employee characteristics (survey respondents)

	Call centres		Software		Total	
	N	% in call centres	N	% in software	N	% of total
Personal characteristics						
Gender						
Male	241	30%	230	72%	471	42%
Female	567	70%	90	28%	657	58%
Age						
16–20	68	8%	3	1%	71	6%
21–30	416	51%	118	37%	534	47%
31–40	206	25%	116	36%	322	28%
41–50	99	12%	66	20%	165	14%
Over 50	28	3%	19	6%	47	4%
Education (highest qualification)						
No qualifications	55	6%	7	2%	62	5%
School/HNC/vocational/FE	530	62%	83	25%	613	52%
Higher degree (undergraduate)	95	11%	24	7%	119	10%
Higher degree (postgraduate)	143	17%	142	43%	285	24%
Nationality						
British	796	96%	297	92%	1093	95%
Other	34	4%	27	9%	61	5%
Job characteristics	N	%	N	%	N	%
Job status						
Non-management	749	88%	242	74%	991	84%
Team/project leader or mgt.	106	12%	86	26%	192	16%
Job classification[a]						
Core operational staff	827	97%	307	94%	1134	96%
Support staff	28	3%	21	6%	49	4%
Contractual status						
Permanent	767	91%	272	83%	1039	89%
Contractor/agency/temp.	76	9%	38	12%	114	10%
Full-time	723	86%	303	93%	1026	88%
Shifts						
% frequency/always work nights	243	28%	7	2%	250	21%
% frequency/always work Sat/Sun	480	56%	11	3%	491	42%

Table B.1 Call centre and software employee characteristics (survey respondents) – *continued*

	Call centres		Software		Total	
	N	% in call centres	N	% in software	N	% of total
Paid overtime						
None	485	57%	138	42%	623	53%
Up to 10 hours/week	355	42%	180	55%	535	45%
More than 10 hours/week	14	2%	8	2%	22	2%
Unpaid overtime						
None	428	50%	93	28%	521	44%
Up to 10 hours/week	404	47%	193	59%	597	51%
More than 10 hours/week	21	2%	41	13%	62	5%
Home life	N	%	N	%	N	%
Dependents/care responsibilities	245	29%	113	34%	358	30%
Living arrangements						
On own	89	11%	61	19%	150	13%
With partner and children	207	25%	98	31%	305	27%
With partner only	231	28%	107	33%	338	29%
With flatmates	63	8%	25	8%	88	8%
With parents	193	23%	19	6%	212	18%
With children only	27	3%	6	2%	33	3%
Other[b]	16	2%	4	1%	21	2%
Contribution to household income						
None or almost none	60	7%	7	2%	67	6%
Less than half	280	34%	37	12%	317	28%
About half	195	24%	49	15%	244	21%
More than half	115	14%	98	31%	213	19%
All or almost all	173	21%	129	40%	302	26%

Notes:

[a] *Job classification* **Core** call centre staff were represented by operators (variously known as Customer Service Agents, telesales advisors, customer advisors, outbound quality checking agents, value knowledge brokers, volume service brokers, account executives, travel consultants, sales consultants), team leaders, managers, and financial planning assistants; core software staff were represented by software developers (variously known as applications support analysts, systems support analysts, technical analysts, software engineers, technical consultants), software managers and project managers. **Support** staff included those not directly involved in the core functions of each workplace (e.g., PAs, secretaries, human resource specialists). The questionnaires were targeted only at core staff, but in some cases 'support' staff responded. Support staff were identified from their job title and excluded from further analysis presented in each chapter. The figures in this table include both core and support staff.

[b] 'Other' living arrangements reported were: with other relative (some with children), with partners' parents or in-laws (some with children), with partner and flatmates, temporary shared accommodation, halls of residence, hotel part of the week.

Bibliography

Ackroyd, S. and Thompson, P. (1999) *Organizational Misbehaviour*, London: Sage.
Ackroyd, S., Glover, I., Currie, W. and Bull, S. (2000) 'The triumph of hierarchies over markets: information systems specialists in the current context', in Glover, I. and Hughes, M. (eds) *Professions at Bay: Encouragement and Control of Ingenuity in British Management*, 267–305, Aldershot: Ashgate.
Adam, A. (2002) 'Exploring the gender question in Critical Information Systems', *Journal of Information Technology*, 17(2): 59–67.
Ahmavaara, A. and Houston, D.M. (2005) *Fatherhood and Family: What do men think?*, Unpublished research report, Canterbury: University of Kent.
Alferoff, C. and Knights, D. (2003) 'We're all partying here: targets and games, or targets as games in call centre management', in Carr, A. and Hancock, P. (eds) *Art and Aesthetics at Work*, 70–92, Basingstoke: Palgrave.
Alvesson, M. (1995) *Management of Knowledge-Intensive Companies*, Berlin/New York: de Gruyter.
Alvesson, M. (2000) 'Social identity and the problem of loyalty in knowledge-intensive companies', *Journal of Management Studies*, 37(8): 1101–123.
Anderson, M., Becchofer, F. and Kendrick, S. (1994) in Anderson, M., Becchofer, F. and Gershuny, J. (eds) *The Social and Political Economy of the Household*, 19–67, Oxford: Oxford University Press.
Anderson, P. (2000) 'Renewals', *New Left Review*, II(1): 5–24.
Andrews, C.K., Lair, C.D. and Landry, B. (2005) 'The labor process in software startups: production on a virtual assembly line?', in Barrett, R. (ed.) *Management, Labour Process and Software Development: Reality Bytes*, 45–76, London: Routledge.
Anthony, P.D. (1977) *The Ideology of Work*, London: Tavistock.
Armstrong, P., Carter, B., Smith, C. and Nicols, T. (1986) *White Collar Workers, Trade Unions and Class*, London: Croom Helm.
Aronowitz, S. and Fazie, D. (1995) *The Jobless Future: Sci-Tech and the Dogma of Work*, Minneapolis: University of Minnesota Press.
Arthur, M.B. and Rousseau, D.M. (eds) (1996) *The Boundaryless Career: a New Employment Principle for a New Organizational Era*, New York: Oxford University Press.
Arthur, M.B., Hall, D.T. and Lawrence B.S. (eds) (1989) *Handbook of Career Theory*. Cambridge: Cambridge University Press.
Arthur, M.B., Inkson, K. and Pringle, J.K. (1999) *The New Careers individual action and economic change*, London: Thousand Oaks, California: Sage Publications.
Bacon, N. and Storey, J. (1996) 'Individualism and Collectivism and the Changing Role of Trade Unions', in Ackers, P., Smith, C. and Smith, P. (eds) *The New Workplace and Trade Unionism*, 41–76, London: Routledge.
Bain, P. and Mulvey, G. (2002) *Workforce flexibility in call centres: stretching to breaking point?* Paper to 20th Annual International Labour Process Conference, 2–4 April, University of Strathclyde, Glasgow.
Bain, P. and Taylor, P. (2002a) 'Ringing the changes? Union recognition and organisation in call centres in the UK finance sector', *Industrial Relations Journal*, 33(2): 246–61.
Bain, P. and Taylor, P. (2002b) 'Consolidation, "cowboys" and the developing employment relationship in British, Dutch and US call centres', in Holtgrewe, U.,

Kerst, C. and Shire, K. (eds) *Re-Organizing Service Work: Call Centres in Germany and Britain*, 42–62, Aldershot: Ashgate.

Bain, P., Taylor, P., Gilbert, K. and Gall, G. (2004) 'Failing to organise – or organizing to fail? Challenge, opportunity and the limitations of union policy in four call centres', in Healy, G., Heery, E., Taylor, P. and Brown, W. (eds) *The Future of Worker Representation*, 62–81, Basingstoke: Palgrave Macmillan.

Bain, P., Watson, A., Mulvey, G., Taylor, P. and Gall, G. (2002) 'Taylorism, targets and the pursuit of quantity and quality by call centre management', *New Technology Work and Employment*, 17(3): 170–85.

Baldamus, W. (1961) *Efficiency and Effort*, London: Tavistock.

Baldry, C. and Connolly, A. (1986) 'Drawing the line: computer-aided design and the organization of the drawing office', *New Technology, Work and Employment*, 1(1): 59–66.

Baldry, C., Bain, P. and Taylor, P. (1997) 'Sick and tired? – working in the modern office', *Work, Employment and Society*, 11(3): 519–39.

Baldry, C., Scholarios, D. and Hyman, J. (2005) 'Organizational commitment among software developers', in Barrett, R. (ed) *Management, Labour Process and Software Development: Reality Bytes'*, 168–95, London: Routledge.

Barley, S.R. (1989) 'Careers, identities and institutions: the legacy of the Chicago school of sociology', in Arthur, M., Hall, T. and Lawrence, B. (eds) *The Handbook of Career Theory*, 41–65, Cambridge: Cambridge University Press.

Barley, S.R. and Orr, J.E. (1997) 'Introduction: The neglected Workforce', in Barley, S.R. and Orr, J.E. (eds), *Between Craft and Science: Technical Work in US Settings*: 1–19, Ithaca New York: Cornell University Press.

Barling, J. and Sorensen, D. (1997) 'Work and family: In search of a relevant research agenda', in Jackson, S. and Cooper, C.L. (eds) *Creating tomorrows organizations: A Handbook of Organizational Behaviour*, 159–70, New York: Wiley.

Baroudi, J. and Igbaria, M. (1995) 'The impact of job performance on career advancement prospects; an examination of gender differences in the Information Systems workplace', *MIS Quarterly*, 19(1): 107–23.

Barrett, R. (1999) *The Labour Process of software development in the Australian Information Industry*, Paper presented to the 17th Annual Labour Process Conference. 30th March–1st April. London: University of London, Royal Holloway.

Barrett, R. (2001) 'Labouring under an illusion? The labour process of software development in the Australian information industry', *New Technology, Work and Employment*, 16(1): 18–34.

Barrett, R. (2005) 'The reality of software developing', in Barrett, R. (ed.) *Management, Labour Process and Software Development: Reality Bytes*, 196–207, London: Routledge.

Barrett, R. and Rainnie, A. (2005) 'Editorial: small firms and new technology', *New Technology, Work and Employment*, 20(3): 184–9.

Batt, R. and Moynihan, L. (2002) 'The viability of alternative call centre production models', *Human Resource Management Journal*, 12(4): 14–34.

Bauman, Z. (1998) *Work, Consumerism and the New Poor*, Cambridge: Polity.

Beck, U. (2000) *The Brave New World of Work*, London: Polity Press.

Beck, U., Giddens, A. and Lash, S. (1997) *Reflexive Modernization: Politics, Tradition and Aesthetics in the Modern Social Order*, Cambridge: Polity Press.

Becker, G. (1964) *Human Capital*, New York: National Bureau of Economic Research.

Becker, G. (1985) 'Human capital, effort and the sexual division of labor', *Journal of Labor Economics*, 3(1, part 2): 533–8.

Becker, H. (1960) 'Notes on the concept of commitment', *American Journal of Sociology*, 66(1): 32–40.

Beer, M. and Spector, B. (1985) *Human Resource Management Trends and Challenges*, Cambridge MA: Harvard Business School Press.

Beirne, M., Ramsay, H. and Panteli, A. (1998) 'Developments in computing work: Control and contradiction in the software labour process', in Thompson, P. and Warhurst, C. *Workplaces of the Future*, 124–41, Basingstoke: Macmillan.

Beirne, M. and Ramsay, H. (1992) 'Manna or monstrous regiment? Technology, control and democracy in the workplace', in Beirne, M. and Ramsay, H. (eds) *Information Technology and Workplace Democracy*, 1–55, London: Routledge.

Bell, D. (1973) *The Coming of Post-Industrial Society: a Venture into Social Forecasting*, Harmondsworth: Penguin.

Bell, D. (1974) *The Coming of Post-Industrial Society: a Venture into Social Forecasting*, London: Heinemann.

Bell, D. (1976) *Coming of Post-Industrial Society: a Venture into Social Forecasting* (2nd edn.) New York: Basic Books.

Belt, V. (2002) 'A female ghetto? Women's careers in call centres', *Human Resource Management Journal*, 12(4): 51–66.

Belt, V., Richardson, R. and Webster, J. (2002) 'Women, social skill and interactive service work in telephone call centres', *New Technology, Work and Employment*, 17(1): 20–34.

Belt, V., Richardson, R., Webster, J., Tijdens, K. and Van Klaveren, M. (1999) *Work Opportunities for Women in the Information Society: Call Centre Teleworking, Final Report for the Information Society Project Office (DG V and DG XIII)*. Brussels: European Commission.

Bendix, R. (1967) 'The Protestant Ethic – Revisited', *Comparative Studies in Society and History*, 9(3): 266–73.

Biernat, M. and Wortman, C.B. (1991) 'Sharing of home responsibilities between professionally employed women and their husbands', *Journal of Personality and Social Psychology*, 60(6): 844–60.

Blackburn, R. (1967) *Union Character and Social Class*, London: Batsford.

Blackler, F. (1995) 'Knowledge, knowledge work and organizations: an overview and interpretation', *Organization Studies*, 16(6): 1021–46.

Blauner, R. (1964) *Alienation and Freedom: the Factory Worker and His Industry*, Chicago: University of Chicago Press.

Boerlijst, J.G., Munnichs, J.M.A. and Van der Heijden, B.I.J.M. (1998) 'The older worker in the organization' in Drenth, P.J.D. Thierry, H.K. and De Wolff, C.H.J. (eds) *Handbook of Work and Organizational Psychology*, (Vol. 2): 183–213, London: Psychology Press.

Bolton, S. (2004) 'Conceptual confusions: emotion work as skilled work', in Grugulis, I., Keep, E. and Warhurst, C. (eds) *The Skills that Matter*, 19–37, Basingstoke: Palgrave Macmillan.

Bonney, N. and Love, J. (1991) 'Gender and migration: geographical mobility and the wife's sacrifice', *Sociological Review*, 39(2): 335–48.

Borman, W.C. and Motowildo, S.J. (1993) 'Expanding the criterion domain to include elements of contextual performance', in Schmitt, N. and Borman, W. (eds) *Personnel Selection in Organizations*, 71–98, San Fransisco: Jossey-Bass.

Bott, F., Coleman, A., Eaton, J., and Rowland, D. (1995) *Professional Issues in Software Engineering (2nd edition)* London: VCL Press Ltd.

Bottero, W. (2004) 'Class Identities and the Identity of Class', *Sociology*, 38(4): 985–1003.

Boyd, C. and Bolton, S. (2003) 'Trolley dolly or skilled emotion manager? Moving on from Hochschild's emotional labour', *Work, Employment and Society*, 17(2): 289–308.

Bradley, H., Erickson, M., Stephenson, C. and Williams, S. (2000) *Myths at Work*, Cambridge: Polity Press.
Braverman, H. (1974) *Labor and Monopoly Capital: The Degradation of Work in the Twentieth Century*, New York: Monthly Review Press.
Brenner, R. (2002) *The Boom and the Bubble: the US in the World Economy*, London: Verso.
Bridges, W. (1995) *Jobshift: How to Prosper in a Workplace Without Jobs*, London: Nicholas Brealey.
Brown, P., Hesketh, A. and Williams, S. (2003) 'Employability in a Knowledge-Driven Economy', *Journal of Education and Work*, 16(2): 107–26.
Brown, R. (1984) 'BSA Presidential Address: Working on Work', *Sociology*, 18(3): 313–23.
Brown, R. (1997) 'Introduction: work and employment in the 1990s', in Brown, R.K. (ed.) (1997) *The Changing Shape of Work*, 1–19, Basingstoke: Macmillan.
Brown, R. and Brannen, P. (1970) 'Social relations and social perspectives amongst shipbuilding workers', Part 1, *Sociology*, 4(1): 71–84.
Brown, R., Brannen, P., Cousins, J.M. and Samphier, M.L. (1972) 'The contours of solidarity: Social stratification and industrial relations in shipbuilding', *British Journal of Industrial Relations*, 10(1): 12–41.
Bruegel, I. (1996) 'Whose myths are they anyway?: a comment', *British Journal of Sociology*, 47(1): 175–7.
Bulmer, M. (ed.) (1975) *Working Class Images of Society*, London: Routledge and Kegan Paul.
Bunting, M. (2004) *Willing Slaves: How the Overwork Culture is Ruining Our Lives*, London: Harper Collins.
Burns, T. and Stalker, G.M. (1961) *The Management of Innovation*, London: Social Science/Tavistock.
Cairncross, F. (1997) *The Death of Distance: How the Communication Revolution Will Change our Lives*, Boston: Harvard Business School Press.
Callaghan, G. and Thompson, P. (2001) 'Edwards revisited: technical control and call centres', *Economic and Industrial Democracy*, 22(1): 13–37.
Callaghan, G. and Thompson, P. (2002) '"We recruit attitude": the selection and shaping of routine call centre labour', *Journal of Management Studies*, 39(2): 233–54.
Callinicos, A. (1983) 'The "New Middle Class" and Socialist Politics', *International Socialism*, 20: 82–119.
Callinicos, A. (2001) *Against the Third Way*, Oxford: Polity.
Callinicos, A. (2003) *An Anti-Capitalist Manifesto*, Oxford: Polity.
Campbell Clark, S. (2000) 'Work/family border theory: A new theory of work/family balance', *Human Relations*, 53(6): 747–71.
Campbell, J.P., McCloy, R.A., Oppler, S.H. and Sager, C.E. (1993) 'A theory of performance', in Schmitt, N. and Borman, W. (eds) *Personnel Selection in Organizations*, 35–70, San Fransisco: Jossey-Bass.
Cappelli, P. (1999) *New Deal at Work*, Boston: Harvard Business School Press.
Cappelli, P. (2000) 'Managing without commitment', *Organizational Dynamics*, 28(4): 11–24.
Cappelli, P. (2001) 'Why is it so hard to find information technology workers?', *Organizational Dynamics*, 30(2): 87–99.
Carmel, E. (1999) *Global Software Teams*, New Jersey: Prentice Hall.
Casey, C. (1995) *Work, Self and Society*, London: Routledge.
Castells, M. (1996) *The Rise of the Network Society*, Oxford: Blackwell.
Castells, M. (1997) *The Power of Identity*, Oxford: Blackwell.
Castells, M. (1998) *End of Millennium*, Oxford: Blackwell.

Castells, M. (2000) *The Rise of the Network Society* (2nd edn.) Oxford: Oxford University Press.
Castells, M. (2001) *The Internet Galaxy: Reflections on the Internet, Business and Society*, Oxford: Oxford University Press.
Castree, N., Coe, N., Ward, K. and Samers, M. (2004) *Spaces of Work*, London: Sage.
Cave, M., Majumdar, S. and Vogelsang, I. (eds) (2002) *Handbook of Telecommunications Economics, volume 1*, Amsterdam: Elsevier.
Cavendish R. (1982) *Women on the Line*, London: Routledge and Kegan Paul.
Charles, N. and James, E. (2003) 'Gender and work orientations in conditions of job insecurity', *British Journal of Sociology*, 54(2): 239–57.
Charles, N. and Kerr, M. (1999) 'Women's work', in G. Allan (ed.) *The Sociology of the Family*, 191–210, Oxford: Blackwell.
Cinamon, R.G. and Rich, Y. (2002) 'Profiles of attribution of importance to life roles and their implications for work-family conflict', *Journal of Counselling Psychology*, 49(2): 212–20.
Ciulla, J.B. (2000) *The Working Life: The Promise and Betrayal of Modern Work*, New York: Three Rivers Press.
Clegg, S. (1990) *Modern Organizations*, London: Sage.
Coleman, D. (ed.) (1996) *Europe's Population in the 1990s*, Oxford: Oxford University Press.
Collins, D. (1998) 'Knowledge work or working knowledge? Ambiguity and confusion in the analysis of the "Knowledge Age"', *Journal of Systemic Knowledge Management*, 1(1998–1999). Available on-line at http://tlainc.com/article7.htm.
Cortada, J. (1998) 'Where did knowledge workers come from?', in Cortada, J. (ed.) *Rise of the Knowledge Worker*, 3–21, Boston: Butterworth-Heinemann.
Council of European Professional Informatics Societies (CEPIS) (2002) *Information Practitioner Skills in Europe*, Frankfurt: CEPIS.
Cousins, C. and Tang, N. (2004) 'Working time and work and family conflict in the Netherlands, Sweden and the UK', *Work, Employment & Society*, 18(3): 531–49.
Cressey, P. and Scott, P. (1992) 'Employment, technology and industrial relations in the UK clearing banks: is the honeymoon over?', *New Technology, Work and Employment*, 7(2): 83–96.
Crompton, R. (2002) 'Employment, flexible working, and the family', *British Journal of Sociology*, 53(4): 537–58.
Crompton, R. (ed.) (1999) *Restructuring Gender Relations and Employment: The Decline of the Male Breadwinner*, Oxford: Oxford University Press.
Crompton, R. and Jones, G. (1984) *White-collar Proletariat: Deskilling and Gender in Clerical Work*, London: Macmillan.
Crompton, R. and Scott, J. (2000) 'Introduction: The State of Class Analysis', in Crompton, R., Devine, F., Savage, M. and Scott, J. (eds) *Renewing Class Analysis*, 1–15, Oxford: Blackwell.
Cully, M., Woodland, S., O'Reilly, A. and Dix, G. (1999) *Britain at Work: As depicted by the 1998 Workplace Employee Relations Survey*, London: Routledge.
Dahrendorf, R. (1959) *Class and Class Conflict in an Industrial Society*, London: Routledge and Kegan Paul.
Darlington, R. and Lyddon, D. (2001) *Glorious Summer: Class struggle in Britain 1972*, London: Bookmarks.
Davis, E. and Hunter, L.W. (2004) 'Where do women's jobs come from? Job resegregation in an American bank', *Work and Occupations*, 31(1): 73–110.
Deery, S. and Kinnie, N. (2002) 'Call centres and beyond: a thematic evaluation', *Human Resource Management Journal*, 12(4): 3–13.

Deery, S., Iverson, R. and Walsh, J. (2002) 'Work relationships in telephone call centres: understanding emotional exhaustion and employee withdrawal', *Journal of Management Studies*, 39(4): 471–96.
Delbridge, R. (1998) *Life on the Line in Contemporary Manufacturing*, Oxford: Oxford University Press.
Dennis, N., Henriques, F. and Slaughter, C. (1956) *Coal is Our Life*, London: Tavistock.
Despres, C. and Hiltrop, J.M. (1995) 'Human resource management in the knowledge age: current practice and perspectives in the future', *Employee Relations*, 17.1: 9–23.
Devine, F. and Savage, M. (2000) 'Conclusion: Renewing Class Analysis', in Crompton, R., Devine, F., Savage, M. and Scott, J. (eds) *Renewing Class Analysis*, 184–99, Oxford: Blackwell.
Dex, S. (2003) *Families and Work in the Twenty-first Century*, York: Joseph Rowntree Foundation.
Dex, S. (1999) *Families and the Labour Market*, York: Joseph Rowntree Foundation.
Dex, S. and Joshi, H. (1999) 'Careers and motherhood: policies for compatibility', *Cambridge Journal of Economics*, 23(5): 641–59.
DfEE (2000a) *Opportunity for All: Skills for the New Economy*, London: Department for Education and Employment.
DfEE (2000b) *Skills for All: Research Report from the National Skills Task Force*, London: Department for Education and Employment.
DfEE (1998) *The Learning Age: A Renaissance for New Britain*, Sheffield: Department for Education and Employment.
Dicken, P. (2003) *Global Shift*, London: Sage.
DiDio, L. (1997) 'Look out for techno-hazing', *Computerworld*, 31(39): 72.
Dolvik, J. and Waddington, J. (2003) 'Private sector services: challenges to European trades unions', *Transfer*, 3(2): 356–76.
Donkin, R. (2001) *Blood, Sweat & Tears: The Evolution of Work*, New York: Texere.
Drucker, P. (1968) *The Age of Discontinuity*, New York: Harper and Row.
Drucker, P. (1970) *Technology, Management and Society*, London: Heinnemann.
Drucker, P. (1993) *Post-Capitalist Society*, London: Butterworth-Heinnemann.
DTI (1998) *Our Competitive Future: Building the Knowledge Driven Economy*, December, Cmmd 4176. London: Department of Trade and Industry.
DTI (2004a) 'Flexible working in the IT industry; long hour cultures and work-life balance at the margins?' Available electronically at www.dti.gov.uk/industries/electronics
DTI (2004b) *Creating Wealth from Knowledge: The DTI Five Year Programme*, London: HMSO.
DTI (2005) *Women in the IT industry. Phase 2 Research: How to Retain Women in the IT Industry*, London: HMSO.
du Gay, P. (1996) *Consumption and Identity at Work*, London: Sage.
du Gay, P. and Salaman, G. (1992) 'The culture of the customer', *Journal of Management Studies*, 29(5): 615–33.
Dubin, R. (1962) 'Organizational effectiveness: some dilemmas of perspective', *American Sociological Review*, (27): 31–41
Dubin, R. (1956) 'Industrial workers' worlds: a study in the central life interests of industrial workers', *Social Problems*, 3(4): 131–42.
Duffield, M. (2002) 'Trends in female employment', *Labour Market Trends*, November 2002, London: Office for National Statistics, 605–16.
Durkheim, E. (1984) *The Division of Labor in Society*, New York: Free Press.

Ehrenreich, B. (2001) *Nickel and Dimed: Undercover in Low-Wage USA*, London: Granta.
Ehrenreich, B. and Ehrenreich, J. (1977) 'The professional-managerial class', in Hyman, R. and Price, R. (eds) (1983) *The New Working Class? White-collar Workers and Their Organisations*, 106–10, London: Macmillan.
England, P. (2005) 'Gender inequality in labor markets: the role of motherhood and segregation', *Social Politics: International Studies in Gender, State & Society*, 12(2): 264–88.
Epstein C.F., Seron, C., Oglensky, B. and Saute, R. (1997) *The Part-time paradox. Time norms, professional life, family and gender*, New York: Routledge.
Equal Opportunities Commission (2003) *Pay and income*, Manchester: EOC.
Equal Opportunities Commission (2005) 'Facts about Women & Men in Great Britain', Manchester: EOC.
European Commission (2004) *Employment in Europe 2004; Recent trends and prospects*, Luxembourg: Office for Official Publications of the European Communities.
European Industrial Relations Review (EIRR) (1995) *Work organization and employment in electronics*, 257: 20–5.
European Information Technology Observatory (2002), *EITO Yearbook*, 10th Edition, Frankfurt: European Information Technology Observatory Yearbook.
European Union (2001) *European skill shortages in ICT and policy responses*. European Competitiveness Report Annex III. Luxembourg: Eur-Op.
Evetts, J. (2000) 'Analyzing change in women's careers: cultural, structural and action dimensions', *Gender, Work, and Organization*, 7(1): 57–67.
Fagan, C. (2001) 'Time, money and the gender order: work orientations and working-time preferences in Britain', *Gender, Work and Organization*, 8(3): 239–66.
Felstead, A. and Jewson, N. (1999) 'Flexible labour and non-standard employment: an agenda of issues', in Felstead, A. and Jewson, N. (eds) *Global Trends in Flexible Labour*, 1–20, London: Macmillan.
Femlee, D. (1995) 'Causes and consequences of women's employment discontinuity, 1967–1973', *Work and Occupations*, 22(2): 167–87.
Fernie and Metcalf (1997) *(Not) Hanging on the Telephone: Payment Systems in the New Sweatshops, London: Centre for Economic Performance*, London School of Economics.
Filby, M. (1992) 'The figures, the personality and the bums: service work and sexuality', *Work, Employment & Society*, 6(1): 23–42.
Fineman, S. (2003) *Understanding Emotion at Work*, London: Sage.
Flecker, J. and Hofbauer, J. (1998) 'Capitalizing on subjectivity: the "new model worker" and the importance of being useful', in Thompson, P. and Warhurst, C. (eds) *Workplaces of the Future*, 104–23, Basingstoke: Macmillan.
Fleming, P. and Sewell, G. (2002) 'Looking for the Good Soldier Svejk: alternative modalities of resistance in the contemporary workplace', *Sociology*, 36(4): 857–73.
Fleming, P., Harley, B. and Sewell, G. (2003) 'A little knowledge is a dangerous thing: getting below the surface of the growth of "Knowledge Work" in Australia', *Work, Employment and Society*, 8.4: 725–47.
Foote, D. (2000) 'Keeping your staff happy? – think "career"', *Computerworld* 34(41): 38–9.
Fox, A. (1974) *Beyond Contract: Work, Power and Trust Relations*, London: Faber.
Fox, A. (1980) 'The meaning of work', in Esland, G. and Salaman, G. (eds) (1980) *The Politics of Work and Occupations*, 139–91, Milton Keynes: Open University Press.
Fransman, M. (2002) *Telecoms in the Internet Age*, Oxford: Oxford University Press.

Fraser of Allender Institute (1996) *Skill Shortages in Scottish Electronics*, March 1996, Glasgow: University of Strathclyde, Fraser of Allender Institute.

Frenkel, S., Korczynski, M., Shire, K. and Tam, M. (1999) *On the Front Line: Organization of Work in the Information Economy*, Ithaca NY: ILR Press.

Friedman, A. (1977) *Industry and Labour: Class Struggle at Work and Monopoly Capitalism*, London: Macmillan.

Frone, M.R., Russell, M. and Cooper, M.L. (1992) 'Antecedents and outcomes of work-family conflict: Testing a model of the work-family interface', *Journal of Applied Psychology*, 77(1): 65–78.

Froud, J., Johal, S. and Williams, K. (2002) 'Financialization and the coupon pool', *Capital and Class*, 78: 119–52.

Gall, G. (2005) *The Political Economy of Scotland – Red Scotland? Radical Scotland?*, Cardiff: University of Wales Press.

Giddens, A. (1973) *The Class Structure of the Advanced Societies*, London: Hutchison.

Giddens, A. (1991) *Modernity and Self-identity*, Stanford: Stanford University Press.

Glucksman, M. (2004) 'Call configurations: varieties of call centre and divisions of labour', *Work, Employment and Society*, 18(4): 795–811.

Goffee, R. (1981) 'Incorporation and conflict: a case study of subcontracting in the coal industry', *Sociological Review*, 29: 475–97.

Goldthorpe, J. (1982) 'On the Service Class: Its Foundation and Future', in Giddens, A. and McKenzie, E. (eds) *Social Class and the Division of Labour*, 162–85, Cambridge: Cambridge University Press.

Goldthorpe, J. (1996) 'Class analysis and the re-orientation of class theory', *British Journal of Sociology*, 45(3): 481–505.

Goldthorpe, J., Lockwood, D., Bechhofer, F. and Platt, J. (1968) *The Affluent Worker: Industrial Attitudes and Behaviour*, Cambridge: Cambridge University Press.

Goldthorpe, J., Lockwood, D., Bechhofer, F. and Platt, J. (1969) *The Affluent Worker in the Class Structure*, Cambridge: Cambridge University Press.

Goodstein, J. (1995) 'Employer involvement in eldercare. An organizational adaptation perspective', *Academy of Management Journal*, 38(6): 1657–71.

Gorz, A. (1967) *Strategy for Labour: A Radical Proposal*, Boston: Beacon Press.

Gorz, A. (1971) 'Technicians and the class struggle', in Hyman, R. and Price, R. (eds) (1983) *The New Working Class? White-collar Workers and Their Organizations*, 82–7, London: Macmillan.

Grainger, H. and Holt, H. (2005) *Trade Union Membership 2004*, London: Department of Trade and Industry.

Green, F. (2000) 'The impact of company human resource policies on social skills: Implications for training sponsorship, quit rates and efficiency wages', *Scottish Journal of Political Economy*, 47(3): 51–272.

Green, F. (2001) 'It's been a hard day's night: the concentration and intensification of work in late twentieth century Britain', *British Journal of Industrial Relations*, 39(1): 53–80.

Grimshaw, D. and Rubery, J. (2001) *The Gender Pay Gap: A Research Review*, Research Discussion Series. Manchester: Equal Opportunities Commission.

Grimshaw, D., Ward, K., Rubery, J. and Beynon, H. (2001) 'Organizations and the transformation of the internal labour market', *Work Employment and Society*, 15(1): 25–54.

Grugulis, I., Vincent, S. and Hebson, G. (2003) 'The rise of the "network organization" and the decline of discretion', *Human Resource Management Journal*, 13(2): 45–59.

Guest, D. (1987) 'Human resource management and industrial relations', *Journal of Management Studies*, 14(5): 503–21.

Guest, D. (1989) 'Human resource management – its implications for industrial relations and trade unions', in: Storey, J. (ed.) *New Perspectives in Human Resource Management*, 41–55, London: Routledge.

Guest, D. (2000) *Effective People Management*, London: Chartered Institute of Personnel and Development.

Guest, D. and MacKenzie-Davey, K. (1996) 'Don't write off the traditional career', *People Management*, 22 February, 2(4): 22–5.

Guest, D., Michie, J., Sheehan, M. and Conway, N. (2000) *Getting inside the HRM-Performance Relationship: ESRC Future of Work Working Paper 8*, Leeds: University of Leeds.

Hakim, C. (1996) *Female Heterogeneity and the Polarisation of Women's Employment*, London: Athlone.

Hakim, C. (2000) *Work-Lifestyle Choices in the 21st Century: Preference Theory*, Oxford: Oxford University Press.

Hakim, C. (2002) 'Lifestyle preferences as determinants of women's differentiated labor market careers', *Work and Occupations*, 29(4): 428–59.

Hall, D.T. (1996) *The Career is Dead – Long Live the Career*, San Francisco, CA: Jossey-Bass.

Hall, D.T. (2002) *Careers in and out of Organizations*, Thousand Oaks: CA: Sage.

Hall, D.T., Briscoe, J.P. and Kram, K.E. (1997) 'Identity, values and learning in the Protean Career', In Cooper, C.L. and Jackson, S.E. (eds) *Creating Tomorrow's Organizations. A Handbook for Future Research in Organizational Behavior*, 321–35, New York: Wiley.

Hampson, I. and Junor, A. (2005) 'Invisible work, invisible skills: interactive customer service as articulation work', *New Technology, Work and Employment*, 20(2): 166–81.

Handel, M.J. (2003) 'Skills mismatch in the labor market', *Annual Review of Sociology*, 29: 135–65.

Handy, C. (1994) *The Empty Raincoat*, London: Hutchinson.

Handy, C. (1985) *The Future of Work*, London: Blackwell.

Hardill, I. (ed.) (2003) 'Special Issue: Teleworking', *New Technology, Work and Employment*, 18(3): 156–7.

Hardill, I. and Watson, R. (2004) 'Career priorities within dual career households: an analysis of the impact of child rearing upon gender participation rates and earnings', *Industrial Relations Journal*, 35(1): 19–37.

Hardt, M. and Negri, A. (2000) *Empire*, Cambridge Mass: Harvard University Press.

Harkness, S. (1999) 'The 24 hour economy: changes in working times', in Gregg, P. and Wadsworth, J. (eds) *The State of Working Britain*, 90–108, Manchester: Manchester University Press.

Harpaz, I. (2001) *The Girls in the Van: Covering Hilary*, New York: Thomas Dunne.

Harpaz, I. and Snir, R. (2003) 'Workaholism: Its definition and nature', *Human Relations*, 56(3): 291–319.

Harvey, D. (2005) *A Brief History of Neo-liberalism*, Oxford: Oxford University Press.

Head, S. (2003) *The New Ruthless Economy: Work and Power in the Digital Age*, New York: Oxford University Press.

Hebson, G. and Grugulis, I. (2005) 'Gender and new organizational forms', in Marchington, M., Grimshaw, D., Rubery, J. and Willmott, H. (eds) *Fragmenting Work: blurring organisational boundaries and disordering hierarchies*, 217–38, Oxford: Oxford University Press.

Heckscher, C. (1995) *White-collar Blues. Management Loyalties in an Age of Corporate Restructuring*, New York, NY: Basic Books.

Held, D., McGrew, A., Goldblatt, D. and Perraton, J. (1999) *Global Transformations – Politics, Economics and Culture*, London: Polity Press.
Heller, F., Pusic, E., Strauss, G. and Wilpert, B. (1998) *Organizational Participation: Myth and Reality*, Oxford: Oxford University Press.
Hendry, C., Arthur, M.B. and Jones, A.M. (1995) *Strategy through People – Adaptation and Learning in the Small-medium Enterprise*, London: Routledge.
Henwood, D. (2003) *After the New Economy*, New York: The New Press.
Henwood, F. (2000) 'From the women question in technology to the technology in question in feminism: rethinking gender equality in IT education', *The European Journal of Women's Studies*, 7(2): 209–27.
Herod, A. (2001) 'Labour internationalism and the contradictions of globalization: or, why the local is sometimes still important in a global economy', *Antipode*, 33: 407–26.
Herriot, P. and Pemberton, C. (1996) 'Contacting careers', *Human Relations*, 49(6): 757–90.
Herriot, P. and Pemberton, C. (1997) 'Facilitating new deals', *Human Resource Management Journal*, 7(1): 45–56.
Hill, R. and Stewart, J. (1999) 'HRD in small organisations', *Human Resource Development International*, 2(2): 103–23.
Hirsch, P. and Stanley, M. (1996) 'The rhetoric of boundaryless or, how the newly empowered managerial class bought into its own marginalization', in Arthur, M. and Rousseau, D. (eds) *The Boundaryless Career: A New Employment Principle for a New Organizational Era*, 218–34, Oxford: Oxford University Press.
Hirst, P. and Thompson, G. (1999) *Globalization in Question*, Oxford: Polity Press.
Hoare, Q. (ed.) (1977) *Selections from political writings (1910–1920): Antonio Gramsci*, London: Lawrence and Wishart.
Hochschild, A.R. (1983) *The Managed Heart: Commercialization of Human Feeling*, Berkeley: University of California Press.
Hochschild, A.R. (1989) *The Second Shift*, New York: Avon.
Hochschild, A.R. (1997) *The Time Bind: When Work Becomes Home and Home Becomes Work*, New York: Metropolitan Books.
Hochschild, A.R. (2003) *The Commercialization of Intimate Life: Notes from Home and Work*, Berkeley: University of California Press.
Hodson, R. (2001) *Dignity at Work*, Cambridge: Cambridge University Press.
Hofstede, G. (1991) *Culture and Organizations*, London: HarperCollins.
Hogarth, T., Hasluck, C. and Pierre, G. (2000) *Work-Life Balance 2000: Baseline Study of Work-Life Balance Practices in Great Britain* Dfee., London: HMSO.
Hogarth, T., Hasluck, C., Pierre, G., Winterbottom, M. and Vivian, D. (2001) *Work-Life Balance 2000: Baseline Study of Work-life Balance Practices in Great Britain – Summary Report*, London: Institute for Employment Research, HMSO.
Holtgrewe, U. (2001) 'Recognition, intersubjectivity and service work: labour conflicts in call centres', *Industrielle Beziehungen. Zeitschrift für Arbeit, Organization und Management. The German Journal of Industrial Relations*, 8(1): 37–54.
Houlihan, M. (2002) 'Tensions and variations in call centre management strategies', *Human Resource Management Journal*, 12(4): 67–85.
Huws, U. (1999) 'Material World: the Myth of the "Weightless Economy"', in Panitch, L. and Leys, C. (eds) *Socialist Register 1999*: 29–55, New York: Merlin Press.
Hyman, J., Baldry, C., Scholarios, D. and Bunzel, D. (2003) 'Work-life imbalance in call centres and software development', *British Journal of Industrial Relations*, 41(2): 215–39.

Hyman, J., Lockyer, C., Marks, A. and Scholarios, D. (2004) 'Needing a new programme: why is union membership so low among software workers?', in Healy, G., Heery, E., Taylor, P. and Brown, W. (eds) *The Future of Worker Representation*, 37–61, Basingstoke: Palgrave Macmillan.

Hyman, R. (1980) 'Introduction: white-collar workers and theories of class', in Hyman, R. and Price, R. (1983) (eds) *The New Working Class? White-collar Workers and Their Organisations*, 3–45, London: Macmillan.

Hyman, R. (1987) 'Strategy or structure? Capital, labour and control', *Work, Employment and Society*, 1(1): 25–55.

Hyman, R. and Price, R. (eds) (1983) *The New Working Class? White-collar Workers and Their Organisations*, London: Macmillan.

Ichniowski, C., Kochan, T.A., Levine, D., Olson, C. and Strauss, G. (1996) 'What works at work: overview and assessment', *Industrial Relations*, 35(3): 299–333.

IDS (1999) *Pay and Conditions in Call Centres 1999*, London: Incomes Data Services.

IDS (2000) *Pay and Conditions in Call Centres 2000*, London: Incomes Data Services.

IDS (2003) *Pay in the Not-for-profit Sector 2002*, IDS Report 873. London: Incomes Data Services.

Igbaria, M. and Chidambaram, M. (1997) 'The impact of gender on careers success of information systems professionals: A human-capital perspective', *Information Technology and People*, 10(1): 63–86.

Jacobs, J. and Gerson, K. (2001) 'Overworked individuals or overworked families?', *Work and Occupations*, 28(1): 40–64.

Jessop, B. (2000) 'The state and the contradictions of the knowledge-driven economy', in Bryson, J.R., Daniels, P.W., Henry, N.D. and Pollard, J. (eds) *Knowledge, Space and Economy*, 63–78, London: Routledge.

Jewson, N. and Mason, D. (1986) 'Theory and practice of equal opportunities policies: liberal and radical approaches', *Sociological Review*, 34(2): 307–34.

Kanter, R.M. (1989) 'Career and the wealth of nations: a macro-perspective on the structure and implications of career form', in Arthur, M.B., Hall, D.T. and Lawrence, B.S. (eds) *Handbook of Career Theory*, 506–21, New York: Cambridge University Press.

Kärreman, D. and Alvesson, M. (2004) 'Cages in tandem, management control, social identity, and identification in a knowledge-intensive firm', *Organization*, 11(1): 149–75.

Kaufman, D. and Fetters, M. (1980) 'Work motivation and job values among professional men and women: A new accounting', *Journal of Vocational Behavior*, 17(1): 251–62.

Keep, E. and Mayhew, K. (1999) 'The assessment: knowledge, skills and competitiveness', *Oxford Review of Economic Policy*, 15(1): 1–15.

Kelley, R.E. (1985) *The Gold-Collar Worker: Harnessing the Brainpower of the New Workforce*, Reading: Addison Wesley.

Kelly, J. (1985) 'Management's redesign of work: labour process, labour markets and product markets', in Knights, D., Willmott, H. and Collinson, D. (eds) (1987) *Job Redesign – Critical Perspectives on the Labour Process*, 30–51, Aldershot: Gower.

Kelly, J. (1998) *Rethinking Industrial Relations*, London: Routledge.

Kerr, C., Dunlop, J.J., Harbison, F.H. and Mayers, C.A. (1960) *Industrialism and Industrial Man*, Cambridge Mass: Harvard University Press.

Kinnie, N. and Parsons, J. (2004) 'Managing client, employee and customer relations: constrained strategic choice in the management of human resources in a commercial call centre', in S. Deery and N. Kinnie (eds) *Call Centres and Human Resource Management*, 102–26, Basingstoke: Palgrave Macmillan.

Kinnie, N., Hutchinson, S. and Purcell, J. (2000) '"Fun and Surveillance": the paradox of high commitment management in call centres', *International Journal of Human Resource Management*, 11(5): 967–85.

Kirchmeyer, C. (1993) 'Multicultural task groups: An account of the low contribution level of minorities', *Small Group Research*, 24: 127–48.

Kirton, G. and Greene, A.M. (2000) *Positive Action in Trade Unions: The Case of Women and Black Members* August, Aston Business School Working Paper RP0021, Birmingham: Aston Business School.

Klingender, F.D. (1935) 'Clerks as proletarians' in Hyman, R. and Price, R. (1983) (eds) *The New Working Class? White-collar Workers and Their Organisations*, 52–7, London: Macmillan.

Knights, D. and Murray, F. (1994) *Managers Divided: Organisation Politics and Information Technology Management*, Chichester: John Wiley.

Korczynski, M. (2002) *Human Resource Management and Service Work*, Basingstoke: Palgrave.

Kraft, P. (1999) 'The industrialisation of computer programming: From programming to "software production"', in Wardell, M., Steiger, T., and Meiksins, P. (eds) *Rethinking the Labour Process*, 17–36, New York: State University of New York Press.

Kraft, P. and Dubnoff, S. (1986) Job content, fragmentation, and control in computer software work, *Industrial Relations*, 25(2): 184–96.

Kumar, K. (1981) *Prophecy and Progress: the Sociology of Industrial and Post-Industrial Society*, Harmondsworth: Pelican.

Kumar, K. (1984) 'The social culture of work: work, employment and unemployment', in Thompson, K. (ed.) (1984) *Work, Employment and Unemployment*, 2–17, Milton Keynes: Open University Press.

Kunda, G. (1992) *'Engineering Culture, Control and Commitment in a High-Tech Corporation'*, Philadelphia: Temple University Press.

Leadbeater, C. (1999) *Living on Thin Air*, London: Penguin.

Ledwith, S. and Colgan, F. (eds) (1996) *Women in Organisations: Challenging Gender Politics*, Basingstoke: Macmillan.

Legge, K. (1995) *Human Resource Management: Rhetorics and Realities*, London: Macmillan.

Legge, K. (2001) 'Silver Bullet or Spent Round? Assessing the Meaning of the High Commitment Management/Performance Relationship', in Storey, J. (ed.) *Human Resource Management: a Critical Text*, 2nd edition, 21–36, London: Thompson.

Liedner, R. (1991) 'Serving hamburgers and selling insurance. Gender, work and identity in interactive service jobs', *Gender and Society*, 5(2): 154–77.

Lockwood, D. (1966) 'Sources of variation in working class images of society', *Sociological Review*, 14 (November): 249–67.

Lockwood, D. (1958) *The Blackcoated Worker*, London: Unwin.

Lyon, D. (1988) *The Information Society: Issues and Illusions*, London: Polity.

MacInnes, J. (1987) *Thatcherism at Work*, Milton Keynes: Open University Press.

Mallet, S. (1975) *The New Working Class*, Nottingham: Spokesman.

Mannheim, B. (1983) 'Male and female industrial workers: job satisfaction, work role centrality and work place preference', *Work and Occupations*, 10(4): 413–36.

Mannheim, B. (1993) 'Gender and the effects of demographics, status, and work values on work centrality', *Work and Occupations*, 20(1): 3–22.

Marchington, M., Rubery, J., Grimshaw, D. and Willmott, H. (2005) *Fragmenting Work*, London: Oxford University Press.

Marks, A. and Lockyer, C. (2004) 'Self-interest and knowledge work: the bugs in the programme for teamwork?', *Economic and Industrial Democracy*, 25(2): 213–38.

Marks, A. and Lockyer, C. (2005) 'Debugging the System: the impact of location on the identity of software team members', *International Journal of Human Resource Management*, 16(2): 219–37.

Marshall, G. (1997) *Repositioning Class*, London: Sage.

Marshall, J.N. and Richardson, R. (1996) 'The impact of "telemediated services" on corporate structures: the example of "branchless" retail banking in Britain', *Environment and Planning A*, 28: 1843–58.

Marx, K. (1976) *Capital: Volume One*, Harmondsworth: Penguin.

Marx, K. (1982) 'The economic and philosophic manuscripts of 1844', in Giddens, A. and Held, D. (eds) (1982) *Classes, Power, and Conflict: Classical and Contemporary Debates*, 157–74, London: Macmillan.

McDowell, L. and Court, G. (1994) 'Gender divisions of labour in the post-Fordist economy: the maintenance of occupational sex segregation in the financial services sector', *Environment and Planning* A-26(9): 1397–418.

McKay, S. (2001) 'Between flexibility and regulation: rights, equality and protection at work', *British Journal of Industrial Relations*, 39(2): 285–303.

McKie, L., Bowlby, S. and Gregory, S. (1999) 'Gender and the household' in McKie, L., Bowlby, S. and Gregory, S. *Gender, Power and the Household*: 3–21, Basingstoke: Palgrave Macmillan.

McRae, S. (1997) 'Household and labour market change. implications for the growth of inequality in Britain', *British Journal of Sociology*, 48(3): 384–405.

McRae, S. (1999) 'Introduction: family and household change in Britain', in McRae, S. (ed.), *Changing Britain: Families and Households in the 1990s*, 1–31, Oxford: Oxford University Press.

McRae, S. (2003) 'Constraints and choices in mothers' employment careers: a consideration of Hakim's Preference Theory', *British Journal of Sociology*, 54(3): 317–38.

Meiksins, P. and Smith, C. (1996) *Engineering Labour: Technical Workers in Comparative Perspective*, London: Verso.

Meyer, J.P. and Allen, N.J. (1991) 'A three-component conceptualization of organizational commitment', *Human Resource Management Review*, 1(1): 61–89.

Miozzo, M. and Ramirez, M. (2003) 'Services innovation and the transformation of work: the case of UK telecommunications', *New Technology, Work and Employment*, 18(1): 62–79.

Morgan, H. and Milliken, F. (1993) 'Keys to action. Understanding differences in organizations' responsiveness to work-and-family issues', *Human Resource Management Journal*, 31: 227–48.

Morris, T., Storey, J., Wilkinson, A. and Cressey, P. (2001) 'Industry change and union mergers in British retail finance', *British Journal of Industrial Relations*, 39(2): 237–56.

Morse, N.C. and Weiss, R.S. (1955) 'The function and meaning of work and the job', *American Sociological Review*, 20: 191–8.

MOW International Research Team (1987) *The Meaning of Working*, London: Academic Press.

Newby, H. (1972) 'The farm worker', *Sociological Review*, 20(3): 413–27.

Newell, S. (1993) 'The superwoman syndrome: Gender differences in attitudes towards equal opportunities at work and towards domestic responsibilities at home', *Work, Employment & Society*, 7(2): 275–80.

Newell, S., Robertson, M., Scarborough, H. and Swan, J. (2002) *Managing Knowledge Work*, London: Palgrave.

Newmark, D. and Reed, D. (2000) *Employment Relationships in the New Economy*, NBER Working Paper 8910, Cambridge MA: National Bureau for Economic Research.

Nicholson, N. (1996) 'Careers in a new context', in Warr, P. (ed.) *Psychology at Work*, 161–87, Harmondsworth: Penguin.

Nohria, N. and Berkley, J.D. (1994) 'The virtual organization: bureaucracy, technology and the implosion of control', in Heckscher, C. and Donnellon, A., *The Post-Bureaucratic Organization: New Perspectives on Organizational Change*, 108–28, Thousand Oaks, California: Sage.

Nolan, P. (2002) 'The ESRC Future of Work Programme', *New Technology Work and Employment*, 17(3): 150–1.

Nolan, P. and Slater, G. (2003) 'The labour market: history, structure and prospects', in Edwards, P. (ed.) *Industrial Relations: Theory and Practice*, 58–80, Oxford: Blackwell.

Nonaka, I. and Takeuchi, H. (1995) *The Knowledge Creating Company*, Oxford: Oxford University Press.

Noon, M. and Hoque, K. (2004) 'Equal opportunities policy and practice in Britain: evaluating the "Empty Shell" hypothesis', *Work Employment and Society*, 18(3): 481–506.

Novitz, T. (2002) A revised role for trade unions as designed by new labour: the representation pyramid and partnership, *Journal of Law and Society*, 29(3): 487–509.

NTO tele.com (1999) *Analysis and mapping of the Call Handling Sector*, TVSC: London

OECD (2000) *Measuring the ICT Sector*, Paris.

OECD (2002) *Measuring the Information Economy*, Paris.

Office for National Statistics (ONS) (2000a) *Size analysis of United Kingdom business*, London: Office for National Statistics.

Office for National Statistics (ONS) (2000b) Labour Force Survey 2000, London: Stationery Office.

Office for National Statistics (ONS) (2001a) *Annual Survey of Hours and Earnings*, London: Office of National Statistics.

Office for National Statistics (ONS) (2001b) Labour Force Survey 2001, London: Stationery Office.

Ohmae, K. (1995) *The Evolving Global economy: Making Sense of the New World Order*, Boston: Harvard University Press.

Oliver, N. and Wilkinson, B. (1992) *The Japanisation of British Industry*, Oxford: Blackwell.

Osterman, P. (1995) 'Work-family programs and the employment relationship', *Administrative Science Quarterly*, 40(4): 681–700.

Pahl, R. (1984) *Divisions of Labour*, Oxford: Blackwell.

Pahl, R. (1995) *After Success. Fin-de-Siècle Anxiety and Identity*, London: Polity Press.

Pakulski, J. and Waters, M. (1996) *The Death of Class*, London: Sage.

Panteli, A., Stack, J. and Ramsay, H. (1999) 'Gender and professional ethics in the IT industry', *Journal of Business Ethics*, 22(1): 51–61.

Parker, P. and Arthur, M.B. (2000) 'Careers, organizing, and community', in Peiperl, M.A., Arthur, M.B., Goffee, R. and Morris, T. (eds) *Career Frontiers: New Conceptions of Working Lives*, 99–121, Oxford, U.K.: Oxford University Press.

Parkin, F. (1979) 'Social Closure and Class Formation', in Giddens, A. and Held, D. (eds) (1982) *Classes, Power, and Conflict: Classical and Contemporary Debates*, 175–84, London: Macmillan.

Perolle, J. (1986) 'Intellectual assembly lines: the rationalization of managerial, professional and technical work', *Work Computers and Social Sciences*, 2: 111–21.

Peters, T. and Waterman, R. (1982) *In Search of Excellence*, New York: Harper and Row.

Pilcher, J. (1998) 'Gender matters? Three cohorts of women talking about role reversal', *Sociological Research Online*, 3(1): http://www.socresonline.org.uk/socresonline/3/1/10.html.

Pongratz, H.J. and Günter, Voß G. (2003) 'From employee to "entreployee": towards a "self-entrepreneurial" work force?', *Concepts and Transformation*, 8(3): 239–54.
Poulantzas, N. (1975) 'The New Petty Bourgeoisie', in Hyman, R. and Price, R. (eds) *The New Working Class? White-collar Workers and Their Organisations*, 110–16, London: Macmillan.
Poulantzas, N. (1975) *Classes in Contemporary Capitalism*, London: Verso.
Prandy, K. (1965) *Professional Employees*, London: Faber & Faber.
Procter, S. and Mueller, F. (eds) (2000) *Teamworking*, Basingstoke: Macmillan.
Proctor, I. and Padfield, M. (1999) 'Work orientations and women's work: a critique of Hakim's theory of the heterogeneity of women', *Gender, Work and Organisation*, 6(3): 152–62.
Purcell, K. (2002) *Qualifications and Careers*, EOC Working Paper Series No. 1. Manchester: Equal Opportunities Commission.
Quah, D. (1997) 'Increasingly weightless economies', *Bank of England Quarterly Bulletin*, 37 (1): 49–56.
Quintas, P. (1994) 'A product-process model; of innovation in software development', *Journal of Information Technology*, 9(1): 3–17.
Rabinowitz, S. and Hall, D. (1977) 'Organizational research on job involvement', *Psychological Bulletin*, 84(2): 245–58.
Rake, K. (2000), *Women's Incomes over the Lifetime*, London: Stationery Office.
Ramsay, H. (1999) 'Close encounters of the nerd kind: Computer professionals in the new millennium', *Work-life Conference*, May. Malmo: Swedish National Institute of Working Life.
Ramsay, H., Scholarios, D. and Harley, B. (2000) 'Employees and high performance work systems: testing inside the black box', *British Journal of Industrial Relations*, 38(4): 501–31.
Redman, T. and Mathews, B. (2002) 'Managing services; should we be having fun?', *The Service Industries Journal*, 22(3): 51–62.
Reeve, R. (2000) *Happy Mondays*, London: Momentum.
Reich, R. (1993) *The Wealth of Nations*, London: Simon and Schuster.
Reich, R. (2001) *The Future of Success*, New York: Albert A. Knopf.
Richardson, R. and Marshall, J.N. (1996) 'The growth of telephone call centres in peripheral areas of Britain: evidence from Tyne and Wear', *AREA*, 28(3): 308–17.
Rifkin, J. (1995) *The End of Work: The Decline of the Global labour Force and the Dawn of the Post-Market Era*, New York: Putnam.
Ritzer, G. (1996) *The McDonaldization of Society*, Thousand Oaks California: Pine Forge Press.
Rose, E. (2002) 'The labour process and union commitment within a banking services call centre', *The Journal of Industrial Relations*, 44(1): 40–61.
Rose, M. (1988) *Industrial Behaviour* (2nd edn.), London: Penguin.
Rousseau, D.M. and Parks, J.M. (1993) 'The contracts of individuals and organizations', in Staw, B.M. and Cummings, L.L. (eds) *Research in organizational behavior*, 15: 1–43, Greenwich, CT: JAI Press.
Rubery, J., Ward, K., Grimshaw, D. and Beynon, H. (2005) 'Working time, industrial relations and the employment relationship', *Time and Society*, 14(1): 89–111.
Ruigrok, W. and van Tulder, R. (1995) *The Logic of International Restructuring*, London: Routledge.
Salaman, G. (1971) 'Two occupational communities', *Sociological Review*, 19(1): 389–99.
Salaman, G. (1974) *Community and Occupation: an Exploration of Work/Leisure Relationships*, Cambridge: Cambridge University Press.

Salaman, G. (1981) *Class and the Corporation*, Glasgow: Fontana.
Savage, M. (2001) 'Class identities in contemporary Britain: the demise of collectivism?', in Van Gyes, G., De Witte, H. and Pasture, P. (eds) (2001) *Can class still unite? The differentiated work force, Class Solidarity and Trade Unions*, 79–100, Aldershot: Ashgate.
Savage, M. (2005) 'Working-class identities in the 1960s: revisiting the affluent worker study', *Sociology*, 39(5): 929–46.
Savage, M., Bagnall, G. and Longhurst, B. (2001) 'Ordinary, ambivalent and defensive: class identities in the Northwest of England', *Sociology*, 35(4): 875–92.
Saxenian, A. (1996) 'Beyond boundaries: open labor markets and learning in Silicon Valley', in Arthur, M.B. and Rousseau, D.M. (eds) *The Boundaryless Career: A New Employment Principle for a New Organizational Era*, 23–39, Oxford: Oxford University Press.
Schein, E.H. (1978) *Career Dynamics*, Reading, MA: Addison-Wesley.
Scholarios, D. and Marks, A. (2004) 'Work-life balance and the software worker', *Human Resource Management Journal*, 14(2): 54–74.
Schor, J. (1991) *The Overworked American: the Unexpected Decline of Leisure*, New York: Basic Books.
Scottish Enterprise (1998) *Dynamics of the Scottish Labour Market*, April 1998, Glasgow: Scottish Enterprise.
Scottish Enterprise (2001) *A National Strategy for Scotland*, Glasgow: Scottish Enterprise.
Scottish Enterprise (2002) *The Scottish Labour Market, 2002*, Glasgow: Futureskills Scotland and Scottish Enterprise.
Scottish Executive (2002) *Scottish Economic Statistics*, Edinburgh: Scottish Executive.
Sennett, R. (1998) *The Corrosion of Character. The Personal Consequences of Work in the New Captialism*, London: W.W. Norton & Company.
Smith, C. (1987) *Technical Workers: Class, Labour and Trade Unionism*, Basingstoke: Macmilllan.
Smith, C. and Thompson, P. (1998) 'Re-evaluating the labour process debate', *Economic and Industrial Democracy*, 19(4): 551–77.
Smithson, J., Lewis, S., Cooper, C. and Dyer, J. (2004) 'Flexible working and the gender pay gap in the accountancy profession', *Work, Employment and Society*, 18(1): 115–35.
Stanworth, C. (2000) 'Women and work in the Information Age', *Gender, Work and Organization*, 7(1): 20–32.
Stonier, T. (1983) *The Wealth of Information*, London: Thames-Methuen.
Storey, J. (1992) *Developments in the Management of Human Resources*, Oxford: Blackwell.
Storey, J. (2005), 'Human resource policies for knowledge work', in T. Ray, P. Quintas and S. Little (eds), *Managing Knowledge: An Essential Reader*, 199–220, London: Sage.
Stroh, L., Brett, J. and Reilly, A. (1996) 'Family structure, glass ceiling, and traditional explanations for the differential rate of turnover of female and male managers', *Journal of Vocational Behavior*, 49(1): 99–188.
Super, D.E. (1957) *The Psychology of Careers*, New York: Harper and Brothers.
Tam, Y.M., Korczynski, M. and Frenkel, S.J. (2002) 'Organizational and Occupational Commitment: Knowledge Workers in Large Corporations', *Journal of Management Studies*, 39(6): 775–801.
Tawney, R.H. (1926) *Religion and the Rise of Capitalism*, New York: Harcourt, Brace and World.
Taylor, P. and Bain, P. (2005) '"India calling to the faraway towns": the call centre labour process and globalization', *Work, Employment and Society*, 19(2): 261–82.

Taylor, P. and Bain, P. (2003a) '"Subterranean Worksick Blues"': humour as subversion in two call centres', *Organization Studies*, 24(9): 1487–509.
Taylor, P. and Bain, P. (2003b) *Call Centres in Scotland and Outsourced Competition from India*, Stirling: Scotecon.
Taylor, P. and Bain, P. (1997) *Call Centres in Scotland: A Report for Scottish Enterprise*, Glasgow: Scottish Enterprise.
Taylor, P. and Bain, P. (1999) '"An assembly line in the head": work and employee relations in the call centre', *Industrial Relations Journal*, 30(2): 101–17.
Taylor, P. and Bain, P. (2001a) 'Trade unions, workers' rights and the frontier of control in UK call centres', *Economic and Industrial Democracy*, 22(1): 39–66.
Taylor, P. and Bain, P. (2001b) *Call Centres in Scotland in 2000*, Glasgow: Rowan Tree Press.
Taylor, P., Baldry, C., Bain, P. and Ellis, V. (2003) '"A unique working environment": health, sickness and absence management in UK call centres', *Work, Employment and Society*, 17(3): 435–58.
Taylor, P., Gall, G., Bain, P. and Baldry, C. (2005) '"Striving under chaos": the effects of market turbulence and organizational flux on call centre work', in Stewart, P. (ed.) *Employment, Trade Union Renewal and the Future of Work*, 20–40, Basingtoke: Palgrave Macmillan.
Taylor, P., Mulvey, G., Hyman, J. and Bain, P (2002) 'Work organization, control and the experience of work in call centres', *Work, Employment & Society*, 16(1): 133–50.
Taylor, R. (2002a) *Britain's world of work – Myths and realities, ESRC Future of Work Commentary Series*, Swindon: Economic and Social Research Council.
Taylor, R. (2002b) *The Future of Work-Life Balance*, Swindon: ESRC.
Taylor, S. (1998) 'Emotional labour and the new workplace', in P. Thompson and C. Warhurst (eds) *Workplaces of the Future*, 84–103, London: Macmillan.
Terkel, S. (1974), *Working*, Harmondswoth: Penguin Books.
Thiessen, V. and Nickerson, C. (1999) *Canadian Gender Trends in Education and Work*, Ottawa: Human Resources Development Canada Applied Research Branch.
Thomas, R.J. (1989) 'Blue-collar careers: meaning and choice in a world of constraints', in Arthur, M.B., Hall, D.T. and Lawrence, B.S. (eds) *Handbook of career theory*, 354–79, Cambridge: Cambridge University Press.
Thompson, E.P. (1967) 'Time, work-discipline and industrial capitalism', *Past and Present*, 38: 56–97.
Thompson, P. (2003) 'Disconnected capitalism or why employers can't keep their side of the bargain', *Work, Employment and Society*, 17(2): 359–78.
Thompson, P. and McHugh, D. (2002) *Work Organizations*, Basingstoke: Palgrave.
Thompson, P., Callaghan, G. and van den Broek, D. (2004) 'Keeping up appearances: recruitment, skills and normative control in call centres', in Deery, S. and Kinnie, N. *Call Centres and Human Resource Management*, 129–52, Basingstoke: Palgrave.
Thompson, P., Warhurst, C. and Callaghan, G. (2001) 'Ignorant theory and knowledgeable workers: interrogating the connections between knowledge, skills and services', *Journal of Management Studies*, 38(7): 923–42.
Thorne, B. (2001) 'Pick-up time and Oakdale Elementary School', in Hertz, R. and Marshall, N. (eds) *Working Families*, Berkeley: University of California Press.
Thurow, L. (1996) The *Future of Capitalism: How Today's Economic Forces Will Shape Tomorrow's World*, New York: William Morrow.
Toffler, A. (1980) *The Third Wave*, New York: Morrow.
Touraine, A. (1971) *The Post-Industrial Society*, New York: Randon House.

Trillas, F. (2002) 'Mergers, acquisitions and control of telecommunications firms in Europe', *Telecommunications Policy*, 26: 268–86.

Turok, I. (1992) 'Inward investment and local linkages: how deeply embedded is "silicon glen"?', *Regional Studies*, 27(2): 401–17.

Twomey, B. (2002) 'Women in the labour market: results from the spring 2001 Labour Force Survey', *Labour Market Trends*, 110(3): 109–27.

Tyler, M. and Taylor, S. (2001) 'Juggling justice and care: gendered customer service in the contemporary airline industry', in Sturdy, A., Grugulis, I. and Willmott, H. (eds) *Customer Service, Empowerment and Entrapment*, 60–78, London: Palgrave.

Van den Broek, D., Callaghan, G. and Thompson, P. (2004) 'Teams without teamwork: explaining the call centre paradox', *Economic and Industrial Democracy*, 25(2): 197–218.

Wacjman, J. (1991) *Feminism Confronts Technology*, University Park, PA: Pennsylvania State University Press.

Wacjman, J. and Martin, B. (2002) 'Narratives of identity in modern management: the corrosion of gender difference?', *Sociology*, 36(4): 985–1002.

Walby, S. (1997) *Gender Transformations*, London: Routledge.

Wallace, J.E. (1997) 'It's about time: a study of hours worked and work spillover among law firm lawyers', *Journal of Vocational Behavior*, 50(2): 227–48.

Walton, R. (1985), 'From control to commitment in the workplace', *Harvard Business Review*, 63(2): 77–85.

Warhurst, C. and Thompson, P. (1998) 'Hands, hearts and minds: changing work and workers at the end of the century', in Thompson, P. and Warhurst, C. (eds) *Workplaces of the Future*, 1–24, London: Macmillan.

Warr, P., Cook, J. and Wall, T. (1979) 'Scales for measurement of some work attitudes and aspects of psychological well-being', *Journal of Occupational Psychology*, 52(2): 129–48.

Webb, J. (2004) 'Organizations, Self-Identities and the New Economy', *Sociology*, 38(4): 719–38.

Weber, M. (1964) *The Theory of Social and Economic Organization*, New York: Free Press.

Weber, M. (1992) *The Protestant Work Ethic and the Spirit of Capitalism* (first published 1930) London: Routledge.

Weinberg, N. (1998) 'Feeding frenzy for Java-savvy whiz kids leaves 40-something IT pros high and dry', 14 September. *Network World*.

Wenger, E. and Snyder, W.M. (2000) 'Communities of practice: the organizational frontier', *Harvard Business Review*, 78(1): 139–45.

White, M., Hill, S., Mills, C. and Smeaton, D. (2004) *Managing to Change? The Future of Work Series*, Basingstoke: Palgrave Macmillan.

Whyte, W. (1956) *The Organization Man*, New York: Simon and Schuster.

Wilkinson, A., Redman, T., Snape, E. and Marchington, M. (1998) *Managing with TQM: Theory and Practice*, Basingstoke: Palgrave Macmillan.

Williams, K., Cutler, T., Williams, J. and Haslam, C. (1987) 'The end of mass production?', *Economy and Society*, 16(3): 405–39.

Wilson, M. (2004) 'A conceptual framework for studying gender in information systems research', *Journal of Information Technology*, 19(1): 81–92.

Wise, S. (2005) 'The right to time off for dependants: contrasting two organisations' responses', *Employee Relations*, 27(2): 126–40.

Wolf, A. (2002), *Does Education Matter?*, London: Penguin.

Wright Mills, C. (1951) *White Collar*, New York: Galaxy.

Young, M. and Willmott, P. (1957) *Family and Kinship in East London*, Harmondsworth: Penguin.
Zuboff, S. (1988) *In the Age of the Smart Machine*, Oxford: Heinemann.

Web references

Intellect (2006) *Intellect* Perceptions of Equal Pay Survey 2006, Available on-line at http://www.intellectuk.org.
Labour Force Survey (LFS) (2000). Available online at www.dfes.gov.uk/statistics
www.scottish-enterprise.com/sedotcom_home/sig/ebusiness-suppliers/software_ke
www.scottish-enterprise.com/sedotcom_home/sig/ebusiness-suppliers/software_ke

Index

Affluent Worker, 13 *see also* Luton studies
Ahmavaara, A., 178
   fatherhood and extension/expansion of work, 178
alienation, 3, 4, 5, 6, 7, 12, 96, 230
   call centres, 162
     fun at work, 158
   capitalism, 225, 230
   commitment culture, promotion of, 96
   knowledge work, 40
   role of work, 1
   work/non-work life, 12
Allen, N.J., 100
   value-based notion of commitment, 100
Alvesson, M., 83
   cultural-ideological modes of control, 83
Anderson, M., 164
Andrews, C.K., 56, 83
   software development, four generic stages of, 56
   structuration and standardization, 83
Anthony, P.D., 14
Aron, R., 1
Arthur, M.B., 110, 119
   careers more than a linear path, 119
   non-linear job-to-job moves, 110
Automatic Call Distribution (ACD), 51, 76, 96, 226
autonomy, in job, 5, 6, 7, 83, 84, 163, 199, 217, 230, 232
   distinction from controls, 30
   occupational identity generation, 220
   'responsible autonomy', 19, 50, 80, 81, 217, 227
   software workers, 78, 79, 130, 131, 139, 209, 234
     hours/patterns of work, 147
     individual expectations, 220
     motivation, 32

   professional status, 152, 196
   work-home boundary, 164

Bain, P., 76
   'assembly line in the head', 76
Baldamus, W., 230
   wage-effort bargain, 230
Baldry C., 52, 59, 135
Batt, R., 81
   categorization of call centres, 81
Bauman, Z., 197
   second wave of 'revisionists' of class, 197
Beck, U., 194
   convergence in male and female domestic/working identities, 194
Becker, H., 105
   'side bets' on losing desirable company aspects, 105
Bell, D., 1, 29, 40, 197
   early Industrial Society and Post-Capitalist models, 40
   first wave of 'revisionists' of class, 197
   post-industrialism, 29
Belt, V., 188
   'soft' interpersonal skills of women, 188
Bendix, R., 14
   changes in the societal work ethic, 14
Beynon, H., 88
   pressure on management for 'lean head count', 88
Blackburn, R., 197
   first wave of 'revisionists' of class, 197
Blackler, F., 29
   structuralist categories of knowledge, 29
Blair, Tony, 42
   Fairness at Work White Paper (1998), 42
Blauner, R., 225, 226, 230
   model of alienation, 230
boundaryless careers, 120, 127, 131, 132
   self-management, for professional managers, 120, 130

Index

Bradley, H., 168
  good customer service and feminine traits, 168
Braverman, H., 6, 218, 227
  lack of intrinsic or extrinsic task satisfaction in job design, 6
Brenner R., 41, 48
British Social Attitudes Survey, 170
  women in employment, 170
Brown, Richard, 224, 235
Bunting, M., 135, 228
  women and intensification of work, 228
Burns, T., 87
  'organic' model of organization, 87

Call Centre Association, 44
call centre employees/workers, 54, 76, 136–41, 154, 157, 163, 179, 188–90, 225, 229, 230, 235, 239, 240
  career patterns/attitudes, 120, 122–3, 209, 236
    industrial action/collectivism, 211, 214, 220
    oppositional attitudes, 210
    three orientations, 121
  class character of, 215, 216–18, 219
    class identity, 204, 206, 221
    wage labourer class, 196, 208
    white-collar proletariat, 234
  commitment, 93–4, 122
  discretionary, 103–4
  fun culture, 94–7, 108
  measurement of, 101
  communications, 90–1
  contractual relationship, 124, 200–1
  emotional labour, 36, 69, 80, 82, 182
  emotional strain, 190–1
  home life, 145–7
    conflict burden, 232
    work/non-work, 160–1
  mobility, 35
    job satisfaction, 105–8
    staying with company, 104–5
  occupational identity/community, 158, 196–7, 233
  pay and rewards, 88–90
    overtime, 178
    women, 182
  resourcing of, 87–8
  training and certification, 113–15
    limited progression opportunities, 117–19, 121
  women in, 166–8, 181, 195–6
  under-representation in management positions, 165, 231
call centres, 6, 2, 17–22, 35–6, 44, 46–7, 57, 58–9, 87
  acronyms used, 52
  built working environment, 60
  categorization of, 81–2
  competitive capitalist dynamics, 82
  customer pressure, 80
  management practices, 96–7
  offshoring from UK, 40
  operating hours, 64, 74, 137–41
  paid overtime, 62
  work organization/control, 65–71, 153, 228
    direct/overt regimes of, 50, 73, 80, 151–2
    flat hierarchy, 86, 109
    monitoring/targets, 66–71, 78, 235
    teamworking, 65–6, 227
  work settings, 52–5
    ACD, 51, 226
Callinicos, A., 29, 40, 218
  computer system upgradation, 29
  globalization-challenging assumptions of, 40
Campbell, Clark, 141
  work-life balance, definition of, 141
Campbell, J.P., 31
  expanded model of desirable work performance, 31
capitalism/new capitalism, 4, 6, 12, 41, 64, 194, 199, 220, 221, 225, 235
  alienation of workers, 3
  call centre and software workers, positioning of, 196, 216–18
  class
    antagonism/polarization, 197, 198
    social stratification, 233
  competitive dynamics, 82
  convergence in male and female identities, 194
  gendered inequalities, 165
  dynamics/rationale of, 216
  structures, 219
Cappelli, P., 9
  'portfolio careers', 9

career breaks, 175, 184, 193
  married women
    lack of options, 176
    maternity/child rearing reasons, 119, 173
    older/female workers, 119
    restricting advancement, 231
career orientations, 9, 17, 231–2 *see also* 'portfolio careers'
  call centres, 126, 128–30
    horizontal-bounded/horizontal-boundaryless, 127, 131
  software sector, 130
    flexible/self-managed, 131
  work preferences, 180–1
career progression, 17, 36, 110–12, 123–6, 129 *see also* boundaryless careers
  barriers to, 132, 133
  call centres
    limited opportunities for, 109, 117–18, 132
    training and certification, 113–15
  high mobility, 35
  internal, 118
  institutional/organizational infrastructure for, 110
  skills, 110–12
  interpretative approaches to, 120
  linear/vertical, 110
  mobility, 129, 130
  'multi-employer relationships', 36
  patterns/attitudes, 120–3, 231–2, 237
  self-management/strategic self-management, 36, 109
    personal trajectory, 231
    self-awareness and adaptability, 120
  shaping identity, 119
  subjective accounts/experiences of, 119
    Protean Career/Intelligent Career, 120
  women, 174–5, 232
career strategies, 109
  call centres, 126–30
    self-marketization, 132
    preference for recruiting women, 133
  software sector, 130–2
  typologies in, 126–32

case study organizations, 19
  call centres, 20–2
  software companies, 22, 24–5
    five features of, 23
career typologies, 109, 121, 128–9
  call centres, 127–30
    four clusters, 126
  software sector, 130–2
cash nexus, 3, 12, 16, 33, 225
Castells, M., 2, 27, 28, 29, 34, 40, 84, 180, 197, 225, 226, 235
  'informationalism', 2, 29
  second wave of 'revisionists' of class, 197
  technological determinism, 29
Cavendish, R., 11
  meaning from personal bonds, 11
class-based collectivism, 212
class/class consciousness, 4, 11, 17, 20, 157, 166, 210, 221–2 *see also* Marx, Karl, Marxian analysis/concepts; white-collar workers
  call centre and software workers, 219–20
  collectivism
    vs individualism, 212–16
    'solidaristic collectivism', 13
  definitions of, 216, 218
  embourgeoizification of the (manual) working class, 198
  existence of, 204–6
    disappearance of, 233
  identity, 206–9
  Marxist concepts, 197
    disintegration of, 196
  problems in, 218
  status, 39, 197–220
  Weberian approaches, 197, 217
  white-collar workers, 198–200
  workplace
    attitudes and behaviours, 203–6, 210–12, 231–2, 237
class relations, 4, 218
collectivism/collectivist, 93, 136, 155, 157, 199, 221, 226
  bargaining/industrial action, 42, 89, 90, 223, 236
  class, 204–9, 234
    and individualism, 50, 203, 213–16
    status, 39, 197–220
    three forms of, 212

Connect – communication industry union, 112
Marxian concepts, 4, 13, 196, 197, 200
occupational identity, 12–13
social action, 39
team spirit, 72
  software projects, 118–19
  workspaces, 52
Collins, D., 30
  distraction of knowledge work, 30
commitment, measures of, 10, 17, 18, 31, 101, 102, 108, 126, 134, 139, 151
  'high commitment work practices' (HCWP), 8, 32, 34, 36, 100, 122, 143, 154
  discretionary effort, 103–4
  employer-employee 'mutuality', 8, 9, 14
  hours worked/flexibility, 15–16, 33, 34, 99–100, 148
  meeting deadlines, 62
  shared values, internalization of, 100–3
HRM, 37, 153, 178
  career progression, 119, 123
  dress codes, 94
  fun, 94–7
  socializing, formal/informal, 98–9
  staying with the organization, 104–5, 132
community life, 16, 20, 36–7
  domestic/family considerations, 135–7
  home life, 134–49, 164
  organizational provisions for, 150–3
  work centrality/value, 153–4
  working life, conflicts/intrusions, 141–7, 160–2
  social aspects, 154–60
  working time/hours, 137–41, 147–50
competition/competitive, 10, 26, 29, 45, 46, 76, 118, 132, 211
  cost-reduction/profit-maximizing, 82
  depreciation in incomes, 47
  internal, 73
  management structures, 86–8
  merger and acquisition activity, 51
  quality-based, 7, 33
  strategies
    combination of changes in, 86
    targets, 69, 70, 97

convergence (between male/female), 165, 184, 195, 231
  working hours and British mothers, 136
Council for Vocational Qualifications (NCVQ), 111
  SCOTVEC in Scotland, 111
Cousins, C., 136
  working hours and British mothers, 136
co-worker/group relationships, 11, 39, 79, 100, 103, 112, 133, 135, 158, 162, 170, 206
  career development, 117, 119, 128, 130, 180
  collectivism, 220, 212, 213
  interdependence, 71, 83
  mobility, 103, 108
  occupational community, 130
  socializing with/in, 98, 99, 158, 216
  software companies, 84
  project organization, 72
Crompton, R., 218
Cully, M., 6
customer focus/orientation, 7, 18, 21, 36, 47, 51–5, 56, 66, 74, 82, 95, 111, 114, 200, 226, 227, 230, 236
  'differentiation of demand', 33–4
  emotion work, 50, 229
  preference for women, 188, 189, 190, 192, 231
  quality of service, 31, 33, 34, 78, 235
  demands of, 65, 67, 229
  tension/stress, 79, 80, 82, 189–90

Dahrendorf, R., 1, 40, 217
  early Industrial Society and Post-Capitalist models, 40
  social differentiation on particularism, 217
deregulation, 22, 27, 42, 222
  business/economic environment, 46, 51
  employment/statutory provisions, 37, 41–3
  equal opportunities policies, 183–5
  'Washington consensus', 41
deskilling/deskilled jobs, 56, 218
  call centres
    work design, 199
    management control, 35

deskilling/deskilled jobs – *continued*
  relegation of women to, 165
  software sector, 82
    automation of computer tools, 83
Dex, S., 195
  parenthood and gender division of roles, 195
DiDio, L., 166
  women overlooked in software projects, 166
Direct Line (24-hour insurance service call centre), 51
division of labour, 4, 218
  complexities of, 83
    language related, 56
  gendering of, 38, 136
  household/domestic, 38, 172
  organizational/internal control, 52, 55, 83
  software sector, 56, 75, 81
Donkin, R., 14
Donovan Commission, 90
dot.com bubble/companies, 41
  crash of, 46, 47, 48, 235
Drucker, Peter F., 1, 27, 31, 197
  first wave of 'revisionists' of class, 197
  'knowledge industries'/'knowledge economy', 1
  principal economic resource, 27
dual income (earner)/dual career households, 16, 168
  domestic division of labour, 38
    unequal, 176
  home influences, 135–7
  part-time, 37
  women's role in, 170
    secondary career, 174
Dubin, R., 13
  'central life interest' (of occupational communities), 13
Durkheim, E., 3, 4, 6, 225
  organic solidarity, 4
  shared moral order, 225

Economic and Social Research Council, 2
Ehrenreich, B., 11, 198, 218, 221
  white-collar workers–'professional – managerial class', 198, 218
Ehrenreich, J., 198, 218, 221
  organic solidarity, 4
  shared moral order, 225

emotional labour, 36, 69, 82, 182, 227
  customer service/pressure, 80, 82, 190
  women's work, 188–91
employability, 127, 193
  software sector, 127
  definition of, 130
  'portfolio careers', 35, 120
employee/worker attitude, 7, 13, 37, 68, 108, 163, 179, 189, 199, 210, 213, 219, 224, 226, 231–2, 234
  career expectations, 109, 119, 120–4
  contract, 140–1
  egalitarianism in practice, 172, 186, 195
  occupational identity, 123–5
employment, 3, 10, 29–34, 36–7, 39–40, 85, 93, 109, 110, 113, 119, 166, 195, 196, 234 *see also* collectivism/collective; organizational conditions
  cash nexus basis of, 12, 16
  changing forms/conditions of, 2, 17, 134–6
    discontinuities, 118, 120
    flexibility in, 19, 63, 150, 151
    gender considerations, 166–70, 231
    work centrality, 176–80
  contractual nature, 14, 18, 141
  levels of, 13, 22
  mobility, 123, 127, 129
  new areas of
    knowledge economy, 27–8, 46–9, 109, 224
    service-sector, 18
  practices/policies, 35
    customer-orientated, 7
    individualized climate, 37, 212–16
    'win-win', 9
  preferences, 175–6, 180–1
  regulation of, 41–3
  sectoral trends in, 43–6
    call centres, 46–7
    software development, 47–9, 150
  spillover, 173–5
employment relations, 6, 9, 26, 42, 44, 229, 234
  building commitment, 93–7, 113
    individualistic, 212
  career development, 120
  cash nexus, 12
  collectivism, 220

'full circuit of capital', 85
regulatory and legal framework, 27, 41
Employment Relations Act (1999), 42
Equal Pay Code of Practice, 182
e-skills UK, 112
  Framework for Sector Skills Council for IT, Telecoms and Contact Centres, 112
European Union (EU), 149
  domestic labour, division of
    European Foundation survey (2000), 136
    Household, Work, and Flexibility, 136
    Working Time Directive, 136
  Draft Charter of Fundamental Rights (adopted in UK in October 2000), 42

Femlee, D., 174
  female partners' secondary career, 174
Ferguson, Adam, 3
Financial Services and Building Society Acts (1986), 51
First Direct (24–hour banking service call centre), 51
Flecker, J., 9
  organizational embrace of the 'complete person', 9
Fleming, P., 108
  'distance' (employee resistance), 108
flexibility/flexible working, 36, 92, 128, 141, 145
  call centres, 142, 147, 231
  employment conditions, 19, 35
  software sector, 140, 148, 150, 152, 188
  spillover, 152
  work at home, 144
  women, 180, 184, 191, 195, 232
  working time, 18, 37, 61–5, 137, 139–41, 164
    flexitime system, 138, 184, 185
    part-time, 163, 174
  work-life balance/boundary, 132, 135, 151, 163, 164, 232
Fordism/post-Fordism, 1, 13 *see also* industrial era/industrialism
Forsythe, Michael (Scottish Secretary), 44
Foucault, M., 85

Fox, A., 34, 230, 233, 236
  criteria for work, 230
  'two great alternative meanings'(of work), 236
  'work beyond contract', 34
Frenkel, S., 22n., 31, 35, 61, 69, 82, 120
  'behaviour measures', 69
  'workflow' (term), 22n
fun at work, 93, 94–5, 98–9, 108, 229, 230, 236
  Doctor Fun, 96
  manipulative tool, 97
  promotion of a commitment culture, 96

Gall, G., 215
gender influences/considerations, 11, 36–9, 45, 73, 123, 131, 133, 139, 181, 182, 183–5, 224, 231, 234, 237n.2
  call centre preference for women, 133, 153, 166–8
  career orientations, 180–1
  difference and disadvantage, 174–5, 177–94
    domestic circumstances, 168–73, 195
    work preferences, 176–80
    division of labour, 136
    emotion work, 188–91
    marriage/home influences, 135–7, 168–73
    motherhood and drop in income, 176
    technical work for men, 191–4
    work centrality, impact upon, 16
Giddens, A., 1, 199, 217, 219, 222
  'sense of involvement and attachment', 11
  social differentiation on particularism, 199, 217
Gilbreth, Frank, 82
globalization, 2, 14, 40
  decline of Marxian concepts, 197
  knowledge economy, 26
  software industry, 18
  new political economy, 40
  characteristics of, 27, 43, 222
  work centrality, 85
Goffee, R., 11
  'shared experiences of work', 11

Goldthorpe, J., 13, 198, 204, 206, 230
  Affluent Worker, 13
  'money model perspective', 204
  'service class', 198
Gorz, A., 198, 199, 219
  rebellion against proletarian treatment, 199
Grimshaw, D., 88
  pressure on management for 'lean head count', 88
group identity, 10, 11, 15, 53, 79, 84, 98, 117, 121, 133, 135, 196, 206, 221, 234
  collectivism, 212, 213, 220
  'high commitment practices', 34
  occupational, 123–6, 130
  organic solidarity, 4
  shared value limits, 99–103
  teamworking, 65–6, 90, 202
    project matrix structure, 72, 73
    turnover impact, 99
  vocational qualifications, role of, 112
Grugulis, I., 168, 195
  womens' equality of opportunity, 166, 195
Guest, D., 34, 229
  four-feature model of HRM, 34
  high-commitment management practices, 229

Hakim, C., 165, 170, 175, 195
Hampson, T., 36
  foundation of training strategy, 36
Hardill, I., 164, 176
  motherhood and drop in income, 176
  rewards from work, 176
Hebson, G., 168, 195
  new risks of gender equality, 168
hegemony/hegemonic management, 27, 33
  class character/consciousness, 39
  work ethic, 14
Heller, F., 8
hierarchy (organizational), 5, 40, 127, 198, 206, 219, 221 *see also* work organization
  flat structure, 4, 8, 84, 87, 236
  linear/non-linear mobility, 110
  management structures, 86–7
    progression, 132, 141
  software, 83
  skills, 32
  work, 55
High commitment work practices (HCWP), 8, 34
Hirst, P., 40
Hochschild, A.R., 14, 69, 172, 176, 179
  performance of emotional labour, 69
  womens' 'stalled revolution', 172
Hodson, R., 4, 9, 10, 11
  co-workers add meaning to work, 9
  theory of dignity at work, 4
Hofbauer, J., 9
  organizational embrace of the 'complete person', 9
Hogarth, T., 39
  work-life spillover, 39
home life, 134, 145–7, 149–59 *see also* work-life balance; work-life spillover
  community life, 36–7
  influences, 135–7
  inter-role conflict, 141–5
    work intrusions/spillover, 145–7, 189
  work/life boundaries, 160–2, 173–4
  working time, 140–1
    extension/expansion of, 137, 138–9, 143–4, 148
homeworking, 57, 148
household income, 140, 168–70
  men's contribution, 169, 195, 240
Houston, D.M., 178
  fatherhood and extension/expansion of work, 178
Human Resource Management (HRM), 10, 85, 86, 225, 229 *see also* training and development
  employee commitment, stress on, 14, 100, 153, 156
  employee travel, 156–7
  employee voice, 19
    call centres, 90–1
    software companies, 92–3
  organizational conditions, 182–8, 228
    individualistic relationship, 212
  people management, 32–3
    approach to collectivism, 212, 221
    approach to mutuality/trust, 34
    family friendly culture, 37, 57, 151, 152, 163, 187, 232
    'win-win' practices/policies, 9

recruitment practices, 88
    'fire-fighting' approach, 115
resourcing
    call centres, 87–8
    software companies, 91–3
rewards for performance, 7
    intrinsic, 7
    material, 8
    shared value limits, 99–103
    skills and training, 110–19
    support for, 108
    Taylorist prescriptions, failings of, 6
Huws, U., 29
    'weightless' economy, 29
Hyman, J., 151
Hyman, R., 199
Hyundai, 43

ICT, 2, 18, 26, 30, 45, 197, 220, 221, 223
    class changes, 197
    informating properties of, 46, 82, 84
    knowledge work, 40
        call centres, 51, 67
        dispersal of economic activity, 226
    revolution, 28, 29
    Scottish economy, decline in, 43
    technology
        spatial overlap with domestic life, 164
incentive/incentive pay, 8, 114, 158 *see also* pay and rewards
    disadvantaged groups, 15
    monthly remuneration package, 89, 90, 92, 125
    rewards in kind, 9, 84, 118
Independent Committee for the Supervision of Standards of Telephone Information Services and OFTEL, 112
    call centres database management, 112
India/Indian, 40, 57, 71
industrial era/industrialism, 12, 18, 156, 197 *see also* Fordism/post-Fordism
    early characteristics, 3, 5, 6, 12, 13
    end of, 1
    mid-century characteristics of, 13
    work ethic, 15
industrial society, 3
information and communications technologies *see* ICT
Information Society, 6

information technologies, 2, 18, 28, 30, 32
Information Technology National Training Organization, 111
    standards and qualifications for software work, 111
informationalism, 2, 28, 29
Inkson, K., 110
    non-linear job-to-job movement, 110
innovations, 40, 51, 46, 223, 226
instrumentalism, 105, 128, 159, 196
    collectivism, 212, 213
    meanings of work, 14
        little intrinsic value, 4, 155
    occupational identity, 158
    orientation of, 13, 126, 160
    skill acquisition, 119
    work design, 230
Intel, 29
Internet protocols, 51

Japan/Japanese, 7, 8, 15, 32
    customer-orientated employment practices, 7
Jewson, N., 183
    equality of opportunities, 183
job, 18, 23, 35, 55, 96, 108, 117, 128, 140, 144, 151, 156, 157, 162, 169, 194, 202
    career/security, 119, 120, 121, 128, 178, 180, 181, 231, 235
    cash nexus, 154
    definition of, 31
    design/redesign, 7, 199, 226
    changing nature of, 78, 79, 100, 103, 106, 107, 120, 164, 174, 189, 228, 230
    cyclicality, 62
    formal descriptions of, 25
    gender factors, 38, 165, 166–8, 171, 191, 192
    individualistic, 212
    part-time, 135
    sharing, 147, 148, 185
    knowledge-intensive, 34
    loss/replacement of, 18, 23, 45
    remuneration, 213
    satisfaction, 32
    skills, 30, 44, 188, 227
    Taylorist concepts of, 5, 6, 8
    training, 127

job autonomy, 198, 209, 217, 220, 221, 234
job control, 20, 164, 230, 233, 237n.1
job satisfaction, 4, 12, 50, 90, 105–8, 141, 176, 230, 235, 236, 237n.1
   intrinsic/extrinsic task satisfaction, 6, 36, 126, 162
   relief from repetition, 32
   working hours/conditions, 15, 64, 65, 129, 174
Jones, G., 218
Joshi, H., 195
   parenthood and gender division of roles, 195
Junor, A., 36
   foundation of training strategy, 36
Juran, Dr. Joseph M., 33

Kanter, R.M., 110
   linear, vertical career progression, 110
Kärreman, D., 83
   cultural-ideological modes of control, 83
Kelly, J., 85
   'full circuit of capital', 85
Kerr, C., 1, 40
   early Industrial Society and Post-Capitalist models, 40
Klingender, F.D., 218
knowledge economy, 1, 6, 13, 27, 32, 48, 57, 109, 130, 198, 220, 227, 229, 235
   career models, 120, 127
   challenges/reservations, 28–30
   class and status, 39, 196, 221, 222, 233
   defining characteristics of, 200
      'economic value' in intangibles, 13
      'informationalism', 2
   gender influences/considerations, 180
   men and women, 37–9, 231
   lifestyle choice, 38
   management practices, 229
   new political economy
      globalization, 40
      Scotland, 43–6
      'Washington consensus', 41
   occupational life, 35–9, 61, 133, 162, 196, 227
      flat hierarchy, 132
      individualization, 165
      work centrality, 153–4
   productivity, 41
   social implications, 222, 225
   Weberian approaches, 39
   work paradigm, 84
knowledge intensive work/industries, 1, 2, 34, 40, 83, 168
knowledge workers, 10, 30, 84, 152
   autonomy and control, 227
   boundaryless careers, 120, 130, 131, 132
   mobility, 133
   characteristics of, 84, 131
      behaviours/attitudes, 196, 226
   class or hierarchy, 221
   commitment/self-motivation of, 10, 31, 35
   confusion of, 108
   co-worker interdependence, 71
   identity, foci of, 39
Korczynski, M., 82
Kraft, P., 56
Kumar, K., 3
   work centrality, 3
Kunda, G., 56

Labour Force Survey (LFS), 18, 48, 211
labour market, 9, 13, 17–19, 22, 27, 147, 164–5
   cash nexus, 225
   collectivism, 219–20
   deregulation of, 41–2
   disadvantaged groups, 15
   fragmentation of, 10
   gendered division of, 136, 139
      women's dual role, 16, 168–73, 175–6
      work centrality, 176–80
   incentives/sanctions, 15
   organizational values, 100, 104
   Scottish economy, 43–9
   software developers, 35, 73, 164–5
   types of, 83
   value of, 84
      career paths, 110, 128, 131–2, 156
      remuneration, 92
labour process/control, 2, 3, 6, 20, 50, 61–4, 66–80
   decentralization of form/centralization of power, 30
   new forms of, 32, 82, 85, 142, 227
      individualization, 65
      structuration and standardization, 56
      work spillover, 150–1, 212, 232

Index 269

strategies, 75, 76, 219, 227
work-life boundaries/spillover, 163, 173–5, 232, 233
Learning and Skills Councils (formerly Lead Bodies/National Training Organizations), 111
Legge, K., 33
  parameters for social action, 33
liberalization, 40, 46
  'Washington consensus', 41
Lockwood, D., 13, 199, 211, 217, 219
  Affluent Worker, 13
  class and unionization, 211
  social differentiation on particularism, 217
Luton studies, 13, 230, 231

Mallet, S., 199, 218, 219
  technical workers a 'new working class', 199
management control, 35, 50, 72–4, 86, 235
  call centres
    monitoring, 66–7
    targets, 67–71
    teamworking, 65–6
  cultural-ideological modes of, 83
  degree of, 76–80
  dress code, 94
  organizational practices, 62, 67, 68, 69, 117, 227–8, 233
  strategies, 8, 75, 76, 219, 227, 232
management/managerial strategy, 6, 7, 42, 50, 83, 92, 93, 190, 232, 235
  employee commitment, 7, 85–108
  employer-employee 'mutuality', 8
  fun as manipulation, 94, 97
  HRM, 6, 10
  organizational life, 32–5
  organizational practices, 62, 67, 68, 69
management/organizational practices, 62, 67, 68, 69, 76–7, 94–108, 117, 227–8, 233
  call centres, 87–91
  software companies, 91–3
management/organizational structures, 31, 91, 195, 211, 226
  flat, 25, 86, 87, 231, 236
  matrix, 59, 72, 86, 87
Mannheim, B., 175
  womens'work-centredness, 175

Martin, B., 194
  gender structuring of career choices, 194–5
Marx, Karl, 3, 4, 6, 12, 197, 199, 200, 225, 230
  concept of alienation, 3
  fragmentation and 'infinity of classes', 199
Marxian analysis/concepts, 29
  alienation, concept of, 3, 12, 225, 230
  class analysis/conflict, 39, 196, 197, 199, 218
  class, definition of, 199
  'collective labourer', concept of, 200
  fragmentation of class structure, 196
  workers' revolution, 6
Maslow, A., 6
  hierarchy of needs, 6
Mason, D., 183
mass production, 28, 81, 225
Maternity and Parental Leave Regulations (1999), 42
Mathews, B., 94
Mayo, Elton, 6
  redesign of work/enhancing intrinsic satisfactions, 6
McHugh, D., 30
  decentralization of form is centralization of power, 30
Meaning of Work (international survey), 15, 16
Meiksins, P., 83
Meyer, J.P., 100
  value-based notion of commitment, 100
Microsoft, 29
Mills, Wright, 198, 218
  white-collar 'new middle class', 198
mobility/high mobility, 119, 124, 126, 129, 130, 132, 156, 157, 193
  across nations, 111
  call centre women with dependants, 180
  inter-organizational, 35
  occupational, 36, 123, 198
  'portfolio careers', 9, 35
  upward, 32, 133
Morse, N.C., 11
Motorola, 43
Moynihan, L., 194
  categorization of call centres, 194

National Minimum Wage Act (1998), 42
neo-liberalism, 41, 51
network society, 39, 220 *see also* knowledge economy; new economy
  existence/basis of class, 196, 221, 233
  informational economy, characteristic form of, 28
  'informationalism', 12
  new societal epoch, 6
new economy, 17, 30, 35, 41, 43, 46, 111, 180 *see also* knowledge economy; network society
  defining characteristics of, 222
  flat hierarchy, 84
  ICT, 40, 46, 48
  men and women
    convergence in, 231
    empowerment of, 165
  self-management of/
    self-marketization in career, 120, 127, 130
  working class, existence of, 196, 222
  working time, 61
Nicholson, N., 110
  linear, vertical career progression, 110
norms/normative, 4, 69, 80, 126, 143, 146, 227
  boundaryless careers, 120, 130
  controls, 7, 156, 236
    pressures, 228
    training strategies, 133
  deviation from, 67
  gender, 189
  inter-personal attachments, 76
  occupational, 11
  societal, 165, 176
Norway, 220
NTO tele.com, 111
  call centre occupational standards, 111

occupational community, 16, 109, 119, 125–6, 178
  characteristics of, 162
  sense of belonging, 233
  social networks, 154, 156–60
    specific factors, 155, 162
  software workers, 130, 131
occupational identity, 12, 133, 158, 220
  employee/career attitude, 123, 125, 231–2, 237
    contractual relationship, 124
    social relations, stability in, 119
  occupational life, 109, 120–4
    career strategies/typologies, 126–32
    community, 125–6
    knowledge economy, 35–7, 39
    voluntary childlessness, 38
    training and development, 110–19
offshoring, 35, 40, 57, 71
old economy, 2, 28
organizational commitment, 10, 85–102
  HRM model, 7
  low-trust control strategies, abandonment of, 8
  'ownership' of project, 9
  quality of working life
    job satisfaction, 105–8
    staying with the company, 104–5
  training and development
    discretionary/prescribed effort, 103–4
  work-life balance, 132
organizational/company culture, 34, 93, 94, 236
  call centre architecture, 52–3
  enhanced commitment, 229
organizational conditions, 166, 232
  equal opportunities, 183–5, 186, 195
  fair treatment, 185–8
  pay equity, 182
organizational life, 67, 183
  nature of work, 30–2, 50–84
    work settings, 50–61
  role of management, 32–5
organizational structure, *see* management/organizational structures
Orwell, George, 108, 229
overtime, paid, 138, 141–2, 191, 201, 202, 203
  call centre employees
    disparities in, 61
    instrumental collectivism, 213
  career progression, sacrifice of, 232
  commitment, 103
  software employees
    specific projects, 62–3
  women, 177
overtime, unpaid, 135, 139, 140, 191, 202, 203
  call centre employees, 143
    instrumental collectivism, 213

meeting targets, 62
specific projects, 63
career progression, sacrifice of, 232
discretionary effort, 103
software employees, 61
demands/reasons for, 63
'on-call' allowance, 138
women, 177, 178
work 'beyond contract', 34

Padfield, M., 120
single women/young mothers in homemaker's role, 170
Pahl, R., 110, 164
linear, vertical career progression, 110
Pakulski, J., 197
second wave of 'revisionists' of class, 197
Parkin, F., 199
Part-time Workers (Prevention of Less Favourable Treatment) Regulations (2000), 42
part-time working, 14, 37, 45, 64, 115, 134, 152, 162
organizational practices, 97, 114
women, 38, 130, 135, 136, 138, 139, 153, 173, 175, 186, 231
domestic pressures, 172, 179
flexibility for, 135, 136, 144, 145, 163
work preferences, 175–8, 180–1
workplace coping strategy, 147, 148
childcare responsibilities, 150, 173, 174
pay and rewards, 36, 42, 50, 73, 87, 108, 114, 117, 138, 158, 203 see also incentive/incentive pay
call centres, 88–90, 201
equity in, 182, 183
extrinsic/intrinsic systems, 16
incentive pay/bonus, 9, 74, 89
target-related, 71, 174
mobility, 104, 132
performance related, 34, 107
individualized schemes, 8, 68
software companies, 91–3, 152, 202
women, 38
performance, 5, 12, 31, 61, 66, 68, 88, 112, 115, 125, 156, 184, 209, 221, 227, 228 see also targets
call centres, 213

commonalities in, 55
training, 36, 113
career progression, 117
criteria, 22, 53, 67, 78, 137, 183
emotional labour, 80, 82
inducements/penalties, 75, 76, 79, 89, 97, 98, 114, 201
targets, 37, 62, 70, 230
intrinsic rewards for, 7
pay scheme, 34, 92, 107
individualized, 8, 89, 118
quality and flexibility, 33
Peters, T., 7, 34, 229
'excellence literature', 7
Pilcher, J., 170
'portfolio careers', 9, 35, 118, 129
marketability/employability
software workers, 35
strategic self-management, 120
post-capitalism/post-capitalists, 6, 28
womens' individualism, 170
post-industrialism/post-industrialists, 6, 15, 29
post-modernism, 1, 39, 221, 233
Poulantzas, N., 198
white-collar workers 'new petty bourgeoisie', 198
Prandy, K., 197
first wave of 'revisionists' of class, 197
privatization/liberalization
employment regulation, 41–3
'Washington consensus', 41
Proctor, I., 170
single women/young mothers in homemaker's role, 170
production, 4, 33, 43, 85, 93, 146, 200, 212, 217
call centre industry
lean principles, 66, 77
realization of value only, 201
class, 221
fragmentation of, 36
industrial society, 3
labour process, 227
outsourcing, 47
ownership of means of, 197, 204, 216, 218
software industry, 152
contribution to value, 202
Taylorist assembly-line technique, 5
in mass production, 28, 81, 225

projects/project work (software companies), 19, 25, 60, 61, 81, 84, 107, 111, 112, 121, 131, 193, 227, 228
  deadlines, 62, 65, 78, 79, 137
    working hours, 104, 138, 144, 178
  learning collectives, 116, 118–19, 130
  matrix structure, 59, 87
  overtime, 63
  'ownership' of, 19
  spatial dynamic of, 51
  team, 71, 72, 73, 74, 152, 202
    fulcrum, 57
    leaders' commitment, 100
    location, 226
    reward, 75, 203
    seating, 59
  women, 166, 174–5, 185, 186, 192
Protestant Work Ethic, The, 14

quality focus/orientation, 7, 22, 32, 34, 56, 78, 117, 121, 189, 190, 191
  competition strategy, 33, 47
  emphases, 21, 33, 53, 68, 82, 105, 155, 202, 235
  quantity, 55, 69, 70, 112

Race Relations (Amendment) Act (2000), 42
Ramsay, H., 83, 226
Reagan, Ronald, 41
Redman, T., 94
Reeve, R., 32
research methods/description, 17–25, 273–8
  case study organizations
    call centre companies, 20–2
    software companies, 22–5
  methodology, 19–20
  survey respondent characteristics, 238–9
Rifkin, J., 197
  second wave of 'revisionists' of class, 197
Rubery, J., 88
  pressure on management for 'lean head count', 88
Ruigrok, W., 40

Salaman, G., 155, 162
  'open-ended concept' of community, 155

Savage, M., 206, 213
scientific management, 5, 32, 68
Scotland Act (1998), The, 44
Scottish economy, 18, 27
  labour market in, 43–9
  Scotland Act (1998), The, 44
sectoral comparisons/differences (call centre and software employees), 59, 83, 138–40, 147–50, 163, 199–200, 203
  class, perceptions of, 206–9, 233
  domestically focused community, 156–7
  oppositional attitudes to employer, 220
  overtime working and payments, 61
  separating work from home, 160–2
  spillover, 162
  social relationships, 158–60
  trade unionism, 234
self-management/strategic self-management, 36, 109
self-awareness and adaptability, 120
Sennet, R., 14, 194, 222
  convergence in male and female identities, 194
  'corrosion of character', 14
Sewell, G., 108
  'distance' (employee resistance), 108
Smith, Adam, 3
Smith, C., 83, 199, 218, 219
  control
    management and craft groups, 83
    technical workers and working class identity, 199
social action, 12, 33, 39, 164, 225
social identity, 11, 75, 83, 108, 213, 235
social life, 11, 75, 83, 108, 213, 235
socializing, 93, 99, 126, 161, 191, 229
  layers of meaning to work, 10, 135
  patterns, 157
    call centre workers, 151, 158
    formal/informal, 98–9
  workplace relationships, 13
software development, 2, 17, 18, 47–9, 80, 81, 93, 109, 130–2
  career spans, 121–2
  commitment, measurement of, 102, 103
  job satisfaction, 105–8
  staying with company, 104–5

division of labour, 56
  heterogeneous character of, 60–2, 73
  home teleworking, 57
  language evolution complexities, 56
  management control
    divergences in work content, 73–6
    'responsible autonomy', 50, 80
    teamworking, 71–3
  management practices, 91–3
  work organization, 32, 71–6
  work settings, 55–61
  mobility, 35, 36
software employees/workers, 2, 31, 33, 58, 66, 76, 93, 103, 119, 169, 192, 234, 239, 240
  characteristics/typology of, 100, 103, 118, 122–3, 125, 130, 132, 140, 159, 162
  women, 174, 178, 179, 182, 185, 186
  class character of, 216–18
  'middle class'identity of, 196, 203, 208
  strong labour market, 35, 225
  contractual relationship, 200–3
  'gold-collar workers', 32
  high mobility, 35, 36
  job satisfaction, 106, 107
  home/family before work, 236
  management positions
    women overlooked, 166
  work/non-work blurred boundaries, 161
  work settings, 55–61, 75, 82, 146
    environment, 60
    timings/hours, 61–2, 63, 65
software sector *see* software development
Stalker, G.M., 87
  'organic' model of organization, 87
Stonier, T., 197
  first wave of 'revisionists' of class, 197
Storey, J., 33
  'idealized and narrated model' (of people management), 33
surveillance/surveillance structures, 1, 66, 67, 73, 229
  fun, 94
  workplace, 223

Tang, N., 136
  working hours and British mothers, 136

targets, 37, 54, 75, 81, 115, 174, 203, 230, 235 *see also* performance
  control over, 78, 79, 80, 226
  employee antipathy, 70
  managerially-determined, 62, 71, 89
  gradation of, 68
  pressures of, 90, 91, 97, 114, 126, 229
  work-induced stress, 142
  multifaceted array of
  quantitative ('hard'), 67, 69, 74
  qualitative, 68
  sales, 68, 69, 70
Tawney, R.H., 14
  changes in the societal work ethic, 14
Taylor, F.W., 5
  assault on craft workers' values, 5
Taylor, P., 76, 137, 142
  'assembly line in the head', 76, 217
Taylorism/Taylorist, 6, 8, 18, 32, 68, 69, 82
  assembly-line technique, 5, 84
  standardization, 28
    control model, 227
  variable repetitive work, 81, 84
    advancement, 168
  work-induced stress, 142, 150, 190, 232
    organizational provisions, 150–3
    part-time, 148
teams/team working, 16, 52–3, 98, 114, 156, 212, 226
  call centres, 65–6, 117
  'high commitment practices', 34–5
  leaders, 75, 86, 87, 88, 90, 97, 129, 201
  target focus, 115
  sensory contrast between sectors, 59
  shared value limits, 99–103
  software companies, 9
    learning collectives, 118–19
technological determinism, 29, 51, 226
Tennyson, Alfred Lord, 223
Terkel, S., 11
Thatcher, Margaret, 41
Thomas, R.J., 110
  linear, vertical career progression, 110
Thompson, E.P., 64
  'time thrift', 64
Thompson, G., 40

Thompson, P., 30, 133
  decentralization of form is centralization of power, 30
  'springboard for normative control', 133
Thorne, B., 164
Thurow, L., 28
  'brainpower industries', 28
Tokugawa Shogunate, 15
Touraine, A., 29
trade unions, 9, 13, 34, 39, 182, 183, 196, 207, 211, 220, 234, 236
  class consciousness, 218–20
  collectivism vs individualism, 37, 198, 210, 212–16, 219, 223
    bargaining, 89, 90, 184
    Connect, 112
  decline in protection from, 37
  HRM, 93
  legislation
    collective bargaining, statutory recognition for, 42
    UK, 42, 91, 111
  training and development, 36, 110–13, 131, 138
    HRM role, 88, 91, 92, 108
    Lead Bodies/National Training Organizations, 111
    organizational provision for
      call centres, 113–15, 126, 127, 130, 132, 133, 190
      software companies, 115–16, 118–19, 184
Transnational Information and Consultation of Employees Regulations (1999), 42

UK/US comparisons and contrasts, 16, 48
  HRM approach to mutuality, 33
  productivity, 41
unitarism, 9, 91
  collectivism, 212, 213, 221
  statutory employee entitlements, 42
  values based upon quality and the customer, 34
United Kingdom (UK), 15, 18, 27, 40, 45, 46, 47, 53, 141, 166, 229
  call centres, 20, 21, 22
  dual-income earners, 136
  HRM initiatives, 33
  income levels, 201, 203, 217
  legislation, 42
    Draft EU Charter of Fundamental Rights (adopted in October 2000), 42
  software companies, 22, 25, 48, 59
  training, 111
    e-skills UK, 112
  women, 38, 170
  working hours, 16, 136
United States (US), 9, 11, 16, 22, 35, 53
  HRM
    mutuality, 33
  new economy
    bursting of the 'dot.com bubble', 48
    productivity in, 41
    shift from male-breadwinner to dual-earner couples, 16
  work centrality, 176

van Tulder, R., 40

Wacjman, J., 194
  gender structuring of career choices, 194–5
wage-effort bargain, 11, 12, 42, 136, 201, 202, 216, 221, 230
  autonomy at work, 199
  class situation, 203, 218–19, 221
    white-collar proletariat, 234
  empowerment, 32
    responsible autonomy, 217
  social status, 196
  work and non-work, 161
Walton, R., 8, 33, 235
  'high commitment work practices' (HCWP), 8, 34
Ward, K., 88
  pressure on management for 'lean head count', 88
'Washington consensus', 41
Waterman, R., 34, 229
  excellence literature, 7
Waters, M.
  second wave of 'revisionists' of class, 197
Watson, R., 17
  motherhood and drop in income, 176
Weber, M., 3, 4, 14
  changes in the societal work ethic, 14
  rational hierarchies or bureaucracies, 4

Weberian approaches/criteria, 39, 197, 198, 217, 221
Weiss, R.S., 11
white-collar workers, 13, 59 *see also* class/class consciousness
  call centres, 227, 234
  class consciousness, 198–200, 216
  bourgeoisification/proletarianization of, 39, 198, 218
  software sector, 217
Whyte, William H., 9
'organization man', 9
women, 37, 140, 169, 170–1, 174–6, 179–87 *see also* gender influences/considerations; women in employment
  call centres, 166–7
  'female ghettoes', 133, 168
  egalitarian attitudes to work/non-work roles, 172, 232
  domestic work, 236
  emotion work for women, 188–91
  technical work for men, 191–4
  equal opportunities, 183–5
  fair treatment, 185–8
  household income
    men's contribution, 169
  household life, 134–62, 176–7
    childcare, 173
  knowledge economy, 37, 39
    voluntary childlessness, 38
  nature of work, 188–94
  parenthood and priorities, 177, 178
  technical work for men, 191–4
  vertical segregation of, 165
women in employment, 18, 37, 38, 39, 132, 135, 136, 166, 168, 173, 177 *see also* gender influences/considerations; women
  career breaks, 231
  equality, 171, 183–5, 186, 195
  fair practices, 185–8, 196
  management level representation, 165, 184, 195
  motherhood and income drop, 169, 170, 176
  secondary career, 174, 175, 178, 232
  technical work for men, 191–4
  work preferences, 175–81, 195
work, 11, 143 *see also* work, nature of

centrality/value of, 153–4, 176–80
change and continuity, 118, 120, 223–35
collegiality, 236
classical legacy of, 3–5
control
  home life role, conflict with, 141–5
  definitions/redefinitions of, 3, 8, 225
  job redesign, 7
  meanings/new meanings in the workplace, 5, 7–12
  intrinsic, 6
  redefinition of, 9
  organizational conditions, 182–8
work, nature of, 2, 182, 188–94 *see also* work
  coping with
    organizational provisions for, 150–3
    part-time, 148
  demands of
    effects on home life, 142–5
    induced stress, 141, 147, 150, 190, 232
  organizational life, 30–2, 50–84
work centrality, 1–12, 13–14, 17–26, 134, 135, 153–4, 176, 179–80, 223, 224
  definition of, 15
  impact of gender, 16, 177
  index of, 233
  life fulfilment, 236
work continuity, 2, 6, 28, 37, 82, 118
  and change, 223–36
  of service, 137
work ethic, 15, 16, 223, 236
  financial compulsion, 11
  hegemonic value of, 14
work organization, 1, 5, 16, 18, 19, 50, 61–4, 80, 83, 86 *see also* hierarchy
  call centres, 65–71, 117
  fun, 96
  centralization/decentralization, 30
  company cultures/practices, 34
  contractual agreements, 22
  flexibility, 14
  impact of knowledge economy, 26, 28
  new/contemporary forms of, 13, 31, 32, 84, 224, 235
  commercial pressures, 90
  narrow HRM focus on, 85
  software companies, 57, 71–6

work preferences, 35, 131, 166, 175, 213
  career orientations, 116, 119, 180–1
  development, 130
  centrality of work, 176–80
  women, 188, 232
  convergence with men, 195, 231
work settings, 146
  call centres, 50, 52, 54–5
    Automatic Call Distribution (ACD)/'predictive dialler', 51
    'direct control' regimes, 50
    uniformity/differences, 53
  software development, 55–61
work tasks, 5, 6, 7, 10
  dual income households, 37
  women, 173, 176
  intensity of, 145
  job satisfaction, 105–6
  key themes/issues, 30–9
working life, 30, 48, 128, 235
  dual income households, 37
  women, 173, 176
  intensity of, 145
  job satisfaction, 105–6
  key themes/issues, 30–9
working time, flexibilities in, 18, 37, 61–2, 64–5, 137, 139–41, 164 see also flexibility/flexible working
  flexible regimes, 63, 134, 141
  flexitime system, 138, 184, 185
  part-time, 148, 163, 174
  primarily for the employers, 164
  work at home, 144
  software employees, 148
  developing competencies/skills, 140
working time, patterns of, 14, 16, 26, 61, 64, 67, 99, 162, 164, 228 see also overtime, paid; overtime, unpaid
  call centres, 142
  customer demand levels, 63, 66, 70
  dual-income households, 37
  extension/expansion of, 16, 61
  legislation, 42
  organizational provisions, 150–3
  part-time, 148
  shifts, 63, 65, 70, 137, 191
  pay premium, 201, 202
  team nights, 98–9

software employees, 78
  autonomy, 147, 150
  'peaks and troughs' system, 138
  work and home, 134, 135
  intrusions into home, 145–8, 152, 153, 175
Working Time Regulations (1998), 42
work-life balance, 37, 142–4, 164, 184, 230 see also home life; work-life spillover
  boundary, 20, 151, 163, 173, 233
  separating work from home, 160–2
  spillover, 39, 151, 189
  definition of, 141
  home/work interrelations, 134–62
  organizational commitment, 132
  organizational provisions, 148, 150–3
  family friendly policies, 232
  part-time, 148
  work intrusions into home, 145–7
work-life spillover, 39, 151, 126, 189, 162 see also home life; work-life balance
  home/work interrelations, 134–62
  separating work from home, 160–2
  tangible/intangible, 150
  work intrusions into home, 145–7
work stress, 189
  coping with, 232
  organizational provisions, 150, 152–3
  part-time, 148
work/non-work life, 12, 20, 153 see also work-life balance; work-life spillover
  complex interaction, 14
  interconnectedness, 36, 155, 160
  household and community life, 36–7, 134–62
  negative spillover, 126, 189
workplace, 13, 19, 22n., 38, 87, 106, 135, 143, 146, 150, 155, 159, 162, 165, 195, 217, 226
  attitudes, 37, 199, 203, 209–10, 231–2, 237
  behaviour, 98, 210–12, 221
  career influence, 131
  collectivism vs individualism, 212–16, 220

control, 33, 80, 86, 223
counter-culture, 97
environment, 52, 153
   coping strategies, 148
   flexibility, 164
   stress, 147
HRM, 85, 225
   managerially-induced communities, 156
   meaning of work in, 5–8, 10–12
   redefinition of, 9
   vertical/horizontal relationships with market/capital, 85
   women, 139, 172
Workplace Employment Relations Survey (WERS) (1998), 6

Zuboff, S., 34